Provisionally Applied Treaties:
Their Binding Force and Legal Nature

Queen Mary Studies in International Law

Edited by

Malgosia Fitzmaurice
Panos Merkouris
Phoebe Okowa

VOLUME 9

The titles published in this series are listed at brill.com/qmil

Provisionally Applied Treaties: Their Binding Force and Legal Nature

By

Anneliese Quast Mertsch

BRILL

LEIDEN • BOSTON
2012

Library of Congress Cataloging-in-Publication Data

Quast Mertsch, Anneliese.
Provisionally applied treaties : their binding force and legal nature / by Anneliese Quast Mertsch.
p. cm. -- (Queen Mary studies in international law ; vol. 9)
Originally presented as the author's dissertation (doctoral--University of London, 2010) under the title: The binding force and legal nature of provisionally applied treaties.
Includes bibliographical references and index.
ISBN 978-90-04-22353-0 (hardback : alk. paper)
1. Treaties--Provisional application. I. Title.

KZ1302.8.M47 2012
341'.026--dc23

2012027740

This publication has been typeset in the multilingual "Brill" typeface. With over 5,100 characters covering Latin, IPA, Greek, and Cyrillic, this typeface is especially suitable for use in the humanities. For more information, please see www.brill.com/brill-typeface.

ISSN 1877-4822
ISBN 978-90-04-22353-0 (hardback)
ISBN 978-90-04-22354-7 (e-book)

This book is printed on acid-free paper.

To my family
Ulrich, Martine, Stefanie and Philipp

CONTENTS

ACKNOWLEDGEMENTS

First and foremost I would like to express my gratitude to my mentors and former supervisors Professor Malgosia Fitzmaurice and Dr Olufemi Elias. I am indebted to both for invaluable guidance and unfailing support and patience, as well as thought-provoking comments and discussions throughout my student years and the writing of this book. I would also like to thank Queen Mary, University of London for the Research Studentship which materially supported my doctoral studies, eventually leading to this book.

With regard to the questionnaire project that I drew up for the present study, I would like to thank the participating legal advisers and treaty experts for sharing their expertise and for kindly devoting their time to supporting this research project – unfortunately the confidentiality assured for the project means I am unable to name and thank them properly. For advice on the questionnaire project, and often for further support of my research, I am grateful to Professor Anthony Aust, Ambassador Hans Corell, Professor Richard Gardiner and Sir Michael Wood, as well as Paul Barnett and Nevil Hagon from the UK Foreign Ministry's treaty section.

I am also grateful to Annebeth Rosenboom and Andrei Kolomoets, Andrew Michie and Agnieska Kochanska, Gerard Limburg, Dr Freya Baetens, Dr Lorand Bartels, Dr Catherine Brölmann, Peter Buschman, Professor Eileen Denza CMG, Professor Ellen Hey, Dr Mojtaba Kazazi, Dr Panos Merkouris, Sophie Nappert and Jenny Ray for supporting my research. For insightful comments and suggestions I am indebted to the examiners of my doctoral thesis, Professor Gerhard Loibl and Dr George Letsas. Furthermore, I would like to thank Lydia Goldblatt, Natasha Harrington, Simone Kuster, Sam Mendelson, Micheál O'Flynn, Kristina Schönfeldt and James Upcher for invaluable help with the manuscript during its different stages. For help with translations of Italian and Spanish academic writings, I am grateful to Isabella Corradini and Soledad Contreras respectively. The following devoted librarians kindly went out of their way to provide me with long-sought after documents: Martine Basset, Jonathan Sims, and Peter Zawada.

I am grateful to my parents, my sister and Antje for their moral support, and to Philipp for his patience, generosity and witty advice.

PREFACE

Treaties are the primary source of modern international law.[1] Yet delay in the entry into force of certain treaties is a serious problem affecting international law and its ability to govern relations between States.[2] One method of addressing this problem is through the provisional application of treaties: to agree on applying the provisions of a treaty to relevant acts, facts and situations *prior* to the treaty's entry into force. States and international organizations regularly rely on this mechanism, so that approximately 3% of all treaties registered with the UN since 1945 have been subject to provisional application.[3] The practice of provisional application has been codified in Article 25 Vienna Convention on the Law of Treaties 1969[4] (hereinafter 'VCLT 1969'). The VCLT 1969 does not define 'provisional application', and the notion has thus been criticised as 'ambiguous'.[5] Theoretical treatment of the mechanism since its codification by and large has been scant. Despite major achievements in using provisional application to overcome treaty crises, for example in respect of the UN Law of the Sea Convention[6] or Protocols 14 and 14*bis* to the European Convention for the Protection of Human Rights and Fundamental

---

[1] Malgosia Fitzmaurice and Olufemi Elias, *Contemporary Issues in the Law of Treaties* (Utrecht: Eleven International Publishing, 2005), xiii.

[2] Jose Maria Ruda, *The Final Acceptance of International Conventions* (Muscatine, IA: Stanley Foundation, 1976), 29; Martin A. Rogoff and Barbara E. Gauditz, "The Provisional Application of International Agreements," *Maine Law Review* 39 (1987): 31–2; see also Anthony Aust, "Limping Treaties: Lessons from Multilateral Treaty-Making," *Netherlands International Law Review* 50 (2003): 243ff. In an effort to counter the problem and, *inter alia*, to achieve a speedier entry into force of multilateral treaties, the UN has been organizing treaty events in the past decade, since it links wider participation of States in multilateral treaties with ultimately fostering the rule of law on the international plane. See the invitation to the UN 2011 treaty event <http://treaties.un.org/doc/source/events/2011/Publication/publication-English.pdf> ix.

[3] Albane Geslin, *La mise en application provisoire des traités* (Paris: Pedone, 2005), 347.

[4] Vienna Convention on the Law of Treaties 1969 (adopted 23 May 1969, entered into force 27 January 1980) 1155 UNTS 331.

[5] Gerhard Hafner, "The 'Provisional Application' of the Energy Charter Treaty," in *International Investment Law for the 21st Century: Essays in Honour of Christoph Schreuer*, eds. Christina Binder et al. (Oxford: University Press Oxford, 2009), 595; Rogoff and Gauditz, "Provisional Application," 51; Daniel Vignes, "Une notion ambiguë: la mise en application provisoire des traités," *Annuaire Français de Droit International* XVIII (1972): 181.

[6] United Nations Convention on the Law of the Sea (concluded 10 December 1982, entered into force 16 November 1994) 1833 UNTS 397.

Freedoms,[7] or high-profile cases such as *Yukos*,[8] this state of affairs has only marginally improved. As a result, the fact that "doctrine has not very frequently dealt with the matter" has been deplored as recently as in 2009.[9]

The need for analysis of the provisional application of treaties has now been acknowledged by the International Law Commission (ILC). In its 63rd session in 2011, the ILC decided to include the provisional application of treaties in its long-term programme of work.[10] In its 64th session in 2012, the ILC decided to include the provisional application of treaties in its Current Programme of Work and appointed Ambassador Juan Manuel Gómez Robledo as Special Rapporteur. This decision signals that, in the view of the ILC, there is a need to progressively develop and codify international law regarding the provisional application of treaties.[11] More precisely, and based on a paper by then ILC member Giorgio Gaja, the current scope of work envisaged by the ILC is to address the meaning of provisional application (in terms of its legal effects), its preconditions and its termination.[12]

The present book is devoted to the first of the issues identified by Gaja and focuses on the question of the binding force and legal nature of treaties subject to the mechanism of provisional application. The question is important for the certainty and stability of treaty relations but contested in practice and academic writings. From a theoretical viewpoint, the problem presents itself as follows: while treaties are by definition binding, this is so only upon their entry into force.[13] Provisional application occurs before that event, so that the binding force of treaties during this period is open to question. To the extent that legal effects are ascribed to provisionally applied treaties, this leads to the more general question of

---

7 Protocol No 14 to the Convention for the Protection of Human Rights and Fundamental Freedoms, amending the Control System of the Convention (done 13 May 2004) CETS No 194.

8 *Yukos Universal Ltd v Russian Federation*, Interim Award on Jurisdiction and Admissibility, PCA Case No. AA 227 (30 November 2009), http://www.encharter.org/index.php?id=213&L=0#Yukos. In this Award, the Tribunal discussed the separate claims of three Claimants in separate arbitrations as a single set of proceedings, except where circumstances distinct to particular Claimants necessitated separate treatment, see [2] of the Award.

9 Hafner, "Provisional Application," 594.

10 ILC, Report of the International Law Commission on the Work of its Sixty-Third Session (2011), Official Records of the General Assembly, Sixty-Six Session (Supplement No. 10), UN Doc A/66/10, chap. XIII, [365]-[367] and chap. III, [49].

11 ILC, Report of the International Law Commission on the Work of its Sixty-Third Session (2011), UN Doc A/66/10, chap. XIII [366], (a).

12 Giorgio Gaja, "Provisional Application of Treaties," in *Report of the International Law Commission on the Work of its Sixty-Third Session* (2011), UN Doc A/66/10, Annex C, [11].

13 See Article 26 VCLT 1969.

the potential legal effects of treaties that have yet to enter into force. This problem also arises with regard to similar mechanisms such as Article 18 and 24(4) VCLT 1969, and in this context has been found by the ILC and academics to be a matter of considerable complexity.[14]

In practice, as stated above, the uncertainty surrounding the binding force and legal nature of these instruments may potentially concern 3% of treaties registered with the UN. The problem recently arose in two major investment disputes involving a provisionally applied treaty. In both the *Kardassopoulos*[15] and the *Yukos*[16] litigations, the question of the binding force of provisionally applied treaties, in particular the provisionally applied 1994 Energy Charter Treaty, was contested between the parties. However, the uncertainty is not limited to alleged breaches of provisionally applied treaties and available responses to them. Other questions that may arise are, for example, whether Article 46 VCLT 1969 applies if the agreement to provisionally apply a treaty has been expressed in violation of a relevant rule of internal law; or whether the VCLT 1969 rules on reservations apply if States append a reservation to their declaration to provisionally apply a treaty. The legal nature of agreements to provisionally apply a treaty is decisive for determining the rules applicable to them and to the regime of provisional application they establish. If, and only if, the agreement on provisional application is intended to be legally binding, then it is conceivable that the law of treaties applies to that agreement and to the provisionally applied treaty. If, however, the agreement is not intended to be legally binding, i.e. is intended to be a soft law agreement, then the question of the rules governing this agreement and the regime of provisional application would belong to the realm of soft law.

The question to which this book is devoted is therefore theoretically challenging and concerns an essential aspect of the practice of treaty relations. The issue is theoretically challenging because it touches upon the potential legal effects of treaties prior to their entry into force.

---

14 See e.g. Martin A. Rogoff, "The International Legal Obligations of Signatories to an Unratified Treaty," *Maine Law Review* 32 (1980): 280 fn. 56; See e.g. Arnold Duncan Mc Nair, *The Law of Treaties* (Oxford: Clarendon Press, 1961), 203 (Article 24(4) VCLT 1969); ILC, Summary record of the 644th meeting, UN Doc A/CN.4/SR.644, on the obligation contained today *inter alia* in Article 18 VCLT 1969 (then Draft Article 9, legal effects of a full signature).

15 *Kardassopoulos v Georgia*, ICSID Case No. ARB/05/18, Decision on Jurisdiction (06 July 2007), http://www.encharter.org/fileadmin/user_upload/document/Kardassopoulos.pdf. For a discussion hereof see the text to notes 32–36 (section 2.5.2.) in chapter 4 below.

16 *Yukos Universal Ltd v Russian Federation* (30 November 2009). For a discussion hereof see the text to notes 127–144 in chapter 2 below as well as the text to notes 32–36 (section 2.5.2.) in chapter 4.

From the practical viewpoint it is important because States and international organisations require certainty about the rules applicable to agreements on provisional application and the ensuing regime of provisional application.

The second purpose of the book is to begin to fil the gap that exists as a reference book on provisionally applied treaties. Such a step is long overdue: not only is there no English language book on provisional application; of the few books that do exist (to this author's knowledge in French, German and Italian)[17] all but one do not cover the treaty practice and academic writings of the past 25 years,[18] nor do they provide an index.[19] The present book will try to begin filling this gap in several ways. First, it is written in English and deals with the question of binding force and legal nature in a more comprehensive manner than existing texts. While focusing on this question, it explains basic notions such as the function of provisional application and some of the features of these treaties; it delineates provisional application from other similar treaty mechanisms; it traces the drafting history and major debates on the subject in the ILC and at the 1968–1969 Vienna Conference on the Law of Treaties (hereinafter '1968–1969 Vienna Conference'), all against the background of academic writings on the matter. Furthermore, this book attempts to combine an analysis of theory and practice relating to the question of the binding force and legal nature of provisionally applied treaties. In addition, the book has a detailed index, enabling readers swiftly to locate points of interest. Finally, a multilingual bibliography on provisional application is annexed to the book.

In conclusion, it is hoped that this book clarifies the matter of the binding force and legal nature of provisionally applied treaties and, in so doing, contributes to a better understanding of the concept of provisional application in general. Furthermore, it is hoped that the book begins to fill the need for a dedicated reference work on the subject and will assist academics and practitioners in their work with, research into or analysis of, provisionally applied treaties.

---

17 Horst-Günther Krenzler, *Die vorläufige Anwendung völkerrechtlicher Verträge* (Freiburg i. Br.: Rota-Druck Johannes Krause Buchbinderei, 1963); Paolo Picone, *L'applicazione in via provvisoria degli accordi internazionali* (Naples: Eugenio Jovene, 1973); Frank Montag, *Völkerrechtliche Verträge mit vorläufigen Wirkungen* (Berlin: Duncker & Humblot, 1986); Geslin, *Application provisoire*.

18 The exception being Geslin, *Application provisoire*.

19 With the exception of the '*indice degli autori*' provided in Picone's book, *L'applicazione in via provvisoria*, 235ff.

TABLE OF ABBREVIATIONS

CFE	Treaty on Conventional Armed Forces in Europe
CoE and BIICL	Council of Europe and British Institute of International and Comparative Law (eds) *Treaty Making: Expression of Consent by States to be Bound by a Treaty* (Kluwer Law International London 2001)
CoW	Committee of the Whole (here at the Vienna Diplomatic Conferences on the Law of Treaties)
CTBT	Comprehensive Nuclear-Test-Ban Treaty
Digest US Practice IL	Digest of US Practice in International Law
ECJ	Court of Justice of the European Union
ECT	Energy Charter Treaty
FCO	Foreign and Commonwealth Office
GATT	General Agreement on Tariffs and Trade
IAEA	International Atomic Energy Agency
ICAO	International Civil Aviation Organization
ICC	International Criminal Court
ICJ	International Court of Justice
ICSID	International Centre for Settlement of Investment Disputes
ILA	International Law Association
ILC	International Law Commission
ILM	International Legal Materials
LNOJ	League of Nations Official Journal
MOU	Memorandum of understanding
MPEPIL online	Wolfrum R (ed) *The Max Planck Encyclopedia of Public International Law* (OUP 2008) online edition
OJ	Official Journal
OR	Official Records (generally of the UN Conference on the Law of Treaties 1968 and 1969).
OSCE	Organization for Security and Co-operation in Europe
Parry's TS	Parry C *Consolidated Treaties Series*
PCIJ	Permanent Court of International Justice
SCC	Swedish Chamber of Commerce
SR	Summary Records (of ILC meetings)
TIAS	Treaties and other International Agreements (US)
UN	United Nations
UNCLOS	United Nations Convention on the Law of the Sea
UNECE	United Nations Economic Commission for Europe
UNGA	United Nations General Assembly
UNTS	United Nations Treaty Series

TABLE OF CASES

TABLE OF TREATIES AND OTHER INTERNATIONAL INSTRUMENTS

Multilateral

Name of treaty or instrument	Reference	Registration no	Date of conclusion	Place of conclusion	Page no
Agreement concerning the International Institute of Refrigeration	826 UNTS 191	I-11837	01/12/1954	Paris	4, 210
Agreement on an International Energy Programme	1040 UNTS 272	I-15664	18/11/1974	Paris	10, 98
Agreement on the International Dolphin Conservation Programme 1998	[2005] OJ L 348/28	–	21/05/1998	Washington	204
Agreement Providing for the Provisional Application of the Draft International Customs Convention on Touring ... (Agreement Providing for the Provisional Application of the Draft International Customs Conventions on Touring, on Commercial Road Vehicles and on the International Transport of Goods by Road)	45 UNTS 149	I-696	16/06/1949	Geneva	201
Amendments to the Intelsat Agreement 2000 (Amendments to the Agreement and Operating Agreement relating to the International Telecommunications Satellite Organisation "INTELSAT" of 20 August 1971)	2004 ATS 30	–	17/11/2000	Washington	208

(continued)

Name of treaty or instrument	Reference	Registration no	Date of conclusion	Place of conclusion	Page no
Articles of Agreement of the International Bank for Reconstruction and Development (World Bank)	2 UNTS 134	I-20	27/12/1945	Washington	88
Articles of Agreement of the International Monetary Fund (IMF)	2 UNTS 39	I-20	27/12/1945	Washington	88
Central European Free Trade Agreement 1992 (Central European Free Trade Agreement concluded by the Czech Republic, the Republic of Hungary, the Republic of Poland, and the Slovak Republic)	(1995) 34 ILM 8	–	21/12/1992	Krakow	204
CFE (Treaty on Conventional Armed Forces in Europe)	(1991) 30 ILM 1	44001	19/11/1990	Paris	5, 202, 203, 205, 206
Convention on Assistance in the Case of a Nuclear Accident or Radiological Emergency	1457 UNTS 133	24643	26/09/1986	Vienna	10, 204, 205
Convention on Early Notification of a Nuclear Accident	1439 UNTS 275	24404	26/09/1986	Vienna	10, 204
Convention on Long-Range Transboundary Air Pollution	1302 UNTS 217	I-21623	13/11/1979	Geneva	220
Convention on the Liability of the Operation of Nuclear Ships[20]	(1963) 57 AJIL 268	–	25/05/1962	Brussels	123
CTBT (Comprehensive Nuclear Test-Ban Treaty)	1996 ILM 1443	–	10/09/1996	New York	18, 19, 253, 260

[20] Did not enter into force.

Decision 2 (2003) ATCM XXVI (Madrid)[21] on the Provisional Application of Measure 1 (2003)	(see the website indicated in the footnote)	–	20/06/2003	Madrid	210
ECT (Energy Charter Treaty)	2080 UNTS 95	36116	17/12/1994	Lisbon	xiii, 4, 14n35, 67, 89,98, 99, 100, 101,102, 110, 115,170, 174, 175, 208, 213, 214, 231
European Pharmacopoeia Convention (Convention on the Elaboration of a European Pharmacopoeia)	1286 UNTS 70	I-21200	22/07/1964	Strasbourg	11, 199
Eutelsat Agreement 1985 (Convention establishing the European Telecommunications Satellite Organization "EUTELSAT" (with annexes, operating agreement and protocol of amendment of 15 December 1983)	1519 UNTS 149	I-26342	15/07/1982	Paris	208
Extension of the 1983 Coffee Agreement (Extension of the International Coffee Agreement, 1983) Resolution 347 (3 July 1989)	1546 UNTS 389	A-22376	03/07/1989	London	226

(continued)

21 <http://www.ats.aq/devAS/info_measures_listitem.aspx?lang=e&id=298>.

Name of treaty or instrument	Reference	Registration no	Date of conclusion	Place of conclusion	Page no
Fish Stocks Agreement 1995 (Agreement for the Implementation of the Provisions of the United Nations Convention on the Law of the Sea of 10 December 1982 relating to the Conservation and Management of Straddling Fish Stocks and Highly Migratory Fish Stocks)	2167 UNTS 3	I-37924	04/08/1995	New York	204
Fisheries Convention 1964 (Fisheries Convention)	581 UNTS 57	I-8432	09/03/1964	London	213
Food Aid Convention 1971	800 UNTS 45	A-11400	29/03/1971	Washington	189, 193
Fourth Extension of the 1983 Coffee Agreement (Fourth Extension of the International Coffee Agreement, 1983, as modified)	1737 UNTS 478	A-22376	01/10/1993	London	226
General Agreement on Privileges and Immunities of the Council of Europe	250 UNTS 14	I-3515	02/09/1949	Paris	11
Geneva Convention Relative to the Protection of Civilian Persons in Time of War	75 UNTS 287	I-973	12/08/1949	Geneva	12, 124
Havana Convention 1928 (Convention on Treaties)	IV Hudson 2378 (No 190)[22]	-	20/02/1928	Havana	25

22 Hudson (ed) *International Legislation* (Carnegie Endowment for International Peace Washington 1931) vol IV, No. 190, 2378.

Implementation Agreement 1994 (Agreement relating to the Implementation of Part XI of the United Nations Convention on the Law of the Sea of 10 December 1982)	1836 UNTS 3	I-31364	28/07/1994	New York	84, 98, 209, 216, 249, 260
Institute for the Management of Technology Convention 1971 (Convention on the Establishment of the International Institute for the Management of Technology)	995 UNTS 164	I-14566	06/10/1971	Paris	209
Intelsat Agreement 1971 (Agreement relating to the International Telecommunications Satellite Organization 'INTELSAT' (with annexes)	1220 UNTS 21	I-19677	20/08/1971	Washington	208
International Agreement on Olive Oil and Table Olives 1986	1445 UNTS 13	I-24591	01/07/1986	Geneva	225
International Agreement on Olive Oil and Table Olives 2005	[2005] OJ L 302/47	–	29/04/2005	Geneva	225
International Cocoa Agreement 1972	882 UNTS 67	I-12652	21/10/1972	Geneva	223, 224, 225
International Cocoa Agreement 1975	1023 UNTS 253	I-15033	20/10/1975	Geneva	223, 225
International Cocoa Agreement 1980	1245 UNTS 221	I-20313	19/11/1980	Geneva	181, 223, 225, 227, 228
International Cocoa Agreement 1986	1446 UNTS 103	I-24604	25/07/1986	Geneva	181, 223, 225, 227, 228
International Cocoa Agreement 1993	1766 UNTS 3	I-30692	16/07/1993	Geneva	4, 102–103, 181, 223, 225, 227, 228, 250

(*continued*)

Name of treaty or instrument	Reference	Registration no	Date of conclusion	Place of conclusion	Page no
International Cocoa Agreement 2001	2229 UNTS 2	I-39640	02/03/2001	Geneva	181, 223, 227, 228
International Coffee Agreement 1962	469 UNTS 169	I-6791	28/09/1962	New York	97, 102, 223
International Coffee Agreement 1968	647 UNTS 3	I-9262	31/03/1968 and 18/03/1968	New York	223
International Coffee Agreement 1976	1024 UNTS 3	I-15034	03/12/1975	London	223
International Coffee Agreement 1983	1333 UNTS 119	I-22376	16/09/1982	New York	223
International Coffee Agreement 1994	1827 UNTS 3	I-31252	–	London	181, 223, 228
International Coffee Agreement 2001	2161 UNTS 308	I-37769	28/09/2000	London	181, 223, 228
International Coffee Agreement 2007[23]	see the website indicated in footnote	n/a	28/09/2007	London	181, 228
International Natural Rubber Agreement 1987	1521 UNTS 3	I-26364	20/03/1987	Geneva	181, 228
International Olive Oil Agreement 1963	495 UNTS 3	I-7239	20/04/1963	Geneva	225, 226
International Olive Oil Agreement 1979	1219 UNTS 135	I-19674	30/03/1979	Geneva	225
International Sugar Agreement 1968	654 UNTS 3	I-9369	24/12/1968 and 03/12/1968	New York	189, 190, 223
International Sugar Agreement 1977	1064 UNTS 219	I-16200	07/10/1977	Geneva	223

23 http://dev.ico.org/documents/ica2007e.pdf

International Sugar Agreement 1984	1388 UNTS 3	I-23225	05/07/1984	Geneva	223
International Sugar Agreement 1987	1499 UNTS 31	I-25811	11/09/1987	London	223
International Sugar Agreement 1992	1703 UNTS 203	I-29467	20/03/1992	Geneva	223
International Tropical Timber Agreement 2006		I-49197	27/01/2006	Geneva	185
International Wheat Agreement 1962	444 UNTS 3	I-6367	15/05/1962 and 19/04/1962	Washington	193
Law of the Sea Convention (United Nations Convention on the Law of the Sea)	1833 UNTS 397	31363	10/12/1982	Montego Bay	17, 92
Long-Term Trade Agreement	929 UNTS 85	I-13231	25/11/1971	The Hague	123
Mir Inter-State Television Agreement 1993 (Agreement on International Legal Guarantees for the Free and Independent Operation of the Inter-State Television and Radio Broadcasting Company "Mir")	1971 UNTS 11	I-33647	24/12/1993	Ashgabat	199
Privileges and Immunities Agreement of the International Tribunal for the Law of the Sea 1997 (Agreement on the Privileges and Immunities of the International Tribunal for the Law of the Sea)	2167 UNTS 271	I-37925	23/05/1997	New York	204
Protocol Amending the European Convention on Transfrontier Television	CETS 171	–	01/10/1998	Strasbourg	205
Protocol Concerning the Provisional Application of the Statute of the European School	443 UNTS 244	6362	15/07/1957	Luxembourg	95

(*continued*)

Name of treaty or instrument	Reference	Registration no	Date of conclusion	Place of conclusion	Page no
Protocol No 14 to the Convention for the Protection of Human Rights and Fundamental Freedoms (Protocol No. 14 to the Convention for the Protection of Human Rights and Fundamental Freedoms, Amending the Control System of the Convention)	CETS 194	–	13/05/2004	Strasbourg	10, 204
Protocol No 14bis to the Convention for the Protection of Human Rights and Fundamental Freedoms	CETS 204	–	27/05/2009	Strasbourg	xvii
Protocol of 15 July 1840 to the Convention for the Pacification of the Levant	90 Parry's TS 291	–	15/07/1840	London	8, 26
Protocol of 1993 extending the International Agreement on Olive Oil and Table Olives, 1986	1763 UNTS 319	A-24591	10/03/1993	Geneva	225
Protocol of Provisional Application of the European Monetary Agreement	–[24]	008344[25]	5/08/1955	Paris	208, 209, 216
Protocol of Provisional Application of the Fisheries Convention of 9 March 1964	581 UNTS 76	A-8432	09/03/1964	London	213, 216
Protocol of Provisional Application of the General Agreement on Tariffs and Trade	55 UNTS 308	I-814	30/10/1947	Geneva	142, 249
Rome Statute of the International Criminal Court	2187 UNTS 91	38544	17/07/1998	Rome	18, 155, 156
Second Extension of the 1983 Coffee Agreement Resolution 352 (28 September 1990) (Second Extension of the International Coffee Agreement, 1983, as modified)	1651 UNTS 572	A-22376	28/09/1990	London	226

24 <http://www.minbuza.nl/en/key-topics/treaties/search-the-treaty-database>.
25 Relates to minbuza treaty database, see preceding footnote.

Treaty	Source	Reg. No.	Date	Place	Pages
Third Extension of the 1983 Coffee Agreement, adopted by the Coffee Council in Resolution 355 (27 September 1991) (Third Extension of the International Coffee Agreement, 1983, as modified)	1691 UNTS 449	A-22376	27/09/1991	London	226
Third Protocol to the General Agreement on Privileges and Immunities of the Council of Europe	ETS 28	A-3515	6/03/1959	Strasbourg	11
Treaty Banning Nuclear Weapon Tests in the Atmosphere, in Outer Space and Under Water	480 UNTS 43	I-6964	05/08/1963	Moscow	114
Treaty of Paris 1856 (Traité Général)	2 Hertslet No. 264, 1265	–	30/03/1856	Paris	83
Treaty on Fisheries 1987 (Treaty on Fisheries between the Governments of Certain Pacific Island States and the Government of the United States of America)	2176 UNTS 93	I-38285	02/04/1987	Port Moresby	178
UN Charter (Charter of the United Nations)	1 UNTS xvi	–	26/06/1945	San Francisco	17, 156–157, 221
VCLT 1969 (Vienna Convention on the Law of Treaties)	1155 UNTS 331	18232	22/05/1969	Vienna	
Article 2(1)					98, 129, 140
Article 18					xiii, 19–20, 39, 51, 54, 85, 87, 173, 174
Article 24(4)					xiii, 12, 147–154, 159
Article 25					21–22, 28–60, 58, 130–131
Article 25(2)					77–80, 84–85, 117, 186
Article 26					50, 52, 54, 93, 123, 162, 216
Article 27					13, 97, 104, 108
Article 28					122, 123
Article 46					xiii, 62
Article 60					167
Articles 65&66					83
Article 70					123
Article 72					123

BILATERAL

Name of treaty or instrument	Reference	Registration no	Date of conclusion	Place of conclusion	Page no
Agreement in the form of an Exchange of Letters concerning the provisional application of the trade and trade-related provisions of the Euro-Mediterranean Agreement establishing an Association between the European Communities and their Member States, of the one part, and the Arab Republic of Egypt, of the other part	[2003] OJ L 345/115	–	21/12/2003	Brussels	202
Agreement in the form of an Exchange of Letters on the Provisional Application of the Protocol Establishing the Fishing Opportunities and the Compensation Provided for in the Agreement between the European Economic Community and the Government of the Republic of Guinea-Bissau on Fishing off the Coast of Guinea Bissau for the period of 16 June 2001 to 15 June 2006	[2002] OJ L 19/34	–	06/12/2001	–	209
Agreement in the form of an Exchange of Letters on the provisional application of the protocol setting out, for the period from 18 January 2005 to 17 January 2011, the fishing opportunities and the financial contribution provided for by the agreement between the European Economic Community and the Republic of Seychelles on fishing off Seychelles	[2005] OJ L 348/3	–	23/02/2006 23/02/2006	Brussels Paris	210

Agreement in the form of an Exchange of Letters on the provisional application of the Fisheries Partnership Agreement between the European Community and the Republic of Guinea-Bissau for the period 16 June 2007 to 15 June 2011	[2007] OJ L 342/3		15/04/2008	Brussels	210
Belgium–Greece Air Transport Agreement 1949 (Agreement between the Royal Government of Belgium and the Royal Greek Government concerning air transport between their respective territories)	137 UNTS 215	I-1854	21/06/1949	Athens	198
Belgo–Luxembourg Economic Union–Morocco Investment Agreement 1965 (Convention between the Belgo–Luxembourg Economic Union and the Kingdom of Morocco concerning the encouragement of capital investment and the protection of property)	620 UNTS 171	I-8954	28/04/1965	Rabat	199
Brazil–Chile Air Transport Agreement 1947 (Air Transport Agreement (with annex and exchange of notes))	971 UNTS 321	I-14065	04/07/1947	Rio de Janeiro	221
Canada–Bulgaria Trade Agreement (Trade Agreement)	977 UNTS 295	I-14192	12/02/1973	Sofia	123
Canada–Netherlands Air Transport Agreement 1974 (Air Transport Agreement between the Government of Canada and the Government of the Kingdom of the Netherlands)	987 UNTS 113	I-14424	17/06/1974	Ottawa	198

(*continued*)

Name of treaty or instrument	Reference	Registration no	Date of conclusion	Place of conclusion	Page no
Cuba–Portugal Air Services Agreement 1951 (Agreement between the Government of Portugal and the Government of the Republic of Cuba for the establishment of air services between and beyond their respective territories)	192 UNTS 136	I-2598	26/06/1951	Lisbon	98
EC–Angola agreement [2002] (Agreement in the form of an Exchange of Letters concerning the provisional application of the Protocol setting out, for the period from 3 August 2002 to 2 August 2004, the fishing opportunities and the financial contribution provided for by the Agreement between the European Economic Community and the Government of the Republic of Angola on fishing off Angola)	[2002] OJ L 351/91	–	03/08/2002	–	209
EC–Mozambique Agreement [2007] (Agreement in the form of an Exchange of Letters on the provisional application of the Fisheries Partnership Agreement between the European Community and the Republic of Mozambique)	[2007] OJ L 331/33	–	20/12/2007	Brussels	210
Economic Partnership Agreement between the CARIFORUM States, of the one part, and the European Community and its Member States, of the other part	[2008] OJ L 289/I/3	–	15/10/2008	Bridgetown Barbados	215

EEC– Côte d'Ivoire agreement [2008] (Agreement in the form of an Exchange of Letters on the provisional application of the protocol setting out the fishing opportunities and financial contribution provided for in the Fisheries Partnership Agreement between the European Community and the Republic of Côte d'Ivoire on fishing in Côte d'Ivoire's fishing zones for the period from 1 July 2007 to 30 June 2013)	[2008] OJ L 48/39	–	18/04/2008	Brussels	210
EEC–Madagascar agreement [2007] (Agreement in the form of an Exchange of Letters on the provisional application of the amendments to the Protocol setting out the fishing opportunities and financial contribution provided for in the Fisheries Partnership Agreement between the European Economic Community and the Republic of Madagascar on fishing off the coast of Madagascar for the period from 1 January 2007 to 31 December 2012)	[2007] OJ L 331/5	–	15/04/2008	Brussels	210
EEC–Senegal agreement [2002] (Agreement in the form of an Exchange of Letters concerning the provisional application of the Protocol setting out the fishing opportunities and the financial contribution provided for in the Agreement between the European Economic Community and the Government of the Republic of Senegal on fishing off the coast of Senegal, for the period from 1 July 2002 to 30 June 2006)	[2002] OJ L 349/45	–	01/08/2003	Brussels	209

(continued)

Name of treaty or instrument	Reference	Registration no	Date of conclusion	Place of conclusion	Page no
EU–US Passenger Name Record Agreement 2007 (Agreement between the European Union and the United States of America on the processing and transfer of Passenger Name Record (PNR) data by air carriers to the United States Department of Homeland Security (DHS) (2007 PNR Agreement))	[2007] OJ L 204/18	–	23/07/2007 26/07/2007	Brussels Washington	84, 208
Finland–Union of Soviet Socialist Republics Treaty of Peace	(1940) 34 AJIL Sup 127	–	12/03/1940	Moscow	10
Germany–Mongolia Cultural Cooperation Agreement 1997 (Agreement between the Government of the Federal Republic of Germany and the Government of Mongolia Concerning Cultural Cooperation)	2071 UNTS 80	I-35903	16/09/1997	Bonn	98
Greece–Ethiopia Agreement on Reciprocal Tax Exemptions on Income Earned by Greek and Ethiopian Air Transport Companies (Exchange of notes constituting an agreement on reciprocal tax exemptions on income earned by Greek and Ethiopian air transport companies)	550 UNTS 189	I-8015	07/11/1962	Addis Ababa	216

Greece–Ethiopia Agreement on Reciprocal Tax Exemptions on Income earned by Greek and Ethiopian Maritime Shipping Enterprises 1962 (Exchange of Notes constituting an agreement between Greece and Ethiopia on Reciprocal Tax Exemptions on Income earned by Greek and Ethiopian Maritime Shipping Enterprises)	550 UNTS 179	8014	07/11/1962	Addis Ababa	216
Japan–Philippines Exchange of Notes 1958 (Exchange of notes constituting a provisional agreement concerning the simplification of the entry and sojourn procedures)	325 UNTS 104	4696	24/07/1958	Manila	16
Netherlands–Japan Exchange of Notes 2008[26] concerning the Provisional Application of the Agreement on Social Security 2008	(see the website indicated in the footnote)	–	21/02/08	The Hague	201
Netherlands–OECD Agreement on the Provisional Participation of the Netherlands in the Activities of the Organisation (Agreement between the Kingdom of the Netherlands and the Organisation for Economic Co-operation and Development concerning the provisional participation of the Kingdom of the Netherlands in the activities of the Organisation)	(1961) 22 Tractaten blad No 126, 3	–	30/09/1961	Paris	216

(continued)

26 <http://www.minbuza.nl/en/key-topics/treaties/search-the-treaty-database>.

Name of treaty or instrument	Reference	Registration no	Date of conclusion	Place of conclusion	Page no
Netherlands–UK Pipeline Agreement 2005 (Agreement between the Government of the Kingdom of the Netherlands and the Government of the Kingdom of Great Britain ... relating to the transmission of natural gas through a pipeline between [them])	2398 UNTS 251	I-43316	21/03/2005	The Hague	199
Sweden–Brazil Air Transport Agreement 1947 (Air Transport Agreement between Sweden and the United States of Brazil)	94 UNTS 139	I-1310	14/11/1947	Rio de Janeiro	221
UK–International Cocoa Organization Headquarter Agreement 1975 (Headquarters Agreement between the Government of the United Kingdom of Great Britain and Northern Ireland and the International Cocoa Organization)	990 UNTS 141	I-14470	26/03/1975	London	224
UK–Argentina Air Services Agreement 1946 (Agreement between the Government of the United Kingdom and the Government of the Argentine Republic for air services between their respective territories)	164 UNTS 53	2159	17/05/1946	Buenos Aires	199
UK–Colombia Air Services Agreement 1947 (Agreement between the Government of the United Kingdom of Great Britain and Northern Ireland and the Government of the Republic of Colombia for air services between and beyond their respective territories)	160 UNTS 297	I-2115	16/10/1947	Bogotá	198

UK–Iceland Air Transport Agreement 1950 (Agreement between the Government of the United Kingdom of Great Britain and Northern Ireland and the Government of Iceland relating to certain air transport services)	95 UNTS 277	I-1326	26/05/1950	London	198, 199
UK–Panama Aviation Agreement 1951 (Aviation Agreement between the Government of the United Kingdom of Great Britain and Northern Ireland and the Government of the Republic of Panama)	560 UNTS 143	I-8172	15/09/1951	Panama City	198
UK–Spain Air Services Agreement 1950 (Agreement between the Government of the United Kingdom of Great Britain and Northern Ireland and the Government of Spain for air services)	398 UNTS 101	I-5719	20/07/1950	Madrid	198
US–Brazil Agreement for a Cooperative Programme of Agriculture (Agreement for a Cooperative Programme of Agriculture and Natural Resources between the Government of the United States of America and the Government of the United States of Brazil)	(1958) 9 UST 1357	–	26/06/1953	Rio de Janeiro	96
US–Cuban Maritime Boundary Agreement (Maritime Boundary Agreement between the United States of America and the Republic of Cuba)	(1978) 17 ILM 110	–	16/12/1977	Washington	11
– extension of provisional application	9732 TIAS 840	–	28/12/1979		11

Other International Instruments

Name of treaty or instrument	Reference	Registration no	Date of conclusion	Place of conclusion	Page no
1975 Helsinki Final Act of the Conference on Security and Co-operation in Europe[27]	(see the website indicated in the footnote)	–	01/08/1975	Helsinki	202
Final Act of the Eleventh Antarctic Treaty Special Consultative Meeting	(1991) 30 ILM 1460	–	04/10/1991	Madrid	218, 220
Final Act, 1992 Helsinki Summit Conference (CFE)[28]	(see the website indicated in the footnote)	–	10/07/1992	Helsinki	202
Exchange of Letters Constituting an Agreement on the Provisional Application of the Cooperation Service Agreement for the Contribution of Personnel to the International Criminal Tribunal for the Former Yugoslavia (United Nations and United States of America)	1823 UNTS 335	31230	23/09/1994	New York	218
Memorandum of Understanding Provisionally Applying the Treaty On Fisheries Between the Governments of Certain Pacific Island States and the Government of the United States of America[29]	(see the website indicated in the footnote)	–	24/03/2002	Kiritimati	218
1979 Resolution on Long-Range Transboundary Air Pollution[30]	(see the website indicated in the footnote)	–	13/11/1979	Geneva	220

27 <http://www.osce.org/documents/mcs/1975/08/4044_en.pdf>.

28 <http://www.state.gov/s/l/65828.htm>.

29 <http://iea.uoregon.edu/pages/view_treaty.php?t=2002-MemorandumOfUnderstanding-1987-FisheriesPacificIslandsUS.EN.txt&par=view_treaty_html>.

Table of Materials

Designation	Page no
A32-WP/10 LE/1 of 30/6/98 – Ratification of Amendments to the Chicago Convention (Legal Commission of the International Civil Aviation Organization), <www.icao.int/icao/en/assembl/a32/wp/010.pdf>	231
Browne 'The Law of the Sea Convention and US Policy' 12, Congressional Research Service <http://ncseonline.org/NLE/CRSreports/06Apr/IB95010.pdf>	14
CDDH-GDR(2003)020 – Draft reform of the European Court of Human Rights – Final clauses for an accelerated entry into force of an Amending Protocol, <http://www.coe.int/t/e/human_rights/cddh/3._committees/07.%20other%20committees%20and%20working%20groups/archives/06.%20guaranteeing%20human%20rights%20(cddh-gdr)/01.%20working%20documents/2003/2003_020_en.asp#TopOfPage>	231
CDDH-GDR(2003)031 – Exchange of views on possibilities for an accelerated entry into force of an amending protocol to the Convention (extracts of the report of the joint CDDH-GDR/DH-PR meeting of 17–20 March 2003), <http://www.coe.int/t/e/human_rights/cddh/3._committees/07.%20other%20committees%20and%20working%20groups/archives/06.%20guaranteeing%20human%20rights%20(cddh-gdr)/01.%20working%20documents/2003/2003_031_en.asp#TopOfPage>	231
Committee of Ministers' document CM(2009)56 addendum <https://wcd.coe.int/ViewDoc.jsp?id=1426443&Site=CM>	231
CTBTO Prepcomm Resolution	18, 19
Resolution Establishing the Preparatory Commission for the Comprehensive Nuclear Test-Ban Treaty Organization (17 October 1996) CTBT/MSS/RES1	
FCO Treaties and MOUs	
(Treaties and MOUs – Guidance on Practice and Procedure, FCO Treaty Section (2nd edn 2004)) <http://www.fco.gov.uk/resources/en/pdf/pdf8/fco_pdf_treatymous>	200, 204, 219
Final Act of the Third United Nations Conference on the Law of the Sea <http://www.un.org/Depts/los/convention_agreements/texts/final_act_eng.pdf>	17

(*continued*)

Designation	Page no
Final Act of the UN Diplomatic Conference of Plenipotentiaries on the Establishment of an International Criminal Court (17 July 1998) UN Doc A/CONF.183/10, Annex I, F	18
Intertemporal Problem – Resolution	110,
Resolution 'The Intertemporal Problem in Public International Law' (1975) 56 AIDI	111
PESC/SEC 899 (09.08.96)	177
Questionnaire Concernant les Procédures Internes des Etats Membres pour la Conclusion d'Accords Internationaux Approuvés selon une Procédure Simplifiée ou d'Accords Juridiquement non Obligatoires	58
Precedents of Provisional Application	18,
('Examples of Precedents of Provisional Application, Pending their Entry into Force, of Multilateral Treaties, Especially Treaties which have Established International Organizations and/or Regimes' requested by the Committee on the Peaceful Uses of the Sea-bed and the Ocean Floor Beyond the Limits of National Jurisdiction, A/AC.138/88 of 12 June 1973 (A/AC.138/88)) Reprinted in Platzöder R (ed) *Dokumente der dritten Seerechtskonferenz der Vereinten Nationen* (Los Angeles: Nossaman, Krueger and Marsh, 1979)	189
Report of the ILC to the General Assembly Doc A/1316, (1950) ILC YIL Vol 2	372
Review of the Multilateral Treaty-Making Process, UN Doc. A/35/312	9
SEC: S12RAA (Annex to the Report of the 12th Session of the Inmarsat Assembly) (20–24.04.1998) (on file with the author)	
Assembly/12/Report Annex 32 [statement by the representative of Japan]	231
Assembly/12/Report Annex 14 [statement by the representative of Costa Rica]	231
Statement of Principles Applicable to the Formation of General Customary International Law – Final Report (Committee on the) Formation of Customary (General) International Law of the International Law Association, <http://www.ila-hq.org/en/committees/index.cfm/cid/30>	105

[31] 73, 186, 187, 192, 256.

INTRODUCTION

This book will investigate the legal character of the provisional application of treaties in international law. The binding force and legal nature of provisionally applied treaties is contested in international practice and academic writings. Accordingly, aspects of both the academic debate and practice will be analysed in order to arrive at a better general understanding of the mechanism and to clarify the binding force and legal nature of provisionally applied treaties.

1. Structure

The present book comprises this introduction, four chapters and a conclusion. Chapter one gives a brief introduction to provisional application and distinguishes this mechanism from other similar mechanisms of the law of treaties or similar types of agreement. Furthermore, the codification process leading to Article 25 Vienna Convention on the Law of Treaties 1969[1] (hereinafter 'VCLT 1969') will be examined in order to understand the background to the mechanism of provisional application and its conceptualisation in international law. Then, provisional application will be briefly analysed, in a general manner, from the perspective of 'internal law'.[2] This perspective is important because internal law can affect a treaty regime on the international plane,[3] for instance by shaping the content and features of agreements on provisional application. Chapter one prepares the ground for the two following chapters because the drafting history as well as some of the issues raised during the conceptualisation of provisional application are instructive on the subject and indeed have been used in arguments for and against the binding force of these treaties.

---

[1] For the treaty details, see Preface, note 4 above. Unless otherwise indicated references to articles are to those of the VCLT 1969.

[2] In this book the terminology is meant to designate all laws and regulations adopted within the framework of the State, by whatever authority and at whatever level, similar to its use in Article 27 as well as Article 3 of the Articles on the Responsibility of States for Internationally Wrongful Acts (hereinafter 'State Responsibility Articles'). The articles and the commentary are available at http://untreaty.un.org/ilc/texts/instruments/english/commentaries/9_6_2001.pdf.

[3] Article 46.

Chapter two examines the arguments put forward in recent academic writings in support of the proposition that treaties are non-legally binding and are a form of soft law during the period of their provisional application. Emphasis is placed on the discretion which provisional application allows, such as the possibility to terminate provisional application unilaterally at any time.[4] The primary question is whether this discretion prevents the provisionally applied treaty from having legally binding force, or whether a "discernible realm of obligation"[5] remains despite this discretion. Throughout the discussion the particular features of provisionally applied treaties that are said to result in discretion are analysed in the wider context of the law of treaties and the international legal system in order better to understand their effects (on the binding force and legal nature of an undertaking).

Chapter three analyses some of the arguments put forward in academic writings in support of the view that provisionally applied treaties are legally binding and are subject to the principle of *pacta sunt servanda.* Key to these works is the argument that provisionally applied treaties are conceptually similar to treaties that have entered into force, in relation to the question of their binding force. Further, it has been argued that States generally intend to be bound by treaties during the period of their provisional application: this 'general intention' is derived from factors including the overall purpose of provisional application and the principle of legitimate expectations. The second part of the chapter is devoted to analysing different theoretical explanations for the (assumed) existence of legally binding rights and obligations during the period of provisional application, given that treaties prior to their entry into force, in principle, do not have obligatory force.

Chapter four explores some elements of the practice of States and international organisations in relation to the provisional application of treaties. First, statements on the binding force of provisionally applied treaties are examined. Second, the intention of States and international organisations is analysed as manifested in agreements on provisional application.

Finally, the conclusion recalls the principal issues identified in previous chapters. Against this background it provides an assessment of the binding force of provisionally applied treaties and submits a proposition as to how the matter should be approached.

---

4 See Article 25(2).

5 Kelvin Widdows, "What is an Agreement in International Law," *British Yearbook of International Law* 50 (1979): 124.

2. Terminology

Throughout this book a number of terms and phrases will be used concerning the provisional application of treaties.

'Provisional application' is a mechanism which allows States and international organisations to give effect to a treaty pending its entry into force by applying its provisions to relevant acts, facts and situations. The ILC referred to the mechanism under consideration as 'provisional entry into force';[6] however, State delegates at the 1968–1969 Vienna Conference changed the name to 'provisional application.'[7] In practice both terms (and others) can be found.[8] Generally they are used interchangeably.[9] Thus, in general, when the phrase 'provisional entry into force' is used what is meant thereby is 'provisional application' as set out in Article 25.[10] Accordingly, in the present book the term 'provisional application' will be used as a generic term (which covers 'provisional entry into force') except when the ILC position is quoted or its legal basis analysed. Finally, in order to avoid any confusion at this point the specific use of the terms in commodity agreements will be introduced later.[11]

The phrases 'provisionally applied treaty' and 'treaty during its (period of) provisional application' are used to describe a treaty that is subject to provisional application. In other words, these phrases refer to a treaty that is given effect to pending its entry into force by applying its provisions to relevant acts, facts and situations. Recourse is normally had to provisional application where there is a gap between the conclusion of the treaty and its entry into force. Thus normally only those treaties, which do not enter

[6] See, e.g., the final ILC draft article on today Article 25; Draft articles on the law of treaties: text as finally adopted by the Commission on 18 and 19 July 1966, UN Doc A/CN.4/190, 177.

[7] Report of the Committee of the Whole (CoW) on its work at the first session of the Conference, UN Doc A/Conf.39/14, §230.

[8] Andrew G. Michie, "The Provisional Application of Treaties with Special Reference to Arms Control, Disarmament and Non-Proliferation Instruments" (LL.M. thesis, University of South Africa, 2004), 77, http://uir.unisa.ac.za/handle/10500/1920; Denise Mathy, "Article 25 VCLT 1969," in *The Vienna Conventions on the Law of Treaties: A Commentary*, vol. 1, Olivier Corten and Pierre Klein, eds. (Oxford: Oxford University Press, 2011), 646–48.

[9] Geslin, *Application provisoire*, 127, 139f.

[10] An exception to this is the use of these terms in the context of commodity agreements. There 'provisional entry into force' relates to the treaty (the commodity agreement), and more precisely its status, whereas 'provisional application' relates to the provisional application of the commodity agreement by States, i.e. it denotes the giving effect to the agreement prior to its entry into force by individual States, frequently as a result of a State's unilateral declaration or notification of provisional application to such effect.

[11] See the preceding note and the text to notes 57–60 in chapter 4 below.

into force 'immediately' upon signature, at least with regard to some of the States concerned, are subject to provisional application.[12]

'Limitation clause' is a term used for stipulations which determine the extent to which provisional application is to take place. These stipulations thus 'delimit' provisional application. Frequently this is done by reference to internal law, for example by providing that the treaty shall be provisionally applied 'to the extent compatible with internal laws/regulations/the constitution' etc. Thus, these clauses make a renvoi to internal law, so that it is internal law that determines the extent to which a treaty is provisionally applied in the international sphere. Writers broadly agree that this subjection of provisional application to internal law means that in case of conflict (the specified) internal law prevails over the treaty during its period of provisional application.[13] In some instances financial considerations may additionally delimit the provisional application, for instance when the parties agree that a treaty will be applied provisionally 'insofar as their constitutional and budgetary regulations permit.'[14]

'Agreement on provisional application' is the term used to designate the agreement between States and/or international organisations to subject a certain treaty to provisional application. These agreements regulate the procedure and technicalities of provisional application in a given case, such as its commencement and termination, possibly also the relationship to an earlier agreement on the same subject-matter, or specific duties which may arise during that period or upon the termination of provisional application etc. Limitation clauses, for instance, can also form part of agreements on provisional application.[15] Frequently, such an agreement

---

[12] See also René Lefeber, "Treaties, Provisional Application," last modified October 2006, in *MPEPIL online*, ed. Rüdiger Wolfrum, [1]-[2]; Hafner, "Provisional Application," 594.

[13] Heike Krieger, "Article 25: Provisional Application," in *Vienna Convention on the Law of Treaties: A Commentary*, eds. Oliver Dörr and Kirsten Schmalenbach (Heidelberg: Springer, 2012), [26]; Lefeber, "Treaties, Provisional Application," [13]; Michie, "Provisional Application," 74; Sebastian Pritzkow, *Das völkerrechtliche Verhältnis zwischen der EU und Russland im Energiesektor* (Heidelberg: Springer, 2011), 69; in the context of the ECT: Ulrich Klaus, "The Yukos Case under the Energy Charter Treaty and the Provisional Application of International Treaties," *Policy Papers on Transnational Economic Law* 11 (2005): 5; see also Montag, *Völkerrechtliche Verträge*, 54.

[14] Agreement Concerning the International Institute of Refrigeration, Article XXXIV(3) (adopted 1 December 1954, entered into force 23 July 1955) 826 UNTS 191. See also the Japanese declaration made upon notification of provisional application of the 1993 Cocoa Agreement (adopted 16 July 1993, provisionally entered into force 22 February 1994) 1766 UNTS 3.

[15] Anthony Aust, *Modern Treaty Law and Practice*, 2nd. ed. (Cambridge: University Press Cambridge, 2007), 174; Hafner, "Provisional Application," 597; Michie, "Provisional Application," 73.

will consist of just one or two sentences, stipulating, for example, that the treaty will be applied provisionally from a certain date or event. Such short agreements on provisional application can be contained in the treaty itself, in a final clause,[16] often either closely preceding or succeeding the Article on the treaty's entry into force. Alternatively, an agreement on provisional application may be contained in a separate document from the treaty, i.e. in a collateral agreement. Such collateral agreements can be found in all types of documents associated with treaties, including protocols, final acts, resolutions etc.[17] In these cases the collateral agreement can be devoted solely to provisional application, or it can regulate several other issues alongside the provisional application of the main treaty.

Provisional application generally is based on an agreement (on provisional application).[18] Even when provisional application is brought about by a unilateral declaration or notification, it is still based on the underlying agreement of relevant States and international organisations to allow recourse to provisional application concerning the treaty in question, including the agreement that such application may be triggered for individual participants by unilateral declarations to such effect. Finally, it is important to note that the debate surrounding the binding force and legal nature of provisionally applied treaties extends to the binding force and legal nature of the agreement on which provisional application is based, i.e. to the 'agreement on provisional application'.

---

[16] An exception to this constitutes, for example, the Protocol on the Provisional Application of Certain Provisions of the Treaty on Conventional Armed Force in Europe, ILM 30 (1991): 67. Technically, this protocol is a separate document but according to Article I(3) CFE treaty it forms an integral part of the treaty. Thus, this is a case where provisional application is agreed 'in the treaty itself' but not in one of its final clauses.

[17] See also Andrew G. Michie, "The Role of Provisionally Applied Treaties in International Organisations," *Comparative and International Law Journal of Southern Africa*, 39 (2006): 41.

[18] See the wording of Article 25.

CHAPTER ONE

AN INTRODUCTION TO PROVISIONAL APPLICATION

This chapter will provide an introduction to provisional application. The main part of the chapter looks at provisional application from an international law perspective. It will introduce the notion of provisional application and trace the way in which the mechanism was conceptualised during the process of its codification leading to Article 25. This will be followed by a brief overview of provisional application from an internal law perspective. Constitutional law constraints may influence the content and features of an agreement between States to have recourse to provisional application (as in the field of expression of consent to be bound by a treaty, where constitutional law requirements might influence which means of expressing consent are chosen in a given treaty).[1] Thus, to the extent that this furthers the understanding of provisional application on the international plane, the mechanism will also be examined from an internal law perspective. But first, the notion of provisional application will be introduced.

A. Provisional Application in International Law

1. The Notion of Provisional Application

This introduction to the notion of provisional application is in two parts. The first part covers some preliminary remarks on the function and implications of provisional application. The second part contains a delimitation of provisional application from similar mechanisms of the law of treaties or similar types of agreements in order to further clarify the meaning of provisional application and avoid misunderstandings.

1.1. *Preliminary Remarks on the Function and Implications of Provisional Application*

It has been mentioned above that provisional application is a mechanism which allows States to give effect to a treaty *pending its entry into force* by

[1] Aust, *Modern Treaty Law*, 182; Alexandru Bolintineanu, "Expression of Consent to be Bound by a Treaty in the Light of the 1969 Vienna Convention," *American Journal of International Law* 68 (1974): 679.

applying its provisions to relevant acts, facts and situations. Usually recourse is had to provisional application in situations having the following two characteristics.[2] First, there is a gap between the conclusion of the treaty negotiations on the one hand and the entry into force of the treaty on the other.[3] (This is the case when the treaty does not enter into force upon signature but is subject to ratification, acceptance or approval etc.). Second, States are unwilling, for one reason or another, to await the treaty's entry into force and seek to apply the treaty provisions at an earlier point in time. These two elements will now be analysed in more detail.

The reasons why there may be a gap between the conclusion of the treaty negotiations and the treaty's entry into force have changed over time.[4] Historically long geographical distances between States parties explain why a certain amount of time necessarily would elapse before the instruments of ratification could be exchanged.[5] Nowadays, States do not choose signature but ratification or other similar procedures because they may need time after the adoption and signature of the treaty before they can express their consent to be bound.[6] Thus ratification, approval or acceptance may be chosen as a means of expressing consent in order to allow for the time needed for instance to lay the treaty before parliament, to obtain parliamentary consent or to adopt implementing legislation prior to committing the State to the treaty in the international sphere.[7] This is one of the reasons why in modern times a certain amount of time may go by between the adoption and authentication of the treaty on the one hand and its entry into force on the other. Another reason is that the entry into force of certain treaties can be subject to quite rigid (entry into force) requirements in an attempt at ensuring the treaty's effectiveness.[8]

---

[2] Aust, *Modern Treaty Law*, 173; Lefeber, "Treaties, Provisional Application," [2]; Michie, "Provisional Application", 1–2; Montag, *Völkerrechtliche Verträge*, 30–1.

[3] See also Lefeber, "Treaties, Provisional Application," [2]; Mark Eugen Villiger, *Commentary on the 1969 Vienna Convention on the Law of Treaties* (Leiden: Martinus Nijhoff Publishers, 2009), 354.

[4] Jan Klabbers, "Treaties, Conclusion and Entry into Force," last modified September 2006, in *MPEPIL online*, ed. Rüdiger Wolfrum, [6]–[7].

[5] See Protocol of 15 July 1840 to the Convention for the Pacification of the Levant, 90 Parry's TS 291; Montag, *Völkerrechtliche Verträge*, 30; Geslin, *Application provisoire*, 22.

[6] Aust, *Modern Treaty Law*, 103–04 (he makes this statement in the context of ratification). Ruda, *Final Acceptance*, 8. See also Bolintineanu, "Expression of Consent," 679.

[7] Aust, *Modern Treaty Law*, 103–04.

[8] These rigid requirements may not be easily achieved but are aimed at establishing, besides the effectiveness of the treaty regime, a balance among the States in question in the sense that they are only prepared to undertake the possibly strenuous treaty obligations if the other key players also join in. For a similar reasoning, yet in the context of

The treaty's effectiveness can either be achieved by quantitative or qualitative entry into force conditions.[9] Sometimes, for example, a high number of participants are stipulated for the treaty's entry into force in order to reinforce the credibility and universality of the treaty in question.[10] In other situations the success of the treaty regime may depend upon the participation of those States which are key players in the field in question (which are identified by qualitative criteria such as, for example, financial, economic, scientific or other relevant conditions outlined in the entry into force clause),[11] for example in disarmament treaties or commodity agreements.[12] These are only two of many possible causes which may protract a treaty's entry into force.[13] In general, the problem is not a recent one[14] and there are many examples of treaties which took several years or even decades to enter into force.[15]

Sometimes, however, States may not be willing to await a treaty's protracted entry into force. There are a variety of reasons for this. The primary reason would appear to be the urgency of the matter at hand,[16] for

---

explaining delays in ratification, Jean Charpentier, "Pratique Française de droit international," *Annuaire Français de Droit International* XXI (1975): 1099.

9 Ahmed Mahiou, "Article 24 VCLT 1969," *Les Conventions de Vienne sur le Droit des Traités: commentaire article par article*, eds. Olivier Corten and Pierre Klein (Brussels: Bruylant, 2006), 1040; McNair, *Law of Treaties*, 1029, 1032.

10 Mahiou, "Article 24 VCLT 1969," 1031.

11 Aust, *Modern Treaty Law*, 165.

12 Commodity agreements frequently require the participation of a certain number of States which, in addition to that, together must be responsible for instance for a certain percentage of the world trade in the commodity in question.

13 On this problem see Ruda, *Final Acceptance*, 1–29; Charpentier, "L'entrée en application d'un traité revêt l'allure d'un véritable parcours du combattant semé d'obstacles qui multiplient les délais" in "Pratique Française du Droit International," 1095 (he also lists further reasons for the delay).

14 A 1980 Report of the UN Secretary General entitled "Review of the Multilateral Treaty-Making Process" expresses "an increasing concern with the non-ratification or the slow ratification of multilateral treaties, resulting in delays in their entry into force…" UN Doc A/35/312, 25. According to Rogoff and Gauditz already the League of Nations was interested in methods of expediting ratifications and requested reports on means of expressing consent to be bound by treaties, Rogoff and Gauditz, "Provisional Application," 32.

15 For instance the VCLT 1969 itself took more than a decade to enter into force; the 1978 Vienna Convention on Succession of States in respect of Treaties took nearly 18 years to enter into force, and the entry into force of the VCLT 1986 is still awaited, more than twenty years after its adoption.

16 Marian L. Nash, "Contemporary Practice of the United States Relating to International Law," *American Journal of International Law* 74 (1980): 932; Council of Europe (CoE) and British Institute of International and Comparative Law (BIICL), eds., *Treaty Making: Expression of Consent by States to be Bound by a Treaty* (London: Kluwer Law International, 2001) responses by Andorra, 111, and Switzerland, 274, to the question in the questionnaire on provisional application. Vienna Convention, Official Records 1968: CoW 26, Venezuela §29.

example when the treaty is in response to a current or anticipated crisis. Historical examples mentioned in this category are peace treaties which terminate the state of war or put an end to the hostilities.[17] Examples include the provisional application of the 1974 Agreement on an International Energy Programme[18] through which the states parties responded to the oil crises of 1973–1974, and the 1986 IAEA Convention on Early Notification of a Nuclear Accident[19] as well as the 1986 IAEA Convention on Assistance in the Case of a Nuclear Accident or Radiological Emergency.[20] These IAEA Conventions, as well as the possibility to provisionally apply them, are generally seen as a reaction to the nuclear incident at the Chernobyl nuclear power plant in April of the same year.[21] A recent instance is the provisional application of some of the European Court of Human Rights reform measures provided for in Protocol 14 to the European Convention on Human Rights.[22] The need to ensure legal continuity between an earlier and later treaty on the same subject-matter is a further reason why States may not be willing to await a treaty's entry into force, especially when the earlier treaty expires before the entry into force conditions of the later treaty are met.[23] Whether or not recourse is had to provisional application may also depend upon the chances of the ratification of the treaty. When the negotiators are fairly certain that ratification will be forthcoming, this may lead them to agree on the treaty's provisional application.[24] They may equally do so, however, when they expect that the ratification of the treaty may not be forthcoming (any time soon); in situations of this kind it is considered better to have a provisionally

---

[17] Treaty of Peace (Finland–Union of Soviet Socialist Republics) *American Journal of International Law* Sup 34 (1940): 127, Article 9. See also Bartoš, Summary record of the 791st meeting, UN Doc A/CN.4/SR.791, §23; Montag, *Völkerrechtliche Verträge*, 23.

[18] Agreement on an International Energy Programme (adopted 18 November 1974) 1040 UNTS 272.

[19] IAEA Convention on Early Notification of a Nuclear Accident (adopted 26 September 1986, entered into force 27 October 1986) 1439 UNTS 275.

[20] IAEA Convention on Assistance in the Case of a Nuclear Accident or Radiological Emergency (adopted 26 September 1986, entered into force 26 February 1987) 1457 UNTS 133.

[21] Lefeber, "Treaties, Provisional Application," [2].

[22] Protocol No 14 to the Convention for the Protection of Human Rights and Fundamental Freedoms, amending the Control System of the Convention, CETS No. 194.

[23] For instance commodity agreements often provide for provisional application to ensure continuity between the earlier and the later treaty, see Michie, "Provisional Application," 22.

[24] Vienna Conference, OR 1968: CoW 26, Venezuela §30; OR 1969: Plen. 11, Waldock, §89.

applied treaty in place than merely an unratified one, at least from an international (treaty relations) perspective.[25]

It may be fairly difficult to establish the particular reason for provisionally applying a given treaty. This is so because only few treaties provide an explanation as to why recourse was had to provisional application.[26] Sometimes, this explanation may not be informative as for instance the 'standard formula' would seem to suggest which is used in treaties negotiated under the auspices of the Council of Europe when the signatory States have agreed to apply the treaty provisionally. The 'standard formula' is roughly along the following lines '*in order to avoid any delay in the implementation of the present Convention,* the signatory States agree to apply it provisionally…' (emphasis added).[27]

1.1.1. *The Temporal Application of a Treaty Distinguished from its Entry into Force*

Provisional application closes a temporal gap, by hastening the application of a treaty. It does so by disconnecting the treaty's application from the treaty's entry into force. For a better understanding of this 'detachment', it might be useful to point out that the entry into force of a treaty has to be distinguished from its operation or application.[28] While the

[25] Krieger, "Article 25: Provisional Application," [7]. An example of this motivation for provisional application (difficulty of obtaining the Senate's advice and consent to the treaty) is the US boundary agreement with Cuba that has been provisionally applied for more than three decades, Maritime Boundary Agreement between the United States of America and the Republic of Cuba, ILM 17 (1978): 110, whose Article V provides for provisional application (for an initial period of two years). Subsequently, further agreements have been concluded in which the extension of provisional application has been agreed (for instance 9732 TIAS 840).

[26] The fact that "[t]here is now a general lack of verbatim, or even summary, records of treaty negotiations" as Aust said with regard to multilateral treaties, does not help. Aust, "Limping Treaties," 244.

[27] Convention on the Elaboration of a European Pharmacopoeia (adopted 22 July 1964, entered into force 8 May 1974) CETS No. 50, Article 17. See also General Agreement on Privileges and Immunities of the Council of Europe (signed 2 September 1949, entered into force 10 September 1952) 250 UNTS 12, Article 22, and Third Protocol to the General Agreement on Privileges and Immunities of the Council of Europe (done 6 March 1959), ETS 28, Article 16(2).

[28] Herbert W. Briggs, *The Law of Nations*, 2nd ed. (London: Stevens & Sons, 1953), 865; Taslim Olawale Elias, *Modern Law of Treaties* (Dobbs Ferry: Oceana Publications, 1974), 39; Paul Guggenheim and Krystyna Marek, "Völkerrechtliche Verträge," in *Wörterbuch des Völkerrechts*, 2nd ed., vol. 3, eds. Karl Strupp and Hans-Jürgen Schlochauer (Berlin: De Gruyter, 1962), 537; Mahiou, "Article 24 VCLT 1969," 191; Paul Reuter, *Introduction au droit des traités*, 2nd ed. (Paris: Presses Universitaires de France, 1985), [108]; 1935 Harvard Draft Convention on the Law of Treaties (hereinafter 'Harvard Draft'), *American Journal of*

entry into force of a treaty and its entry into operation or application often coincide, it is perfectly possible for them to occur separately.[29] The entry into operation may *succeed* the entry into force, as is the case for instance in the 1949 Geneva Conventions:[30] they entered into force decades ago but to a large extent only become operative in case for instance of an international armed conflict.[31]

On the other hand, it is also possible that the application of a treaty or some of its provisions *precedes* the entry into force of the treaty. Article 24(4) demonstrates this with regard to those final clauses of a treaty which regulate matters necessarily arising prior to the entry into force of a treaty, such as its adoption, authentication, depositary matters etc. According to Article 24(4), treaty provisions on those issues apply from the time of the adoption of the treaty, although the treaty at that point has not yet entered into force. Provisional application follows the pattern of the application *preceding* the entry into force of the treaty. The difference with Article 24(4) is that provisional application concerns either the treaty as a whole or treaty provisions on substantive issues, i.e. the legal regime which the treaty establishes, as opposed to being limited to a treaty's final clauses, or some of them.

1.1.2. *How Provisional Application Works*

As the mechanism of provisional application accelerates the application of a treaty, the question arises as to how this is technically done – and how time is saved compared with the entry into force of a treaty. The starting point of this analysis is the fact that provisional application, as opposed to entry into force, does not involve an expression of consent to be bound. Frequently the expression of consent to be bound in the international sphere is under constitutional law conditioned upon the prior completion of an internal treaty-making procedure.[32] Thus, it is only upon

---

International Law Sup 29 (1935): 787; J. L. Brierly, Report on the Law of Treaties, UN Doc A/CN.4/23 (hereinafter 'Brierly's 1st Report'), commentary Article 11, §108.

[29] McNair, *Law of Treaties*, 193–4.

[30] E.g., Geneva Convention relative to the Protection of Civilian Persons in Time of War (adopted 12 August 1949, entered into force 21 October 1950) 75 UNTS 287 (Geneva Convention IV).

[31] Common Article 2(1) 1949 Geneva Conventions. This is a simplified explanation of one of the possibilities under which the Conventions become operative, as there are several other conditions or situations in which the Conventions or certain of their provisions become operative, according to common Articles 2 and 3.

[32] Ruda, *Final Acceptance*, 23; see also Hersch Lauterpacht's 1st Report, UN Doc A/CN.4/63, commentary Article 6(1) §1; Robert Yewdall Jennings and Arthur Watts (eds.), *Oppenheim's International Law*, 9th ed., vol. 1 (Harlow: Longman, 1992), [602].

the completion of this internal treaty-making procedure that consent to be bound can be expressed. Provisional application, however, is an invitation to dispense with these procedures or rather to apply the treaty prior to the completion of the usual constitutional procedures given that this is on a provisional basis and formal consent to be bound has not yet been expressed. If the treaty negotiators include a limitation clause to the effect that the treaty is provisionally applied only to the extent that it is in conformity with domestic legislation, they agree the mutual suspension of the international legal obligation to implement the treaty through domestic legislation. Thus, what normally might amount to a breach, see Article 27, becomes accepted, temporarily during provisional application. Accordingly, such a limitation clause confirms the invitation to apply the treaty prior to the completion of certain lengthy constitutional procedures, which in its case is the adoption of implementing legislation.

Naturally, whether for provisional application a State does or does not await the completion of the usual treaty-making procedure is a matter which each domestic legal system can decide for itself. Accordingly, the extent to which the advantages of provisional application are used can differ from one State to another[33] and essentially depends upon how provisional application is accommodated under the domestic constitutional law of each State. Some States have indicated that in the case of provisional application a treaty may be applied prior to the completion of the internal treaty-making procedures.[34] Accordingly, these States are an example of legal systems which use the advantages of provisional application in that they can apply the treaty (provisionally) without prior completion of the normal internal treaty-making procedures. On the other hand, there are legal systems in which a treaty subject to provisional application has to undergo the exact same internal treaty-making procedure as it would for an expression of consent to be bound by the treaty in the international sphere.[35] In these cases, the full potential of provisional

[33] Evidence of this diversity in accommodating provisional application in national treaty law and practice can be found in a question on provisional application in a Council of Europe questionnaire. The question enquires whether in the State's respective legal system the provisional application of a treaty prior to its entry into force is possible, and if so under what conditions, see CoE and BIICL, eds., *Treaty Making*, 316.

[34] Council CoE and BIICL, eds., *Treaty Making*, Switzerland, 274; Greece, 183; Luxembourg, 215; see also Spain, 263.

[35] Ibid., Finland, 163. See also Iceland, 192. Austria: "Verträge können daher [i.e. wegen der Abwesenheit einer Bestimmung über die vorläufige Anwendung von Verträgen in der österreichischen Bundesverfassung] erst dann vorläufig angewendet werden, wenn das österreichische Vertragsabschlußverfahren verfassungsgemäß durchgeführt wurde."

application would not seem to be realised, since the application of the treaty is not brought forward for instance to the moment of the treaty's adoption or signature. But the application may still be accelerated to some extent, beginning once the internal treaty-making procedures have been completed instead of awaiting the fulfilment of the entry into force requirements of the treaty[36] (for instance the deposit of the requisite number of instruments of ratification by the other States).

Put more succinctly, provisional application, in contrast to entry into force, does not require an expression of consent to be bound by the treaty in the international sphere. It is an invitation to apply the treaty provisionally without prior completion of normally necessary internal treaty-making procedures, so that the completion of these procedures might occur only once the expression of consent to be bound by the treaty is actually prepared. Therefore, this would appear to be the point where time may be saved through provisional application compared with the "entry into force" mechanism. A matter arising from this is whether provisional application undermines parliamentary powers relating to treaties.[37] This has been said to be the case when provisional application

---

Ferdinand Trauttmansdorff, "Der Abschluß völkerrechtlicher Verträge: einige Streiflichter aus der Österreichischen Praxis," in *Völker- und Europarecht, 24. Österreichischer Völkerrechtstag*, eds. Wolfram Karl and Ulrike Brandl (Wien: Verlag Österreich, 2000), 144. Loibl highlights this problem in the context of the provisional application of the Energy Charter Treaty: "Most countries would have to follow the same procedures on the national level in order to provisionally apply the Energy Charter Treaty as if they would ratify the Treaty." Gerhard Loibl, "The Energy Charter Treaty: Implementation and Compliance Issues," in *The Energy Charter Treaty*, ed. Thomas W. Wälde (London: Kluwer Law International, 1996), 581.

[36] Trauttmansdorff, "Abschluß völkerrechtlicher Verträge," 144.

[37] A 2001 US Senate Study observes: "In the United States, provisional application of a treaty may be subject to question especially if it gives temporary effect to a treaty prior to its receiving the advice and consent of the Senate." Similarly it is stated that "provisional application of the agreement [1994 UN Law of the Sea Convention] and US participation in the International Seabed Authority, including the funding for such participation, might be viewed as bypassing or circumventing the role of Senate in giving its advice and consent to US adherence to a treaty." Marjorie Ann Browne, "The Law of the Sea Convention and US Policy," 12, Congressional Research Service, http://ncseonline.org/NLE/CRSreports/06Apr/IB95010.pdf. For the rejection by the Italian Constitutional Affairs Committee of a bill presented by the Foreign Affairs Minister "concerning the possibility of financing the provisional execution [application] of international agreements" on the ground that such a bill involved a two-fold violation of the parliamentary prerogatives, see *Italian Yearbook of International Law* VII (1986–87): 329; see also the reservation by Colombia to Article 25: "With regard to article 25, Colombia formulates the reservation that the Political Constitution of Colombia does not recognize the provisional application of treaties; it is the responsibility of the National Congress to approve or disapprove any treaties and conventions which the Government concludes with other States or with international legal

concerns a treaty whose entry into force (or rather the preceding expression of consent to be bound) is under constitutional law subject to parliamentary approval. In these cases, the (provisional) application of the treaty may *precede* the parliamentary approval procedure, whereas normally, i.e. in case of the treaty's entry into force, the treaty's application would *succeed* such approval. We will return to this area of concern at a later point in the introduction. Yet, from the standpoint of international law, and that is the standpoint from which provisional application will mainly be analysed in this book, it is perfectly normal for a legal system to have a mechanism in place for 'emergency laws', and it is clear that this mechanism would not be very effective if it were to take the same amount of time as the normal procedure, or was applicable only to certain treaties and their subject-matter but not to others, due to relevant internal treaty-making procedures.

1.2. *The Delimitation of Provisional Application from Similar Mechanisms*

After this short introduction to the notion of provisional application, its function and potential implications it may be useful to distinguish provisional application from several other mechanisms or agreement types which either have a similar function or a similar name. This serves the purpose of further clarifying the notion of provisional application, thus avoiding potential confusion.

1.2.1. *Provisional or Interim Agreements*

Provisional agreements and provisional application have similar functions. They are both intended to bridge the gap which may arise prior to a treaty's entry into force. The difference between the two concerns the way in which the gap is bridged. In the case of a provisional or interim agreement, the gap is bridged by the conclusion of a provisional agreement which States generally intend to replace in the future by the permanent or

---

entities." <http://treaties.un.org/Pages/ViewDetailsIII.aspx?&src=TREATY&mtdsg_no=XXIII~1&chapter=23&Temp=mtdsg3&lang=en>, accessed 18 April 2012. See also CoE and BIICL, eds., *Treaty Making:* responses by France, 167, and Turkey, 281. For academic views on the problem: the tension in the German constitutional system is described by Ress in the following way: "Artikel 25 gibt der Bundesregierung damit [mit der völkerrechtlich verbindlichen Vereinbarung der vorläufigen Anwendung bei der Unterzeichnung] völkerrechtliche Möglichkeiten, für die ihr intern nach deutschem Verfassungsrecht die Ermächtigung fehlt." Georg Ress, "Verfassung und Völkerrechtliches Vertragsrecht," in *Staat und Völkerrechtsordnung*, eds. Kay Hailbronner et al. (Berlin: Springer, 1989), 819. In general see Geslin, *Application provisoire*, 235–237; Mathy, "Article 25 VCLT 1969," 1053–55; see also Lorand Bartels, "Withdrawing Provisional Application of Treaties: Has the EU Made a Mistake," *Cambridge Journal of International and Comparative Law* 1 (2012): 113.

final treaty regime[38] on the same subject-matter which may be more detailed or elaborate than the provisional or interim agreement.[39] Thus, the gap preceding the entry into force of the final or permanent regime is bridged by the conclusion of *another* agreement on the same subject-matter with a slightly different content (less elaborate, less detailed etc.), i.e. a provisional agreement. By contrast, in the case of provisional application the gap is bridged simply by applying the treaty prior to its entry into force. Thus, the application of the treaty is detached from its entry into force and brought forward in time. In this case it is the giving effect to certain treaty provisions, prior to the treaty's entry into force, which is 'provisional' and which will become definitive once the treaty has entered into force. While it is possible that provisional application may be agreed in an instrument other than the treaty subject to provisional application, i.e. in a separate agreement, the temporarily applied provisions are those of the treaty whose entry into force is awaited. Thus, in case of provisional application, it is the final, permanent legal regime which is applied temporarily or provisionally, pending the treaty's entry into force, whereas in case of a provisional agreement, it is an interim regime and provisional agreement which enters into force normally[40] and is applied normally until the final or permanent regime is ready to take its place.[41]

1.2.2. *Preparatory Commissions*

Preparatory or interim commissions and provisional application sometimes are mentioned without any differentiation.[42] They share the feature of bridging the gap preceding a treaty's entry into force, yet they do so in different ways. Since preparatory commissions can be seen as based on a

---

38 See for instance Japan–Philippines Exchange of Notes 1958, introductory sentence, 325 UNTS 104.

39 William Elliott Butler, *The Law of Treaties in Russia and the Commonwealth of Independent States: Text and Commentary* (Cambridge: Cambridge University Press, 2002), 125 (Butler describes provisional agreements as used in Russian treaty practice. It is submitted that this description is valid also for the use of the term in general treaty practice in the international sphere).

40 It is possible for a provisional agreement, as it is for any other treaty, that the parties decide to apply it provisionally while awaiting its entry into force. In such a case the agreement is still provisional in the sense that the parties intend to replace it in the future by a permanent legal regime which may be more comprehensive or more elaborate yet whose negotiation may not be completed or whose entry into force may be delayed.

41 "Law of the Sea and International Waterways," *Digest of United States Practice in International Law* (1973): §5, 268.

42 See for instance Louis B. Sohn, "International Law Implications of the 1994 Agreement," *American Journal of International Law* (1994) 88: 703.

'provisional agreement',[43] reference can be made to the analysis above when explaining both the similarities and the differences between preparatory commissions and provisional application.

A preparatory commission is a 'temporary entity'[44] laying the legal and practical groundwork for a regime, body or international organisation, in order to allow it to function *immediately* upon its coming into existence, i.e. immediately upon the entry into force of the treaty constituting the regime, body or organisation. Such a preparatory commission generally is composed of all the signatory or negotiating States[45] and can be assisted by a provisional Secretariat or other provisional organ(s) if the States so wish. Typical tasks of a preparatory commission include preparing a draft agenda and draft procedural rules either for the first Conference of the Parties, or, if the treaty constitutes an international organisation, for the first session of the organs of the organisation; engaging secretariat staff; making recommendations for the election of officers or the location of the headquarters; finding premises; preparing a draft budget; drawing up draft financial and staff regulations, a draft headquarters agreement or model agreements; and any other tasks which it may be helpful to perform prior to the coming into force of the legal regime, body or international organisation. Such preparatory commissions were set up for instance to lay the groundwork for the United Nations,[46] for the entry into force of the Law of the Sea Convention 1982,[47] and in recent years for the International

[43] It is said that they "*can* be seen as based on a provisional agreement" because this would be a special kind of 'provisional agreement': in the case of preparatory commissions the negotiations to the final and permanent treaty setting up the later regime, body or international organisation are generally completed. It is a case of bridging the gap until the entry into force of the permanent or final regime. However, with regard to provisional agreements in general, this is not necessarily the case. The parties may have in mind to conclude at a later point the final or permanent regime – for this reason they call the current agreement 'provisional' – but this later final or permanent regime may for the time being just be a plan, and the negotiations may not yet have begun.

[44] Michie, "Provisional Application," 37.

[45] Aust, *Modern Treaty Law*, 175.

[46] Ruth B. Russell, *A History of the United Nations Charter* (Washington, D.C: Brookings Institution, 1958), 1065–66; Charter of the United Nations (signed 26 June 1945, entered into force 24 October 1945) 145 BSP 805.

[47] More precisely, such preparatory commissions were set up for the "International Seabed Authority and for the International Tribunal for the Law of the Sea", see Resolution I, Annex I, "Final Act of the Third United Nations Conference on the Law of the Sea" 175, accessed 18 April 2012, http://www.un.org/Depts/los/convention_agreements/texts/final_act_eng.pdf; United Nations Convention on the Law of the Sea, 1833 UNTS 397.

Criminal Court[48] and the Comprehensive Nuclear Test-Ban Treaty Organization[49] (CTBTO).

The legal basis of a preparatory commission is an ancillary agreement to the main treaty which will constitute the permanent regime, body or international organisation.[50] Since the ancillary agreement setting up the preparatory commission is intended to be replaced in the near future by the treaty setting up the permanent regime, body or international organisation, the ancillary agreement can be seen to be a 'provisional agreement' as discussed above. This ancillary agreement covers the period from the establishment of the preparatory commission to the entry into force of the main treaty. Its content is devoted mainly to the preparatory commission and its establishment, composition, tasks and powers etc. It follows that the content of the ancillary agreement is different from the content of the main treaty which sets up the definitive regime, body or international organisation whose entry into force is prepared by the preparatory commission. Thus, as with provisional agreements generally, this second ancillary agreement with its different content is how in theory preparatory commissions can be distinguished from a treaty's provisional application. Only preparatory commissions involve a second ancillary agreement with a different content, whereas provisional application means that the main treaty itself, or some of its provisions, are applied on a provisional basis, pending its entry into force.[51]

On a final note it may be useful to mention that an ancillary agreement setting up a preparatory commission may be combined with a provisional application of the main treaty's provisions to the extent that it is stipulated that certain provisions of the main treaty shall be applied by the

---

48 Final Act of the UN Diplomatic Conference of Plenipotentiaries on the Establishment of an International Criminal Court (17 July 1998) UN Doc A/CONF.183/10, Annex I, F. Rome Statute for an International Criminal Court, UN Diplomatic Conference of Plenipotentiaries on the Establishment of an International Criminal Court (17 July 1998) UN Doc A/CONF.183/9

49 Resolution Establishing the Preparatory Commission for the Comprehensive Nuclear Test-Ban Treaty Organization (17 October 1996) CTBT/MSS/RES1; Comprehensive Nuclear Test-Ban Treaty, ILM (1996): 1443.

50 Shabtai Rosenne, "Final Clauses," last modified January 2008, in *MPEPIL online*, ed. Rüdiger Wolfrum, [17].

51 Report of the UN Secretary-General "Examples of Precedents of Provisional Application, Pending their Entry into Force, of Multilateral Treaties, Especially Treaties which have Established International Organizations and/or Regimes" requested by the Committee on the Peaceful Uses of the Seabed and the Ocean Floor Beyond the Limits of National Jurisdiction (1973) UN Doc A/AC.138/88, 3.

preparatory commission or other organs prior to the treaty's entry into force.[52]

1.2.3. *The Obligation not to Defeat a Treaty's Object and Purpose Prior to its Entry into Force*

Provisional application and the obligation not to defeat a treaty's object and purpose prior to its entry into force both concern the effect of a treaty prior to its entry into force.[53] They are also both limited to treaties which do not enter into force immediately upon completion of the negotiations but where there is a gap between the conclusion of the treaty and its entry into force. They can be distinguished by the different effects treaties have prior to their entry into force as a consequence of either the obligation stipulated in Article 18 or of a provisional application. In case of the obligation not to defeat the object and purpose of a treaty prior to its entry into force, the effect of the treaty is rather limited and indirect. States which have expressed their consent to be bound by the treaty, and those which have undertaken first steps into that direction, are placed under an obligation roughly not to render the treaty inoperative or 'meaningless'[54] prior to its coming into force.[55] Any other conduct, below the threshold of defeating the treaty's object and purpose, is not covered by the obligation.[56] Thus, the obligation does not require States to refrain from conduct which, if the treaty was in force, would amount to a breach; and it certainly does not require States to perform the treaty as if it was in force.[57] The effect the treaty provisions have prior to the treaty's entry into

---

[52] Michie, "Provisionally Applied Treaties in International Organisations," 51. If, however, the ancillary agreement establishing the preparatory commission provides that provisions of the main treaty serve as guidance or ought to be applied in the preparatory period *mutatis mutandis*, this may fall short of a provisional application of the main treaty. See for instance Resolution Establishing the Preparatory Commission for the Comprehensive Nuclear Test-Ban Treaty Organization, CTBT/MSS/RES1, Annex, paras. f 5(c), 8(c).

[53] In the VCLT the provisions relate to the period "pending the treaty's entry into force" and "prior to the treaty's entry into force", see Article 25(1) and 18 (title) respectively.

[54] Villiger, *Commentary*, 249.

[55] Such conduct would not yet amount to a breach of the treaty because the treaty is not yet in force and not binding on the parties to it. It is this gap which the obligation not to defeat a treaty's object and purpose prior to its entry into force closes.

[56] Aust, *Modern Treaty Law*, 119; Oliver Dörr, "Codifying and Developing Meta-Rules: The ILC and the Law of Treaties," *German Yearbook of International Law* 49 (2006): 135; Rogoff, "Unratified Treaty," 297.

[57] Aust, *Modern Treaty Law*, 117, 118; Dörr, "Codifying and Developing Meta-Rules," 135; Rogoff, "Unratified Treaty", 297; see also Geslin, *Application provisoire*, 186–7; Jean-Pierre Cot, "La bonne foi et la conclusion des traités," *Revue Belge de Droit International* (1968): 155.

force is that they serve to establish the treaty's object and purpose (by way of an interpretation of the treaty and its provisions), and in this sense the treaty's effect is rather limited and indirect as it has been mentioned above. Any conduct which would defeat the treaty's object and purpose so established would be prohibited by the obligation. Thus the obligation will often be one of abstention rather than of positive action.[58] To the extent that positive action should be required under that obligation it would generally fall short of applying the treaty's provisions to relevant acts, facts and situations.[59] By contrast, the purpose of provisional application is precisely to allow the treaty's application prior to its entry into force[60] in situations where some or all of the States in question feel a need to act swiftly and accordingly choose not to await entry into force. There is, therefore a clear distinction to be noted between, provisional application[61] and the obligation not to defeat a treaty's object and purpose.[62] Thus, while under Article 18 the effects of a treaty prior to its entry into force are limited to preserving the treaty's core by prohibiting acts which would defeat the treaty's object and purpose, provisional application involves giving effect to the treaty in a much broader way by actually applying it (or some of its provisions) to relevant acts, facts and situations prior to the treaty's entry into force.

1.2.4. *The Retroactive Application of a Treaty*

Both the retroactive application of a treaty and its provisional application concern the temporal sphere of application of the treaty. In both instances the treaty applies to acts, facts and situations which take place prior to the treaty's entry into force. The difference between the two is the moment in time when the duty to apply the treaty to such acts, facts and situations arises. In case of a retroactive application, the duty arises *ex post facto*, i.e. after such acts, facts and situations have actually occurred. Thus it is, for example, upon the treaty's entry into force, that the duty arises to apply the treaty to past acts, facts and situations. By contrast, provisional

58 Nash, "Contemporary Practice of the United States," 933. Villiger, *Commentary*, 249.

59 Villiger, *Commentary*, 249; Laurence Boisson de Chazournes, Anne-Marie La Rosa, and Makane Moise Mbengue, "Article 18 VCLT 1969," in Corten and Klein, *The Vienna Conventions on the Law of Treaties*, 400f.

60 State practice indicates that provisional application involves the "fulfilment" or "performance" of the "obligations", or the "application" of the treaty, see CoE and BIICL, eds., *Treaty Making*, Denmark, 153; Iceland, 192; Ireland, 196; Lithuania, 211; Romania, 241.

61 Nash, "Contemporary Practice of the United States," 933.

62 Geslin, *Application provisoire*, 330; Villiger, *Commentary*, 252.

application is non-retroactive.[63] Provisional application means that the treaty is applied *prior* to its entry into force, but it is applied only to acts, facts and situations *of the present and the future*. Thus in case of provisional application, the treaty does not apply to acts, facts and situations of the past.

In conclusion, in the case of a retroactive application of a treaty, the duty to apply the treaty to acts, facts and situations prior to the treaty's entry into force arises after the events have occurred and in this sense relates to the past, whereas in case of provisional application the treaty's application *actually* occurs prior to its entry into force, and relates to current and future acts, facts and situations.

After this initial introduction to the notion of provisional application, the emergence of the concept of provisional application and its further development will be traced against the background of its codification in Article 25, in order to provide yet a deeper and more comprehensive understanding of the mechanism and its features in international law.

2. The Emergence of the Concept of Provisional Application and its Codification in Article 25

2.1. *Introduction*

The starting point of an analysis of provisional application in international law is its default rule, Article 25. Article 25 reads as follows:

> Article 25 Provisional application
> 1. A treaty or part of a treaty is applied provisionally pending its entry into force if:
> a) the treaty itself so provides; or
> b) the negotiating States have in some other manner so agreed.
>
> 2. Unless the treaty otherwise provides or the negotiating States have otherwise agreed, the provisional application of a treaty or a part of a treaty with respect to a State shall be terminated if that State notifies the States between which the treaty is being applied provisionally of its intention not to become a party to the treaty.*

---

63 Denise Bindschedler-Robert, "De la rétroactivité en droit international public" in *Recueil d'Etudes de Droit International en Hommage à Paul Guggenheim* (Geneva: Faculté de Droit de l'Université de Genève, 1968), 187, fn. 8.

The Article has been criticised for being fairly general and laconic,[64] and for lacking legal precision.[65] Broadly speaking, Article 25 is divided in two subsections: subsection one is devoted to how provisional application comes into being; subsection two is concerned with its termination.[66] More specifically, subsection one stipulates that provisional application is brought about by agreement between the negotiating States – whether that agreement is contained in the treaty subject to provisional application or reached in some other manner. Subsection one further clarifies that provisional application may relate to the treaty as a whole or only parts of it, and that it occurs pending the entry into force of the treaty. Subsection two allows for the unilateral termination of provisional application by notification to the other participating States of the (notifying) State's intention not to become a party to the treaty. Yet, this is conditioned upon there not being an agreement to the contrary between the negotiating States, either contained in the provisionally applied treaty or reached otherwise. The effect of the notification is to end the provisional application only with regard to the notifying State, not with regard to the treaty as such – which becomes relevant in case of the provisional application of a multilateral treaty. Finally, from this it can be inferred that the phrase 'pending the entry into force of the treaty' from the chapeau in subsection one also covers a multilateral setting. That is, it relates to the entry into force of the treaty with regard to a specific State as opposed to solely the entry into force of the treaty as such.

This analysis of the content of Article 25 shows that the Article provides the technical framework of how States may go about the provisional application of a treaty. Neither provisional application nor its legal effects and implications are actually defined. Additionally, theory in general seems to have had difficulty in keeping up with the practice of provisional application. Although States have had recourse to this mechanism since 1840[67] or even earlier,[68] more than a century later the mechanism was still perceived by some legal writers to be fairly "new"[69] and unfamiliar. As recently

---

64 Geslin, *Application provisoire*, 112, see also Vignes, "Une notion ambiguë: la mise en application provisoire des traités," 192.

65 Rogoff and Gauditz, "Provisional Application," 41, 51.

66 Michie, "Provisional Application," 47.

67 Geslin, *Application provisoire*, 6.

68 Krenzler, *Vorläufige Anwendung*, 16; Montag, *Völkerrechtliche Verträge*, 23.

69 TO Elias, *Law of Treaties*, 38; Ian McTaggart Sinclair, *The Vienna Convention on the Law of Treaties*, 2nd ed. (Manchester: Manchester University Press, 1984), 46; see also Alex Niebruegge, "Provisional Application of the Energy Charter Treaty: The Yukos Arbitration

as 2009, the fact that "doctrine has not very frequently dealt with the matter" has been deplored.[70] Thus, in order to gain a deeper and more comprehensive insight into provisional application, the emergence of the concept of provisional application and its further development will be examined against the background of the drafting history to Article 25.

The first part of the analysis will be devoted to the emergence of the concept of provisional application as reflected in the *emergence of a provision* thereon. The second and main part of the analysis will be devoted to the further conceptualisation of the mechanism, as reflected in the *drafting of the provision* in the ILC and at the 1968–1969 Vienna Conference. As there were four Special Rapporteurs in the ILC working on the law of treaties, there are different approaches to provisional application among the Rapporteurs. Furthermore, it was only with regard to Waldock's drafts that the full working potential of the ILC was used in that the Commission became involved and influenced the codification process of a provision on provisional application. All other approaches to provisional application contained in the reports of Waldock's predecessors were not discussed in the Commission due to time constraints.

2.2. *The Emergence of a Provision on Provisional Application*

This section is concerned with codifications of the law of treaties which demonstrate the emergence of a provision on provisional application. The process leading to the first provision on provisional application can be broken down in different stages: from the period in which there are no traces of any awareness of the mechanism; through the stages where there might possibly be an awareness of the mechanism and where the codes or rather their commentaries contain unambiguous references at least to provisionally applied treaties; finally to the stage where the code contains a provision devoted to the mechanism.

2.2.1. *No Reference to Provisional Application or Provisionally Applied Treaties*

The analysis begins with the period in which there are no traces of any awareness of the mechanism of provisional application, nor are there any references to provisionally applied treaties. In this stage belong the

and the Future Place of Provisional Application in International Law," *Chicago Journal of International Law* 8 (2007): 355; contrast Montag, *Völkerrechtliche Verträge*, 21.

[70] Hafner, "Provisional Application," 594. See also Geslin, *Application provisoire*, 11.

earliest attempts at codifying the law of treaties. These attempts were private initiatives, drawn up by highly reputed individuals in the late 19th century and early 20th century, such as Field,[71] Bluntschli[72] and Fiore.[73] The common feature of these codes is that they deal with issues closely related to provisional application and yet do not mention the mechanism at all – neither when dealing with parliamentary consent to treaties or the interplay of constitutional law and international law with regard to entry into force of treaties, nor under ratification or signature. Consequently, these codes serve as examples of the period prior to the conceptualisation of provisional application.

2.2.2. *Ambiguous Reference to Provisional Application*

The next stage in the emergence of a provision on provisional application is a potential or ambiguous reference to provisional application in a draft code, such as for instance the 1935 Harvard Draft Convention on the Law of Treaties[74] and Briely's first report on the law of treaties.[75] A case in point is a passage from the commentary to Article 10 of the Harvard Draft on the "Date of entry into force". The passage relates to the distinction between a treaty's entry into force on the one hand and its entry into operation or the commencement of its application on the other:

> ... while treaties may become 'operative' on a date subsequent to that on which they 'come into force', they or certain of their stipulations may become operative prior to the latter date. Sometimes in fact, treaties which by their own terms fix a date subsequent to signature on which they shall come into force, expressly provide that certain of their stipulations shall be performable as from the date of signature.[76*]

The text then moves on to final clauses, since some of a treaty's final clauses are examples of treaty provisions that operate prior to the entry into force of the treaty.[77] No additional information is provided which

---

[71] David Dudley Field, *Outlines of an International Code*, 2nd. ed. (New York: Baker, Voorhis & company, 1876).

[72] Johann Caspar Bluntschli, *Droit International Codifié*, trans. MC Lardy, 3rd. ed. (Paris: Librairie Guillaumin, 1881).

[73] Pasquale Fiore, *International Law Codified: and its Legal Sanction* (New York: Baker, Voorhis & company, 1918).

[74] Harvard Draft, 655.

[75] Brierly's 1st Report, UN Doc A/CN.4/23, commentary Article 11(4), 243, fn. 89.

[76] Harvard Draft, 788.

[77] Article 24(4).

could help ascertaining whether or not this passage also is intended to refer to provisional application. The passage could be read as covering provisional application since provisional application largely fits the description. Provisional application is precisely about certain provisions of a treaty becoming applicable or operative prior to the treaty's entry into force. Yet, doubts remain because there is no reference to the mechanism as such or at least a reference to examples of provisionally applied treaties. Also the passage relates to "treaties which ... fix a *date* subsequent to signature on which they shall come into force..." Thus, based on a literal interpretation the phrase could simply mean that the entry into force of the treaty is fixed to occur at a certain date, irrespective of (or not requiring) ratification. However, according to the contemporary understanding of provisional application, it is a frequent feature of provisionally applied treaties that their entry into force is subject to ratification (acceptance or approval). In fact, the treaty being subject to for instance ratification, and the constitutional law procedures which may precede the international act of ratification, would appear to be one of the main reasons why the treaty's entry into force can be protracted and the need to have recourse to provisional application may arise.

In light of the uncertainties appertaining to the above quoted passage it is unsurprising that the issue of whether this passage of the Harvard Draft is a reference to provisional application is contested in academic writings.[78] Similar examples of such potential or ambiguous references to provisional application can be found in Brierly's first report on the law of treaties[79] or in a section relating to Article 8 of the 1928 Havana 'Convention on Treaties'.[80]

The conclusion to be drawn from this stage is that drafters were aware of mechanisms similar to provisional application. While it is possible that they were aware of and meant to refer to provisional application, this cannot be proved and therefore remains uncertain.

2.2.3. *Unambiguous Reference to Provisionally Applied Treaties*

The next stage in the emergence of a provision on provisional application are codes referring to treaties which themselves use the terminology of

---

78 For such a reference: Vignes, "Une notion ambiguë: la mise en application provisoire des traités," 181, fn. 1; see also Montag, *Völkerrechtliche Verträge*, 36, fn. 5. Against such a reference Rogoff and Gauditz, Provisional Application," 42–3.

79 Brierly's 1st Report, UN Doc A/CN.4/23, commentary Article 11(4), 243, fn. 89.

80 Hudson, ed., *International Legislation* (Washington, DC: Carnegie Endowment for International Peace, 1931) vol. IV, no. 190, 2378. Montag, *Völkerrechtliche Verträge*, 36, submits that the Havana Convention does not contain a reference to provisional application.

'provisional entry into force', 'provisional application' or 'immediate execution'.[81] Nevertheless, the references to provisionally applied treaties in these codes seem to reflect a different understanding or concept of provisional application than the present one. The Harvard Draft,[82] for instance, refers to the 1840 Convention for the pacification of the Levant.[83] This treaty is commonly classified as a provisionally applied treaty,[84] yet the Harvard Draft refers to it in a section on treaties stipulating that certain of their articles come into force on different dates.[85] Thus provisional application is compared to the situation in which the entry into force is not a singular event of a treaty but may occur twice and on different dates in relation to different articles of the same treaty. This clearly differs from the contemporary understanding according to which there is only one entry into force; if treaty provisions are being executed immediately in spite of a later ratification (other than the ones dealt with by Article 24(4)), this amounts to a 'provisional application' of those provisions, not to a 'first' entry into force to be followed by another.

Another example of a reference to provisionally applied treaties is contained in Lauterpacht's first report on the law of treaties.[86] There he refers to two treaties which employ the terminology of 'provisional entry into force' and 'provisional application', and they do so in their respective final clause on the entry into force of each treaty. By contrast, Lauterpacht refers to these two treaties in his draft article on 'ratification'. There he notes the exception that a treaty in absence of ratification is binding if, while providing for ratification, it also provides for its coming into force prior to ratification. Thereby, he treats the mechanism as belonging to the realm of 'ratification' and disconnects it from the context of 'entry into force' within which it was mentioned in both treaties. He also does not retain the terminology used in the treaties ('provisional') to designate the mechanism.

---

[81] Harvard Draft, Article 7, 760; Article 10, 788; 791–2; 794; Hersch Lauterpacht, Report on the Law of Treaties, (hereinafter 'Lauterpacht's 1st Report'), UN Doc A/CN.4/63, commentary Article 6(b), 114–5.

[82] Article 10, 794.

[83] Article 10, 794, n 109.

[84] Ludwig Bittner, *Die Lehre von den völkerrechtlichen Vertragsurkunden* (Stuttgart: Deutsche Verlagsanstalt, 1924), 262, fn. 1053; Fernand Dehousse, *La ratification des traités* (Paris: Recueil Sirey, 1935), 103; Geslin, *Application provisoire*, 6, 22; Krenzler, *Vorläufige Anwendung*, 17, fn. 2; Montag, *Völkerrechtliche Verträge*, 23.

[85] Article 10, 794.

[86] Lauterpacht's 1st Report, UN Doc A/CN.4/63, commentary Article 6(b), 114–5.

In conclusion, references of this type show that the practice of provisional application had been noticed but that the theoretical approach to these treaties yet still differed from the contemporary understanding of provisional application.

2.2.4. *A Provision on Provisional Application*

The last step in the emergence of a provision on provisional application in codes on the law of treaties is the drafting of such a provision. As opposed to a mere reference to provisionally applied treaties in the commentary, a provision on provisional application in codes means that the mechanism is *regulated* in an article or a subsection thereto. This would imply to set out for instance its legal effects or some of the details to be followed when having recourse to the mechanism. It was Fitzmaurice who, as the ILC's third Special Rapporteur on the Law of Treaties, first drafted such a provision on provisional application.[87] He regulated (parts of) the mechanism in an article, coined the terminology 'provisional' and placed this rule in the context of the 'entry into force' of treaties.[88]

2.2.5. *Conclusion*

The emergence of a provision on provisional application allows some conclusions to be drawn on the conceptualisation of provisional application. Leaving the ambiguous references to provisional application aside, it is clear that the drafters of the Harvard Draft Articles as well as Lauterpacht in his first report had come across treaties which explicitly provide for their provisional application (and still today are classified as cases of provisional application). While they incorporated them in their commentaries, they did not display a great interest in them, nor attach much value to their possible legal consequences. Thus, the analysis of these treaties is very brief, and arguably inexistent.

This point can be further illustrated by reference to the Harvard Draft. It is the richest source of ambiguous references to provisional application. Three of them occur over a span of six pages within the commentary to Article 10 on the "Date of entry into force".[89] However, these enumerated incidents of either provisional application or similar mechanisms are

[87] G. Fitzmaurice, Report on the Law of Treaties, (hereinafter 'Fitzmaurice's 1st Report'), UN Doc A/CN.4/101, Article 42(1), 116.

[88] Fitzmaurice's 1st Report, UN Doc A/CN.4/101, Articles 42, 43.

[89] Harvard Draft, 788; 791–2; 794.

perceived as isolated cases. Despite their similarities in content and problems, the drafters fail to establish a connection between them. Instead they use them as instances of unusual entry into force clauses. Thus, this exemplifies the 'non-conceptualisation' of provisional application.

In conclusion, the absence of an article on provisional application in those codes preceding Fitzmaurice's first draft provision reflects the fact that provisional application had not yet been recognised as a mechanism of the law of treaties. The lack of awareness of the phenomenon implies that no terminology was coined to describe it: the term 'provisional' was not used at all in those codes before Fitzmaurice. At the end of the development stands the first provision on provisional application drafted by Fitzmaurice, when he became Special Rapporteur on the Law of Treaties. His draft provision implied an awareness and conceptualisation of the mechanism. When he left the ILC, the Commission, due to work pressure, had not yet discussed his draft article.[90] Therefore, it was Waldock's first draft[91] which became the basis of the ILC's drafting work on this provision.

2.3. *The Drafting of the Provision*

The drafting history of Article 25 in the ILC and at the United Nations Conference on the Law of Treaties in Vienna is quite complex.[92] First, the work in the ILC will be analysed and then the work at the 1968–1969 Vienna Conference. For this analysis certain draft provisions are selected in order to highlight and capture the most important stages of the codification process. Additionally, recurring themes or topics of the ILC sessions devoted to provisional application are identified, and the debates surrounding these themes will be summarised and later evaluated.

2.3.1. *The Drafting of the Provision Within the ILC*

The development of the provision on provisional application within the ILC becomes apparent if one compares the first and the final draft provisions which were debated in the ILC. The first draft provision on

---

90 H. Waldock, First Report on the Law of Treaties (hereinafter 'Waldock's 1st Report'), UN Doc A/CN.4/144 and Add. 1, 29. In its 11th session in 1959, the ILC discussed Articles 1–25 of Fitzmaurice's 1st Report, UN Doc A/CN.4/101. However, there was no time to discuss the remaining articles (nor the remaining reports) drafted by him, including his draft Article 42(1) on provisional application. See also Richard D. Kearney and Robert E. Dalton, "The Treaty on Treaties," *American Journal of International Law* 64 (1970): 514.

91 Waldock's 1st Report, UN Doc A/CN.4/144 and Add. 1, 71.

92 Michie, "Provisional Application," 5.

provisional application to be debated in the ILC is Waldock's first draft stipulation on provisional application.[93] It became the basis of the ILC's work on a provision on provisional application. The final draft article debated and adopted in the ILC[94] is the one which later became the basis of the discussions by the Diplomatic Conference at Vienna.[95]

Waldock's first provision on provisional application embedded in an article on the 'Legal Effects of Entry into Force', A/CN.4/144 and Add.1.	The Final Draft Article adopted by the ILC on 'Entry into Force Provisionally', A/CN.4/190
Article 21* Legal Effects of Entry into Force: 1. … 2(a) When a treaty lays down that it shall come into full force provisionally upon a certain date or event, the rights and obligations contained in the treaty shall come into operation for the parties to it upon that date or event and shall continue in operation until the treaty enters into full force in accordance with its terms. 2(b) If, however, the entry into full force of the treaty is unreasonably delayed and, unless the parties have concluded a further agreement to continue the treaty in force on a provisional basis, any of the parties may give notice of the termination of the provisional application of the treaty; and when a period of six months shall have elapsed, the rights and obligations contained in the treaty shall cease to apply with respect to that party.	Article 22.** Entry into force provisionally 1. A treaty may enter into force provisionally if: a) The treaty itself prescribes that it shall enter into force provisionally pending ratification, acceptance, approval or accession by the contracting States; or b) The negotiating States have in some other manner so agreed. 2. The same rule applies to the entry into force provisionally of part of a treaty.

[93] Waldock's 1st Report, UN Doc A/CN.4/144 and Add. 1, 71.

[94] Draft articles on the law of treaties: text as finally adopted by the Commission on 18 and 19 July 1966, UN Doc A/CN.4/190, 180.

[95] UNGA Res 2166 (XXI) (5 December 1966) §7.

Four years of debate lie between these two drafts. Some of the developments become apparent from comparing the drafts, for instance the form chosen for the provision. Whereas Waldock suggested a provision on provisional application within an article on the broader topic of the "legal effects of entry into force", the ILC devoted an entire draft article solely to provisional application. Additionally, the final draft article is less detailed. For instance, it does not provide for the termination of provisional application, nor does it clarify the legal force of provisionally applied obligations, something Waldock did in his initial draft by referring to 'full force'. Yet the final draft article does clarify in paragraph two, as opposed to Waldock's first draft, that provisional application may relate either to the treaty as a whole or only to parts of it and that it can be agreed 'in some other manner'.

In order to obtain a better understanding of the development, a subject-related overview of the debate will be presented. The most contested issues will be identified (as well as one neglected issue), and the quality of the debates assessed. The starting point of this subject-related overview will be the discussion on the retention versus the deletion of a provision on provisional application.

2.3.1.1. *The Retention or Deletion of (then) Draft Article 24*

The discussion of the retention or deletion of the Article was triggered by the presentation of State comments on then Article 24.[96] The US questioned the necessity of such a provision in a convention on treaties,[97] and Japan favoured a deletion of the article in case it was impossible to define the precise legal nature of provisional application.[98]

In the ILC, two Commission members unconditionally supported the deletion of the article.[99] They considered the codification of the mechanism unnecessary in the light of (then) Article 23(1) and (3)[100] on the entry into force of treaties.[101] Japan earlier had made this point, the argument being that Article 23 on entry into force was phrased in a way to also

---

96 ILC, Summary record of the 790th meeting, UN Doc A/CN.4/SR.790, §71.

97 *Yearbook of the International Law Commission* II (1966): 351.

98 Ibid., 303.

99 ILC, Summary record of the 790th meeting, UN Doc A/CN.4/SR.790, Elias, §84; ILC, Summary record of the 791st meeting, UN Doc A/CN.4/SR.791, Tsuruoka, §§9–10. Originally for retention, then only under specific condition: ILC, Summary record of the 790th meeting, UN Doc A/CN.4/SR.790, Reuter, §74 and ILC, Summary record of the 791st meeting, UN Doc A/CN.4/SR.791, §38.

100 UN Doc A/CN.4/148, 182.

101 ILC, Summary record of the 790th meeting, UN Doc A/CN.4/SR.790, Elias, §84; ILC, Summary record of the 791st meeting, UN Doc A/CN.4/SR.791, Tsuruoka, §§9–10.

cover the provisional entry into force, so Article 24 was dispensable.[102] Furthermore the concern was expressed that in light of the varied practice of provisional application and the many unresolved issues surrounding it, the codification of the mechanism might result in restricting the latitude States thus far enjoyed with regard to provisional application.[103] However, the majority of the Commission members endorsed the retention of the article.[104] The argument brought forward for this majority position was that the article was important in view of State practice,[105] as well as from theoretical and legal points of view.[106] Also, the point was made that the codification proved the legitimacy of the practice and thereby supported States which encountered constitutional difficulties due to provisional application.[107]

There are several points worth mentioning in relation to this discussion. First, the issue debated was indeed the merit of a *codification* of the mechanism of provisional application, not its very *existence*.[108] This is interesting in light of the apparently limited awareness of the mechanism of provisional application in the first half of the 20th century. Yet the minority view to stay away from codification in light of the varied practice and the many unsettled issues may possibly show that, at least in the eyes of those ILC members, the overall understanding of the mechanism (its features and implications) was not advanced enough or sufficiently precise as to result in a successful codification. From such a viewpoint it would probably be best not to codify the practice and instead regard it as 'covered' by the more general article on the entry into force of treaties.

---

102 *Yearbook of the International Law Commission* II (1966): 303.

103 ILC, Summary record of the 790th meeting, UN Doc A/CN.4/SR.790, Elias, §84; ILC, Summary record of the 791st meeting, UN Doc A/CN.4/SR.791, Elias, §39 and Reuter, §38.

104 ILC, Summary record of the 790th meeting, UN Doc A/CN.4/SR.790, Castrèn, §78; Ruda, §85; El-Erian, §96; De Luna, §91; ILC, Summary record of the 791st meeting, UN Doc A/CN.4/SR.791, De Aréchaga, §50; Bartoš, §§18, 24; Pessou, §31; Tunkin, §28; implied: Ago, §8; originally for retention, then only under specific condition: Reuter, ILC, Summary record of the 790th meeting, UN Doc A/CN.4/SR.790, §74 and ILC, Summary record of the 791st meeting, UN Doc A/CN.4/SR.791, §38.

105 ILC, Summary record of the 791st meeting, UN Doc A/CN.4/SR.791, Ago, §8 and Bartoš, §18.

106 Ibid., Bartoš, §18.

107 ILC, Summary record of the 791st meeting, UN Doc A/CN.4/SR.791, De Aréchaga, §50.

108 Ibid., §26; see also the US position on then draft Article 24, *Yearbook of the International Law Commission* II (1966): 351.

Many of the arguments brought forward for the majority view either praised the advantages of the mechanism as such[109] or simply referred to State practice. These arguments probably rested on the view that no exception should be made regarding provisional application in an overall effort to codify the law of treaties. Another argument referred to the legitimacy that a codification of the mechanism would bring, and that this would support States encountering constitutional difficulties due to provisional application. Finally, Waldock presented several arguments for the retention of the Article in his 4th report. There he responded to the alleged redundancy of (then) Article 24 in light of (then) Article 23. He pointed out that while (then) Article 23 allowed a reading also covering provisional application, this only amounted to an endorsement of the mechanism, whereas the devotion of an entire article to the mechanism allowed its actual regulation.[110] Moreover, he explained that the inclusion of provisional application in the draft articles forestalled interpretations denying its legal character.[111] Thus it is partly in his 4th report that he develops the counterarguments to the minority position and arguments brought forward by the ILC members favouring the deletion of the article. But even if some of the stronger arguments were not exchanged in the ILC debate, the majority of the Commission still favoured the retention of the Article.

2.3.1.2. *The Legal Force of Provisionally Applied Obligations*

It is interesting to see how Waldock in his first draft addressed the issue of the legal force of provisionally applied obligations. He drafted: "When a treaty lays down that it shall come into *full* force provisionally upon a certain date or event..." (emphasis added).[112] His insistence on 'full' force can be seen as an attempt at forestalling a debate which until today, at least in academic writings, continues.

Several times, concern as to the precise legal nature of provisional application or its legal effect was brought to the Commission's attention and a clarification within the draft article was demanded.[113] The ILC

[109] ILC, Summary record of the 790th meeting, El-Erian, §96.

[110] H. Waldock, Fourth Report on the Law of Treaties (hereinafter 'Waldock's 4th Report'), UN Doc A/CN.4/177 and Add.1 and 2, 58, §1.

[111] Ibid.

[112] Waldock's 1st Report, UN Doc A/CN.4/144 and Add. 1, Article 21(2)(a), 71.

[113] ILC, Summary record of the 656th meeting, UN Doc A/CN.4/SR.656, Castrén, §43; ILC, Summary record of the 791st meeting, UN Doc A/CN.4/SR.791, Tsuruoka, §27; Japan's comment on then draft Article 24, in *Yearbook of the International Law Commission* II (1966): 303.

members had divergent views on this vital topic for the stability and certainty of treaty relations. One member argued that provisionally applied obligations could not be said to have 'full' legal force,[114] however he did not further elaborate upon what their (precise) legal force was. Reuter suggested that in State practice the legal force of provisionally applied obligations varied from the strictest to the loosest categories of obligations.[115] Finally, Briggs found that provisional application needed to be distinguished from the good faith obligation of States not to defeat the object and purpose of a treaty pending its entry into force.[116] Presumably he shared the opinion of the majority of the Commission which considered provisionally applied obligations to have 'normal' or 'full' legal force.[117]

In spite of this variety of positions on the binding force of provisionally applied rights and obligations there was no debate on the matter.[118] Yet the assumption of their binding force by the majority of the Commission members gave rise to another question, namely that of the formal source of these rights and obligations. It is broadly accepted that only treaties in force can be the source of rights and obligations. Accordingly, the assumption that provisionally applied rights and obligations are legally binding raises the question of their formal source, given that the provisionally applied treaty is not yet in force. From the comments which were advanced during the ILC deliberations two different explanations can be inferred for the assumed binding force.[119] One explanation links the assumed legal force of provisionally applied rights and obligations to formal sources which act as a substitute for the treaty not yet in force. Tsuruoka, for instance, argued that there was a collateral or tacit agreement between the relevant States which gave rise to "clear legal obligations"[120]* during provisional application.[121] Reuter employed a similar reasoning when supporting his position of the varied degrees of legal force: if provisional

114 ILC, Summary record of the 657th meeting, UN Doc A/CN.4/SR.657, Castrèn, §9.

115 ILC, Summary record of the 791st meeting, UN Doc A/CN.4/SR.791, §§34–37.

116 Ibid., §2.

117 ILC, Draft articles on the law of treaties: text as finally adopted by the Commission on 18 and 19 July 1966, UN Doc A/CN.4/190, 211, §3. Individual members: Summary record of the 814th meeting, UN Doc A/CN.4/SR.814, Ago, §53; Tsuruoka, §52; ILC, Summary record of the 791st meeting, UN Doc A/CN.4/SR.791, Bartoš, §24, Tsuruoka, §27. See also ILC, Summary record of the 791st meeting, UN Doc A/CN.4/SR.791, Briggs §2.

118 Over the four years of ILC drafting of an Article on provisional application, there were less than ten comments relating to this issue.

119 ILC, Summary record of the 790th meeting, UN Doc A/CN.4/SR.790, El-Erian, §97.

120 ILC, Summary record of the 791st meeting, UN Doc A/CN.4/SR.791, §27.

121 Ibid., Briggs, §§3–4 and Ago, §5.

application was consensually agreed upon, for instance in the treaty itself or in a separate agreement, then according to his reasoning the provisionally applied obligations were binding.[122] If, however, provisional application was brought about by unilateral statements of States expressing only an "intention to follow a certain line of conduct", the resulting commitment was "less strict".[123]

The other reasoning which can be inferred from the ILC deliberations in order to explain the legal force of provisionally applied obligations links the mechanism of provisional application to the concept of entry into force.[124] The argument seems to proceed as follows: when a treaty enters into force it acquires full legal force as a source of obligations, i.e. the instrument as a whole becomes binding. Because the provisional application (or 'provisional entry into force' as it was called by the ILC) of a treaty resembles its entry into force, provisionally applied obligations are binding in much the same way as the obligations arising under a treaty in force. The only difference, then, seems to be that this is not a 'definite'[125] but a provisional state of affairs. The approach of emphasising the similarity between provisional application and entry into force becomes most apparent in the ILC Commentary to then Article 23 on *pacta sunt servanda*. There it was provided that for the purposes of the *pacta sunt servanda* rule, which applies to 'treaties in force', 'treaties provisionally in force' were covered by the words 'treaties in force':

> The words 'in force' of course cover treaties in force *provisionally* under Article 22 as well as treaties which enter into force definitively under Article 21.[126]

Whether there was more to this similarity than the terminology of 'provisional entry into force' the ILC did not elaborate. But it is possible that the ILC considered provisionally applied treaties as akin to treaties having 'entered into force' and thus as a formal source of rights and obligations. In the end the ILC did not take a final stand in the matter, as had previously

122 Ibid., §§35–36.

123 Ibid., §37.

124 ILC, Summary record of the 814th meeting, UN Doc A/CN.4/SR.814, Ago, §53 and Tsuruoka, §52.

125 A definitive entry into force would mean that there is, under the general law of treaties, no power of unilateral termination comparable to that under Article 25(2); instead the treaty is subject to the general rules of the termination, suspension and invalidity of treaties.

126 ILC, Draft articles on the law of treaties: text as finally adopted by the Commission on 18 and 19 July 1966, UN Doc A/CN.4/190, 211, §3.

been suggested by one of its members.[127] Thus, the commentary to the ILC's final draft article on provisional application formulates the question, yet leaves it open, as the following quotation evidences:

> Whether in these cases [of "entry into force provisionally"] the treaty is to be considered as entering into force in virtue of the treaty or of a subsidiary agreement concluded between the States concerned ... may be a question. But there can be no doubt that such clauses have legal effect and bring the treaty into force on a provisional basis.[128]

Yet, even if the ILC did not take a final stand on the matter of the formal source of provisionally applied rights and obligations, it is clear from the second sentence of the last quote (and also the preceding quote) that the ILC considered them to be legally binding and subject to the principle of *pacta sunt servanda.*

2.3.1.3. *The Termination of Provisional Application*

The termination of provisional application was one of the most (if not the most) debated issue(s) in the ILC. From the very first discussion[129] to the last substantial discussion[130] of provisional application in the ILC 'termination' was a consistent source of debate.[131] Many different approaches were suggested over time with the surprising result that the final ILC draft article did *not* provide for the termination of provisional application at all. The matter is addressed in the Commentary to the final draft article and the relevant section reads as follows:

> 4. The text of the article, as provisionally adopted in 1962, contained a provision regarding the termination of the application of a treaty which has been brought into force provisionally. On re-examining the article and in the light of the comments of Governments, however, the Commission decided to dispense with the provision and to leave the point to be determined by the agreement of the parties and the operation of the rules regarding the termination of treaties.[132]

---

127 ILC, Summary record of the 790th meeting, UN Doc A/CN.4/SR.790, Reuter, §75. See also ILC, Summary record of the 791st meeting, UN Doc A/CN.4/SR.791, Briggs, §3.

128 ILC, Draft articles on the law of treaties: text as finally adopted by the Commission on 18 and 19 July 1966, UN Doc A/CN.4/190, 210 §1.

129 ILC, Summary record of the 657th meeting, UN Doc A/CN.4/SR.657, §§14–17.

130 ILC, Summary record of the 814th meeting, UN Doc A/CN.4/SR.814, §§43–44, 49–51.

131 ILC, Summary record of the 672nd meeting, UN Doc A/CN.4/SR.672 §93; ILC, Summary record of the 790th meeting, UN Doc A/CN.4/SR.790 §§77; 79–80; 86–87; ILC, Summary record of the 791st meeting, UN Doc A/CN.4/SR.791 §§30, 32, 57.

132 ILC, Draft articles on the law of treaties: text as finally adopted by the Commission on 18 and 19 July 1966, UN Doc A/CN.4/190, 210.

What were the arguments of substance which led to such a drastic change in the position of the ILC? To answer this question and to analyse the development on this topic as a whole, the summary on the ILC deliberations will be considered in two different ways. A systematic overview will be presented in order to describe the different regulatory approaches to termination which were outlined. Prior to this, however, a chronological summary is provided because the actual development of the topic was anything but systematic, and the underlying uncertainty regarding provisional application which at times shines through is also a point worth illustrating.

A Chronological Summary of the Debates on Termination

As already mentioned the draft article from Waldock's first report (quoted above) became the basis of the future work of the Commission on provisional application. It provided for the termination of provisional application in case the treaty entered into force or, *de lege ferenda*, for a unilateral power of termination which was subject to certain conditions. In the ILC discussion this power of unilateral termination was strongly criticised[133] and therefore dropped.[134] The ILC Drafting Committee in its next draft accordingly provided for termination either when the treaty entered into force or when all the States concerned had agreed to the termination of the provisional application.[135] This, too, was criticised in the ILC.[136] Thus, Waldock in his 4th report reintroduced a draft article providing for a unilateral power of termination[137] – only for it to be removed again, yet this time based on the argument that the matter should be dealt with in the general Part on termination in the VCLT as opposed to the Part on "conclusion, entry into force and registration of treaties".[138] Surprisingly, neither the final ILC draft articles submitted to the 1968–1969 Vienna Conference on the termination of treaties nor the commentaries thereto specifically mention the termination of provisionally applied treaties; the same applies

[133] ILC, Summary record of the 657th meeting, UN Doc A/CN.4/SR.657, §§14–16.

[134] Ibid., §18.

[135] ILC, Summary record of the 668th meeting, UN Doc A/CN.4/SR.668, §37.

[136] This was criticised for being consensual: ILC, Summary record of the 790th meeting, UN Doc A/CN.4/SR.790, §86–87; and also on other grounds: ILC, Summary record of the 668th meeting, UN Doc A/CN.4/SR.668, §38; ILC, Summary record of the 790th meeting, UN Doc A/CN.4/SR.790 §§77; 79–80; ILC, Summary record of the 791st meeting, UN Doc A/CN.4/SR.791, §§30, 32, 57.

[137] Waldock's 4th Report, UN Doc A/CN.4/177 and Add.1 and 2, Draft Article 24, 58.

[138] ILC, Summary record of the 814th meeting, UN Doc A/CN.4/SR.814, §44; see also ILC, Summary record of the 791st meeting, UN Doc A/CN.4/SR.791, §57.

for earlier draft articles and commentaries presented in Waldock's 5th[139] and 6th[140] reports. The last ILC discussion of the matter discloses that Waldock's proposal ('to deal with the matter under the termination of treaties') can be interpreted in two different ways: either as referring to a specific regulation of the termination of provisional application to be inserted in the VCLT's Part on Termination, or, on the contrary, as meaning that this matter could fall under the general provisions on termination and hence would not require specific mentioning. The 'disappearance' of the provision on the termination of provisional application would seem to suggest that Waldock's proposal was understood according to the latter interpretation. Yet, some ILC members, and most notably Ruda, understood Waldock's suggestion along the lines of the first interpretation, i.e. as referring to a specific regulation of the termination of provisionally applied treaties which should be transferred to the Part on termination in the VCLT.[141]

Unfortunately, the above quoted explanation in the Commentary does not shed light on the matter. Neither the Commission's decision nor government comments in support of dispensing with the provision could as yet be found in the preparatory work, and the fact that there is no reference or footnote to either does not help matters. Thus the 'disappearance' of the provision on termination remains puzzling, especially in view of the ILC's overall great interest in the topic. In any case, the 1968–1969 Vienna Conference received a draft article which did not provide for the termination of provisional application.[142] Eventually one of the most discussed topics in the work of the ILC did not make it into the final draft article but was only mentioned in the commentary thereto.[143]

The Different Regulatory Approaches to Termination

A constant element of almost all drafts[144] presented in the ILC was that provisional application ended with the 'definitive' entry into force of the treaty.[145] With regard to a second terminating factor, the decision needed

139 Waldock's 5th Report, UN Doc A/CN.4/183 and Add.1–4.

140 Waldock's 6th Report, UN Doc A/CN.4/186 and Add.1–7.

141 ILC, Summary record of the 814th meeting, UN Doc A/CN.4/SR.814, §51.

142 ILC, Draft articles on the law of treaties: text as finally adopted by the Commission on 18 and 19 July 1966, UN Doc A/CN.4/190, 180.

143 Ibid., 210.

144 Contrast: Fitzmaurice's 1st Report, UN Doc A/CN.4/101, Article 42(1), 116.

145 Waldock's 1st Report, UN Doc A/CN.4/144 and Add. 1, Article 21(2)(b), 71; ILC, Summary record of the 668th meeting, UN Doc A/CN.4/SR.668, §37; Waldock's 4th Report, UN Doc A/CN.4/177 and Add. 1 and 2, 58.

to be taken whether termination could be brought about unilaterally[146] or only upon consent.[147] Many drafts provided for a power of unilateral termination.[148] Even the one draft version which explicitly stipulated the consent-based termination and was silent upon any possible unilateral power of termination,[149] according to the Commentary, still allowed for unilateral termination.[150] The explanation as to why such a power of unilateral termination may be appropriate in the case of provisional application was delivered by Ruda: so long as States had not expressed their consent to be bound by a treaty, they should remain free to withdraw from the treaty and consequently terminate its provisional application.[151] The drafts stipulating a unilateral power of termination generally subjected this to several (cumulative) conditions, such as an unreasonable delay of the 'final' entry into force of the treaty[152] and the absence of an agreement to the contrary (for instance an agreement providing for consensual termination) among the States concerned. Furthermore, in some drafts recourse to the power of unilateral termination was made subject to prior notification,[153] and such notification often became effective only after a certain period of time, for instance after a period of six months.[154]

Conclusion

The numerous variations of drafts and ideas on the theme of the termination of provisional application as well as the twists and turns taken

[146] Waldock's 1st Report, UN Doc A/CN.4/144 and Add. 1, Article 21(2)b, 71; Waldock's 4th Report, UN Doc A/CN.4/177 and Add.1 and 2, 58.

[147] ILC, Summary record of the 668th meeting, UN Doc A/CN.4/SR.668, §37.

[148] These include drafts merely presented in ILC discussions as opposed to being contained in reports of the Special Rapporteur or drawn up by the drafting committee; Waldock's 1st Report, UN Doc A/CN.4/144 and Add. 1, Article 21(2)(b), 71; ILC, Summary record of the 668th meeting, UN Doc A/CN.4/SR. 668, §37; ILC, Summary record of the 790th meeting, UN Doc A/CN.4/SR.790, §73; Waldock's 4th Report, UN Doc A/CN.4/177 and Add.1 and 2, 58.

[149] ILC, Summary record of the 668th meeting, A/CN.4/SR.668, §37.

[150] Report of the International Law Commission covering the work of its Fourteenth Session, 24 April – 29 June 1962, UN Doc A/CN.4/148, Commentary Article 24, 182. See Sweden's remark in *Yearbook of the International Law Commission* II (1966): 339 which Waldock meant to accommodate in Waldock's 4th Report, UN Doc A/CN.4/177 and Add.1 and 2, Draft Article 24, 58.

[151] ILC, Summary record of the 790th meeting, UN Doc A/CN.4/SR.790, §§86–87.

[152] For instance Fitzmaurice's 1st Report, UN Doc A/CN.4/101, Article 42(1), 116; Waldock's 1st Report, UN Doc A/CN.4/144 and Add. 1, Article 21(2)(b) 71.

[153] Waldock's 1st Report, UN Doc A/CN.4/144 and Add. 1, Article 21(2)(b) 71; ILC members for the requirement of a notification in meeting: ILC, Summary record of the 791st meeting, UN Doc A/CN.4/SR.791, Tunkin, §30; Rosenne, §32; De Aréchaga, §51.

[154] Waldock's 1st Report, UN Doc A/CN.4/144 and Add. 1, Article 21(2)(b), 71.

demonstrate, at least in part, the uncertainty which existed with regard to provisional application, especially at the beginning of the ILC drafting process. Thus it is only with time that the ILC warmed to the idea of a power of unilateral termination and agreed that, although generally problematic, such a power may be appropriate in case of provisional application.[155] It is not quite clear why an express provision on the power of unilateral termination was removed from the ILC draft articles. This of course did not prevent the 1968–1969 Vienna Conference from (re)inserting a provision to such an effect. Yet the Conference, if provided with a draft provision and commentary thereto based on the understanding gained in the numerous discussions on the topic, might have had a different starting point and background for their deliberations on the topic.

2.3.1.4. *The Terminology of the Mechanism*

In the ILC, the terminology chosen for the title or the wording of a provision may be indicative of the Commission's understanding of the underlying legal concept. An example of this is the decision not to refer to 'good faith' within Article 18 in order to avoid the connotation of a moral rather than a legally binding obligation.[156] With regard to the mechanism under consideration, the ILC discussed whether 'provisional entry into force' or 'provisional application' was the appropriate terminology. Reuter initiated this discussion by classifying his statement as a "small drafting amendment which might also affect the substance".[157] He found the terminology of 'provisional entry into force' to be incorrect, as the mechanism did not bring the whole treaty into force with its conventional machinery, including the final clauses. Rather, he argued, it provided for "the immediate application of the substantive rules of the treaty".[158] Further, 'entry into force' was different from the 'application of stipulations of a treaty' in that it could depend on certain conditions, a specified term or procedure. Several members of the Commission instantly agreed with Reuter.[159]

155 One reason for its appropriateness is that consent to be bound may not yet have been expressed, another that parliaments may withhold the necessary approval of the treaty once the relevant internal treaty-making procedures are completed.

156 Joni S. Charme, "The Interim Obligation of Article 18 of the Vienna Convention of the Law of Treaties: Making Sense of an Enigma," *George Washington Journal* of International Law and *Economics* 25 (1991–1992): 95; *Yearbook of the International Law Commission* II (1953): 108; *Yearbook of the International Law Commission* II (1956): 113, 121.

157 ILC, Summary record of the 790th meeting, UN Doc A/CN.4/SR.790, §75.

158 Ibid.

159 ILC, Summary record of the 790th meeting, UN Doc A/CN.4/SR.790, De Luna, §91; Lachs §100; Verdross, §81.

The contribution of some members was confined to reiterating that the article really was about the application of the clauses of a treaty on a provisional basis.[160] Another member backed his support of Reuter's position by saying that the mechanism was indeed about the application of some provisions of the treaty only, not the treaty as a whole and not its final clauses.[161]

Nevertheless, Reuter's position was also met with criticism.[162] Although Bartoš seemed to agree in general with Reuter's point concerning the role of final clauses in provisional application (i.e. that they often were not subject to the mechanism), he argued that there was still the possibility of treaties being provisionally applied as a whole. Moreover, in some instances the provisional application was quite long-lasting.[163] This last comment is understood as contending that the longer the provisional application continued, the more it resembled the 'entry into force' of the treaty. In other words, Bartoš seemed to suggest that the distinction drawn by Reuter was irrelevant. The ILC Drafting Committee also rejected Reuter's approach, so that the new draft article was again phrased in terms of 'provisional entry into force'.[164] Waldock explained this position on several grounds:[165] First, by reference to State practice, 'provisional entry into force' was the terminology used – a point which Reuter had conceded when introducing his suggestion. Second, Waldock disagreed that there was a difference in kind between 'provisional application' and 'provisional entry into force'; in fact he labelled this a "doctrinal question". Finally, he suggested that the mechanism was closely related to 'entry into force'.[166]

In assessing this terminological discussion, one sees that several of the contributions referred to Reuter's argument regarding final clauses, i.e. that entry into force related to the instrument as a whole whereas the mechanism under consideration related solely to the substantive provisions of a treaty but never to the treaty's final clauses.[167] The force of this

---

160 Ibid., Lachs, §100.

161 Ibid., Verdross, §81; De Luna, §91.

162 Ibid., Bartoš, §83; De Aréchaga, §76; ILC, Summary record of the 791st meeting, UN Doc A/CN.4/SR.791, Tunkin, §29; ILC, Summary record of the 814th meeting, UN Doc A/CN.4/SR.814, Waldock, §39; Tsuruoka, §52.

163 ILC, Summary record of the 790th meeting, UN Doc A/CN.4/SR.790, Bartoš, §83.

164 ILC, Summary record of the 814th meeting, UN Doc A/CN.4/SR.814, §38.

165 Ibid., §39.

166 Ibid.

167 ILC, Summary record of the 790th meeting, UN Doc A/CN.4/SR.790: agreed: Lachs, §100, Verdross, §81; disagreed: Bartoš, §83; ILC, Summary record of the 791st meeting, UN Doc A/CN.4/SR.791, Tunkin, §29.

argument lies in its plausibility, it is quite intuitive. However, it is a rather formal approach and reducing the matter to it means disregarding the underlying substantive question, namely whether the assimilation of the mechanism to entry into force is appropriate and ought to be sustained or not.

Only a few contributions approached this underlying question which would seem to lie at the heart of the matter. It was argued that there was something 'illogical' or 'inconsistent' in a mechanism which brought a treaty 'into force' provisionally although the same treaty was subject to ratification – precisely for the purpose of acquiring (again?) binding 'force'.[168] Yet other than these remarks and Reuter's initiative to change the terminology on the grounds that the mechanism was more about the application of treaty provisions than a treaty's entry into force, there was no further enquiry into the conception of the mechanism as a subset of 'application' rather than 'entry into force'. Instead the Special Rapporteur, when referring to this debate, returned to supporting the assimilation of the mechanism with 'entry into force'.[169]

The Commission followed the conceptual understanding of the similarity between 'entry into force' and the mechanism under consideration. It has been illustrated above, in the section on the legal force of provisionally applied obligations, how the Commission expressed this conceptual approach to the mechanism under consideration. It may be recalled that the Commission supported its opinion as to the binding nature of these obligations by reference to the principle of *pacta sunt servanda* and its applicability to all treaties '*in force*', including treaties that were 'provisionally in force'.[170] This statement clearly shows the Commission's conceptual understanding, by emphasising the similarity between the provisional and regular entry into force of a treaty. From this it follows that the choice of 'provisional entry into force' indeed expresses the Commission's conceptual understanding of the mechanism, even though the course of the debate on the change of terminology would seem to suggest that the Commission did not necessarily fully explore its appropriateness.

---

168 ILC, Summary record of the 790th meeting, UN Doc A/CN.4/SR.790: De Aréchaga, §76; see also ILC, Summary record of the 668th meeting, UN Doc A/CN.4/SR.668, Bartoš, §40.

169 ILC, Summary record of the 814th meeting, UN Doc A/CN.4/SR.814, §39.

170 Draft articles on the law of treaties: text as finally adopted by the Commission on 18 and 19 July 1966: Final Commentary Article 23, UN Doc A/CN.4/190, 211, §3.

2.3.1.5. *Constitutional Law and Provisional Application*

Throughout the ILC debates on provisional application several ILC members referred to the implications of provisional application under a State's constitutional law. They perceived provisional application as a solution for States whose constitutions caused delay in bringing treaties into force.[171] Provisional application, as understood by the ILC, was a mechanism for overcoming these delays. This understanding served as an underlying assumption in debates on other issues surrounding provisional application and as such was never questioned or opposed.

One aspect of provisional application that arises under a State's constitutional law, namely the question of the reception of provisionally applied treaties in a State's internal law, was brought to the attention of the Commission by Bartoš. Since most ILC deliberations centred on the effects of provisional application in the international law sphere, he introduced his comment by stating that provisional application was not only relevant at the international but also in the internal law sphere.

> The question of the provisional entry into force of treaties arose not only at the international level, but also at the national level. If the treaty had truly entered into force, its provisions automatically prevailed over those of internal law in the increasingly numerous countries which acknowledged the supremacy of international law. If, on the other hand, the treaty was applied provisionally, most legal systems would regard that situation as a practical expedient which did not introduce the rules of international law into internal law.[172]

Thus, Bartoš drew attention to the question of the reception of provisionally applied treaties in monist legal systems. The essence of the monist approach is that treaties may, without legislation, become part of

---

[171] ILC, Summary record of the 790th meeting, UN Doc A/CN.4/SR.790: De Aréchaga, §76; De Luna §92; El-Erian, §96; ILC, Summary record of the 791st meeting, UN Doc A/CN.4/SR.791, De Aréchaga, §50. See also Reuter who viewed the link between constitutional law and provisional application from a different perspective, depending on whether the agreement to provisionally apply a treaty was contained in the treaty itself or in a separate document: ILC, Summary record of the 791st meeting, UN Doc A/CN.4/SR.791, §§35–36. Finally, Waldock referred to the link between provisional application and constitutional law when countering Japan's argument that the article on provisional entry into force (then Article 24) was redundant as it could be subsumed under the article dealing with entry into force in general (then Article 23). He argued that it was because of constitutional law, that a treaty originally had been subjected to ratification or approval. Hence, it would be problematic from the point of view of constitutional law to treat the provisional entry into force as an ordinary case of entry into force (i.e. both covered by the general article on entry into force, then Article 23) although they might be treated differently in the constitutional sphere: Waldock's 4th Report, UN Doc A/CN.4/177 and Add.1 and 2, 58.

[172] ILC, Summary record of the 791st meeting, UN Doc A/CN.4/SR.791, §21.

domestic law, oncc thcy have been concluded in accordance with the constitution and have entered into force.[173] Accordingly, the question arises whether the same is true for provisionally applied treaties. This is a crucial question for determining the legal effects of these treaties in the internal legal sphere, and the matter is particularly delicate when a treaty is provisionally applied prior to the completion of the constitutional treaty-making procedure (if, for example, expression of consent to be bound by the treaty under constitutional law is subject to parliamentary approval).

This shows some of the difficulties that provisional application can raise in the domestic legal sphere in monist systems. We will look at these matters in more detail in the second part of this chapter. For the time being it suffices to point out that the effect of provisionally applied treaties in the international law sphere is distinct from and may differ from its effect in the internal law sphere, and that the latter is a matter of constitutional law.[174] For this reason, the matter played a secondary role in the ILC considerations of provisional application. But because constitutional law influences how final clauses are drawn up, how consent to be bound by the treaty will be expressed[175] and possibly also the features of an agreement on provisional application,[176] we will return to the matter and take a closer look at the constitutional law side of provisional application.

2.3.1.6. *Conclusion*

In conclusion the ILC highlighted the conceptual issues that provisional application raised and contributed with its discussions to the conceptualisation of the mechanism, for instance regarding its termination, the search for an appropriate name and the question of the binding force of these treaties. In comparison to the variety of topics raised in these discussions, the Final Article that the ILC eventually adopted merely stipulates that provisional application can be done with regard to the treaty as a whole or parts thereof, if the States have so agreed in the treaty itself or in some other manner.[177]

---

173 Aust, *Modern Treaty Law*, 183.
174 Vignes, "Une notion ambiguë: la mise en application provisoire des traités," 191.
175 Bolintineanu, "Expression of Consent," 679.
176 Aust, *Modern Treaty Law*, 182.
177 "Article 22. Entry into force provisionally
1. A treaty may enter into force provisionally if:
a) The treaty itself prescribes that it shall enter into force provisionally pending ratification, acceptance, approval or accession by the contracting States; or
b) The negotiating States have in some other manner so agreed.
2. The same rule applies to the entry into force provisionally of part of a treaty."

It is possible that the ILC opted for a cautious codification of the concept because of the uncertainty surrounding it and the wish not to limit the freedom that States enjoyed in practice with regard thereto. Possibly the greatest contribution in terms of conceptualisation is that the ILC recognised the practice as a concept or mechanism in its own right. Waldock's first draft still dealt with the matter as a side-issue of entry into force, but under the ILC, the mechanism had its own Article in the Convention and obtained recognition as a distinct mechanism in the law of treaties.

Against this background the next section will explore how the delegates at the 1968–1969 Vienna Conference contributed to the conceptualisation of the mechanism both with their deliberations and their final decision on its present form in Article 25.

2.3.2. *The Drafting of the Provision at the 1968–1969 Vienna Conference*

The 'United Nations Conference on the Law of Treaties' was convened by the UN General Assembly[178] at the recommendation of the ILC,[179] once the ILC had adopted its final draft articles on the law of treaties. The conference was held in Vienna in two sessions[180] and more than one hundred States participated in it. On 22 May 1969, the conference adopted the Vienna Convention on the Law of Treaties,[181] including Article 25 on the provisional application of treaties. The debates surrounding the draft article on provisional application will now be summarised and evaluated. As a preliminary remark it may be mentioned that the topics on which the debate focused at the 1968–1969 Vienna Conference were frequently those already identified in the ILC deliberations above.

2.3.2.1. *The Retention or Deletion of a Draft Article on Provisional Application*

The question of the retention or deletion of an article on provisional application in the convention was raised again at the first session of the 1968–1969 Vienna Conference.[182] The US delegation had put forward an amendment proposing the deletion of the article.[183] This amendment was

[178] UNGA Res 2166 (XXI) (5 December 1966); UNGA Res 2287 (XXII) (6 December 1967).

[179] ILC, Draft articles on the law of treaties: text as finally adopted by the Commission on 18 and 19 July 1966, UN Doc A/CN.4/190, 177, §36. See also ILC, Summary record of the 892nd meeting, UN Doc A/CN.4/SR.892 §§5, 13, 17, 18, and Article 23 ILC Statute.

[180] 1st session: 26 March to 24 May 1968. 2nd session: 9 April to 22 May 1969.

[181] Summary on the ILC's work on the law of treaties, <http://untreaty.un.org/ilc/summaries/1_1.htm>, last modified January 2009.

[182] Vienna Conference, OR 1968: CoW 26, 27.

[183] UN Doc A/Conf.39/C.1/L.154.

co-sponsored by Vietnam and Korea[184] and supported by Japan during the course of the debate.[185] (Then) Article 22 was criticised on the basis that it failed to explain the legal effects of provisional entry into force[186] as well as its legal nature.[187] Furthermore, it was suggested that the avoidance of provisional application in general would lead to greater certainty and security in treaty relations.[188] This argument presumably implied that if provisional application indeed was avoided in treaty relations, there would be no need to retain the article in the Vienna Convention. Another argument put forward for the article's deletion was, again, its redundancy in the light of (then) Article 21 on entry into force, the abstract wording of which made it possible to also subsume *provisional* entry into force under it.[189]

The majority of States, however, were in favour of the retention of the article.[190] Their main argument was that contemporary practice necessitated the inclusion of such an article,[191] pointing out that the Article 'codified modern practice' or 'corresponded to' it.[192] In a similar vein, the Venezuelan delegate stated it would be regrettable if the convention represented a retrograde step in relation to present practice.[193] Another supporting argument was that the Article met "real needs" in international relations since it allowed responding quickly to urgent problems at the international plane.[194] The few States favouring the deletion of the article as expressed in the US amendment were clearly outnumbered, and the US delegate requested that the amendment would not be put to a vote.[195] As a result no voting took place, (then) Article 22 was retained and with this the debate at the 1968–1969 Vienna Conference on the retention or deletion of the Article was closed.

184 UN Doc A/Conf.39/C.1/L.154 and Add 1.
185 Vienna Conference, OR 1968: CoW 26 §39.
186 Ibid., CoW 26, USA §23.
187 Ibid., CoW 26, Japan §40.
188 Ibid., CoW 26, Vietnam §26.
189 Ibid., CoW 26, Japan §41; USA §23.
190 Explicit support: Vienna Conference, OR 1968: CoW 26 Czechoslovakia §38; France §45; Israel §44; Switzerland §46; UK §48; Venezuela §29; Yugoslavia §28; OR 1968: CoW 27, Cambodia §4; Malaysia §7. Implicit support: Vienna Conference, OR 1968: CoW 26, Belgium §42; Italy §43; India §57; Bulgaria §59; CoW 27: Poland §3; Romania §5; Thailand §8; Australia §10.
191 Ibid., CoW 26: France §45; Israel §44; Switzerland §46; UK §48; Venezuela §29;Yugoslavia §28; CoW 27, Cambodia §4.
192 Ibid., CoW 26: Switzerland §46; UK §48; Yugoslavia §28.
193 Ibid., CoW 26, §29.
194 Ibid., CoW 26, Venezuela §29; Yugoslavia §28; OR 68: CoW 27, Cambodia §4; see also CoW 27, Malaysia §7.
195 Ibid., CoW 27, USA §22.

In assessing this debate at the 1968–1969 Vienna Conference, the point which needs to be highlighted is again the uncertainty surrounding the concept of provisional application. The arguments relating to the failure of (then) Article 22 to explain its legal effect and legal nature are unambiguous in this regard, as well as the argument on the uncertainty in treaty relations which the retention of (then) Article 22 would cause. Likewise, the Israeli delegate linked the position to delete (then) Article 22 to the problems surrounding it:

> Mr. Rosenne said he was tempted at first sight to agree to the deletion of Article 22, which raised many difficulties. But, although deletion seemed the simplest solution, it did not solve the problem, because the deletion of the article would fail to take account of existing practice, which had its merits.[196]

With regard to the second sentence of this quotation, one can only agree that the deletion of the article would not solve the problems surrounding the provisional application. It might have solved the problems surrounding its *codification*, but certainly not the problems or uncertainty surrounding *the mechanism as such*. However, it is reasonable to assume that the uncertainty surrounding the mechanism was the source of the codification problems. It is indeed conceivable that such uncertainty may lead to an inaccurate (too broad, too narrow etc) codification of the mechanism. Possibly, this was a genuine risk – yet the planned Convention on the Law of Treaties was presumably an unparalleled chance to codify this mechanism in international treaty law. Thus while the debate on the retention or deletion of the article *inter alia* highlights the uncertainty surrounding the mechanism, the outcome of the debate, namely the decision to retain the article, shows that the mechanism was (nevertheless) perceived as forming part of the modern law of treaties and for this reason needed to be included in the codification of the law of treaties.

Since the vast majority of States participating in the Conference were supporting the codification of the article, most of the deliberations on Article 22 centred on how this should be done rather than why. These considerations will now be analysed in more detail starting with the question of the correct terminology for the mechanism, a question which, it may be recalled, had already been considered in the ILC debates.

---

196 Ibid., CoW 26, §44.

2.3.2.2. *The Terminology for the Mechanism*

The debate on the correct terminology for the mechanism was resumed at the first session of the 1968–1969 Vienna Conference. Yugoslavia had submitted an amendment, sponsored by Czechoslovakia, which suggested that the terms of 'provisional entry into force' should be replaced by 'provisional application'.[197] The arguments advanced in support of the amendment were that first, the entry into force and application of a treaty needed to be distinguished.[198] This claim was backed by a reference to the accepted distinction between the entry into force of treaties on the one hand and their entry into operation on the other.[199] Furthermore, the claim for this distinction was based on the ground that the application of a treaty was 'practical', whereas entry into force was a 'formal legal notion'.[200] The second argument challenged the terminology of 'provisional entry into force' on the rationale that there could hardly be two entries into force.[201]

The opposing view was upheld by two States only.[202] They had recourse to the argument of the relatedness of 'entry into force' and 'provisional entry into force'; i.e. that from a legal point of view, the situation described under (then) Article 22 was similar to when the treaty entered into force in the usual manner. The only difference was that under (then) Article 22, the entry into force was 'provisional'.[203] Waldock, in his position as an Expert Consultant, also preferred the terminology of 'provisional entry into force'.[204] Once again, he advanced the argument that 'provisional entry into force' was the terminology used in State practice.[205] He further pointed out that the application of treaty provisions necessarily presupposed the entry into force of some kind of international document, which here was either the treaty itself or some kind of separate agreement.[206] He concluded with a reference to cases in which ratification never took place; according to him, the terminology of 'provisional entry force'

---

197 UN Doc A/Conf.39/C.1/L.185 and Add.1.

198 Vienna Conference, OR 1968: CoW 26, Czechoslovakia §36; Italy §43; see also Switzerland §47.

199 Ibid., CoW 26 Czechoslovakia §36.

200 Ibid., CoW 26 Italy §43.

201 Ibid., CoW 26, Czechoslovakia §37.

202 Ibid., Iraq and Cambodia: CoW 26 §52 and 27 §4.

203 Ibid., CoW 26, Iraq §52.

204 Ibid., CoW 27 §§16–18.

205 Ibid., CoW 27 §16, as earlier in the ILC discussion, Summary record of the 814th meeting, UN Doc A/CN.4/SR.814, §39.

206 Ibid., CoW 27 §17.

was better suited in order to provide such acts with some kind of legal basis.[207]

Nevertheless, the majority at the Conference supported the Yugoslav and Czechoslovak amendment. The article was referred to the Drafting Committee, and the newly drafted version, including the 'provisional application' terminology,[208] was adopted by the Committee of the Whole without formal voting.[209]

There are some conclusions which can be drawn from this debate. The position first suggested by Reuter in the ILC debates, to change the terminology from 'provisional entry into force' to 'provisional application', was not only taken up but also expanded. Reuter had claimed that the application of certain of the rules of a treaty needed to be distinguished from the entry into force of the treaty as a whole. Most emphasis in the following debate then had been placed on the different objects of entry into force and provisional application: whereas the latter only related to the substantial provisions of a treaty, the former related to the treaty as a whole. At the 1968–1969 Vienna Conference, the claim for such a distinction was further elaborated by reference to the accepted distinction between a treaty's entry into force on the one hand and its entry into operation or application to relevant acts, facts and situations on the other. By claiming that the mechanism entailed in (then) Article 22 was similar to the *entry into operation of a treaty* or parts of it, the counter-position was established to the concept which had prevailed in the ILC debates according to which the mechanism was similar to the *entry into force of a treaty*. In the same way, Waldock's arguments supporting the terminology of 'provisional entry into force' had further developed over time. Not only were there new arguments, such as that relating to cases where ratification actually never took place; but also his rejection of 'provisional application' had become more sophisticated. Earlier, the argument presented by Waldock to the ILC was that the distinction was a mere 'doctrinal question'. Now, by contrast, he argued that the application of certain treaty provisions necessarily required the entry into force of some international instrument, hence 'provisional entry into force' was more to the point.

However, these sophisticated arguments were rare at the 1968–1969 Vienna Conference debate. Most contributions confined themselves to

---

207 Ibid., CoW 27 §18.

208 Vienna Conference, OR 1968, CoW 72 §24.

209 Report of the Committee of the Whole on its work at the first session of the Conference, UN Doc A/Conf.39/14, §230.

voicing the State's position without providing a substantial[210] (or even any) explanation for it.[211] Eventually, the Yugoslav and Czechoslovak amendment, or more specifically the part relevant to the terminology issue,[212] was adopted by 73 votes to 3, with 11 abstentions.[213] Hence 84 per cent of the participating States preferred the terminology of 'provisional application' over 'provisional entry into force'. This was a clear outcome, although the course and main content of the debate creates doubts as to whether the majority of States were aware of the possible further implications which this change could involve.[214] One of these implications concerned the legal force of provisionally applied obligations. How the change in terminology affected the debate on the legal force of provisionally applied obligations will be analysed in the following section.

2.3.2.3. *The Legal Force of Provisionally Applied Obligations*

At the first session of the 1968–1969 Vienna Conference, the matter of the legal force of provisionally applied obligations was treated rather peripherally. The only two remarks by delegates which placed emphasis on the point were made in the context of the terminology discussion. Both remarks aimed at clarifying that *pacta sunt servanda* did apply to provisionally applied treaties: the first in case the terminology "provisional entry into force" prevailed; the second once the terminology "provisional application" had been chosen instead.

First, Rosenne pointed out that if the terminology of 'provisional entry into force' prevailed, one might need to clarify that 'provisional' related to temporal and not to legal effects.[215] In other words, obligations stemming from a treaty which had only provisionally entered into force had the same legal effect as obligations from a treaty which had (definitely) entered into force: both were subject to the principle of *pacta sunt servanda*. The only

---

210 E.g., Vienna Conference, OR 1968: CoW 26, Ecuador §14; Greece §55; Switzerland §47.

211 E.g., ibid., CoW 26, Ceylon §35; India §58; CoW 27, Poland §3; Thailand §8; USA §22 (the amendment originally proposed by the US aimed at deletion of the article; however, after requesting that this amendment was not put to vote, the US declared to vote in favour of the Yugoslav-Czechoslovak amendment.) CoW 26 Yugoslavia §27. State preferring 'provisional entry into force': CoW 27, Cambodia §4.

212 UN Doc A/Conf.39/C.1/L.185 and Add.1, §1.

213 Vienna Conference, OR 1968: CoW 27 §27. In percentage, this means that a little less than 84% of the States participating in the vote agreed to the adoption of the amendment, around 3.5% disagreed and a little less than 13% abstained.

214 See also Vignes, "Une notion ambiguë: la mise en application provisoire des traités," 188–9.

215 Vienna Conference, OR 1968: CoW 26, Israel §44.

difference between them, according to this understanding,[216] was one relating to time, more specifically the duration of their applicability. One was in force only provisionally, whereas the other was in force 'definitely', i.e. subject only to the rules of the termination, suspension and invalidity of treaties.

The second remark was made by the Norwegian delegate, in the context of then Article 23 on *pacta sunt servanda*.[217] This was one day after the change of terminology from "provisional entry into force" to "provisional application" had been adopted by a large majority. The Norwegian delegate was concerned that this change of terminology could affect the scope of the principle of *pacta sunt servanda*. This is so because in Article 26 the scope of the principle is defined by the phrase "every treaty in force": "*Every treaty in force* is binding upon the parties to it…" Prior to the change of terminology, it was reasonable to assume that a treaty which 'entered provisionally in force' was a "treaty in force" for the purpose of that article.[218] It followed that such treaties fell within the principle's scope and accordingly were binding. Now with the change of terminology, it became possible to interpret the phrase 'treaties in force' to exclude treaties which were 'provisionally applied'. Then, provisionally applied treaties fell outside the scope of the *pacta sunt servanda* principle and were not binding. The principle of *pacta sunt servanda*, however, was intended to cover provisionally applied treaties, as an explicit statement in the ILC's commentary to the principle showed. Therefore, the delegate requested the Drafting Committee to consider the possible ambiguity which could follow from the change of terminology for the binding force of provisionally applied treaties.

It is presumably in response to this request that the Drafting Committee undertook the following change. After incorporating the amendment on the change of terminology from "provisional entry into force" to "provisional application" into then Article 22,[219] it replaced the amendment's original wording "a treaty … *may be* applied provisionally" by the expression "a treaty … *is* applied provisionally"[220] [continuation: "if the treaty … so provides"] (emphasis added). When the re-drafted Article was

---

216 Ibid., CoW 26, Iraq §52 and CoW 27, India §24.

217 Ibid., CoW 29, Norway §58.

218 This was so also in light of the ILC commentary to final draft Article 23 on *pacta sunt servanda* which stated exactly that, Draft articles on the law of treaties: text as finally adopted by the Commission on 18 and 19 July 1966, UN Doc A/CN.4/190, 211, §3.

219 UN Doc A/Conf.39/C.1/L.185 and Add.1

220 Vienna Conference, OR 1968: CoW 72 §26.

introduced to the Committee of the Whole, the Chairman of the Drafting Committee explained this change in the following way: the original wording had been open to an interpretation according to which the contracting States were left free not to provisionally apply a treaty even when the treaty prescribed its provisional application.[221] The Drafting Committee had amended the wording in order to exclude such an interpretation. In other words, the Drafting Committee's change was intended to emphasise that the contracting States were *under an obligation* to provisionally apply the treaty if this had been agreed. Once the Chairman of the Drafting Committee had finished his explanations on the Committee's work on Article 22, the Committee of the Whole approved the Article without any changes.[222] It thereby also approved the Drafting Committee's emphasis on the obligation – as opposed to a choice – to provisionally apply a treaty once this had been agreed.

Nevertheless, at the second session of the Conference, the UK brought the topic back to the attention of the delegates. While the UK supported the view that *pacta sunt servanda* was applicable to provisionally applied treaties by reference to the ILC's *travaux préparatoires*,[223] India rejected this by reference to the change of terminology. It suggested instead that the binding force of provisionally applied treaties fell under the scope of Article 18, the obligation not to defeat the object and purpose of a treaty pending its entry into force.[224] In the following Plenary Meeting, two amendments were discussed which sought to clarify (further) within the text of the Article on *pacta sunt servanda* that provisionally applied treaties were binding.[225] Overall, since the change of terminology twelve States expressed the view that *pacta sunt servanda* was applicable to provisionally applied treaties.[226] India did not reiterate her position that provisionally applied treaties came under the heading of Article 18. Nor did any other Delegation support this position or suggest any other viewpoint on the binding force of provisionally applied treaties.

---

221 Ibid., CoW 72 §26, explanation by Yasseen, Chairman of the Drafting Committee.

222 Ibid., CoW 72 §28.

223 Vienna Conference, OR 1969: Plen. 11: UK §58.

224 Ibid., Plen. 11: India §70.

225 UN Doc A/Conf.39/L.24 or A/Conf.39/L.21, amendment by Yugoslavia; for a similar oral amendment by Colombia see OR 1969: Plen. 12: §45.

226 Vienna Conference, OR 1968: CoW 28, Ecuador §50; CoW 29, Indonesia §59. OR 1969: Plen. 11: Guatemala §53; UK §58; Iran §62; Greece §73; Plen.12: Norway §33–34; Colombia §45; Yugoslavia §50; Romania §58; Ukrainian Soviet Socialist Republic §61; Plen. 29: Poland §§2–3. See also OR 1969: Plen. 12: Israel §62.

Furthermore, two officers of the conference each made a rather general statement to the effect that it was "obvious" that the principle of *pacta sunt servanda* was applicable to provisionally applied treaties. The first of the statements was made by the President of the Plenary Meetings when he summarised and closed the debate on the Article on *pacta sunt servanda.*[227] In reference to the abovementioned interpretative statements by the delegates he said that "it was *obvious* that the expression "treaty in force" [in today Article 26] also covered treaties applied provisionally..." Moreover, he concluded that "all delegations were agreed" on the interpretation of the *pacta sunt servanda* rule according to which provisionally applied treaties were falling within its scope. The other such statement was made by the Chairman of the Drafting Committee.[228] More precisely, the Chairman informed the Plenary Meeting of the Drafting Committee's decision to reject the abovementioned amendments seeking to clarify in the text of the Article on *pacta sunt servanda* that provisionally applied treaties were covered by it and binding. As already mentioned, one reason for this rejection was that the Chairman of the Drafting Committee found it "obvious" that provisionally applied treaties were binding. The other reason was the drafting style of the Article on *pacta sunt servanda.* In order to highlight the overall importance of the principle of *pacta sunt servanda*, the Article was intended to be kept general and of a declaratory nature. It was argued that the regulation of specific details placed emphasis on the fact that the principle applied to a specific case, which in turn, so it was felt, could result in weakening the principle's general character.

The two statements made by officers of the conference seem to carry a different weight than mere interventions of delegates. Due to the wording ("obvious") as well as the officers' authority, those statements claim to reflect a generally accepted position, as indeed the President of the Plenary Meetings makes clear when he says that "*all* delegations were agreed"[229] (emphasis added) on the understanding that provisionally applied treaties fell within the scope of the *pacta sunt servanda* principle. If some delegates were not convinced of this position, these statements would seem to offer two very good opportunities for either formulating a question on the matter of the binding force of provisionally applied treaties, or for putting on record a different opinion. Nevertheless, these statements remained undisputed. Furthermore, the Polish delegate used the

---

227 OR 1969: Plen. 12: §63.

228 For the following see Yasseen (Chairman) OR 1969: Plen. 28: §§46–47.

229 Ibid., Plen. 12: §63.

opportunity in the next Plenary Meeting to put on record her delegation's agreement with the position that *pacta sunt servanda* was applicable to provisionally applied treaties.[230] Again, this remark on the matter remained undisputed.[231]

Until recently, the position of the 1968–1969 Vienna Conference on the applicability of *pacta sunt servanda* to provisionally applied treaties was contested in academic opinion. While some authors suggest that (ever since the change of terminology) the *travaux préparatoires* are inconclusive for determining the binding force of provisionally applied treaties,[232] others find that the discussions at the 1968–1969 Vienna Conference support the position of the applicability of the principle of *pacta sunt servanda.*[233] Again others suggest that the change of terminology at the Vienna Conference involves a change of concept which ultimately also affects the legal effects and binding force of treaties during the period of provisional application (or rather agreements on provisional application).[234] An analysis of the divergent views reveals that they are at least partly the result of either an oversight or a selective examination of *travaux préparatoires* relating to the question of the applicability of the *pacta sunt servanda* principle to provisionally applied treaties: out of six Conference Meetings at which delegates and officers made comments relevant to (or implying) the applicability of the *pacta sunt servanda* principle to provisionally applied treaties,[235] until recently at best three meetings had been taken into account.[236]

---

230 Ibid., Plen. 29: Poland §§2–3 (while stating that her delegation found the rejected amendment justified).

231 See also Michie, "Provisional Application," 21.

232 Rogoff and Gauditz, "Provisional Application," 50–51. See also Picone, *L'applicazione in via provvisoria*, 187–88.

233 Michie, "Provisional Application," 20–21; 65; Montag, *Völkerrechtliche Verträge*, 60.

234 Geslin, *Application provisoire*, 328–330.

235 Vienna Conference, OR 1968: CoW 28, 29. OR 1969: Plen 11, 12, 28, 29.

236 Academic writings so far seem to have mostly analysed the *travaux préparatoires* (from after the change of terminology) pertaining to then Article 22 on provisional application, but not to then Article 23 on *pacta sunt servanda*, although the latter, as Mathy has shown, also contains useful material. For instance, Geslin (*Application provisoire*, 329–330) refers to the 11th Plenary Meeting 1969; Picone, *L'applicazione in via provvisoria*, 187, refers to the 28th Plenary Meeting 1969; Rogoff and Gauditz, "Provisional Application," 49, refer to the 11th and 29th Plenary Meeting 1969; also Montag, *Völkerrechtliche Verträge*, 60 fn. 129, refers to the 11th and 29th Plenary Meeting; Michie, "Provisional Application," 21, refers to three of the Meetings, the 11th, 28 and 29th Plenary Meeting 1969. Accordingly, it would appear that the 12th Plenary Meeting 1969 in which the then Article 23 on *pacta sunt servanda* was debated, as well as the 28 and 29th Committee of the Whole Meetings 1968, were overlooked until Mathy's research from 2006.

The most comprehensive research of the *travaux préparatoires* would appear to be by Mathy.[237] She found some of the material which has been presented and analysed above, which has not previously been put into context. In light of this and the above analysis concerning the *travaux préparatoires* relevant to the applicability of the *pacta sunt servanda* principle, the following propositions are submitted. The view according to which the *travaux préparatoires* are inconclusive for the applicability of the *pacta sunt servanda* principle cannot be supported. While it is admitted that a handful of States favoured a clarification of the matter and supported (or submitted) the above-mentioned amendments, *all* of them supported the applicability of the *pacta sunt servanda* principle.[238] Moreover, India's digressing position, preferring the applicability of Article 18 to Article 26, stands in contrast to the intervention of not only one or two States, as the matter was sometimes presented,[239] but of twelve States, which either in passing or to the point assert the applicability of Article 26, the *pacta sunt servanda* principle. Additionally, not one, as argued so far,[240] but two officers of the conference made general statements in support of this view, which both remained undisputed. Therefore, the course of events of the debate – especially the lack of support for India's position, and the numerous times in which general statements on the applicability of the *pacta sunt servanda* principle to provisionally applied treaties remained undisputed – suggests that the majority view of States was that the *pacta sunt servanda* principle applies to provisionally applied treaties, despite the change of terminology.[241]

2.3.2.4. *The Termination of Provisional Application*

There was almost no debate on the issue of termination of provisional application during the first session of the Conference. The contributions were mainly limited to the presentation of positions, sometimes without

---

237 Mathy, "Article 25 VCLT 1969," 652, fn. 105; Villiger, *Commentary*, 354 fn. 15 (he refers to Mathy's research). Lefeber, "Treaties, Provisional Application," [16] (he relies solely on the ILC commentary to the final draft articles on the law of treaties in order to show that provisionally applied treaties are "binding and enforceable legal instrument[s]."))

238 Vienna Conference, OR 1969: Plen.12: Colombia §45; Yugoslavia §50 (States submitting the amendments). See also OR 1968: CoW 29, Norway §58 (contrast: OR 1969: Plen.12: Norway §33–34). See also Ukrainian Soviet Socialist Republic §61.

239 Geslin, *Application provisoire*, 329–330; Rogoff and Gauditz, "The Provisional Application of International Agreements," 49.

240 Michie, "Provisional Application," 21.

241 Michie, "Provisional Application," 21, 65 and Montag, *Völkerrechtliche Verträge*, 60 (both reaching this conclusion but based on less supporting material from the *travaux préparatoires*); see also Mathy, "Article 25 VCLT 1969," 652.

any explanation provided or with explanations stating the obvious. The main result of this is reflected in the vote on the principle of including a paragraph on the termination of provisional application as proposed in a Belgian amendment[242] and the Polish-Hungarian amendment.[243] Three quarters of the delegates voting agreed and the remainder abstained. One State out of 81 voting States voted against the inclusion.[244] The sponsors of these two amendments argued that Part V (on termination of treaties) was inapplicable to provisionally applied treaties;[245] either on the ground that those created only a provisional state of affairs[246] or that States could not denounce a treaty to which they were not a party.[247] Both amendments provided for a power of unilateral termination. Of the 15 States expressing their views on the issue of termination,[248] four voiced their support for such a power of unilateral termination.[249] To that, however, there was no reaction.

Finally, one comment took the topic a step further, exploring the legal consequences of provisional application in case the entry into force did never occur.[250] The suggestion was made that the article should provide for such contingencies, for instance, that once the provisional application was terminated, acts done during that period (on the basis of the provisionally applied treaty) "should not be open to question".[251] This raised again the crucial issue of the legal force of provisionally applied obligations but unfortunately there was no response to this specific approach to the problem.

In conclusion, the participating States agreed on the principle of including a regulation of the termination of provisional application and to include that regulation in a new paragraph to (then) Article 22. Therefore, the States did not share the concerns which arose in late ILC discussions that the termination of provisional application should be dealt with in the Part on the termination of treaties in general (in the VCLT) as

242 UN Doc A/Conf.39/C.1/L.194.

243 UN Doc A/Conf.39/C.1/L.198.

244 Vienna Conference, OR 1968: CoW 27, §28.

245 Ibid., CoW 26: Belgium §42; CoW 27: Poland §3.

246 Ibid., CoW 27: Poland §3.

247 Ibid., CoW 26: Belgium §42.

248 Australia; Belgium; Ceylon; Finland; France; Greece; Israel; Italy; Poland; Romania; Switzerland; Thailand; UK; USA; Yugoslavia.

249 Vienna Conference, OR 1968: CoW 26: USA §24; Belgium §42; France §45; Italy §43; not clear: Australia OR 1968: CoW 27, §11.

250 Ibid. CoW 26: Ceylon §32.

251 Ibid.

opposed to the Part on 'conclusion, entry into force and registration of treaties'.

At the second session of the Conference, the debate was of a wholly different character, critically engaging with the issue in a far greater depth than had been done during the first session. There was a general awareness of the distinctiveness of provisional application and a sense of the possible differences to treaties in force. As a consequence, a multitude of different questions arose of which a few shall be presented as examples: was provisional application terminated *ex nunc* or *ex tunc*[252] (whereas for regularly applied treaties, under the VCLT 1969 termination generally has an *ex nunc* effect)? Was it possible to resort to unilateral termination regardless of what the treaty itself provided? Some delegates thought so[253] and accordingly criticised the wording of (then) draft Article 22 which only allowed unilateral termination "unless the treaty otherwise provided."[254] Finally: did provisional application end for all States if the treaty entered into force for only some of them?[255] I.e. was provisional application possible between some States only, especially if for others the same treaty had already entered into force?

Besides these questions highlighting various aspects of the termination of provisional application, there was one concern shared by a group of States: that the power of unilateral termination put the stability of treaty relations under a provisionally applied treaty at risk.[256] Whereas at the first session not a single State had objected to this power of unilateral termination, these concerns were now raised several times and voiced so seriously as to provoke the Expert Consultant Waldock to admit that he was "surprised at the degree of anxiety to which paragraph 2 had given rise"[257] as well as that "he personally was unable to see all the bogeys which had had been evoked during the debate."[258] Another delegate was prompted to remind the concerned States of the broad approval the power of unilateral termination had received by the Committee of the Whole at the previous year's session.[259] Yet the concerned States did not argue for the rejection of the power of unilateral termination but suggested minor

252 Vienna Conference, OR 1969: Plen. 11: Italy §84.
253 Ibid., Plen. 11: Italy §84; Ago (President) §65.
254 Ibid., Plen. 11: Ago (President) §65.
255 Ibid., Plen. 11: UK §56.
256 Ibid., Plen. 11: Austria §61; Iran §§62, 71; Greece §75; Poland §88.
257 Ibid., Plen. 11: §89.
258 Ibid., Plen. 11: §91.
259 Ibid., Plen. 11: Uruguay §79.

drafting amendments, such as the additional requirement of a notification which only became effective a certain time after being made.[260] At the end of the debate, none of the suggested minor drafting amendments relating to the termination of provisional application were put to the vote.[261] They were only referred to the Drafting Committee which, however, did not propose any changes.[262] Consequently, the power of unilateral termination was retained as it stood.

The deliberations on the termination of provisional application at the 1968–1969 Vienna Conference highlight how the understanding of provisional application evolved between the first and second session. This is revealed by the multitude of different, pertinent questions surrounding the termination of provisional application as well as the growing awareness of the possible tension between the application of the *pacta sunt servanda* principle on the one hand, and the unilateral power of termination on the other. Yet, the explanation as to why such a power of unilateral termination was appropriate in the case of provisional application was not delivered by a State, but by the Expert Consultant. He reminded the concerned States of the constitutional law aspect of provisional application.[263] The purpose of the power of unilateral termination, he added, was precisely to safeguard the balance of powers, and the rights of parliaments not to approve a treaty, even if it had been applied provisionally.[264]

After having examined the debate concerning the termination of provisional application it is the last mentioned issue, and more precisely the implications of provisional application for a State's constitutional law, which will now be analysed.

2.3.2.5. *Constitutional Law and Provisional Application*

The implications of provisional application for a State's constitutional law received little attention at the first session of the conference. The Malaysian delegate mentioned in passing that treaty negotiators were sometimes "reluctant" to include in the treaty a clause on provisional application "for fear of constitutional difficulties"[265] but did not further elaborate upon what those difficulties were. At the second session of the conference the topic was more of an issue, probably because some Latin American States

260 Ibid., Plen. 11: Poland §88; see also Austria §61.
261 Ibid., Plen. 11: §§95–100.
262 Ibid., Plen. 28: §§46–7.
263 Ibid., Plen. 11: §90.
264 Ibid., Plen. 11: §90.
265 Vienna Conference, OR 1968: CoW 27: §7.

announced their intention to abstain from the final vote on the Article on provisional application[266] due to the constitutional difficulties the mechanism caused within their internal legal system.[267] Over the course of this debate these 'constitutional difficulties' were explained in more detail. Provisional application was perceived as undermining parliamentary prerogatives in the treaty-making process, such as the parliamentary power to approve of treaties prior to their entry into force or application. Since these prerogatives were anchored in the constitution, provisional application was seen as being in conflict with the constitution. To some the solution to this conflict was that their State would not normally participate in the provisional application of a treaty.[268]

It is clear in light of other state practice that provisional application has given rise to constitutional difficulties also in European and Western States.[269] Yet the problem seems particularly acute in Latin American States. They were the ones considering abstaining from the final vote on the Article on provisional application, and they were the only ones formulating reservations with regard to Article 25[270] (some of them specifically on account of the role of parliament in treaty making or the fact that the mechanism was 'unconstitutional'). The reason for this may be that these States attach greater weight to the parliamentary prerogative in the treaty-making process.[271] Whereas in those constitutional systems treaties in general are subject to parliamentary approval, with only few exceptions, in many European and Western States it is only certain kinds of treaties or treaties on a specific subject-matter which are subject to parliamentary approval,[272] but not treaties in general. For the acceptance in

---

266 Vienna Conference, OR 1969: Plen. 11: Costa Rica §67; see also Guatemala §54.

267 Ibid; Plen. 11: Uruguay §77; see also Colombia §85–86.

268 Ibid., Plen. 11: Uruguay §78, see also Colombia §86.

269 See, e.g., Hans Sondaal, "Dutch Treaty Practice," *Netherlands Yearbook of International Law* 19 (1988): 227; expressing Australian concerns Jonathan Chew "Treaties in the Global Environment," 17 November 2004, http://www.dfat.gov.au/treaties/workshops/treaties_global/chew.html. See also the remark by the Australian Government, Department of Foreign Affairs and Trade, Treaties Secretariat that "provisional application ... should be avoided" in *Signed, Sealed and Delivered: Treaties and Treaty Making: An Official's Handbook*, 6th ed. (Canberra: Department of Foreign Affairs and Trade, 2005), [64]; see note 37 (in chapter 1) above and the text to notes 296–332 (in chapter 1) below (i.e. section 4 of chapter 1).

270 Colombia, Costa Rica, Guatemala and Peru, <http://treaties.un.org/Pages/ViewDetailsIII.aspx?&src=TREATY&mtdsg_no=XXIII~1&chapter=23&Temp=mtdsg3&lang=en> accessed 18 April 2012; see also note 37 (in chapter 1) above.

271 See also Reuter, *Introduction au droit des traités*, [42] 25.

272 PESC/SEC 899 (9 August 1996): Questionnaire Concernant les Procédures Internes des Etats Membres pour la Conclusion d'Accords Internationaux Approuvés selon une Procédure Simplifiée ou d'Accords Juridiquement non Obligatoires, 2.

constitutional systems of a mechanism such a provisional application, this might have the following implication. If parliamentary powers with regard to treaties are from the outset limited and not absolute, then it may be easier to accept further limitations, for instance in order to accommodate agreements in simplified form or provisional application and *vice versa*.

Returning to the debate on the implications of provisional application for a State's constitutional law at the 1968–1969 Vienna Conference, it shows that the question of parliamentary powers in the treaty-making procedure during provisional application can be problematic for certain States. In terms of the dynamics of the conference, the fact that the implications of provisional application for and under a State's constitutional law played a marginal role at the first sessions and a more prominent role at the second may reflect the growing familiarity with and understanding of the procedure and its potential implications by the conference delegates.

2.3.2.6. *Conclusion*

The most fundamental decision for the codification process once a provision on provisional application had emerged was for it to be retained. At the 1968–1969 Vienna Conference, State practice on this had been found to be too important. Also it was thought that a contemporary convention on the law of treaties could not omit the mechanism. While the debate on this point highlighted the uncertainties surrounding the mechanism, the final decision on the retention of the Article showed to which degree the mechanism was – despite the uncertainties – anchored in the law of treaties. Another major step in the codification process was the change in terminology from 'provisional entry into force' to 'provisional application' at the Vienna Conference. This probably did entail a change of concept, namely to perceive the mechanism as a subset of treaty 'application' rather than 'entry into force'. Yet it was clarified in a follow-up meeting that this change of concept was not intended to affect the applicability of the *pacta sunt servanda* principle to these treaties. Provisionally applied treaties, in a string of interpretative declarations, were said to fall within the ambit of the *pacta sunt servanda* principle, even if this position was often not substantiated. Another important decision was to regulate the termination of provisional application and to incorporate the default rule of the power of unilateral termination in Article 25(2).

Accordingly, the Vienna Conference made several major changes to the Final Draft Article that the ILC had submitted. Overall, these changes stay within the framework of the ideas previously discussed by the ILC. Thus, the Vienna Conference made important final decisions for the codification of the mechanism, as well as important progress with regard to its conceptualisation, and in doing so drew from the groundwork that the ILC had laid in its earlier debates.

2.3.3. *Conceptualisation and Codification in Light of the Uncertainty Surrounding Provisional Application*

At the beginning of the deliberations in the ILC, a lack of familiarity with provisional application was apparent. In the very first debate of the ILC on provisional application, two essential elements of Waldock's first draft were criticised and accordingly dropped: the reference to the 'full legal force' of provisionally applied obligations and the power of unilateral termination in case of an unreasonable delay in the regular entry into force of the treaty. Yet both elements, slightly modified, form part of the final concept of provisional application as derived from the 1968–1969 Vienna Conference. As much as this compliments Waldock's work, it would also seem to indicate the Commission's initial lack of familiarity with provisional application.

The very first contribution relating to Waldock's first draft provision on provisional application was the revealing request that an explanation be inserted as to what was meant by the provisional entry into force of a treaty.[273] However, this request was not implemented, and concerns over the legal nature and legal effects of provisional application were voiced continuously throughout the whole codification process.[274] This analysis of the relatively common lack of acquaintance with provisional application is confirmed by a cautiously phrased remark by Waldock. In retrospect, he linked some of the difficulties of codification encountered by the Commission with the generally shared "feeling of novelty" towards the mechanism:

> Some of the Commissions' difficulties no doubt arose from the feeling of novelty which the Commission had had when it introduced an article on provisional entry into force in 1962.[275]

Besides these remarks, the uncertainty was particularly tangible in some of the debates in the ILC and at the 1968–1969 Vienna Conference. The

[273] ILC, Summary record of the 656th meeting, UN Doc A/CN.4/SR.656, §43.

[274] See for instance the Japanese comment on ILC draft Article 24 in *Yearbook of the International Law Commission* II (1966): 303; see also Vienna Conference, OR 1968: CoW 26: USA §23 and Japan §40.

[275] ILC, Summary record of the 791th meeting, UN Doc A/CN.4/SR.791, §55.

chronological summary of the debate on the termination of provisional application in the ILC may serve as an excellent example of this, since it highlights the twists and turns taken by the ILC to develop its approach. As was mentioned earlier, the uncertainty also found an expression at the 1968–1969 Vienna Conference in the initial willingness of some States to delete the provision.

The lack of acquaintance and familiarity decreased over time and partially gave way to an evolving understanding of the mechanism in both *fora*. In the ILC, this evolving understanding becomes most apparent in the contributions of the Special Rapporteur, whose explanations and arguments became more precise and refined over time. The terminology debate in particular allows this development to be traced: his arguments improve over time in that they incorporate previous criticism and become more and more sophisticated in explaining and backing his own position. Also the fact that the 1968–1969 Vienna Conference was subdivided into two sessions renders such developments visible. An example of this is the power of unilateral termination of provisional application: while at the first session no concerns at all arose relating to this, at the second session, States had become aware of the tensions this caused with regard to the stability and certainty of treaty relations on the one hand, and also of the distinctiveness of the mechanism with regard to treaties in force on the other.

In conclusion, the ILC Final Draft Article 'recognized'[276] the practice of provisional application, and the 1968–1969 Vienna Conference finalised the codification of the concept and contributed to the conceptualisation by changing the name and regulating the entire lifecycle of provisional application. The Vienna Conference thereby ensured that the basic aspects of provisional application (its beginning, termination and object) were addressed. The fact that Article 25 has only basic regulatory content may well be a reflection of the overall uncertainty and possibly remaining unsettled issues. Yet, in light of the general difficulty theory seems to have had in keeping up with the mechanism and the lack of familiarity that affected the codification process the task was not an easy one. Thus, the determination to codify the practice nevertheless so as to produce a modern Convention on the Law of Treaties is admirable. Accordingly, looking behind the scenes of Article 25 reveals the overall conceptualisation of the mechanism that resulted from the codification process. It also shows that

276 ILC, Draft articles on the law of treaties: text as finally adopted by the Commission on 18 and 19 July 1966, UN Doc A/CN.4/190, 210 §1.

the Article can be seen not only as an expression of uncertainty but also, and possibly even more so, as an achievement.

B. Provisional Application in Internal Law

This book looks at provisional application mainly from an international law perspective. While the VCLT gives little room to internal law, it indicates, for example in Article 46, that treaties are governed by both international and internal law. Because internal law can affect a treaty regime also on the international plane – see Article 46, but also the choice of means of expressing consent to be bound[277] or the content and features of an agreement on provisional application[278] – provisional application will be briefly examined from an internal law perspective. In order to obtain an indication on the status of the concept in internal law, a general overview will be given of the regulation of provisional application in internal law and the different approaches that exist towards the mechanism. Then the issues that arise with regard to the domestic treaty-making procedure will be identified, since they potentially influence the content and features of agreements on provisional application, and an analysis of the responses and possible solutions thereto will follow. Finally, the internal law perspective also allows addressing some of the criticism that provisional application has raised.

3. Internal Regulation of and Approaches towards Provisional Application

Some domestic legal systems have an equivalent to Article 25, in the sense that there is a specific provision in the domestic laws or constitution regulating provisional application.[279] Examples are for instance the Netherlands, the Russian Federation and Belarus.[280] By contrast, in many

277 Bolintineanu, "Expression of Consent," 679.

278 Aust, *Modern Treaty Law*, 182.

279 Andrew G. Michie, "The Provisional Application of Treaties in South African Law and Practice," *South African Yearbook of Inernational Law* 30 (2005): 11.

280 Article 15, State Law on Approval and Promulgation of Treaties (Rijkswet goedkeuring en bekendmaking verdragen), Staatsblad, 1994, no. 542. Article 23, Federal Law on International Treaties of the Russian Federation, 1995, as printed in Butler, *Law of Treaties*, 125; Article 14, Law on International Treaties of the Republic Belarus, 1991, as printed in Butler, *Law of Treaties*, 280.

other legal systems, it would appear that provisional application has not found its place in the written legal framework and instead is a matter of uncodified practice.[281] Whether codified or uncodified, broadly three approaches to provisional application can be distinguished in domestic law: either provisional application is prohibited; allowed; or allowed under certain conditions. Several States have expressed the view that provisional application is in principle prohibited by their constitution or not accepted by their legal system,[282] including Austria;[283] Luxembourg;[284] Italy;[285] Portugal;[286] Egypt;[287] as well as several Latin-American States such as Brazil;[288] Colombia;[289] Costa Rica,[290] and Mexico.[291] A variant of this position is that provisional application is possible only in exceptional circumstances, as is the case, for instance, in Belgium, Colombia, France, Greece and Turkey.[292] Others, such as Finland, Spain, the Slovak Republic and Bosnia Herzegovina, state that provisional application is generally allowed.[293] Again in other systems, provisional application is allowed but

---

281 Michie, "Treaties in South African Law," 11. See, e.g., Council CoE and BIICL, eds., *Treaty Making*, Albania, 106; The Former Yugoslav Republic of Macdonia, 278; Hungary, 187; Romania, 241; Leigh, Blakeslee, Ederington, eds., *National Treaty Law and Practice*, no. 30, Chile, 36.

282 See also CoE and BIICL, eds., *Treaty Making*, Cyprus, 143.

283 Trauttmansdorff, "Abschluß völkerrechtlicher Verträge," 127; Austria would appear to make exceptions to the prohibition, also in the context of EU treaty making, see Trauttmansdorff above and Austria's response to a questionnaire which the Secretariat of the then EC Council of Ministers circulated in the 1990s to the then fifteen Member States on "[...] les procédures internes des Etats Membres pour la conclusion d'accords internationaux approuvés selon une procédure simplifiée ou d'accords juridiquement non obligatoires", PESC/SEC 899 (9 August 1996), 10.

284 PESC/SEC 899 (9 August 1996), 8; CoE and BIICL, eds., *Treaty Making*, 215.

285 CoE and BIICL, eds., *Treaty Making*, Italy, 203.

286 CoE and BIICL, eds., *Treaty Making*, Portugal, 237.

287 Monroe Leigh, Merritt R. Blakeslee, L. Benjamin Ederington, eds., *National Treaty Law and Practice. Studies in Transnational Legal Policy*, no. 30 (Washington, DC: American Society of International Law, 1999), 42.

288 Reservation to the Co-operation Agreement for the Promotion of Nuclear Science and Technology in Latin America and the Caribbean (ARCAL) of 25 September 1998 http://www.iaea.org/Publications/Documents/Conventions/arcal_reserv.pdf.

289 Reservation to Article 25 VCLT 1969, <http://treaties.un.org/pages/DB.aspx?path=DB/MTDSG/page1_en.xml&menu=MTDSG>.

290 See also Costa Rica's reservation to ARCAL, note 288 (in chapter 1) above.

291 CoE and BIICL, eds., *Treaty Making*, Mexico, 313.

292 CoE and BIICL, eds., *Treaty Making*, Belgium, 127; France, 167; Greece, 183 and Turkey, 281. Leigh, Blakeslee, Ederington, eds., *National Treaty Law and Practice*. no. 30, Colombia, 74.

293 CoE and BIICL, eds., *Treaty Making*, Finland, 163; Spain, 263; Slovak Republic, 252; Bosnia Herzegovina, 294.

subject to certain conditions, this is the case, for example, in Slovenia, the Netherlands, Denmark, Lithuania, Canada etc.[294]

This variety of approaches towards provisional application in internal law shows that it is for each State to decide, and thus that it is a matter of internal law, whether to allow provisional application and if so upon what conditions.[295] Furthermore, the relatively great number of States in which provisional application is in principle prohibited or in which recourse to the mechanism can only be had in exceptional circumstances suggests that provisional application, at least in some domestic legal systems, gives rise to considerable difficulties.

4. Internal Issues to Which Provisional Application can Give Rise

In the internal law sphere, provisionally applied treaties can raise issues regarding the parliamentary approval of treaties, their implementation and their effect in the domestic legal sphere.[296] The issue that has raised most concern is the effect of provisional application on the constitutional rule of the separation of powers, for example, when the provisionally applied treaty is subject to parliamentary approval (for the expression of consent to be bound).[297] It may be remembered that provisional application arises in situations having the two following characteristics: First, there is a gap between the conclusion of the treaty negotiations on the one hand and the entry into force of the treaty on the other.[298] (This is the case when the treaty does not enter into force upon signature but is subject to ratification, acceptance or approval etc.). Second, States are unwilling, for one reason or another, to await the treaty's entry into force and seek to apply the treaty provisions at an earlier point in time. Provisional application can oblige and enable the treaty's application from the moment of the adoption of the text of the treaty or the treaty's signature. One way of achieving this is to apply the treaty provisionally without awaiting the

---

[294] CoE and BIICL, eds., *Treaty Making*, Slovenia, 257; Netherlands, 223; Lithuania, 211; Denmark, 153; Canada, 301; Israel, 305; Sweden, 267; Norway, 227; UK, 290.

[295] Mathy, "Article 25 VCLT 1969," 645; Michie, "Provisional Application," 112; Geslin, *Application provisoire*, 208; see also Lefeber, "Treaties, Provisional Application," [14]; Villiger, *Commentary*, 358.

[296] Krieger, "Article 25," [23]; Klaus, "Yukos Case," 4; Vignes, "Une notion ambiguë: la mise en application provisoire des traités," 191.

[297] Krieger, "Article 25," [23]; Klaus, "Yukos Case" 4; see also Mathy, "Article 25 VCLT 1969," 644.

[298] See also Lefeber, "Treaties, Provisional Application," [2]; Villiger, *Commentary*, 354.

completion of the usual constitutional treaty-making procedures;[299] thus, these procedures may take place sometime later, for instance, when the expression of consent to be bound by the treaty is prepared. In the meantime, provisional application enables the treaty's application to relevant acts, facts and situations. The result of this is that a treaty is applied, provisionally, without parliamentary approval, although in the normal course of events, such approval is necessary and would usually precede both the expression of consent to be bound by the treaty and its application. Accordingly, provisional application has been said to reduce parliamentary participation in treaty making to a mere formal act.[300]

Provisional application is least problematic in this regard, if it has been agreed because the treaty is subject to parliamentary approval in some (but not all) of the participating States. While there may be a certain similarity as to the kinds of treaties requiring parliamentary approval under different constitutions, this is not absolute, and it is conceivable that the same treaty requires parliamentary approval in some States but not in others.[301] Accordingly, several States have mentioned that provisional application is possible if the treaty in question does not require parliamentary approval within their own domestic legal system.[302]

Yet for those States, where the treaty is subject to parliamentary approval, provisional application may give rise to tensions,[303] especially so if the treaty is provisionally applied prior to the completion of the parliamentary approval procedure. Parliamentarians have described this situation as presenting them with a '*fait accompli*': the parliamentary right of *ex ante* control of certain treaties can be transformed into an *ex post* control or validation of such treaties.[304] This is less problematic, if provisional

299 Sweden ILC 339; Council CoE and BIICL, eds., *Treaty Making*, Switzerland, 274; Greece, 183; Luxembourg, 215; see also Spain, 263.

300 Theo Öhlinger, "Vertragsabschlußverfahren," in *Lexikon des Rechts: Völkerrecht*, 2nd ed., ed. Ignaz Seidl-Hohenveldern (Neuwied: Luchterhand, 1992), 381; Alfred Verdross and Bruno Simma, *Universelles Völkerrecht: Theorie und Praxis*, 3rd ed. (Berlin: Duncker & Humblot, 1984), 460.

301 Bolintineanu, "Expression of Consent," 680–81.

302 See, e.g., CoE and BIICL, eds., *Treaty Making*, Turkey, 281; see also Italy, 203.

303 Krieger, "Article 25," [23]; CoE and BIICL, eds., *Treaty Making*, France, 167.

304 Italian Parliamentary Practice in *Italian Yearbook of International Law* (1975) 1: 294; French Parliamentary Practice in Alexandre Charles Kiss, *Repertoire de la pratique française en matiere de droit international public*, vol. 1 (Paris: editions du centre national de la recherche scientifique, 1962), [491] 251; Switzerland, Council of States (Ständerat) Report of the Commission of National Policy (Bericht der Staatspolitische [sic] Kommission, 18 January 2003) 02.456 [2], http://www.parlament.ch/afs/data/d/bericht/2002/d_bericht_s_k24_0_20020456_0_20030118.htm.

application is done because parliamentary approval and ratification of the treaty is certain,[305] but it is more so if recourse to the mechanism is had precisely because parliamentary approval is not expected to be forthcoming[306] (for instance within the required time-frame, or for political reasons).[307] In case unilateral termination of provisional application is possible, parliament retains its right of control, but it succeeds the treaty's application rather than precede it as it normally would (in case of the treaty's entry into force).[308] Unilateral termination then may act as damage limitation from the parliamentarian perspective: The *ex nunc* effect of termination[309] means that a treaty has been (provisionally) applied, whose (non-provisional) application would normally follow, or be dependent upon, prior parliamentary approval, for reasons such as democratic legitimacy – but this state of affairs can be ended legally in a fairly easy manner. The degree of damage caused also depends upon the extent to which the factual situation created through the application of the treaty to acts, facts and situations can be undone.[310] Yet, in case unilateral termination is *de jure* or *de facto* impossible, the parliamentary *ex ante* control of the treaty can be reduced to a mere formal act of *ex post* validation.[311] In such a situation it is possible that provisional application would continue even if parliament did not give its consent to the treaty in question. Thus, parliament would have lost its power of control and would only be able to validate the decision, if so inclined. In addition, it is possible to argue that not only parliamentary powers and the rule of separation of powers are at issue but also the underlying interests that these seek to protect, for instance, the democratic legitimacy of state conduct.[312] In conclusion,

---

305 Vienna Conference, OR 1968: CoW 26, Venezuela §30. OR 1969: Plen. 11, Waldock, §89.

306 Michie, "Provisional Application," 113.

307 Krieger, "Article 25," [7].

308 See also Sondaal, "Dutch Treaty Practice," 227.

309 Ibid., 225.

310 On this concern, see CoE and BIICL, eds., *Treaty Making*, Spain, 263 and Andorra, 111.

311 See also Öhlinger, "Vertragsabschlußverfahren," 381; Verdross and Simma, *Universelles Völkerrecht*, 460.

312 On the link between ratification as a means of expressing consent to be bound and parliamentary control or participation in treaty making and democratic legitimacy see Antoine F. Frangulis, *Théorie et pratique des traités internationaux* (Paris: Académie Diplomatique Internationale, 1934), 59. See also Paul F. Smets, *La conclusion des accords en forme simplifiée* (Brussels: Emile Bruylant, 1969), 3–4. On arguments that consent expressed by the executive on the international plane without the constitutionally required assent of the legislative is not 'real' consent, and that international law ought to support the principles of democracy and modern representative government by protecting the participatory rights, which national constitutions grant the legislative in the treaty-making process, see

to the extent that the parliamentary control of treaties is seen to relate to their actual (including provisional) application to acts, facts and situations rather than to the formal expression of consent to be bound by the treaty, the above are the infringements that might occur should a treaty be provisionally applied prior to the completion of its parliamentary approval procedure.

At this point it is useful to remember that provisional application is an invitation to deviate from the usual constitutional treaty-making procedure. Each domestic legal system is free to choose how to accommodate provisional application,[313] and accordingly each system is free to chose how to react to this invitation. Some systems appear to decline the invitation: they follow for provisional application the exact same procedure under constitutional law as they would for expressing consent to be bound.[314] Other systems can accept the invitation and allow for the application of the treaty without necessarily awaiting the completion of the procedure that usually precedes expression of consent to be bound by the treaty, its entry into force and its application.[315] Both approaches have drawbacks. The first does not bring the application of the treaty forward in time to the fullest extent possible since the treaty is not applied from (for instance) its adoption or signature but only once the usual constitutional procedure is completed. The second bears the potential of undermining parliamentary treaty powers, by transforming the right of *ex ante* control of treaties to an *ex post* control or even mere validation. By contrast, the optimal provisional application would allow as swift an application of the treaty as possible while safeguarding parliamentary powers to the greatest

---

Thilo Rensmann, "Article 46 VCLT 1969: Provisions of Internal Law Regarding Competence to Conclude Treaties," in Dörr and Schmalenbach, *Vienna Convention on the Law of Treaties. A commentary*, [8].

313 Mathy, "Article 25 VCLT 1969," 645–46; Michie, "Provisional Application," 112; Geslin, *Application provisoire*, 208; see also Lefeber, "Treaties, Provisional Application," [14]; Villiger, *Commentary*, 358.

314 Council CoE and BIICL, eds., *Treaty Making*, Finland, 163. See also Iceland, 192. Regarding Austria: "Verträge können daher [i.e. wegen der Abwesenheit einer Bestimmung über die vorläufige Anwendung von Verträgen in der österreichischen Bundesverfassung] erst dann vorläufig angewendet werden, wenn das österreichische Vertragsabschlußverfahren verfassungsgemäß durchgeführt wurde." Trauttmansdorff, "Abschluß völkerrechtlicher Verträge," 144. Loibl highlights this problem in the context of the provisional application of the Energy Charter Treaty: "Most countries would have to follow the same procedures on the national level in order to provisionally apply the Energy Charter Treaty as if they would ratify the Treaty." Loibl, "Energy Charter Treaty," 581.

315 CoE and BIICL, eds., *Treaty Making*, Switzerland, 274; Greece, 183; Luxembourg, 215; see also Spain, 263.

extent possible. Accordingly, a decision could be made for a certain class of treaties or a certain type of situation in which the deviation from the usual treaty-making procedure for the benefit of provisional application is seen as appropriate. Then provisional application could be restricted by a time limit,[316] in order to prevent a 'never-ending' (provisional) application[317] of a treaty independent from the parliamentary control to which an expression of consent to be bound by the same treaty would be subjected. Alternatively, or additionally, the executive could be obliged to liaise with parliament or a committee thereof when agreeing to provisional application, for instance in the form of a regular reporting or consultation obligation.[318] In other systems, provisional application can trigger a correlative obligation of the executive to submit the treaty to parliament for its approval.[319] It is also conceivable that the consent to provisional application is given by the authority which under constitutional law gives the consent to be bound by the treaty, i.e. in certain cases parliament or a committee thereof.[320]

In short, it is submitted that while provisional application has given rise to separation of powers issues, this is not an automatic implication of the mechanism. Instead, constitutional systems can choose how to accommodate provisional application. In light of evidence that some systems have not yet settled the conditions under which provisional application can take place, and the relatively great number of States which prohibit or severely restrict recourse to provisional application, it is submitted that the regulatory freedom and the chance to address separation of powers issues might not yet have been used to the extent possible.

Moving on to implementation, provisional application is less problematic in this regard if the treaty does not require any implementation in the domestic legal sphere, or if such implementation can be done within the

---

[316] Article 23(2), Federal Law on International Treaties of the Russian Federation, 1995, as printed in Butler, *Law of Treaties*, 125.

[317] Emmanuel Roucounas, "Uncertainties regarding the Entry into Force of some Multilateral Treaties," in *International Law: Theory and Practice*, ed. Karel Wellens (The Hague: Martinus Nijhoff Publishers, 1998), 187.

[318] See for instance CoE and BIICL, eds., *Treaty Making*, Japan, 310.

[319] See for instance Leigh, Blakeslee, Ederington, eds., *National Treaty Law and Practice*, no. 30, Colombia, 74 and Leigh, Blakeslee, Ederington, eds., *National Treaty Law and Practice*, no. 33, Egypt, 42; CoE and BIICL, eds., *Treaty Making*, Luxembourg, 215; Norway, 227.

[320] See for instance CoE and BIICL, eds., *Treaty Making*, Slovenia, 257; see also Slovak Republic, 253.

existing legal framework (for instance on the basis of administrative acts).[321] Provisional application, however, may raise problems if the treaty's application does require the adoption of new legislation. Theoretically, in these cases, the treaty cannot be fully applied until this legislation has been passed. Yet in practice the passing of implementing legislation is one of the constitutional processes that can contribute to a slow entry into force of a treaty and thus contribute to the situation that provisional application tries to avert. Domestic legal systems react in different ways to this problem: according to some States, provisional application is excluded if the treaty requires the adoption of implementing legislation.[322] According to others provisional application is only possible if the required legal framework is put in place.[323] Again others seem to opt for a middle way: they allow provisional application but implement and apply the treaty only to the extent that it does not require implementing legislation,[324] at least until the legislation has been adopted.

It may be added that limitation clauses in agreements on provisional application can address and mitigate this problem. A relevant clause would provide that the treaty is to be applied provisionally only to the extent to which it is in conformity with internal law; therefore, in case of conflict, internal law would prevail and the treaty would (to that extent) not be applicable. Accordingly, at least from an international law perspective there is no need to adopt implementing legislation in the internal sphere; partial provisional application to the extent enabled by administrative action and already existing legislation is sufficient in case of limitation clauses to such effect. In other words, a limitation clause can be the international law mechanism that accommodates implementation approaches as the one chosen in the Netherlands. Such an approach seems to strike a good balance between the need for swift treaty application and the respect for the absence of internal implementing legislation.

Regarding the effect of a provisionally applied treaty in the domestic legal sphere, the point has been made that it has to be distinguished and

---

321 See also Hans Blix, *Treaty-Making Power* (London: Stevens & Sons Limited, 1960), 297; CoE and BIICL, eds., *Treaty Making*, Netherlands, 223; Germany, 178; Turkey, 281.

322 See for instance CoE and BIICL, eds., *Treaty Making*, Turkey, 281; see also Japan, 310.

323 CoE and BIICL, eds., *Treaty Making*, UK 290; Denmark, 153; Canada, 301; Israel, 305; Sweden, 267.

324 CoE and BIICL, eds., *Treaty Making*, Netherlands, 223 and Jan Klabbers, "New Dutch Law on the Approval of Treaties," *International and Comparative Law Quarterly* 44 (1995): 636; see also CoE and BIICL, eds., *Treaty Making*, Malta, 219 and Andorra, 111.

can differ from its effect in the international sphere.[325] The effect on the domestic plane is a matter of constitutional law,[326] and the question arises whether provisionally applied treaties have the same effects as other treaties in the internal sphere, and if so on what conditions. The different implementation approaches to provisionally applied treaties examined above already indicate that provisionally applied treaties can have different legal effects in the domestic legal sphere.

In some States, certain provisionally applied treaties can have the same legal effects as other agreements;[327] by contrast in others they might generally have "no legal force".[328] Again other States condition the legal effect in the internal sphere on the parliamentary approval of the treaty,[329] or make it dependent on the treaty's implementation: a treaty may for instance be operative to the extent that it can be implemented by certain administrative acts; but if legislation has to be enacted, those effects of the treaty will only be operative in the internal sphere once the relevant legislation is enacted.[330] No two constitutions are the same, and as Lefeber has pointed out, the effects of provisionally applied treaties in the domestic legal sphere generally depend upon factors such as the hierarchy of norms (whether treaties can be directly applied in domestic law or require implementation) and the nature of the norms involved (direct effect of the treaty).[331] Besides these general factors, much may depend upon the circumstances of a given case, for instance whether the rights of individuals are concerned, whether the provisionally applied treaty is published etc.[332]

5. Internal Acceptance of Provisional Application

The above overview shows that provisional application can give rise to major problems in the domestic law sphere. Not surprisingly then the

325 Blix, *Treaty-Making Power*, 297; Polish court decision: *SP SA v Director of the Customs Chamber in Lódz*, Complaint procedure, I SA/ Ld 1707/2002; ILDC 270 (PL 2003), 26 March 2003, H1 and para. 12.

326 Vignes, "Une notion ambiguë: la mise en application provisoire des traités," 191.

327 Nash, "Contemporary Practice of the United States," 933.

328 Blix, *Treaty-Making Power*, 297; see also comment by Bartoš in ILC, Summary record of the 781st meeting, UN Doc A/CN.4/SR.791, §21.

329 CoE and BIICL, eds., *Treaty Making* Belgium, 127; see also Germany, 178.

330 Ibid., Malta, 219.

331 Lefeber, "Treaties, Provisional Application," [19].

332 See for instance the Polish court in *SP SA v Director of the Customs Chamber in Lódz*, Complaint procedure, I SA/ Ld 1707/2002; ILDC 270 (PL 2003), 26 March 2003.

mechanism has been exposed to scepticism and criticism.[333] Yet, as has been said above, the separation of powers issues are not an automatic implication of the mechanism. It is for each constitutional system to decide how to accommodate the provisional application of treaties in the domestic law sphere, and some systems encounter fewer problems with provisional application than others.

Part of the problem may be a failure to provide a domestic legal framework for provisional application.[334] This is so where the domestic conditions of provisional application have not yet been settled, or where, in spite of such conditions, separation of power problems persist. This might even be the case for those States, where provisional application is prohibited or its use severely restricted because it is seen as conflicting with the parliamentary control of the executive and over treaties. At the latest since its inclusion in the VCLT 1969, provisional application has been widely recognized in the international legal sphere, and by now the time might be ripe for internal legal systems to follow suit. This is not because codification is thought to be the answer to every rule of law problem, but because it would offer a chance to address the separation of powers issues, and because a provision for provisional application might lead to its recognition in the domestic legal sphere as a mechanism in its own right. Provisional application then might not be seen anymore as undermining the general rule of parliamentary control of the executive and over treaties, and therefore be prohibited. Instead, it might be seen as a recognized exception thereto, allowed under certain circumstances and on specified conditions. In the end it is a matter of perception and custom whether parliamentary powers are thought to be undermined, or whether there might be good grounds to deviate from the general rule in the case of provisional application – again, under certain circumstances and subject to strict conditions and control.

The decision whether or not to regulate phenomena perceived to be problematic and as undermining the constitution or parliamentary powers (as provisional application is viewed by some)[335] is a political one. The options range from omitting regulation, so as not to encourage recourse to it, to providing regulation, possibly addressing the matter and to that

---

333 See notes 37 and 269, and the text to notes 296–332 (i.e. section 4 of chapter 1), above (all in chapter 1).

334 Michie, "Treaties in South African Law," 11, makes the point that that more often than not, provisional application is a matter of uncodified practice (rather than written regulation) in domestic legal systems.

335 Blix, *Treaty-Making Power*, 297; see also comment by Bartoš in ILC, Summary record of the 781st meeting, UN Doc A/CN.4/SR.781, §21.

extent inevitably granting it some recognition and acceptance. It is submitted that the latter might be advisable with regard to provisional application, for all the above reasons; furthermore, because it might not be possible to avoid provisional application completely, and then it might be better to be prepared; finally, because it is desirable from an international law perspective to have a tool akin to emergency legislation. Ideally, this tool could be used with regard to all treaties – even those that under certain systems would normally require implementing legislation and/or parliamentary approval. This is not to say that the domestic law sphere ought to defer to this need, but that acceptance and regulation of provisional application in the domestic law sphere might allow striking a better balance between swift treaty application and safeguarding parliamentary powers (or mitigating their infringement) than is done today at least in some domestic legal systems.

6. Conclusion

The purpose of this first chapter was to provide an introduction to provisional application. The natural starting point of any analysis in the law of treaties is the relevant provision in the VCLT 1969. Article 25 does not explain what provisional application means and what its effect is. Thus, we looked behind the Article in an attempt at gaining a better understanding not only of the provision but also its underlying mechanism. More precisely, the codification process was used to learn about the mechanism of provisional application and its conceptualisation in international law. Then, provisional application was analysed from an internal law perspective, because internal law can affect a treaty regime on the international plane,[336] including the content and features of agreements on provisional application.[337] It is hoped that looking at the mechanism 'from both sides' has helped gaining a more comprehensive and deeper understanding of it. Moreover, the drafting history and the issues raised throughout the conceptualisation – be it the name of the mechanism, the constraints imposed by constitutional law, such as the need for a power of unilateral termination etc. – have been used in arguments that address the question of the binding force and legal nature of these treaties. Thus, against the background provided in this first chapter, we can now move on to the analysis of this question.

---

336 This follows from Article 46.

337 Aust, *Modern Treaty Law*, 182.

CHAPTER TWO

THE VIEW THAT PROVISIONALLY APPLIED TREATIES ARE NON-LEGALLY BINDING

1. Introduction

Opinion is divided as to whether treaties are binding during the period of their provisional application.[1] The following chapter will analyse certain arguments advanced in support of the non-legally binding nature of provisionally applied treaties.[2]

The arguments in question for the non-binding nature of these treaties are based on certain features of provisional application, such as the power of unilateral termination, Article 25(2), or the use of limitation clauses. (Limitation clauses 'delimit' provisional application by reference to 'internal law',[3] for example by providing that the treaty shall be provisionally applied 'to the extent compatible with internal laws'. This means that it is internal law that determines the extent to which a treaty is provisionally applied in the international sphere. In other words, in case of conflict (the specified) internal law prevails over the treaty during its period of provisional application.) Based upon these features, provisionally applied treaties are said to resemble 'soft' law agreements in that they grant so much flexibility and discretion to a State in the shaping of the content of

---

[1] Gaja, "Provisional Application of Treaties," in *Report of the International Law Commission on the Work of its Sixty-Third Session* (2011), UN Doc A/66/10, Annex C, [2] and [4]; Michie, "Provisionally Applied Treaties in International Organisations," 56; Rogoff and Gauditz, "Provisional Application," 49–51; 80; Pritzkow, *Energiesektor*, 57; see also Niebruegge, "Provisional Application of the Energy Charter Treaty," 729; Matthew Belz, "Comment: Provisional Application of the Energy Charter Treaty." *Emory International Law Review* 22 (2008): 356.

[2] For the non-legally binding force of these treaties, see, e.g., Geslin, *Application provisoire*, 319–20; 326–30; Picone, *L'applicazione in via provvisoria*, 184; UN Final Clauses of Multilateral Treaties-Handbook (New York: United Nations, 2003), 44; see also Hartmut Hillgenberg, "A Fresh Look at Soft Law," *European Journal of International Law* 10 (1999): 508.

[3] The terminology is meant to designate all laws and regulations adopted within the framework of the State, by whatever authority and at whatever level, similar to its use in Article 27 as well as Article 3 of the Articles on the Responsibility of States for Internationally Wrongful Acts (hereinafter 'State Responsibility Articles'. The articles and the commentary are available at http://untreaty.un.org/ilc/texts/instruments/english/commentaries/9_6_2001.pdf.

provisional application that this is said to be contrary to a legally binding obligation.[4]

Prior to analysing this argument in more depth, a short introduction to the notion and features of soft law will be given, to the extent required by the similarities identified between it and provisionally applied treaties.

In academic opinion it is agreed that there is no generally accepted definition of 'soft' law.[5] It is further agreed, that 'soft' law is different from that which is described in Article 38(1) ICJ Statute,[6] in that non-compliance with soft law does not give rise to state responsibility.[7] The term may be used to refer to 'soft' provisions in otherwise legally binding treaties or/and to 'soft' instruments, i.e. instruments which as a whole are not legally binding.[8] This, at the latest, is where the agreement ends. There is disagreement as to whether 'soft' law and legally binding instruments are "strictly alternative or whether they are two ends on a continuum from legal obligation to complete freedom of action, making some such instruments more binding than others"[9] (i.e. of relative

---

[4] Geslin, *Application provisoire*, 327–8.

[5] Aust, *Modern Treaty Law*, 52; Eisemann, "Engagements Non Contraignants," in *Répertoire de Droit International*, ed. Dominique Carreau (Paris: Dalloz, 2001), [2]; Tadeusz Gruchalla-Wesierski, "A Framework for Understanding Soft Law," *McGill Law Journal* 30 (1984–1985): 44; Dinah Shelton, "International Law and 'Relative Normativity'," in *International Law*, 3rd ed., ed. Malcom D. Evans (Oxford: Oxford University Press, 2010), 164; see also Christine Chinkin, "The Challenge of Soft Law," *International & Comparative Law Quarterly* 38 (1989): 850.

[6] Patricia Birnie, Alan Boyle and Catherine Redgwell, *International Law and the Environment*, 3rd ed. (Oxford: Oxford University Press, 2009), 34; Daniel Thürer, "Soft Law," in *Encyclopedia of Public International Law*, vol. 4, ed. Rudolf Bernhard (Amsterdam: North Holland, 2000), 453; see also Shelton, "International Law and 'Relative Normativity'," 164.

[7] Michael Bothe, "Legal and Non-Legal Norms," *Netherlands Yearbook of International Law* XI (1980): 87–8; Chinkin, "Challenge of Soft Law," 866; Eisemann, "Engagements Non Contraignants," [40]; Fritz Münch, "Comments on the 1968 Draft Convention on the Law of Treaties: Non-Binding Agreements," *Zeitschrift für ausländisches öffentliches Recht und Völkerrecht* 29 (1969): 11; Oscar Schachter, "The Twilight Existence of Nonbinding International Agreements," *American Journal of International Law* 71 (1977): 300; Wilhelm Wengler, "Die Abgrenzung zwischen völkerrechtlichen und nichtvölkerrechtlichen Normen im internationalen Verkehr," in *Legal Essays: a Tribute to Frede Castberg*, ed. Johannes Andenæs (Copenhagen: Scandinavian University Books, 1963), 335.

[8] Alan E. Boyle, "Some Reflections on the Relationship of Treaties and Soft Law," *International & Comparative Law Quarterly* 48 (1999): 901–2; Chinkin, "Challenge of Soft Law," 851, 865; Fitzmaurice and Elias, *Law of Treaties*, 46; Shelton, "International Law and 'Relative Normativity'," 164–65; Jerzy Sztucki, "Reflections on International Soft Law," in *Festskrift till L Hjerner*, eds. Lars Ramberg et al. (Stockholm: Norstedts Förlag, 1990), 551–3 and 573; Thürer, "Soft Law," 456.

[9] Shelton, "International Law and 'Relative Normativity'," 165. See also Sztucki, "International Soft Law," 569–71.

normativity).[10] Thus, it is contested whether 'soft' law refers to legal norms[11] or non-legal[12] (social or moral) ones – or possibly both.[13] As a consequence thereof, there is disagreement as to whether 'soft' law can have any *legal* effects, and if so which, or whether its effects are confined to the extra-legal realm (or again, possibly both).[14]

More precisely with regard to the effects of soft law, if 'soft law' is understood as designating non-legal norms, i.e. social/moral norms, its effect is generally described as being (merely) politically or morally binding. If, however, 'soft law' is understood as designating legal norms, the issue arises as to the 'legal' effects of these norms. Some assert broadly that 'soft' law is not deprived of any legal effect. There is, however, also a more specific approach, which holds that good faith may give rise to the applicability of the principle of estoppel,[15] so that (even) under 'soft' law agreements certain expectations would be protected.

The view (as put forward by Geslin) that provisionally applied treaties are 'soft law' understands 'soft law' as designating legal norms[16] of relative normativity and which, in conjunction with the principles of good faith and estoppel, may give rise to limited legal consequences (in that certain expectations may be protected). The grounds upon which the soft law nature of provisionally applied treaties is assumed by this view will be explained in more detail in the following section.

---

10 The debate on 'relative normativity', however, is not necessarily linked to 'soft law' and also takes place outside the context of 'soft law', e.g., Prosper Weil, "Towards Relative Normativity in International Law," *American Journal of International Law* 77 (1983): 429.

11 Richard R. Baxter, "International Law in 'her Infinite Variety'," *International & Comparative Law Quarterly* 29 (1980): 565–66; Eisemann, "Engagements Non Contraignants," [3]; Geslin, *Application provisoire*, 320.

12 Bothe, "Legal and Non-Legal Norms," 93–5; Jan Klabbers, *The Concept of Treaty in International Law* (The Hague: Kluwer Law International, 1996), 117–8; Weil, "Relative Normativity," 415.

13 Chinkin, "Challenge of Soft Law," 851; Gruchalla-Wesierski, "Understanding Soft Law," 44, 46.

14 Eiseman, "Engagements Non Contraignants," [41]-[48]; Gruchalla-Wesierski, "Understanding Soft Law," 45; Schachter, "Nonbinding International Agreements," 301–3.

15 Thürer, "Soft Law," 457; Eisemann, "Engagements Non Contraignants," [45]; Münch, "Non-Binding Agreements," 11; Schachter, "Nonbinding International Agreements," 301; Michel Virally, "La distinction entre textes internationaux ayant une portée juridique dans les relations mutuelles entre leurs auteurs et textes qui en sont dépourvus," vol. 1, *Annuaire de l'Institut de Droit International* 60 (1983): 36; see also Aust, *Modern Treaty Law*, 53ff. (on potential international legal consequences of MOUs); contrast Bothe, "Legal and Non-Legal Norms," 94–5.

16 Geslin, *Application provisoire*, 320 and chapter 2, section 2.

2. The Discretion Allowed by Provisional Application

According to this view, the soft law nature of provisionally applied treaties is demonstrated by and is a result of the amount of discretion enjoyed by States in the interpretation and application of provisionally applied treaties.[17] This argument assumes that international law can have varying degrees of binding force, with binding obligations at one end of the scale and soft law agreements at the other end. In between are various kinds of obligations and undertakings with decreasing binding or obligatory force. The more discretion an undertaking allows its addressee with regard to its interpretation and application, so the argument goes, the less binding it is[18] and *vice versa*.[19] The extent of discretion allowed depends on several factors such as the way in which the undertaking is drafted[20] (for instance, recourse to self-judging riders such as 'to the extent possible' would allow considerable freedom) and the role and power of third parties, such as international courts and tribunals, in interpreting the agreement or settling disputes which may arise between the parties in this regard. Thus according to this understanding one of the key factors in assessing the degree to which an agreement is obligatory is the question of who exercises the control over its interpretation and application. If it is both parties together or a third party, such as an international court or tribunal, then one party *alone* has little discretion in deciding how to interpret and apply the agreement in question. Thus agreements of this kind are classified as having a rather high degree of obligatory force. However, if the party which is subject to the obligation also ultimately exercises the control over its interpretation and application, then this party enjoys a great degree of discretion in shaping the content and extent of the undertaking. Accordingly, the agreement or obligation in question is seen as enjoying a lesser degree of obligatory force.

The 'exercise of control over the interpretation and application of a norm' may be a difficult criterion to use in international law, given the absence of compulsory jurisdiction in most cases, in the sense that there is no system of courts having general jurisdiction over all disputes involving States and international organisations, comparable to judiciaries in

---

[17] Ibid., 326–8. In general see Jean-Pierre Cot, "Margin of Appreciation," last modified June 2007, in *MPEPIL online*, ed. Rüdiger Wolfrum, [3], [14], [32].

[18] Geslin, *Application provisoire*, 328.

[19] Ibid.

[20] Cot, "Margin of Appreciation," [3].

internal legal systems. However, the point made is that States, which are still for the most part both the creators and addressees of their norms, can choose the way in which they design a legal undertaking.[21] They can choose the degree of discretion or obligatory force involved, by using different legal mechanisms, thereby indicating the intended level of binding force and the nature of the agreement.

With regard to provisional application several factors are identified which are seen to increase the discretion which participants enjoy with regard to provisionally applied treaties. The first factor to be analysed here is the power to *unilaterally* terminate such application, as codified in Article 25(2).[22] This raises the age old question of how binding an agreement can be if the States so 'bound' are in fact *free* to walk away from the agreement at any time if they so wish. The second factor is the possibility of invoking conflicting internal law to delimit the extent of provisional application.[23] The result of this possibility is that the extent to which each State provisionally applies a treaty is ultimately defined by its internal law. Accordingly, this possibility gives rise to a great deal of uncertainty as to what can be expected from one's counterparts during provisional application. In light of this uncertainty it may be easier to evade the performance of such a treaty, simply by alleging that internal legislation does not allow or enable the performance of the treaty. The validity of such a claim or 'justification' may be rather difficult to assess for the other States involved. These two factors and their effect on the binding force and legal nature of provisionally applied treaties will now be further considered, starting with the power to unilaterally terminate a treaty's provisional application.

2.1. *The Effect of the Power of Unilateral Termination*

The power of unilateral termination is codified in Article 25(2) in the following way:

> Unless the treaty otherwise provides or the negotiating States have otherwise agreed, the provisional application of a treaty or a part of a treaty with respect to a State shall be terminated if that State notifies the other States between which the treaty is being applied provisionally of its intention not to become a party to the treaty.

[21] Geslin, *Application provisoire*, 328.

[22] Ibid., 327; see also Picone, *L'applicazione in via provvisoria*, 187.

[23] Geslin, *Application provisoire*, 326–7.

This power of unilateral termination has been said to confirm the freedom which States enjoy with regard to the performance of the provisionally applied treaty.[24] It has also been suggested that this power renders the recourse to dispute settlement procedures for breaches of a provisionally applied treaty marginal or futile.[25] Certainly, the power to unilaterally terminate does raise the question of how binding or obligatory an undertaking is if it permits the 'obligor' to withdraw from it at any time. If *pacta sunt servanda* means that States are bound even if interests and policies change,[26] one may wonder whether or how *pacta sunt servanda* applies given this freedom of termination.

2.1.1. *Article 25(2) and the Principle of* Pacta Sunt Servanda

At the 2nd session of the 1968–1969 Vienna Conference on the Law of Treaties, after the adoption of the power of unilateral termination of provisional application, a small group of States shared concerns similar to those just expressed; they felt that the power of unilateral termination could put the stability and certainty of treaty relations at risk.[27] The Iranian delegate went as far as suggesting that the power of unilateral termination undermined the principle of *pacta sunt servanda*.[28]

The relationship between *pacta sunt servanda* and the power of unilateral termination in Article 25(2) has not received much attention in academic writing. Instead, many writers highlight the difference between Article 25(2) and the termination of treaties under Article 54, which relates to treaties in force.[29] Others explain the appropriateness of unilateral termination in case of provisional application with reference to the fact that consent to be bound has not yet been expressed. Their reasoning is as follows: because ratification is discretionary,[30] there is no duty to ratify

[24] Geslin, *Application provisoire*, 327; see also Picone, *L'applicazione in via provvisoria,* 133–4.

[25] Geslin, *Application provisoire*, 317; see also Mathy, "Article 25 VCLT 1969," 652.

[26] Jennings and Watts, *Oppenheim's International Law*, [620]; Rudolf Bernhardt, "Treaties," in *Encyclopedia of Public International Law*, vol. 4, ed. Rudolf Bernhardt (Amsterdam: North Holland, 2000), 930; Kenneth W. Abbott et al., "The Concept of Legalization," *International Organization* 54 (2000): 409.

[27] Vienna Convention, OR 1969: Plen. 11: Austria §61; Iran §§62, 71; Greece §75; Poland §88.

[28] Ibid., Plen. 11: Iran §§62, 71.

[29] TO Elias, *Law of Treaties*, 39; Geraldo Eulálio do Nascimento e Silva, "Le Facteur Temps et les Traités," *Recueil des cours de l'Académie de droit international de La Haye* 154 (1977): 235; see also the case *Kuwait v Aminoil* (1982) 21 ILM 976 [34].

[30] This is so also because of the possible domestic disapproval of a treaty (prior to the final expression of consent to be bound by it).

neither with regard to treaties in general nor in the specific case of provisional application.[31] Accordingly, in the period of provisional application, preceding ratification, States should be free to withdraw unilaterally from the provisional application. *Inter alia* this accommodates the possibility that constitutional treaty-making procedures still have to take place. Thus during provisional application there is always a chance that parliamentary approval of the treaty may not be obtained, and already for this reason the power of unilateral termination is appropriate in case of provisional application.

Then there is one view which does reflect on the relationship between *pacta sunt servanda* and Article 25(2), and rejects the opinion that they may conflict with one another.[32] This view uses the abovementioned principle of discretionary ratification as an argument against such a conflict in the following way (and calls the mechanism in Article 25(2) a "withdrawal clause"):

> The withdrawal clause in paragraph 2 of article 25 thus reflects the principle that ratification is a discretionary act. Without the right of withdrawal, there would be no practical or legal distinction between the provisional undertaking and the expression of final consent to be bound. Indeed, but for the possibility of withdrawal the very purpose of provisional application would be defeated as the negotiators may be unable to agree to its [the treaty's] provisional application until it had been subjected to the same process of domestic approval that precedes ratification. The termination provision in article 25 therefore does not conflict with or undermine the *pacta sunt servanda* rule.[33]

Even if we agree with the explanation as to why unilateral termination may be appropriate in the case of provisional application,[34] the fact that unilateral termination may be *appropriate* in case of provisional application does not logically imply that there is, therefore, no tension between it and *pacta sunt servanda*. Additionally, the one motivation provided for the power of unilateral termination does not exclude other motivations such as an intention to exclude binding force.

---

31 Öhlinger, "Vertragsabschlußverfahren," 381; see also Lefeber, "Treaties, Provisional Application," [12]; Delano R. Verwey, *The European Community, the European Union and the International Law of Treaties* (The Hague: T.M.C. Asser Press, 2004), 126.

32 Michie, "Provisional Application," 67–8; see also Sondaal, "Dutch Treaty Practice," 225.

33 Michie, "Provisional Application," 68.

34 See Waldock, Vienna Convention, OR 1969: Plen. 11: §90.

In order to better understand the tension between Article 25(2) and *pacta sunt servanda* and its implication for the binding force of these treaties, the problem will be looked at from a broader angle and set against the general background of unilateral treaty termination.

2.1.2. *The Problem in Context: Academic Writings and the VCLT 1969*

As a preliminary remark, it may be useful to point out that *pacta sunt servanda* and (unilateral) treaty termination reflect the tension between, on the one hand, the need for certainty and stability in treaty relations and on the other hand the reality that facts, situations and interests constantly change.[35]

In 1971, Nahlik, in the context of unilateral treaty termination, suggested that: "The question how far the will or action of one party to a treaty is capable of influencing its obligatory force is again one of the most difficult ones in the whole law of treaties."[36]

McNair devotes a chapter to "*pacta sunt servanda*, and the general presumption against unilateral [treaty] termination",[37] the title of which aptly shows the perceived tension between the two. Indeed, this tension was central to the much debated question as to whether unilateral termination was allowed in case of 'silent treaties',[38] i.e. treaties being silent upon the matter of their termination. The tension is also reflected in the debate surrounding the relationship of *pacta sunt servanda* and *rebus sic stantibus*;[39] it has been argued that the latter undermines the

---

[35] The criterion of 'easy-terminability', which, according to some authors, helps distinguishing soft law from treaties, would appear to be the other side of the same coin. On this see Gruchalla-Wesierski, "Understanding Soft Law," 43; Sztucki, "International Soft Law," 572; Michel Virally, "La deuxième décennie des Nations Unies pour le développement," *Annuaire Français de Droit International* 16 (1970): 29; Prosper Weil, "Observations," (sur le Rapport Provisoire de Virally) *Annuaire de l'Institut de Droit International*, vol. 1, 60 (1983): 368.

[36] Stanislav E. Nahlik, "The Grounds of Invalidity and Termination of Treaties," *American Journal of International Law* 65 (1971): 748; see also Walter G. F. Phillimore, *Three Centuries of Treaties of Peace* (London: John Murray, 1917), 135.

[37] McNair, *Law of Treaties*, 493–505.

[38] See Article 56 and, e.g., Theodore Christakis, "Article 56 VCLT 1969," in Corten and Klein, *The Vienna Conventions on the Law of Treaties*, 1252. In general on this see Kelvin Widdows, "The Unilateral Denunciation of Treaties Containing No Denunciation Clause," *British Yearbook of International Law* 53 (1982): 83; see also Richard Plender, "The Role of Consent in the Termination of Treaties," *British Yearbook of International Law* 57 (1986): 145.

[39] György Haraszti, "Treaties and the Fundamental Change of Circumstances," *Recueil des cours de l'Académie de droit international de La Haye* 146 (1975): 59–60; Athanassios Vamvoukos, *Termination of Treaties in International Law: the Doctrines of Rebus Sic Stantibus*

former,[40] that the latter is an exception to the former,[41] or that there is no particular relationship between the two notions.[42]

An analysis of academic writings on those discussions highlights the relevance of one of the particularities of the international legal system for this tension, namely the "absence in most cases of compulsory jurisdiction".[43] It has been written that "in a system of voluntary submission to judicial settlement, ..., any one of a myriad of specific exits from treaty obligations may be alleged and seized upon without the threat of impartial judicial scrutiny."[44]

It is in response to this problem that the grounds for unilateral treaty termination and the termination procedure under the VCLT have been devised.[45] Accordingly, the VCLT system draws a clear distinction between consensual and unilateral termination. If there is agreement on the termination among all the treaty parties, be it expressly under Article 54(b), or impliedly by the conclusion of a later treaty relating to the same subject-matter (Article 59(1)), the treaty is terminated or is "considered as terminated" (Article 59(1)). By contrast, there are built-in safeguards regulating unilateral termination which are not needed in the case of consensual termination. First, there are restrictions on the power of unilateral termination, in the sense that it is conditioned upon objective events beyond the power of the State wanting to terminate the treaty, such as a supervening impossibility, a material breach by another party and

---

and Desuetude (Oxford: Clarendon Press, 1985), 215–6; see also Nahlik, "Invalidity and Termination of Treaties," 748.

40 Bruno Schmidt, *Über die völkerrechtliche* clausula rebus sic stantibus *sowie einige verwandte Rechtsnormen* (Leipzig: Dunker & Humblot, 1907), 72.

41 E.g. TO Elias, *Law of Treaties*, 43–4; Philip C. Jessup, *A Modern Law of Nations* (New York: The Macmillan Company, 1949), 150.

42 Vamvoukos, *Termination of Treaties*, 216.

43 John B. Whitton, "La Règle *Pacta Sunt Servanda*," *Recueil des cours de l'Académie de droit international de La Haye* 49 (1934): 253; W. Michael Reisman, "Procedures for Controlling Unilateral Treaty Termination," *American Journal of International Law* 63 (1969): 544; Widdows, "Unilateral Denunciation of Treaties," 94; see also Daniel P. O'Connell, *International Law*, vol. 1, 2nd ed. (London: Stevens & Sons, 1970), 279 (in the context of *rebus sic stantibus*). For the term 'absence in most cases of compulsory jurisdiction' see David J. Harris, *Cases and Materials on International Law*, 6th. ed. (London: Sweet & Maxwell, 2004), 1024.

44 Widdows, "Unilateral Denunciation of Treaties," 94; see also Aust, *Modern Treaty Law*, 297.

45 Jennings and Watts, *Oppenheim's International Law*, [656], [643]; ILC, Draft articles on the law of treaties: text as finally adopted by the Commission on 18 and 19 July 1966: commentary on final draft Article 62 (today Article 65), UN Doc A/CN.4/190, 262 §1.

changed circumstances.[46] Second, Articles 65 and 66 ensure that the effect of the unilateral invocation of a ground of termination is not to automatically terminate the treaty but only to set in motion a procedure aimed at declaring the treaty terminated.[47] Third, for this result, the consent of the States concerned is necessary (or alternatively, a binding judgment of a court). Technically speaking, the procedure under Articles 65 and 66 replaces a purely unilateral termination of treaties on the grounds of Articles 60–62 by the possibility of unilaterally setting in motion a procedure which only by consent (or adjudication) can result in the termination of a treaty.

In conclusion, the VCLT system and its *travaux préparatoires* could not make clearer the risk of abuse which the discretion of unilateral treaty termination entails in a legal system lacking compulsory jurisdiction in most cases.[48] In light of this result the following section will analyse the extent of the discretion that the power of unilateral termination under Article 25(2) allows to States participating in the provisional application of a treaty.

2.1.3. *The Extent of the Discretion Accorded to States to Unilaterally Terminate*

The extent of the discretion accorded to States under Article 25(2) will be examined by looking at how the power of unilateral termination is designed in Article 25(2) and whether the provision imposes any restrictions on the exercise of this power. This will be followed by an analysis of the question whether the extent of discretion allowed by Article 25(2), or some of its specific features, can be seen as affecting the binding force of provisional application.

Article 25(2) appears to confer some degree of discretion with regard to the power of unilateral termination. First, the termination of provisional application is not subjected to a requirement of notice[49] – it presumably

[46] The problem is that changed circumstances, and possibly material breach as well, besides being conditioned upon objective elements, allow for greater subjectivity and unilateralism than other grounds for termination, see Fitzmaurice and Elias, *Law of Treaties*, 200; Aust, *Modern Treaty Law*, 300.

[47] Nahlik, "Invalidity and Termination of Treaties," 750–51.

[48] Already the Harvard Draft Articles on the Law of Treaties were concerned with this problem, as Article 27(a) and the commentary show, (1935) 29 *American Journal of International Law* Sup 1089.

[49] Geslin, *Application provisoire*, 325, 306. This is relatively rare in denunciation clauses, see Laurence Helfer, "Exiting Treaties," *Vanderbilt Law Review* 91 (2005): 1597.

has immediate effect once the States concerned have received the notification to such effect.[50] According to Article 78(b), the notification of termination will be considered as having been made upon its receipt by the other States concerned. At the 1968–1969 Vienna Conference, it was feared that in case of a synallagmatic treaty this may offer a State to first take the advantages of the treaty and then terminate the provisional application prior to fulfilling its own duties under the treaty,[51] but in the end, no change was made regarding the immediate effect of the termination, i.e. upon receipt of the notification. The only negative condition for the exercise of this right is that the participating States have not waived or modified it. Besides this obvious exception, the exercise of the power of unilateral termination is not subject to any substantive conditions applicable specifically in the context of provisional application; also Articles 65 and 66 do not apply in the case of Article 25(2).

Does this render the principle of *pacta sunt servanda* inapplicable? Kelsen supports the view that an unconditional power of unilateral termination excludes the binding force of agreements.[52] This view is reflected in the British reply to Russia's claim to a unilateral modification or termination of certain provisions of the 1856 Treaty of Paris.[53] The then British Secretary of State of Foreign Affairs in 1870 rejected the unilateral treaty modification and termination on the following grounds:

> Yet it is quite evident that the effect of [unilateral termination] [...], is to bring the entire authority and efficacy of Treaties under the discretionary control of each one of the Powers who may have signed them: the result of which would be the entire destruction of Treaties in their essence. *For whereas their whole object is to bind Powers to one another* [...], *one of the*

Whether a State should give notice before notifying termination is a question that may need to be addressed by the ILC study, see Giorgio Gaja, "Provisional Application of Treaties," Report of the International Law Commission on the Work of its Sixty-Third Session (2011), Official Records of the General Assembly, Sixty-Six Session (Supplement No. 10), UN Doc A/66/10, Annex C, [8].

50 Michie, "Provisional Application," 82. See also the statement by the Polish delegate at the Vienna Conference: OR 1969: Plen. 11: Poland §88.

51 Ibid., OR 1969: Plen. 11: Austria §60.

52 Hans Kelsen, *Principles of International Law*, 2nd. ed. (New York: Holt Rinehart and Winston, 1967), 493; concerning withdrawal from membership in an organization at any time without previous notice: Finn Seyersted, "Objective International Personality of Intergovernmental Organizations," *Nordisk Tidsskrift for International Ret* 34 (1964): 50.

53 Edward Hertslet, *Map of Europe by Treaty*, vol. 3 (London: Butterworth, 1875), No. 429–431, 1892–1900; Treaty of Paris 1856, Hertslet, *Map of Europe by Treaty*, vol. 2, No. 264, 1265.

> *parties in its separate and individual capacity brings back the entire subject into its own control, and remains bound only to itself.*[54] (Emphasis added).

In the emphasised part of the quotation, it is argued that the discretion to unilaterally free oneself from an obligation is incompatible with an obligation because it runs counter to the very objective of an obligation: to be bound and subjected to it – not free to do as one pleases. On this view, at the heart of the tension lies the fact that the discretion to unconditionally and unilaterally free oneself from the obligation is incompatible with the very nature or idea of a binding obligation.

The question, however, is whether the discretion that Article 25(2) allows is boundless or whether the principle of good faith, for instance, is applicable to treaties during the period of their provisional application and thus limits the discretion enjoyed by States. Academic opinion unquestioningly assumes that the principle of good faith applies to provisionally applied treaties,[55] and there is reason for this. The principle of good faith applies to the 'pre-contractual' relationship between States by obliging them to refrain from acts which would defeat the object and purpose of the treaty pending its entry into force; it would seem *a fortiori* applicable in case of provisional application, given that under Article 25 the treaty is given greater effect than under Article 18.[56] Accordingly, the principle of good faith would outlaw the 'timely' or convenient exercise of the power of unilateral termination just after having received the benefits of the provisionally applied treaty but prior to fulfilling one's own synallagmatic obligations or commitments. Similarly, Article 25(2), and more precisely the *duty to notify* the intention not to become a party to the treaty, as well as the principle of good faith, excludes the possibility of a breach of a provisionally applied treaty being seen as a *rightful* exercise of the power of unilateral termination. Furthermore, a claim that unilateral termination based on Article 25(2) generally would exclude binding force could seem rather formalistic, and would be at the expense of the

---

[54] Hertslet, *Map of Europe by Treaty*, vol. 3, No. 431, 1898–1900.

[55] Geslin, *Application provisoire*, 316; 320; Michie, "Provisional Application," 71, 70; Luigi Condorelli, review of *L'applicazione in via provvisoria degli accordi internazionali*, by Paolo Picone, *Italian Yearbook of International Law* 1 (1975): 384–5; D. H. Anderson, "Resolution and Agreement Relating to the Implementation of Part XI of the UN Convention on the Law of the Sea," *Zeitschrift für ausländisches öffentliches Recht und Völkerrecht* 55 (1995): 283 (in the context of the implementation agreement concerning part XI of UNCLOS).

[56] Practice seems to support the applicability of the principle of good faith to provisionally applied treaties, see, e.g., the Declaration on behalf of the European Union to the EU–US Passenger Name Record Agreement 2007, [2007] OJ L 204/17.

intention of the States. It certainly seems possible to conceive of an intention according to which the participating States may want a provisionally applied treaty to be binding – up until the moment when the power of unilateral termination is exercised in good faith.[57] In particular, if the benefits from the provisionally applied treaty are extremely useful for the participating States, the treaty regime and its (long-lasting) application may be of far greater interest to the States than the power of unilateral termination.

In sum, unilateral freedom to terminate the provisional application of a treaty exposes the undertaking to less certainty and stability, even to a certain risk of abuse. Yet, the discretion conferred by Article 25(2) is not boundless; therefore, an undertaking allowing such discretion is not necessarily irreconcilable with the nature or idea of a legal obligation. Also, it would not seem to negate an intention to be bound, for it is conceivable that such an intention exists up until the exercise of the power to unilaterally terminate the obligation. Thus, it is submitted that the discretion in Article 25(2) does not, at least in itself, seem to be a fatal argument against the legally binding force of provisionally applied treaties.

2.1.4. *The Absence of General Compulsory Jurisdiction*

The British rejection of the Russian claim for unilateral treaty termination or modification by the British Secretary of State of Foreign Affairs in 1870 has been interpreted by Bederman[58] as being evocative of the principle that one should not be a judge of one's own cause (*nemo debet esse judex in propria causa;*[59] the abbreviating terminology Bederman himself coins for this rule is "non-self-judgement"). If one accepts the premise that *nemo debet esse judex in propria causa* is a principle of international law[60] and can be applied not only within a strictly procedural judicial context but

[57] Schachter, "Nonbinding International Agreements," 300 (on treaties in force); Mark Eugen Villiger, *Customary International Law and Treaties* (Dordrecht: Martinus Nijhoff Publishers, 1985), [472] (in the context of Article 18(a)): "Such freedom [i.e. the power of unilateral termination] does not diminish the value of Article 18 since the obligation extends as long as such intention [i.e. the intention not to become a party to the treaty] has *not* become clear".

[58] David J. Bederman, "The 1871 London Declaration, *Rebus Sic Stantibus* and a Primitivist View of the Law of Nations," *American Journal of International Law* 82 (1988): 9.

[59] On this principle in general: Georg Schwarzenberger, *International Law*, vol. 3 (London: Stevens & Sons, 1976), 64–71; Bin Cheng, *General Principles of Law as Applied by International Courts and Tribunals* (London: Stevens & Sons, 1953), 279ff.

[60] See, e.g., Schwarzenberger who is critical of the status as a principle of international law, Schwarzenberger, *International Law*, 68–69.

also with regard to substantive law issues,[61] then the analysis comes full circle with regard to the point made of the international legal system lacking compulsory jurisdiction in most cases. Self-judgement is particularly problematic if, as a result of the system of voluntary submission to jurisdiction in the international sphere, States have the final say in a matter and in this way become a judge in their own cause.[62] Bederman's interpretation of the quotation as "non-self-judgment" could therefore be seen as indirectly confirming the explanation that the tension between *pacta sunt servanda* and unilateral treaty termination is not *solely* caused by the discretion involved in unilateral termination but also by the particularity of the international legal system lacking general compulsory jurisdiction. It follows that the discretion to unilaterally terminate a legal undertaking does not necessarily imply that such an undertaking lacks binding force.

2.1.5. *Evidence that a Power of Unilateral Termination does not Necessarily Imply Absence of Legally Binding Force*

In the following section the conclusion, that a power of unilateral termination does not necessarily imply absence of binding force, will be tested. To that end different legal undertakings have been identified which can be terminated unilaterally, and more precisely almost unconditionally, at any time and with immediate effect. It will be examined how in light of such power of unilateral termination the binding force of these undertakings is perceived by academic opinion, the ILC, Diplomatic Conferences, and the ICJ.

The ILC position to this question can be seen for instance from its deliberations to Article 25 and 18(a). The *travaux préparatoires* to Article 25 show that the ILC did not perceive the power of unilateral termination as excluding or affecting the binding force of treaties during the period of provisional application. In 1965, in the second of the two most intense ILC debates on provisional application,[63] the majority of contributions on the legal force of treaties during the period of provisional application presumed their binding force. Simultaneously, all remarks relating to termination supported an unconditional power of unilateral termination. Although those contributions were made by different ILC members,

[61] Bederman, "The 1871 London Declaration," 23 and fn. 210.

[62] Whitton, "*Pacta Sunt Servanda*," 253; Harvard Draft, commentary Article 27(a), 1089.

[63] The 790 and 791st meeting provide the most intense ILC debates on provisional application during the drafting period, see Summary record of the 790th meeting, UN Doc A/CN.4/SR.790 and Summary record of the 791st meeting, UN Doc A/CN.4/SR.791.

no member mentioned a tension or contradiction between those agreed positions.

Moreover, the predecessor of Article 18(a), stipulating the obligation of signatories not to defeat the object and purpose of a treaty prior to its entry into force, was, since 1953, seen by the Special Rapporteurs[64] and the ILC[65] to be a legally binding obligation. It also provided (and still does) for the possibility of terminating the obligation at will. Therefore, the drafting history to today Article 18(a) shows that in the eyes of the ILC and its Special Rapporteurs, the legal nature and binding force of an obligation in general is not excluded by the possibility of terminating this obligation at will, any time and with immediate effect.

An example of the position taken by a Diplomatic Conference on the question at issue is the treatment of Article 25 at the 1968–1969 Vienna Conference. The majority view of States at the 1968–1969 Vienna Conference was that treaties during the period of their provisional application were binding. They nevertheless adopted the provision on the power of unilateral termination. A few States raised the concern(s) mentioned above, that the unconditional power of unilateral termination put the stability of treaty relations at risk, or even undermined the principle of *pacta sunt servanda*. However, the majority of States did not share this concern and hence again, the unconditional power of unilateral termination was paired with an obligation which by most States was perceived to be legally binding.

Therefore, based on the drafting history of Articles 18(a) and 25, neither the Special Rapporteurs, nor the ILC, or the majority of States at the Vienna Conference had any misgivings about combining a legally binding obligation with an unconditional power of unilateral termination.

---

64 Lauterpacht's 1st Report, UN Doc A/CN.4/63, Article 5; Fitzmaurice's 1st Report, UN Doc A/CN.4/101, Article 30(1)c; Waldock's 1st Report, UN Doc A/CN.4/144, Article 9(2)c.

65 The ILC, in its final draft article on the obligation not to defeat the object and purpose of a treaty prior to its entry into force, used the term 'obligation' twice, once in the heading and once in the chapeau. Additionally, in paragraph 1 of the commentary to this draft article, there was mention of a possible *violation* of this obligation (emphasis added). Furthermore, in a previous meeting (see ILC, Summary record of the 815th meeting, UN Doc A/CN.4/SR.815) it was decided to drop any reference to good faith in the article; this was done in order to avoid any misconception of the obligation being merely a moral and not a legal one (ILC, Summary record of the 812th meeting, UN Doc A/CN.4/SR.812, Chairman, §104; Reuter, §109; Yasseen, §113). Finally, in a number of earlier meetings (see ILC, Summary record of the 644th meeting; Summary record of the 645th meeting; Summary record of the 788th meeting; Summary record of the 789th meeting), the question of the formal source of this obligation – given that the treaty was pending its entry into force – was debated. This interest in the formal source also suggests that the obligation was perceived as a legal one; it is submitted that otherwise, i.e. outside the legally binding framework, the source would not be that relevant.

The example of treaties which allow States to withdraw from them unilaterally at any time and with immediate effect will now be analysed. According to Article 54(a),[66] a treaty can stipulate the modalities of its termination and the withdrawal of a party. Accordingly, some treaties contain a power of unconditional and immediate withdrawal which can be exercised at any time (i.e. comparable to the power of unilateral termination under Article 25(2)), such as the Articles of Agreement of the International Monetary Fund (IMF)[67] and Articles of Agreement of the International Bank for Reconstruction and Development (World Bank).[68] Yet, with regard to those treaties, there is no doubt as to their binding force.[69]

Finally, the attitude of the ICJ towards optional clause declarations is also illuminating. For example, in the Nicaragua case, the ICJ was concerned with the unilateral termination of an optional clause declaration made pursuant to Article 36(2) of the ICJ Statute. The Court's jurisdiction was, amongst other things, based on two such declarations by Nicaragua and the US in accordance with Article 36(2) ICJ Statute.[70] In the decision, the Court acknowledged the right of the US to unilaterally withdraw its optional clause declaration (albeit that such withdrawal would only become effective after six months from the receipt of the notification).[71]

---

[66] Article 56 is on the "denunciation of or withdrawal from a treaty containing no provision regarding termination, denunciation or withdrawal" and accordingly deals with unilateral treaty termination. This would seem to be the natural starting point in arguing that the VCLT 1969 itself does not support the view of the 'incompatibility' of *pacta sunt servanda* and unilateral treaty termination: although the Article does provide for unilateral termination subject to specific conditions, this does not seem to affect the treaty nature of documents subjet to that procedure. However, since Article 56(2) provides for a twelve months' notice, the denunciation or withdrawal in Article 56 lacks the immediate effect it has in Article 25(2). It is on this ground that one may criticise the reference to Article 56 as ill-suited for rejecting the thesis of an incompatibility of *pacta sunt servanda* and unilateral treaty termination, on grounds of the VCLT 1969.

[67] Articles of Agreement of the International Monetary Fund (adopted 22 July 1944, entered into force 27 December 1945) 2 UNTS 39, Article XXVI (1).

[68] Articles of Agreement of the International Bank for Reconstruction and Development (adopted 22 July 1944, entered into force 27 December 1945) 2 UNTS 134, Article VI (1).

[69] Haraszti, *Some Fundamental Problems of the Law of Treaties*, 246; McTaggart Sinclair, *The Vienna Convention on the Law of Treaties*, 182; Francesco Capotorti, "L'extinction et la suspension des traités," *Recueil des cours de l'Académie de droit international de La Haye* 134 (1971): 479.

[70] *Military and Paramilitary Activities in and against Nicaragua (Nicaragua v United States of America) (Jurisdiction)* [1984] ICJ Rep 392 (hereinafter '*Nicaragua Case*') 441 [110].

[71] This was due to the wording of the original US Optional Clause declaration in which it was specified that it would "remain in force for a period of five years and thereafter *until the expiration of six months a notice may be given* to terminate this declaration," *Nicaragua Case* 398, [13].

This right of unilateral withdrawal did not affect the Court's view of the legal nature of the acceptance of the compulsory jurisdiction: it still referred to it as an 'obligation'.[72] As Thirlway put it: "The Court's decision in the Nicaragua v United States case establishes that the existence of this power to 'switch off' the obligation *does not mean that the obligation does not exist so long as no switching off has occurred*."[73] (Emphasis added).

2.1.6. *Conclusion*

It is because of the realities of the international legal system, especially the absence of compulsory jurisdiction in most cases, that the discretion of unilateral termination is perceived as a threat to the stability and certainty of treaty relations, and that good faith plays a crucial role in the relationship between *pacta sunt servanda* and unilateral termination. Treaty provisions, the ICJ and academic opinion confirm that legally binding obligations can be and are combined with a power of unilateral termination. Thus the discretion to unilaterally terminate provisional application in itself would not appear to be a cogent reason for the alleged soft-law nature of provisionally applied treaties.

2.2. *The Hierarchy between a Provisionally Applied Treaty and Internal Law*

2.2.1. *Introduction*

The second factor identified as increasing the discretion which States enjoy regarding provisionally applied treaties is the possibility of invoking provisions of their internal law to delimit the extent of provisional application.[74] It has been said that in case of conflict, internal law prevails over the provisionally applied treaty,[75] and the fact that provisionally applied treaties frequently are not, or only in a limited way, implemented into internal law has been used as a factor in arguing for the non-binding force of treaties during the period of provisional application.[76]

---

72 *Nicaragua Case* 441, [110].

73 Hugh Thirlway, "The Law and Procedure of the International Court of Justice 1960–1989 Part Three," *British Yearbook of International Law* 62 (1991): 11.

74 Geslin, *Application provisoire*, 316–7, 327.

75 Krieger, "Article 25," [26]; Lefeber, "Treaties, Provisional Application," [13]; Michie, "Provisional Application," 74; Pritzkow, *Energiesektor*, 69; in the context of the ECT: Klaus, "Yukos Case," 5. See also Montag, *Völkerrechtliche Verträge*, 54.

76 Geslin, *Application provisoire*, 317.

The argument can be further developed, in two ways. According to one view, clauses similar to limitation clauses, which delimit the international undertaking by reference to internal law, negate any intention to be bound. According to another view, the possibility of invoking internal law to delimit an international obligation is problematic because it allows a State to free itself from the international obligation by subsequently enacting legislation to such effect. Therefore, one could argue that the discretion to unilaterally alter the extent of provisional application is incompatible with the nature of an obligation.

A number of pertinent preliminary considerations will be discussed first.

2.2.1.1. *The Reception of Treaties in Internal Law*

The effects of treaties, despite being instruments of international law, are not limited to the international law sphere but can extend to the internal law sphere.[77] The way in which treaties are given effect in internal law is a matter of constitutional law.[78] Theory broadly distinguishes between two approaches: monism and dualism. At a very basic level, their main difference can be described in the following way. According to the monist approach, international and internal law are considered to belong to one legal system. At least according to some proponents of the monist theory, international law is at the apex of this system, and all internal legal norms, constitutional or other, rank below it in the hierarchy of norms.[79] Since international and internal law are understood to belong to the same legal system, international treaties, once they have been validly concluded and have entered into force, *automatically* also form part of the internal law. They do not need to be transformed into rules of internal law, and in case of conflict, the international rule prevails.[80]

According to the dualist approach, international law and internal law are two distinct legal systems that operate on different levels or regulate

---

[77] Pierre Pescatore, "Conclusion," in *The Effect of Treaties in Domestic Law*, eds. Francis G. Jacobs and Shelley Roberts (London: Sweet & Maxwell, 1987), 274; Francis G. Jacobs, "Introduction" in Jacobs and Roberts, *Treaties in Domestic Law*, xxiii.

[78] Aust, *Modern Treaty Law*, 181; Eileen Denza, "The Relationship between International and National Law," in *International Law*, 3rd ed., ed. Malcom D. Evans (Oxford: Oxford University Press, 2010), 411; Richard K. Gardiner, *International Law* (London: Pearson Longman, 2003), 139; Jacobs, "Introduction", xxiv.

[79] Denza, "International and National Law," 417; Hersch Lauterpacht, ed., *Oppenheim's International Law*, 8th ed., vol. 1 (London: Longmans, Green & Co., 1955), 38; see also Georges Scelle, *Précis de droit des gens*, vol. 2 (Paris: Recueil Sirey, 1934), 5–7.

[80] Denza, "International and National Law," 417.

different subject-matter.[81] Neither legal order has the power to create or alter rules of the other.[82] It follows that treaties as such do not have any effect in the internal legal sphere, unless they have been transformed or implemented into internal law, for instance by an act of parliament. Here, to form part of internal law, the treaty requires an act of transformation, whilst according to the monist approach such an act may not be necessary since the treaty automatically forms part of internal law.

Hypothetically one could argue that because treaties in monist systems automatically form part of the internal law and prevail over other internal law in case of conflict, the situation that internal law conflicts with the provisionally applied treaty cannot arise. Accordingly there would not be any conflicting internal law which could be invoked, on the basis of a limitation clause, to delimit the extent of the provisional application. The possibility of doing so would be reserved to dualist systems. In dualist systems, a conflict between the provisionally applied treaty and internal legislation could arise given that the treaty does not form part of internal law until the act of transformation takes place.

However, such an assumption would be problematic for several reasons. First, although monism, at a very basic level, implies that treaties automatically form part of internal law, the question arises whether this is also the case for provisionally applied treaties. It is conceivable that in monist systems provisionally applied treaties are treated differently from treaties in force, and therefore do not automatically form part of internal law. Such a different approach could be explained by reference to the provisional or temporary function of provisional application.[83] Given that the constitutional procedures necessary for the entry into force of the treaty have possibly not yet taken place,[84] there may be an interest in safeguarding the status quo in the internal law sphere, possibly until the definitive entry into force of the treaty. Otherwise, the situation could arise that the provisionally applied treaty forms part of internal law for a short period of time and then ceases to do so once unilateral termination occurs pursuant to Article 25(2). According to Aust's general explanation of the monist theory, treaties become part of internal law only once they have been

[81] Sir Ian Brownlie, *Principles of International Law*, 7th ed. (Oxford: Oxford University Press, 2008), 31–2.

[82] Ibid., 32.

[83] See the title of Article 25, the wording of subsection 1, and the power of unilateral termination in Article 25(2); see also *Kuwait v Aminoil* (1982) 21 ILM 976 [34].

[84] Mathy, "Article 25 VCLT 1969." 643–44; Loibl, "Energy Charter Treaty," 576, see also 581.

validly concluded and have entered into force.[85] Therefore, it is questionable whether in a monist system provisionally applied treaties would automatically form part of internal law in the same way as treaties in force can do.[86]

Secondly, monism and dualism are essentially a theoretical attempt at explaining the different ways in which constitutional systems address the effect of international law on the internal law plane.[87] In reality, no two constitutional systems are the same,[88] and this variety also relates to the way in which international law is given effect on the internal law plane;[89] it is an oversimplification to divide all constitutional systems in either monist or dualist systems.[90] Many systems combine elements of both approaches. It is often suggested, that monism and dualism are more like two ends of a spectrum with many different grey shades in between.[91] Arguing that only dualist States would ever find themselves in the position to invoke conflicting internal law to delimit the extent of provisional application therefore would be inappropriate since an essentially monist State with only few dualist elements could just as well find itself in such a position.

Finally, whether treaties require implementation into internal law does not solely depend upon the constitutional system.[92] Also the substantive content of the treaty is relevant,[93] i.e. whether its provisions are self-executory. By this is meant here, broadly speaking, the distinction between treaty provisions which instantly are applicable at the internal level and those which are not, possibly because they are worded too broadly, or require further administrative actions to be taken. By way of illustration, Article 3 United Nations Convention on the Law of the Sea (UNCLOS) may serve as an example of a non-self-executory treaty provision,[94] according to which every State has the right to establish the breadth of its territorial sea up to a limit not exceeding 12 nautical miles, since this Article would even in a monist State require the relevant authorities to decide upon the

---

85 Aust, *Modern Treaty Law*, 183.

86 See also Lefeber, "Treaties, Provisional Application," [15].

87 Aust, *Modern Treaty Law*, 182.

88 Ibid., 181.

89 Pescatore, "Conclusion," 278.

90 Jacobs, "Introduction," xxiv.

91 Ibid.; Aust, *Modern Treaty Law*, 182; Denza, "International and National Law," 418.

92 Pescatore, "Conclusion," 274.

93 Gardiner, *International Law*, 140–41; Dionisio Anzilotti, *Cours de droit international*, vol. 1, trans. Gilbert Gidel (Paris: Sirey, 1929), 405–07.

94 United Nations Convention on the Law of the Sea, 1833 UNTS 397.

actual breadth of the territorial sea and to make this public.[95] It follows that even in the purest monist system, the need for implementing action by the legislature or executive may arise. Conversely, in the purest dualist system, the need for implementing legislation may not arise, because the internal law already is in accordance with the substantive content of the treaty.

In conclusion, it is submitted that the need to implement a treaty or the possibility of invoking conflicting internal law to delimit the extent of provisional application does not solely exist in 'dualist' States. In other words, the label attached to a system of internal law (whether 'monist' or 'dualist') does not prejudge whether in a specific case the need to implement a treaty or the possibility of invoking conflicting internal law to delimit the extent of provisional application may arise.

2.2.1.2. *International Law and the Relationship between Treaties and Internal Law*

According to Article 26, treaties have to be performed in good faith once they have entered into force. As mentioned above, the performance and effects of treaties are often not limited to the international law sphere but also affect the internal law sphere. It may be that a change of legislation[96] or acts of the executive are required in order for the treaty to be performed.[97] Although the VCLT 1969 does not contain a provision in which the *positive duty* to implement the treaty into the internal legal order is spelt out *explicitly*, this duty follows from both Article 26 and Article 27.[98] While international law leaves discretion to States as to how they implement a treaty into their internal law,[99] it is concerned with the result of the implementation. If that result does not correspond to the international law obligation, then state responsibility may arise.[100] This shows that

---

95 Gardiner, *International Law*, 143.

96 *Exchange of Greek and Turkish Populations (Advisory Opinion)* PCIJ Rep Series B No 10, 20.

97 Anzilotti, *Cours de droit international*, 405–07; Gardiner, *International Law*, 138–41.

98 Gardiner, *International Law*, 138.

99 Denza, "International and National Law," 424, 427; Jennings and Watts, *Oppenheim's International Law*, [21]; Karl J. Partsch, "International Law and Municipal Law," in *Encyclopedia of Public International Law*, vol. 2, ed. Rudolf Bernhardt (Amsterdam: North Holland, 1995), 1190; Paul Reuter, *Introduction au droit des traités*, [44]-[46].

100 The careful wording of "state responsibility *may* arise" is chosen as it seems to depend on the kind of obligation whether 'wrong' implementation in itself constitutes a breach, or whether the implemented legislation needs to be applied to a specific case and this application does not conform to the result agreed upon in the international

(conflicting) internal law does not excuse the failure to perform an international obligation.[101] This primacy of international over internal law is necessary in order to ensure the effective working of international law. Without this primacy,

> the integrity and utility of the whole treaty system would be undermined, because in that case the duty of performance would be dependent upon the action or inaction of the law-making authority of either party, or upon the character of the governmental organization or constitutional system which it chooses to maintain.[102]

In other words, the reach of international law would be limited by approximately 200 internal legal orders and its regulatory force would be so marginal that any harmonisation, standardisation or unification of conduct through international law and treaties would be almost impossible to achieve.

The Harvard Draft adds another reason for the general irrelevance of the action or inaction of the law-maker and the constitutional set-up of the State[103] for the duty to perform a treaty: "Manifestly, these are not proper criteria for determining the obligatory force of treaties *between* States."[104] Indeed, in order to govern international relations *between* States, it is logical to have recourse to the one legal system they all share, the international legal system, and to keep the influence of the multitude of (unshared) internal legal systems to a minimum. As 'treaties are made to be performed',[105] the general primacy of treaties over conflicting internal law ensures the treaties' effective performance (which remains undisturbed by conflicting internal law). Therefore, this primacy is of utmost importance for the effective working of treaties in general. Additionally, this primacy guarantees the equality of the parties to the treaty and ensures that the respective undertakings agreed upon during the negotiations, as laid down in the treaty, are carried through in the period of performance (and not undermined by unilaterally adopted conflicting internal law).

---

obligation, see Commentary to Article 12 State Responsibility Articles [12]; see also Harvard Draft commentary Article 20, 979; Jennings and Watts, *Oppenheim's International Law*, [21].

[101] Article 3(2) State Responsibility Articles, see also Article 27.

[102] Harvard Draft, commentary Article 23, 1030.

[103] Article 46 is an exception to this, as stated in Article 27.

[104] Harvard Draft, commentary to Article 23, 1030.

[105] Kaye Holloway, *Modern Trends in Treaty Law* (London: Oceana Publications, 1967), 77; Pescatore, "Conclusion," 274; see also Stanislav E. Nahlik, "L'entrée en vigueur des traités internationaux," *American Arbitration Association Yearbook* 31 (1961): 94.

Due to the importance of the primacy of treaties over conflicting internal law for the effective performance of treaties, Article 27 is seen as a corollary to Article 26[106] or as "domestic dimension of the maxim"[107] of *pacta sunt servanda*. This link between Article 26 and 27 shows why it is conceivable that the above-mentioned limited implementation of treaties into internal law, during the period of their provisional application, may be seen as indicative of their binding force during this period.

2.2.2. *Provisional Application and the Possibility of Invoking Internal Law*

In this section, the possibility of invoking internal law in order to delimit provisional application will be analysed more closely. The analysis begins with the bases for such an invocation, followed by the question of whether this possibility is a general feature of provisional application; only if it is, it would be possible to consider it as a general argument against the binding force of treaties during the period of provisional application. Finally, the link between limited implementation and the binding force of provisionally applied treaties will be assessed.

2.2.2.1. *The Written Bases for the Possibility of Invoking Internal Law*

It has been suggested that the possibility of invoking internal law to limit the extent of provisional application can be brought about by two different mechanisms: limitation clauses and unilateral declarations.

Limitation Clauses:

Articles providing for provisional application can contain clauses determining the extent to which provisional application shall take place.[108] This is often done by reference to internal law, as the highlighted part of the following quotation shows: "[this treaty] shall be applied on a provisional basis ... to the extent permitted by the Constitutions and legislation of the Contracting Parties."[109]

The wording of these clauses varies. Some refer not to both but either to the constitution or the legislation, others additionally include

106 Aust, *Modern Treaty Law*, 180.

107 Walter Kälin, "Implementing Treaties in Domestic Law: from 'Pacta Sunt Servanda' to 'Anything Goes'?" in *Multilateral Treaty-Making*, ed. Vera Gowlland-Debbas (The Hague: Martinus Nijhoff Publishers, 2000), 111.

108 Aust, *Modern Treaty Law*, 174, Geslin, *Application provisoire*, 242 and Michie, "Provisional Application," 73; Hafner, "Provisional Application," 597; Mathy, "Article 25 VCLT 1969," 645.

109 Protocol Concerning the Provisional Application of the Statute of the European School, 443 UNTS 244, Sole Article.

'regulations'. Provisional application is provided by some in "so far as lies within their [the States'] administrative powers"[110] or "within the limits of their [the States'] respective executive authority".[111] The effect of these clauses is to determine the extent of the provisional application by reference to different kinds of internal law. Thus, these clauses make a renvoi to internal law, so that it is internal law that determines the extent to which a treaty is provisionally applied in the international sphere. Writers broadly agree that this subjection of provisional application to internal law means that in case of conflict (the specified) internal law prevails over the treaty during its period of provisional application.[112]

The reference to 'constitutional law' in such a limitation clause would appear to be concerned with the status of provisional application under constitutional law. Logically, there would seem to exist at least three possibilities: either provisional application is prohibited;[113] allowed; or allowed under certain conditions. A further option could be seen to exist, namely that provisional application is not regulated under the State's constitution. This, however, does not preclude an unwritten constitutional practice on provisional application, which, it is submitted, would then fall again under one of the three above options. As was mentioned earlier, the subjection of the provisional application of a treaty to a State's constitutional law has the effect of a renvoi, meaning that the constitutional law regulation of provisional application now has effect on the international plane and determines the extent to which that State provisionally applies the treaty vis-à-vis the other participants. If constitutional law prohibits provisional application, then for that State the provisional application of that treaty is excluded. If it allows provisional application, then it is allowed; if it allows provisional application under certain conditions, then these conditions are transposed to the international sphere and to the extent that they are fulfilled, the State will provisionally apply the treaty.

The reference to 'legislation' in the limitation clause means that the provisions of the provisionally applied treaty will only be applied to

110 Air Transport Agreement 1947 (Sweden-Brazil) 94 UNTS 157, Article XII.

111 Agreement for a Cooperative Programme of Agriculture 1958 (US-Brazil) 9 UST 1357, Article XIV.

112 Lefeber, "Treaties, Provisional Application," [13]; Michie, "Provisional Application," 74; see also Montag, *Völkerrechtliche Verträge*, 54.

113 A variant of this position is that provisional application is possible only in exceptional circumstances, as is the case, for instance, in Belgium, Colombia, France, Greece and Turkey, see note 292 in chapter 1 above.

the extent that they are in conformity with the State's legislation.[114] Thus, to the extent that the adoption of *new* legislation (implementing legislation) would be necessary to perform the treaty, the States are absolved from this obligation for the period of provisional application.[115] In other words, the point at which normally the duty to (further) implement the treaty would arise – where conflicting or incongruent internal legislation exists – is now the point which limits the provisional application or rather its scope. Hence, the above described primacy of international over internal law seems reversed.[116] The rationale underlying this type of limitation clause is that the internal treaty-making process may not yet be completed. It follows that implementing legislation may not be in place, so that States may not be able to fully comply with the provisionally applied treaty provisions. To avoid state responsibility for this (see the principle expressed in Article 27 VCLT 1969[117]) the limitation clause cuts down the undertaking to provisionally apply the treaty by reference to relevant internal legislation,[118] in other words it preserves incongruent internal legislation and (re)adjusts or delimits the extent of provisional application by reference to it.

---

114 Cf. *Yukos Universal Ltd v Russian Federation* (30 November 2009), where the arbitral Tribunal interpreted a limitation clause, that referred to the State's constitution, laws or regulations as meaning that signatory States agreed to the treaty's provisional application unless the principle of provisional application was inconsistent with its internal law. A brief discussion of this will follow below.

115 Where States have laws concerning the conclusion and operation of international treaties in which they also regulate provisional application (for example several Central and Eastern European States), then this legislation may also have the three effects mentioned above with regard to constitutions: to prohibit provisional application; to allow it; or to allow it under certain conditions.

116 Lefeber, "Treaties, Provisional Application," [13]; Michie, "Provisional Application," 74; see also Montag, *Völkerrechtliche Verträge*, 54.

117 The article reads as follows: "Article 27, Internal law and observance of treaties

A party may not invoke the provisions of its internal law as justification for its failure to perform a treaty. This rule is without prejudice to article 46."

118 For support of this view in practice, see the following: The US submitted a declaration of provisional application of the 1962 International Coffee Agreement indicating that it would not assume any obligations for which implementing legislation was necessary, (thus applied the treaty only to the extent consistent with existing legislation), see "Treaties and other international agreements: the role of the US Senate," Congressional Research Service Library of Congress (Washington, DC: US Government Printing Office, 2001), 114; Austria: explaining the limited conditions under which provisional application of a treaty is possible, including the voluntary application *of those provisions* of a treaty which can be performed on the basis of existing legislation (author's translation, emphasis added), Trauttmansdorff, "Abschluß völkerrechtlicher Verträge," 144; CoE and BIICL, eds. *Treaty Making*, Germany, 178; the Netherlands, 223; Norway, 227; see also Malta, 219; Council of Europe, report of the Committee on Science and Technology on the Energy Charter Treaty (Rapporteur Tómas Olrich), [35], http://assembly.coe.int/main.asp?Link=/documents/workingdocs/doc97/edoc7838.htm.

A mechanism which fulfils this function with regard to treaties in force is that of reservations. According to Article 2(1)(d) a reservation purports to "exclude or modify the legal effect of certain provisions of the treaty in their application to that State." Reservations frequently exclude or modify the legal effect of treaty provisions by reference to a State's internal law. Put differently the aim of reservations is to preserve internal legislation which conflicts with the treaty, by readjusting or excluding accordingly the application of the provisions of the treaty with regard to the State in question. Hence the aim and effect[119] of limitation clauses and reservations is similar in that conflicting internal law can either exclude or modify the applicability of the international provision for the State relying on the limitation clause or reservation, Article 2(1)(d). However, there are also significant differences between limitation clauses and reservations. Limitation clauses can relate to the treaty as a whole[120] whereas reservations normally relate to one or several of the provisions of the treaty,[121] but not to the treaty as a whole. Additionally, limitation clauses occur in both multilateral[122] and bilateral[123] treaties. Reservations, on the other hand occur in multilateral treaties,[124] to adjust specific needs of individual States which were not accommodated in the general agreement reached. If in a bilateral treaty one of the parties is not satisfied with the outcome of the negotiations, then the treaty cannot be concluded for lack of

119 Michie, "Provisional Application," 74.

120 E.g. Energy Charter Treaty (signed 17 December 1994, entered into force 16 April 1998) 2080 UNTS 95, Article 45(1); Agreement relating to the Implementation of Part XI of the United Nations Convention on the Law of the Sea of 10 December 1982 (adopted 28 July 1994, entered into force provisionally 16 November 1994 and definitively 28 July 1996) 1836 UNTS 3, Article 7(2); OECD, Agreement on an International Energy Programme (signed 18 November 1974, entered into force 19 January 1976) 1040 UNTS 271, Article 68; Germany-Mongolia Cultural Cooperation Agreement 1997, 2071 UNTS 80, Article 16(2); Cuba-Portugal Air Services Agreement 1951, 192 UNTS 136, Article XIV(b).

121 Article 2(1)(d).

122 Energy Charter Treaty, 2080 UNTS 95, Article 45(1); Agreement relating to the Implementation of Part XI of the United Nations Convention on the Law of the Sea of 10 December 1982, 1836 UNTS 3, Article 7(2); OECD, Agreement on an International Energy Programme, 1040 UNTS 272, Article 68.

123 Air Services Agreement 1951 (Cuba-Portugal), 192 UNTS 136, Article XIV(b); Cultural Cooperation Agreement 1997 (Germany-Mongolia), 2071 UNTS 80, Article 6(2).

124 The US practice of conditioning the ratification of bilateral treaties upon modifications to be made to the treaty could be seen as a possible exception to this. This practice is sometimes referred to as 'reservations' see Aust, *Modern Treaty Law*, 132; William Bishop, "Reservations to Treaties," *Recueil des cours de l'Académie de droit international de La Haye* 103 (1961): 266–71. Nevertheless, it is submitted that the more convincing academic opinion is the one explained in the text above, based on the VCLT system, in which the term 'reservation' logically can only relate to multilateral treaties.

agreement on its content. It will either fail or be re-negotiated – but reservations will not be used to address this situation in a bilateral treaty setting.[125] Finally, a limitation clause can be contained in the final clauses of the treaty, thereby deploying its full legal effect. In other words, its legal effect can be brought about solely by the general agreement to provisional application – as opposed to a reservation which always requires a unilateral act, specifying at least the provision(s) to which it relates (and the effect it seeks to achieve).

It should be added that this interpretation of a limitation clause has been rejected by the *Yukos* Tribunal. The Tribunal when deciding on its jurisdiction on the basis of the provisionally applied 1994 Energy Charter Treaty,[126] analysed the effect that the limitation clause in Article 45(1) ECT should be given.[127] Article 45(1) ECT reads as follows (with the limitation clause highlighted):

> (1) Each signatory agrees to apply this Treaty provisionally pending its entry into force for such signatory in accordance with Article 44, *to the extent that such provisional application is not inconsistent with its constitution, laws or regulations*. (Emphasis added)

For the interpretation of the limitation clause the Tribunal discussed the two approaches put forward by the parties to the proceedings, the "all-or-nothing" and the "piecemeal" approach. The all-or-nothing approach had been advanced by the Claimant and required the determination whether the principle of provisional application per se is inconsistent with the constitution, laws or regulations of the Russian Federation.[128] If it is consistent, then the entire ECT will be provisionally applied by the Russian Federation; if it is not, the ECT is not provisionally applied by the Russian Federation. By contrast, the piecemeal approach, put forward by the Russian Federation, required the analysis of the consistency of each provision of the ECT with the Constitution, laws and regulations of the

---

125 Aust, *Modern Treaty Law*, 131–32; Rudolf Bindschedler, "Treaties, Reservations," in Bernhardt, *Encyclopedia of Public International Law*, vol. 4, ,965.

126 *Yukos Universal Ltd v Russian Federation* (30 November 2009). See heading VIII. A. of the Award: "Does the Provisional Application of the ECT in the Russian Federation, as Defined by Article 45, Provide a Basis for the Tribunal's Jurisdiction over the Merits of the Claims in this Arbitration?"

127 See heading VIII. A.4. of the Award: "What Effect Should Be Given to the Limitation Clause in Article 45(1)?"

128 *Yukos Universal Ltd v Russian Federation* (30 November 2009), [292] 107; [295]–[299], 108–110. In academic writings, this approach is supported by Niebruegge, "Provisional Application of the Energy Charter Treaty," 368–69.

Russian Federation.[129] According to this approach, each provision of the ECT is provisionally applied, but only to the extent that such application is not inconsistent with the Russian Federation's constitution, laws or regulations.

The latter approach corresponds to the interpretation that has been put forward above when explaining the meaning of references in limitation clauses to internal law. Yet, the *Yukos* Tribunal rejected it and adopted the all-or-nothing approach[130] on the basis of several arguments, two of which will be examined here, because they touch upon points of general relevance regarding limitation clauses. The first argument is the wording of the limitation clause in Article 45(1);[131] the second is an *argumentum ad absurdum* against the piecemeal approach, holding that it would run squarely against the object and purpose of the treaty and the grain of international law.[132] The Tribunal further argued that allowing a State to modulate (or eliminate) the obligation of provisional application, depending on the content of its internal law in relation to the specific provisions of the Treaty, would undermine the principle that provisional application of a treaty creates binding obligations[133] and would create an unacceptable uncertainty in international affairs.[134] This second argument is similar to the argument put forward by Geslin, assuming as it does that a renvoi to internal law undermines or excludes the binding force of a provisionally applied treaty. This will be looked at in more detail shortly. With regard to the first argument, the Tribunal held that the key to the interpretation of the limitation clause rests in the use of the adjective "such" in the phrase "such provisional application";[135] the Tribunal further held that this meant that the parties intended to submit the entire ECT to provisional application and not only parts thereof,[136] and from this for the Tribunal followed ("therefore")[137] that the limitation clause contains and

---

129 *Yukos Universal Ltd v Russian Federation* (30 November 2009), [292] 107; [293]–[294], 107–108. In academic writings, this approach is supported by Pritzkow, *Energiesektor*, 62–4; Thomas Roe and Matthew Happold, *Settlement of Investment Disputes under the Energy Charter Treaty* (Cambridge: Cambridge University Press, 2011), 76–77.

130 *Yukos Universal Ltd v Russian Federation* (30 November 2009), [301] 110–111.

131 Ibid., [302]–[311], 111–115.

132 Ibid., [312] 115.

133 Ibid., [314] 116.

134 Ibid., [315] 116.

135 Ibid., [304] 112.

136 Ibid., [308] 113.

137 Ibid., [311] 115.

all-or-nothing proposition: either the entire Treaty is provisionally applied, or it is not provisionally applied at all.

The finding that the parties intended to submit the entire treaty to provisional application is supported by other provisions of the ECT,[138] yet it may be questioned whether this finding necessitates the adoption of the all-or-nothing approach with regard to the limitation clause.[139] To answer this question it is helpful to look at different ways in which provisional application generally can be limited, responding to different motivations or questions.[140]

The first is the question of how much of the treaty is subject to provisional application, see Article 25 "A treaty or a part of a treaty is applied provisionally…". The second is the question of what provisional application regime to adopt to the provisions subjected to the mechanism: whether provisional application requires the provisions' application during that period as though they were in force/to the extent that they are consistent with internal law/to the extent practicable/in line with budgetary regulations etc.

These are different ways of limiting provisional application, and the approach adopted to one does not necessarily prejudge the approach towards the other. In other words: if the parties agree that they wish to subject the entire treaty to provisional application, this does not preclude the possibility that for certain technical reasons the provisional application of individual treaty provisions[141] (which ones may differ from one party to another) may be limited or excluded. Because there is no necessary link between these two different limitation mechanisms, all types of combinations of these two questions can be found in practice: the entire treaty is provisionally applied with or without limitation clause; and parts of the treaty are provisionally applied, with or without limitation clause. In light of this the Tribunal's argument could be criticized. However, even if there is no necessary link between these two limitation mechanisms, it is clear that they can be linked, i.e. that the adoption of one *may* influence the adoption of the other.[142] It is possible that the Tribunal may have

---

138 See Article 45(3) ECT.

139 For a similar reasoning see Pritzkow, *Energiesektor*, 63; Roe and Happold, *Investment Disputes*, 76.

140 Geslin, *Application provisoire*, 80 and 83ff.

141 Klabbers, "New Dutch Law on the Approval of Treaties," 636; Hans D. Treviranus, "Neue Verfahren zur Vereinfachung und Beschleunigung des Zustandekommens von multilateralen Verträgen," *Die Friedens-Warte* 59 (1976): 56; see also n461.

142 The following may serve as an example of this. If the negotiators decide to include a limitation clause in their agreement on provisional application, this may enable them to

omitted to refer to the specific circumstances which in this case led to the conclusion that one limiting mechanism does influence the other.

Thus, while there may be reasons to decide the matter the way the *Yukos* Tribunal did, it is submitted that these relate to the ECT and its regime of provisional application. Therefore, the *Yukos* award does not generally preclude the adoption of the piecemeal approach (for other limitation clauses),[143] which has been put forward above when explaining the meaning of a reference to internal law in a limitation clause in general.[144]

Unilateral declarations:

The second mechanism which enables the possibility of invoking internal law is unilateral declarations.[145] They are sometimes made upon the signature of a treaty or the notification of provisional application,[146] and their content is similar to that of limitation clauses.[147]

In practice, States rarely seem to have recourse to such unilateral declarations. Only a few examples can be found, mostly in the context of commodity agreements.[148] Their rarity can possibly be explained given the

---

agree to the provisional application of the entire treaty rather than only parts thereof, because the effect of the limitation clause is to limit for each State its undertaking to that what its internal law enables it to do. No responsibility is incurred (see, e.g., the principle expressed in Article 27) by subjecting the entire treaty to provisional application, since for each State the undertaking is cut down to the size that it is able to perform. By contrast, without limitation clause, States may feel the need to reduce the scope of the provisions subject to provisional application, to explicitly only cover those provisions which they are in a position to perform without the intervention of parliament (e.g., parliamentary approval or the adoption of legislation that implements the treaty).

143 *Yukos Universal Ltd v Russian Federation* (30 November 2009), [320].

144 For support of the piecemeal approach in practice, see the following: The US submitted a declaration of provisional application of the 1962 International Coffee Agreement indicating that it would not assume any obligations for which implementing legislation was necessary, (thus applied the treaty only to the extent consistent with existing legislation), see "Treaties and other international agreements: the role of the US Senate," Congressional Research Service Library of Congress (Washington, DC: US Government Printing Office, 2001), 114; Klabbers, "New Dutch Law on the Approval of Treaties," 636: "If a treaty deviates from the law, ..., provisional application is also out of the question, *but only in respect of the treaty provisions which deviate from the law...*" (emphasis added); Trauttmansdorff, "Abschluß völkerrechtlicher Verträge," 144; CoE and BIICL, eds., *Treaty Making*, Germany, 178; the Netherlands, 223; Norway, 227; see also Malta, 219; Council of Europe, report of the Committee on Science and Technology on the Energy Charter Treaty (Rapporteur Tómas Olrich) para. 35, available at <http://assembly.coe.int/main.asp?Link=/documents/workingdocs/doc97/edoc7838.htm>.

145 Geslin, *Application provisoire*, 318, 326; Michie, "Provisional Application," 75–6.

146 Michie, "Provisional Application," 76.

147 Geslin, *Application provisoire*, 318, 326.

148 US declaration to the 1962 International Coffee Agreement, 469 UNTS 169; Japanese declaration, 1766 UNTS 273, to the 1993 International Cocoa Agreement adopted

frequent recourse to limitation clauses; if there is a generally agreed limitation clause, a unilateral declaration to the same effect would be superfluous. There is, however, at least one example of State practice in which a unilateral declaration was made with regard to a treaty which did contain a limitation clause.[149] In that specific case, the effect of the unilateral declaration went beyond the one of the limitation clause, since the extent of the treaty's provisional application was additionally limited by reference to the declaring State's budget.[150]

Based on these considerations, it would seem that such unilateral declarations are made either if the treaty does not contain a limitation clause at all; or, if there is a limitation clause, to address individual needs which could not be asserted in the agreement on the content of the limitation clause.

2.2.2.2. *Is this Possibility a General Feature of Provisional Application?*

Given that the possibility of invoking internal law is used as part of an argument against the binding force of provisionally applied treaties in general, the question arises whether this is a general feature of provisionally applied treaties. It may be recalled that the possibility of invoking internal law, as well as the power of unilateral termination, have been said to allow States such discretion so as to exclude the legally binding nature of provisionally applied treaties.

Hence the question arises whether the possibility of invoking internal law only arises if provided for in the agreement of provisional application (for example, when the agreement contains a limitation clause) or if it also arises when the agreement is silent in this regard.[151] If the former, then the conclusions drawn from the possibility of invoking internal law for the nature of provisionally applied treaties *in general* would be at risk of being improper generalisations.

According to the majority view the possibility of invoking internal law only arises if specifically provided for in the agreement on provisional

16 July 1993, provisionally entered into force 22 February 1994) 1766 UNTS 3; See also Sohn, "International Law Implications of the 1994 Agreement," 704.

149 1993 International Cocoa Agreement, 1766 UNTS 3, Article 55.

150 Japanese declaration, 1766 UNTS 273, to the 1993 International Cocoa Agreement, 1766 UNTS 3.

151 Krenzler raises the question whether the possibility of invoking internal law is a general feature of provisionally applied treaties but eventually answers it in the negative, see Krenzler, *Vorläufige Anwendung*, 59–61; contrast Vignes, "Une notion ambiguë: la mise en application provisoire des traités," 192.

application.[152] According to this view, if there is no specific (explicit or implied) provision for the possibility of invoking internal law, then the principle expressed in Article 27 applies and conflicting internal law cannot be invoked in the international sphere to delimit the extent of the treaty's provisional application. It follows, that on this view, the possibility of invoking internal law is not a general feature of these treaties and could therefore not be used as a general argument against their binding force, but at best against the binding force of those provisionally applied treaties that specifically provide for the possibility of invoking internal law.

By contrast, Geslin submits that the possibility of invoking internal law is an element which forms part of the legal regime of the agreement on provisional application.[153] She seems to submit, if cautiously, that the practice of States has given rise to a rule of customary law according to which Governments have to respect parliamentary powers when agreeing to provisional application. For this reason, so the argument goes, provisional application generally only encompasses those provisions of a treaty which fall within the administrative competences of the government and for whose application parliamentary intervention is not necessary.[154] Thus, on this view, it might be possible to develop an argument against the binding force of these treaties generally on the basis of this feature.

If the limitation of provisional application by conflicting internal law was a constituent element of the legal regime of provisional application, its source would need to be customary international law since the VCLT 1969 does not regulate the matter. This indeed seems to have been argued, though cautiously, as the highlighted part of the following quotation shows:

> Il semble [...] se dégager de la pratique concomitante des Etats *une réglementation d'ordre* pour ainsi dire *'coutumier'*, selon laquelle le gouvernement, en concluant un accord d'application provisoire, se doit de respecter l'encadrement législatif préexistant dans l'ordre interne, se doit d'agir dans la stricte limite de ses compétences administrative. Ainsi, seules les dispositions pour la mise en application desquelles l'intervention du Parlement n'est pas ou plus nécessaire, peuvent être mises provisoirement en application.[155]

---

[152] Michie, "Provisional Application," 75; Krenzler, *Vorläufige Anwendung*, 60. See also: Lefeber, "Treaties, Provisional Application," [13]; Mathy, "Article 25 VCLT 1969," 646; Montag, *Völkerrechtliche Verträge*, 54; Sondaal, "Dutch Treaty Practice," 225.

[153] Geslin, *Application provisoire*, 317.

[154] Ibid., 238.

[155] Geslin, *Application provisoire*, 238; for a similar statement see 243.

This conclusion seems to be drawn subsequent to an analysis of statements of roughly ten States. If this is the position of the writer, then it is open to the criticism that it is not sufficiently supported by the two elements of customary international law,[156] state practice and *opinio juris*. Admittedly, it is difficult to show that conduct is supported by practice and *opinio juris* in such a way as to amount to a rule of customary international law.[157] Nevertheless, the analysis of the statements of roughly ten States, mostly made in response to a Council of Europe Questionnaire[158] (including at least one uncertain case) is probably insufficient, qualitatively and quantitatively, to draw the conclusion that the conduct in question is 'general conduct' as stipulated in Article 38(1)b ICJ Statute.[159] It is possible that the author is aware of this difficulty, given that she softens her conclusion on the existence of such a 'customary principle' or rule by using qualifying terms such as "un principe que l'on pourrait en quelque sorte qualifier, tout en restant très prudent, de 'coutumier'".[160] Be that as it may, for the purposes of the present analysis it would not appear safe to adopt the view that limitation of provisional application by conflicting internal law is customary in light of its not entirely convincing basis.

Alternatively, one may consider whether the succession or repetition of these limitation clauses may enhance the formation of a corresponding customary rule, in reliance on an argument taken from standard bilateral treaties such as extradition or bilateral investment treaties. However, according to the experts assembled in the Committee of the International Law Association on the Formation of Customary International Law,[161] there is no presumption that a succession of similar treaty provisions gives rise to a new customary rule with the same content. In the context of the law of treaties, the main reason for this is that the inclusion of a provision

156 *North Sea Continental Shelf (Judgment) (Federal Republic of Germany v Denmark and Federal Republic of Germany v the Netherlands)* [1969] ICJ Rep 3 (hereinafter '*North Sea Continental Shelf Cases*') 44 [77].

157 On these difficulties with regard to *opinio juris* see, e.g., Brownlie, *Principles of Public International Law*, 8; Harris, *Cases and Materials on International Law*, 38; Dissenting Opinion, Judge Tanaka, *North Sea Continental Shelf Cases*, 177; Dissenting Opinion, Judge Ad Hoc Sørensen, *North Sea Continental Shelf Cases*, 247.

158 Geslin, *Application provisoire*, 238–240.

159 Article 38(1)(b) ICJ Statute; rephrased as 'constant and uniform' *Colombian-Peruvian Asylum Case (Judgment)* [1950] ICJ Rep 266, 276; 'uniform and consistent' (Brownlie, *Principles of Public International Law*, 7); 'widespread and consistent' (Hugh Thirlway, "The Sources of International Law," in *International Law*, 3rd ed., ed. Malcom D. Evans (Oxford: Oxford University Press, 2010)), 102.

160 Ibid., 243.

161 Statement of Principles Applicable to the Formation of General Customary International Law – 'Final Report [25].

in a treaty does not in itself provide any indication that the customary treaty law is (or is not) the same as that set out in the treaty. States may be guided by entirely different considerations (such as for instance the consideration that written law tends to remove ambiguity), when deciding what to include in the written text of a treaty. Accordingly, there is no reason to assume that the terms agreed in the treaty (even if 'repeated' in a succession of similar treaty provisions) represent the general law (or the view of the negotiating States on the general law). Therefore, the succession of the limitation clauses would not of itself prove the existence of a corresponding rule of customary law.

Finally, on a theoretical note, it seems difficult to conceive the exact content of such a hypothetical customary rule. The content of limitation clauses in treaties varies, especially with regard to the different kinds of internal law which can be invoked to delimit the extent of provisional application (whether only legislation or also constitutional law, regulations etc.). Therefore, it is doubtful whether limitation clauses share a common basic core and content, which would seem a necessary precondition for the formulation of a corresponding (yet) general rule of customary international law.[162]

In conclusion, it has been shown that it is contested in academic opinion whether provisional application as a rule is limited by conflicting internal law, or whether that is only the case if a specific mechanism is provided for this, such as an explicit or implied limitation clause or a unilateral declaration. Furthermore, the basis of Geslin's assumption of the customary law nature of the limitation of provisional application by internal law has been found not entirely convincing, and no alternative basis has been found from which the customary law nature could be deduced. Accordingly, it is thought that the possibility of invoking internal law is not customary in nature, and it is submitted that for lack of generality of this feature it would not be safe to deduce therefrom that provisionally applied treaties in general are non-legally binding.

2.2.2.3. *The Link between the Possibility of Invoking Internal Law and the Binding Force of a Provisionally Applied Treaty*

In the following section the link between the possibility of invoking internal law to delimit the extent of provisional application and the binding force of a provisionally applied treaty will be examined.

---

[162] Compare *North Sea Continental Shelf Cases,* [72] (criterion of the 'fundamentally norm-creating character').

As was mentioned earlier, the *Yukos* Tribunal has held that the possibility of invoking internal law based on a limitation clause, i.e. the possibility of modulating or even excluding the obligation of provisional application, would "undermine the principle that provisional application of a treaty creates binding obligations".[163] The argument put forward to support this view is that limitation clauses "create an unacceptable uncertainty in international affairs", because "the content of domestic law directly controls the content of an international legal obligation".[164] It follows, so the argument, that States "would be bound by nothing but their whims and would make a mockery of the international legal agreement to which they chose to subject themselves".[165]

These considerations indicate that the problems raised by limitation clauses are not specific to provisional application but pertain more broadly to the relationship between international and internal law.[166] Because limitation clauses delimit the extent to which the treaty will be applied provisionally by reference to internal law, i.e. subject the treaty's provisional application to internal law, they are an exception to the supremacy of international law and accordingly lead straight back to the debate that used to surround this question.[167] Thus, all the arguments supporting the supremacy of international law can be used as arguments militating against limitation clauses, highlighting the tension to which they give rise with regard to the *pacta sunt servanda* principle.

In order to better understand the tension between the possibility of invoking internal law and the *pacta sunt servanda* principle, the problem will be looked at in its broader context. This will allow to benefit from that debate and possibly to rely on the solutions suggested in that context.

Two instances of State practice have been chosen to clarify the problem currently under consideration. In both instances, States tried to circumvent the application of international law to the matter in question by

---

163 See note 133 (in chapter 2) above.

164 *Yukos Universal Ltd v Russian Federation* (30 November 2009), [315] 116.

165 Ibid., [315] 116.

166 According to Bothe, "Article 46 VCLT 1969," [2] and [4], behind the problem of the relationship between international and internal law there is the tension between the legislative and the executive power, which is an apt description of the problems caused by provisional application.

167 The supremacy of international law on the international plane finds an expression, for example, in Articles 27 and 46, Article 3 Articles on State Responsibility etc. Prior to the adoption of the supremacy approach, this was highly contested, see, e.g., Bothe "Article 46 VCLT 1969," [4]. For a summary of the debate see, e.g., Rensmann, "Article 46 VCLT 1969," [4]–[12].

arguing that the matter was one falling under their internal law. The US response to this argument presented by Mexico in the *Cutting* case was:

> ... if a government could set up its own municipal laws as the final test of its international rights and obligations, then the rules of international law would be but the shadow of a name and would afford no protection either to States or to individuals.[168]

It is argued that without the primacy of international law over internal law, international law would not comprise real obligations and would be ineffective. The reason for this is indicated in the beginning of the quotation[169] but becomes even more apparent in the emphasised part of the following quotation:

> The fundamental principle on which our deliberations must be based, a principle the disregard of which would result in international anarchy, is the predominance of conventional law over national law. This predominance results from the very nature of things. What would be the object of concluding treaties or of undertaking international obligations *if it were open to those who had undertaken them to escape from their effects* by a legislative, executive or constitutional act or *by an act* of any other kind *arising from their own authority*?[170]

In other words, the inapplicability of the principle enshrined in Article 27 entails the risk that States can *unilaterally* free themselves from the obligations contained in a treaty, by enacting (subsequent) internal legislation to such effect. The implications of this for the discretion States enjoy with regard to provisional application will be discussed shortly in more detail. For the time being it suffices to say that in the overall scheme of provisional application, it is questionable whether this poses such a great risk, given that Article 25(2) already provides for an 'easy way out' which may be more readily available than the enactment of such subsequent legislation. Accordingly, the risk posed by this would depend upon the circumstances of each case and the long-term benefits to be derived from the provisional application of the treaty.

Fawcett has approached the problem of the tension under consideration from the angle of intention. While analysing generally what it was

---

[168] "National Jurisdiction: Its Legal Effects," *Moore Digest of International Law* 2: §201, 235.

[169] Replace "if" by "because": because a government could set up its *own* municipal laws...

[170] *Expropriation by the Romanian Government of the Property of Hungarian Optants (Hungary v Romania)* 4 LNOJ 887 (Nr. 989) (Count Appony, representative of Hungary).

that made agreements binding in international law, he suggested that a clause similar to limitation clauses in the present context would "negative" any intention to be bound:

> Certain provisions in international agreements appear to negative any intention to create legal relations. ... For example, an undertaking qualified by the words 'subject to the law in force' would it is submitted, create no international obligation at all; for it would enable any party to appeal successfully to municipal law against any attempt by another party to enforce the obligation.[171]

Leaving the matter of enforcement aside for the moment, the question arises whether indeed an agreement to limit the extent of an international undertaking by conflicting internal law amounts to an agreement that the undertaking should not be legally binding. The intention not to be bound could then be evidenced in the uncertainty and instability created by this clause, especially if States were allowed to subsequently alter the extent or content of their obligation by altering their internal law. However, it seems equally possible to argue the other way around: precisely because the undertaking is intended to be binding, it may be necessary to draw up limitations in order to avoid state responsibility for non-conformity. Usually, reservations come into play to address this need of modifying or excluding the extent to which one is bound by an obligation. Limitation clauses have a similar (if broader) effect. Therefore, they could simply accommodate the constitutional separation of powers, or incongruent internal legislation, in order to avoid breaches and state responsibility[172] which might otherwise result from a lack of implementation. A similar point has been made by Widdows when responding to Fawcett's argument:

> The clause 'subject to the law in force' cuts down the size of the obligation that might otherwise have arisen but cannot be said to annihilate it completely. There is something left, something ascertainable by both parties, a discernible realm of obligation.[173]

Thus, according to Widdows the decisive consideration is to determine the extent to which there is such a 'discernible realm of obligation' – if

[171] James Fawcett, "The Legal Character of International Agreements," *British Yearbook of International Law* 30 (1953): 390–1.
[172] Bothe, "Legal and Non-Legal Norms," 91: he suggests that States undertake legal obligations only when they expect to be able to comply with them. From this perspective, limitation clauses could be seen as one way of insuring that they can comply with the obligations.
[173] Widdows, "Agreement in International Law," 124.

there is one at all. With regard to provisional application, the above question will now be examined relating to the kind of 'internal law' that can validly delimit its extent: whether only 'pre-existing' or also 'subsequently enacted' law.[174]

2.2.2.4. *The Critical Date for Determining the Reference to 'Internal Law'*

The question whether only 'pre-existing' or also 'subsequently enacted' law can validly delimit provisional application can be rephrased in terms of 'the critical date.' Since the term 'law' is one the content of which changes over time,[175] questions arise as to the critical date pertaining to references to 'internal law' which can be found in limitation clauses or unilateral declarations. Do such clauses/declarations refer to 'internal law' only at the time of the expression of consent to provisional application[176] or (also) to any subsequent moment in time? There is no in-depth discussion of this point in general academic writings on provisional application, although some writers indicate their position in passing.[177]

The question arises whether this is a matter of 'intertemporal interpretation.' By this is meant that treaties may raise interpretative problems relating to time, in the sense that the parties to a treaty use a (legal or other) concept without specifying how it is to be interpreted in light of possible changes in the concept's meaning over time. The matter is then to determine whether the concept is to be interpreted according to its meaning at the time of the conclusion of the treaty (so-called inter-temporal or contemporaneous interpretation) or at the time of its application (i.e. any time after its conclusion).[178] In academic writings, there are a variety of

---

[174] The *Yukos* Tribunal raised this question (phrased in a broader way) in the context of the ECT, see *Yukos Universal Ltd v Russian Federation* (30 November 2009), [340].

[175] Hugh Thirlway, "The Law and Procedure of the International Court of Justice," *British Yearbook of International Law* 60 (1989): 141.

[176] An alternative point in time (for such a static reference) could be the beginning of provisional application. An example of a treaty where the consent to provisional application was chosen is GATT, see *GATT Secretariat Guide to GATT Law and Practice*, 6th ed. (Geneva: WTO Secretariat, 1994), 996, 1002. The *Yukos* Tribunal adopted this interpretation for the reference to internal law in the limitation clause in Article 45(1) ECT, *Yukos Universal Ltd v Russian Federation* (30 November 2009), 126; cf. Pritzkow, *Energiesektor*, 71.

[177] Geslin speaks of "la portée de l'engagement [...] *lors de la conclusion* de l'accord d'application provisoire" (*Application Provisoire*, 239) (emphasis added); see also Michie, "Provisional Application," 74.

[178] See Resolution, "The Intertemporal Problem in Public International Law," *Annuaire de l'Institut de Droit International* 56 (1975): [4]–[3]. For examples of evolutionary interpretation by the ICJ see *Legal Consequences for States of the Continued Presence of South Africa in Namibia (South West Africa) notwithstanding Security Council Resolution 276 (1970)(Advisory Opinion)* [1971] ICJ Rep 16, [53]; *Aegean Sea Continental Shelf* [1978] ICJ Rep 3 (hereinafter 'Aegean Sea Continental Shelf'), [77]–[80]; *Gabčíkovo-Nagymaros*

approaches to this, a discussion of which would go beyond the scope of this book. Indeed, it is arguable whether the problem of the critical date of the reference to internal law in clauses on provisional application is one of intertemporal interpretation. Besides obvious similarities, such as an open concept used in a treaty, and difficulties relating to determining the critical date for the concept's interpretation, there are also possible differences one would have to consider: does the concept apply to agreements which may not be binding? Does it only cover changes in international law[179] or also those of internal law?[180]

For now, it is sufficient to highlight the relevance of this matter, if the possibility of invoking internal law to delimit the extent of provisional application is linked to the discretion States enjoy when having recourse to provisional application. The two alternatives involve great differences in terms of discretion. In the first alternative, the discretion consists of allowing States to invoke their *pre-existing internal law* in the international sphere to delimit the extent of provisional application. In the second alternative, the discretion consists in allowing States to invoke *any law*, whether adopted prior or subsequently to the 'starting point' of provisional application. It follows that the second alternative involves considerably more discretion for the participating States, given that they can modulate or exclude the 'undertaking' to provisionally apply a treaty after the undertaking has been agreed. In the first alternative, such modulation or exclusion of the undertaking *ex post facto* is not possible since subsequently enacted law cannot be invoked in the international sphere to delimit the extent of provisional application.

By way of conclusion the following propositions can be made. Allowing only for the invocation of pre-existing law would enhance certainty and stability in treaty relations. It would minimise the uncertainty by excluding future changes to the extent of the provisional application by each participant. This would accommodate the interest on the international plane to bridge the inconvenient gap between the conclusion[181] and entry into force of the treaty. On the other hand, allowing the invocation of any kind of legislation, i.e. also subsequent legislation, would

---

Project (Hungary v Slovakia) [1997] ICJ Rep 7 [111]–[112]; see also Malgosia Fitzmaurice, "Dynamic (Evolutive) Interpretation of Treaties," *Hague Yearbook of International Law* 21 (2008): 101–57; *Hague Yearbook of International Law* 22 (2009): 3–31.

179 This may be the case if the concept is phrased in terms of Article 31(3)(c).

180 Resolution, "The Intertemporal Problem in Public International Law," preamble [1].

181 (or rather the moment when provisional application began).

preserve the constitutional freedom of law- and treaty-making procedures. It would acknowledge that those procedures possibly have not yet taken place, that consent to be bound may not yet have been expressed and would therefore preserve the liberty of parliament or any other (involved) constitutional organ to act according to its own agenda, thereby enabling the possibility of modulating or excluding the 'undertaking' to provisionally apply a treaty.

2.2.2.5. *Conclusion*

The above discussion has centered on the analysis of the hierarchy between a provisionally applied treaty and internal law. More precisely, the possibility of invoking internal law has been examined and several points were highlighted which seem crucial in assessing the possibility's significance for the determination of the binding force of treaties during the period of provisional application. First, it has been clarified that the possibility of invoking internal law can only serve as an argument for explaining the legal nature and binding force of provisionally applied treaties *in general* if itself it is a *general* feature. While this view is adopted by some academic writers, it is a minority view and, more importantly, due to the varying content of limitation clauses it would appear that they do not have a 'fundamentally norm-creating character',[182] which would stand in their way of being customary law. Therefore, drawing conclusions from them for the binding force of provisionally applied treaties *in general* involves the risk of making improper generalisations. Additionally, it has been shown that the amount of discretion flowing from the limitation of provisional application by internal law depends upon whether such internal laws can be adopted only prior to or also subsequent to the starting point of the provisional application. This matter has not received much attention in academic writings but indeed is crucial if one is interested in discretion in the context of assessing the binding force.

Accordingly, the following will examine whether the point on the scale has been reached in terms of discretion at which binding agreements end and soft law begins as regards provisionally applied treaties.

2.3. *Third Party Interpretation and the Discretion Allowed by Provisional Application*

When the nature of an agreement is in doubt because of the extent of discretion it grants to the norm addressee or 'obligor', then academic

---

[182] *North Sea Continental Shelf Cases*, [72].

opinion refers to the criterion of 'third party interpretation', i.e. whether the agreement is by reference to its substance[183] capable of adjudication.[184] If it is capable of adjudication, then it is seen as legally binding in nature. If it is found to be "inherently unsuited to adjudication",[185] then it is seen as soft law. An undertaking is thought to be inherently unsuited to adjudication if the obligor exclusively can decide if or when the 'obligation' arises, or to which extent it does so (sometimes this is referred to as a 'potestative obligation').[186] Certainly, if in those cases the control over the interpretation and application of the undertaking rests *solely* with the obligor, third party interpretation is excluded.[187]

Academic opinion has identified several mechanisms designed to serve this purpose. A vague wording can be chosen or hortatory clauses[188] inserted (such as 'endeavour', 'seek to promote') in order to leave to the obligor the ability to define the content of the undertaking.[189] There are also devices which *explicitly* allow a subjective assessment of the obligor,

---

183 This criterion is concerned with the potential capability of the undertaking to be an object of adjudication by reference to its substance and content, i.e. *by reference to its substantive provisions.* It is not concerned with the undertaking's *enforceability stricto sensu*, to be determined by reference to *procedural provisions*, such as dispute settlement clauses in treaties, optional clause declarations under Article 36(2) ICJ statute or 'special agreements' conferring jurisdiction to the ICJ in accordance with Article 36(1) ICJ statute.

184 For this criterion in academic writings on soft law, see Chinkin, "Challenge of Soft Law," 862, Gruchalla-Wesierski, "Understanding Soft Law," 49–51, 70; Münch, "Non-Binding Agreements," 11. For this criterion in writings on the intention to be bound see Sir Gerald Fitzmaurice, "Hersch Lauterpacht – The Scholar as Judge," *British Yearbook of International Law* 39 (1963): 171; O'Connell, *International Law*, 222; Philippe Gautier, *Essai sur la définition des traités entre Etats* (Brussels: Bruylant, 1993), 75. See also Widdows, "Agreement in International Law," 140. Virally seems to find this a criterion for not only a legal but also a binding obligation (to use his terminology), given that, according to his view, in case of breach of an undertaking capable of third party interpretation, state responsibility would arise as well as the right to resort to countermeasures: Michel Virally, "La distinction entre textes internationaux ayant une portée juridique dans les relations mutuelles entre leurs auteurs et textes qui en sont dépourvus," *Annuaire de l'Institut de Droit International*, vol. 1, 60 (1983): [16]; see also Separate Opinion, Judge Lauterpacht, *Case of Certain Norwegian Loans (France v Norway)* [1957] ICJ Rep 9 (hereinafter '*Norwegian Loans Case*') 48–51; Dissenting Opinion Judge Lauterpacht, *Interhandel Case (Switzerland v United States of America) (Preliminary Objections)* [1959] ICJ Rep 6 (hereinafter '*Interhandel Case*') 106–7.

185 Chinkin, "Challenge of Soft Law," 862.

186 Separate Opinion, Judge Lauterpacht, *Norwegian Loans Case* 49; Gautier, *Définition des traités*, 75.

187 Separate Opinion, Judge Lauterpacht, *Norwegian Loans Case* 48–51; Dissenting Opinion, Judge Lauterpacht, *Interhandel Case* 106–7; see also Gruchalla-Wesierski, "Understanding Soft Law," 49–51.

188 Abbott et al., "Concept of Legalization," 412; Baxter, "International Law in 'her Infinite Variety'," 553.

189 Gruchalla-Wesierski, "Understanding Soft Law," 49.

which are sometimes referred to as "escape clauses".[190] These can often be found in disarmament treaties. The 'Treaty Banning Nuclear Weapon Tests in the Atmosphere, in Outer Space and Under Water' sets out the following example of such a clause: "Each party shall ... have the right to withdraw from [this agreement] if *it decides* that extraordinary events, related to the subject-matter of [this agreement] have jeopardized the supreme interests of its country." (Emphasis added).[191] Finally, the 'Connally Reservation'[192] is a famous example of a self-judging mechanism. A reservation of this style was first attached by the US to their declaration accepting the compulsory jurisdiction of the ICJ. The reservation exempted from the jurisdiction of the Court 'disputes with regard to matters essentially within the domestic jurisdiction of the United States *as determined by the United States of America*' (emphasis added). These examples highlight the great decision-making power an 'obligor' can have with regard to the existence or the extent of the 'obligation' it has agreed to. It is with regard to such mechanisms that academic opinion on what constitutes a binding undertaking has developed the criterion of third party interpretation.

Asking whether an undertaking is capable of third party interpretation is to enquire whether it could be subject to adjudication. Article 38(1) of the Statute of the ICJ makes clear (also in juxtaposition to its subsection 2) that only binding law can be the basis of a judicial decision and subject to adjudication.[193] Therefore, asking whether an agreement could be subject to adjudication technically only rephrases the question whether that agreement is binding law. Nevertheless, this paraphrasing has the merit of introducing another criterion into the discourse, which will now be applied in the present context to see how the extent of discretion involved in provisional application affects its legal nature and binding force.

The two elements which have been identified as increasing the States' discretion when having recourse to provisional application were the

---

190 Abbott et al., "Concept of Legalization," 411.

191 Treaty Banning Nuclear Weapon Tests in the Atmosphere, in Outer Space and Under Water (signed 5 August 1963, entered into force 10 October 1963) 480 UNTS 43, Article IV.

192 Rudolf Dolzer, "Connally Reservation," in *Encyclopedia of Public International Law*, vol. 1, ed. Rudolf Bernhardt (Amsterdam: North Holland, 1992), 755–7; Christian Tomuschat, "Article 36," in *The Statute of the International Court of Justice: A Commentary*, eds. Andreas Zimmermann et al. (Oxford: Oxford University Press, 2006), 637.

193 Alain Pellet, "Article 38," in Zimmermann et al., *The Statute of the International Court of Justice: A Commentary*, 700. See also, without reference to Article 38 ICJ Statute: Bothe, "Legal and Non-Legal Norms," 87; Chinkin, "Challenge of Soft Law," 866; Eisemann, "Engagements Non Contraignants," [44]; Separate Opinion, Judge Lauterpacht, *Norwegian Loans Case*, 48–51.

possibility of terminating provisional application unilaterally, and the possibility of invoking (conflicting) internal law to delimit the extent of provisional application.

It would seem that the discretion to determine unilaterally the duration of provisional application would not generally affect the potential for third party interpretation of a provisionally applied treaty. Once it is established that a breach of the treaty is not a rightful exercise of the power of unilateral termination[194] there would appear to be no problems for third party interpretation caused by the power of unilateral termination. Any non-conform conduct ('breach') prior to the unilateral termination could certainly be the subject of adjudication,[195] as well as the legality of the termination itself (for instance, the question whether the parties 'had otherwise agreed', Article 25(2)). It follows that the possibility of terminating provisional application unilaterally does not affect the potential for third party interpretation of a provisionally applied treaty.

It remains to be analysed whether the possibility of invoking internal law affects the potential for third party interpretation of a provisionally applied treaty. As mentioned above, the effect of the possibility of invoking internal law is similar to that of reservations. Both preserve internal legislation which conflicts with the treaty and (re)adjust accordingly the extent to which the relevant provisions of the treaty are applied to that party. It follows that the extent to which provisional application takes place can vary among the different participants. It is even conceivable that this extent is different with regard to every one of them, 'individualised' by conflicting internal law. Therefore, it would appear difficult for States to know how much performance of the provisionally applied treaty can be expected from one another.[196] The result is considerable uncertainty and lack of transparency.[197] (Both would yet be increased if the internal law could also be changed after the commencement of provisional application.) Yet, it is submitted that a third party could, by reference to the

---

194 See Article 25(2), and more precisely the *duty to notify* the intention not to become a party to the treaty, as well as the principle of good faith; all these exclude the possibility of a breach of a provisionally applied treaty being seen as a *rightful* exercise of the power of unilateral termination.

195 See, e.g., the *Yukos* Award where the proceedings surrounding a possible breach by the Russian Federation of the provisionally applied ECT were not affected by the termination of the provisional application of the ECT by the Russian Federation, *Yukos Universal Ltd v Russian Federation* (30 November 2009), [338]–[339].

196 Geslin, *Application provisoire*, 319.

197 Michie, "Provisional Application," 75. *Yukos Universal Ltd v Russian Federation* (30 November 2009), [315]; Pritzkow, *Energiesektor*, 69.

relevant internal law and possibly by relying on expert opinions on the foreign internal law, determine exactly to which extent a State is able, at any given moment, to perform a provisionally applied treaty. Thus, there is for each State a clear yardstick against which its conduct can be measured to determine whether a 'breach' has occurred: this is the relevant norm of the provisionally applied treaty, to the extent that it is in conformity with the internal law of that State. Consequently, any conduct that is not in conformity with the provisionally applied treaty could be identified, and consequences may flow from that non-conformity. The possibility of invoking internal law would therefore not seem to affect the potential for third party interpretation of a provisionally applied treaty.

Yet, even if the possibility of invoking internal law does not raise issues concerning the test of the potential for third party interpretation, one concern remains: the delimitation of the provisional application of a treaty by reference to '*ex post* legislation', i.e. legislation that has been enacted *after* the conclusion of the agreement or commencement of provisional application. This would enable States to unilaterally 'modulate or exclude' the provisional application of the treaty. In other words, after having signed up to an undertaking, they would still be in a position to determine for themselves whether or to what extent they wish to be 'obliged'. This might possibly be the point where the balance tips over from legally binding to non-legally binding. But even then – and it is not clear whether this interpretation of limitation clauses has been agreed in practice – this would only affect the binding force of *some* provisionally applied treaties and could not be used as an argument against the binding force of provisionally applied treaties *in general*. Unaffected by this would be the binding force and legal nature of provisionally applied treaties which lack a specific provision for the possibility of invoking internal law; and of those treaties where it is clear that provisional application can only be delimited by reference to legislation that already existed at the time provisional application was agreed or commenced.

2.4. *Conclusion*

Provisionally applied treaties often allow their 'obligors' more freedom than treaties in force, and therefore create less certainty as to their performance than treaties tend to do.[198] Nevertheless, provisionally applied

---

198 Krieger, "Article 25," [30]; Montag 51; see also Reuter, *Introduction au droit des traités*, [111].

treaties are to be distinguished from soft law in that they are not "inherently unsuited" to but capable of adjudication, on the premise that the relevant internal law provides a clear yardstick against which the conduct can be measured. It follows that, based on the criterion of the potential for third party interpretation, the discretion enjoyed by the obligor does not generally exclude the legally binding force of provisionally applied treaties. Yet, if and to the extent that limitation clauses are intended to cover *ex post* legislation and thus allow States to modulate or exclude the undertaking to provisionally apply a treaty subsequent to its commencement, the point may well be reached where the agreement would appear not to be legally binding but of a soft law nature.

3. Conclusion

The purpose of the present chapter was to examine the arguments for the non-legally binding force or soft law nature of provisionally applied treaties recently put forward. The overall approach taken to the legal nature and binding force of these treaties is interesting in that it looks at these treaties as a group, developing arguments based on their (real or supposed) shared features, rather than approaching these treaties on an individual basis as tends to be done when the binding force of a specific instrument is at issue. The question so examined was whether the discretion allowed by provisional application is such as to necessarily exclude the legally binding force of these treaties.

It was seen that the perceived tension between the power of unilateral termination and the *pacta sunt servanda* principle is less a matter of fundamental legal principle and more a problem related to the absence of general compulsory jurisdiction in international law (as comparable to that in domestic legal systems). In other words, the tension is *factual*, due to the realities of the international legal system, but from a *legal* point of view, a power of unilateral termination and a legally binding undertaking are not incompatible. Thus, a power of unilateral termination such as the one provided for in Article 25(2) would not necessarily exclude the binding force of provisionally applied treaties. The same is true for the possibility of invoking (conflicting) internal law to delimit the extent of provisional application. First, it is thought that this is not a *general* feature of provisionally applied treaties, and therefore cannot be used as an argument against the binding force of these treaties *in general*. Moreover, while this possibility may lead to considerable uncertainty as to the extent to which each State is in a position to provisionally apply the treaty, it does not grant them an exclusive right to interpret and determine the extent of their undertaking and thus is qualitatively different from the discretion allowed by soft law agreements.

One factor was identified that may exclude the existence of a legally binding obligation to provisionally apply a treaty: if the possibility of invoking (conflicting) internal law is understood to allow the invocation of law enacted *after* a State has agreed to or commenced the provisional application of a treaty. So understood, a State would be free to unilaterally modify or extinguish the undertaking, after having signed up to it – which raises doubts as to whether the State has bound itself to anything or anyone other than itself. But even if the possibility of invoking internal law would be interpreted in this way at least in some instances, and this has not been shown, then this would not be an argument that would exclude the legally binding force of all provisionally applied treaties but only of some of them.

The identified factors demonstrate that provisionally applied treaties can allow less stability and certainty than treaties in force, at least if they provide for unilateral termination and the possibility of invoking internal law.[199] Nevertheless (and bearing the above possible exception in mind), it is not thought that these factors by themselves necessarily exclude the binding force of these treaties or express an intention not to be bound. Thus, it is submitted that it is still possible for States to bind themselves to provisionally apply a treaty.

---

[199] See note 198 (in chapter 2) above.

CHAPTER THREE

THE VIEW THAT PROVISIONALLY APPLIED TREATIES ARE LEGALLY BINDING

1. Introduction

Academic opinion is divided as to whether treaties are binding during the period of provisional application.[1] In Chapter two we analysed the view that treaties are not binding during the period of provisional application. This chapter explores the opposing view, i.e. that treaties are binding during the period of provisional application,[2] and in its first part the theoretical arguments supporting this view will be analysed.

The first of these arguments,[3] which probably has its roots in the ILC deliberations preceding the 1968–1969 Vienna Conference on the Law of Treaties, holds that provisionally applied treaties are like treaties in force: "Every treaty in force is binding upon the parties to it and must be performed by them in good faith."[4] To the extent that this assumes a

---

[1] Giorgio Gaja, "Provisional Application of Treaties," in Report of the International Law Commission on the Work of its Sixty-Third Session (2011), UN Doc A/66/10, Annex C, [2] and [4]; Michie, "Provisionally Applied Treaties in International Organisations," 56; Rogoff and Gauditz, "Provisional Application," 49–51; 80; Pritzkow, *Energiesektor*, 57; see also Niebruegge, "Provisional Application of the Energy Charter Treaty," 729; Belz, "Comment: Provisional Application of the Energy Charter Treaty," 356.

[2] For the binding force of provisionally applied treaties in academic writings: Blix, *Treaty-Making Power* (London: Stevens & Sons Limited, 1960), 297–8; TO Elias, *Law of Treaties*, 42–43; Knut Ipsen, *Völkerrecht*, 5th ed. (Munich: C.H. Beck, 2004), 137 [30]; Jennings and Watts, *Oppenheim's International Law*, [584] and fn. 1; Herbert Kraus, "Système et Fonctions des Traités Internationaux," *Recueil des cours de l'Académie de droit international de La Haye*, 50 (1934): 359; Krenzler, *Vorläufige Anwendung*, 57–8; Lefeber, "Treaties, Provisional Application," [16]; Erich Lettow, *Die völkerrechtliche Bindung nicht ratifizierter Verträge* (PhD diss., University of Bonn University, 1954), 64; Igor I. Lukashuk, "The Principle of *Pacta Sunt Servanda* and the Nature of Obligation under International Law," *American Journal of International Law*, 83 (1989): 513; Mathy, "Article 25 VCLT 1969," 652ff.; Michie, "Provisional Application," 65–66; Montag, *Völkerrechtliche Verträge*, 48; 50–52; 61–2; Florence Poirat, *Le Traité Comme Acte Juridique* (PhD diss., Université Panthéon Assas, 1997), 276; Sondaal, "Dutch Treaty Practice," 225. See also Schwarzenberger, *International Law*, 433. Hafner, "Provisional Application," 594.

[3] Jennings and Watts, *Oppenheim's International Law*, [584]; Lefeber, "Treaties, Provisional Application," [16]; Vladimir Degan, *Sources of International Law* (The Hague: Martinus Nijhoff Publishers, 1997), 402; Lukashuk, "*Pacta Sunt Servanda*," 516; Krenzler, *Vorläufige Anwendung*, 58; see also *Kardassopoulos v Georgia* (06 July 2007) [205]–[223], [210]–[211].

[4] Article 26.

conceptual resemblance between provisional application and entry into force, its appropriateness will be analysed and discussed. The second argument to be analysed is broader in that it relies on both an interpretation of Article 25 as well as the principle of legitimate expectations in order to identify the intention to be bound of international actors during the period of provisional application.[5] This second argument, being based on the intention of actors participating in provisional application, is followed by considerations of substitute formal sources for the treaty that, during provisional application, is merely awaiting its entry into force. These substitute formal sources are often seen in the construct underlying provisional application, such as, for instance, a collateral agreement. In this vein, the third and final argument suggests that provisionally applied treaties are binding because the mechanism of provisional application is generally based on a collateral (and binding) agreement.[6]

The second part of the Chapter is devoted to the other main aspect discussed in academic writings supporting the view that provisionally applied treaties are legally binding: explanations for the binding force of the rights and obligations of a treaty awaiting its entry into force. This question arises in particular if the obligations of a treaty in force are seen to flow from this treaty (and possibly also derive their binding force therefrom). Yet prior to dealing with such possible explanations, the theoretical arguments for the binding force of treaties during the period of provisional application will be examined.

A. Arguments for the View that Provisionally Applied Treaties are Legally Binding

2. Similarity to Treaties in Force

The main strand of academic opinion holds that provisionally applied treaties are binding in much the same way as treaties in force.[7]

[5] Montag, *Völkerrechtliche Verträge,* 51. See also Krenzler, *Vorläufige Anwendung*, 57.

[6] Montag, *Völkerrechtliche Verträge*, 61; Mathy, "Article 25 VCLT 1969," 652ff.; see also Kraus, "Système et Fonctions," 359; Hans Otto Meißner, *Vollmacht und Ratifikation bei völkerrechtlichen Verträgen nach deutschem Recht* (Göttingen: Vandenhoeck & Ruprecht, 1934), 90.

[7] Jennings and Watts, *Oppenheim's International Law*, [584]; Lefeber, "Treaties, Provisional Application," [16]; Degan, *Sources of International Law*, 402; Lukashuk "*Pacta Sunt Servanda*," 516; Krenzler, *Vorläufige Anwendung*, 58.

This assumption may serve several purposes. First, the assumption serves to explain how provisionally applied treaties are binding, i.e. to explain the applicability of the *pacta sunt servanda* principle to provisionally applied treaties.[8] Second, it serves to explain why provisionally applied treaties are binding. It is argued that provisionally applied treaties are like treaties in force, and, as Article 26 makes clear, treaties in force are binding.[9] This argument, which assimilates provisionally applied treaties to treaties in force, will now be analysed in more detail.

2.1. *Provisionally Applied Treaties as Treaties Provisionally in Force*

The basis of the view that provisionally applied treaties are binding due to their similarity with treaties in force probably lies in the ILC's understanding of provisional application, then still referred to as 'provisional entry into force.'[10] This terminology alone suggests that the ILC saw the mechanism as a subset of entry into force. Confirmation of this can be found in the ILC's commentary to the final draft article. It states that clauses on provisional application "*bring the treaty into force* on a provisional basis"[11] and that provisionally applied treaties are "*treaties in force*"[12] for the purpose of then Article 23 on *pacta sunt servanda*. While the ILC did not explain its reasons for this understanding, its position is very clear. For it, provisionally applied treaties were similar to treaties in force, even a subset of them, and therefore provisionally applied treaties were binding in much the same way as treaties in force.

However, the terminology used in Article 25 is that of 'provisional application', not of 'provisional entry into force'. This notwithstanding, some commentators, when substantiating the view that provisionally applied treaties are legally binding, still refer to the ILC position on the matter and

8 See e.g., Villiger, *Commentary*, [4]; Michie, "Provisionally Applied Treaties in International Organisations," 41. An alternative to the applicability of the *pacta sunt servanda* principle to these treaties would be if these treaties fell under the obligation not to defeat the object and purpose of a treaty prior to its entry into force (Article 18), as submitted by India at the Vienna Conference, OR 1969: Plen. 11: §70. See also Rogoff and Gauditz, "Provisional Application," 50.

9 Krenzler, *Vorläufige Anwendung*, 58; Lefeber, "Treaties, Provisional Application," [16]; See also Jennings and Watts, *Oppenheim's International Law*, [584].

10 See the references to the ILC by the following authors: Jennings and Watts, *Oppenheim's International Law*, [584]; Lefeber, "Treaties, Provisional Application," [16]; see also Krieger, "Article 25," [29].

11 Final Commentary on Article 22, see ILC, Draft articles on the law of treaties: text as finally adopted by the Commission on 18 and 19 July 1966, UN Doc A/CN.4/190, 210, §1 (emphasis added).

12 Ibid., Final Commentary on Article 23, 211, §3 (emphasis added).

the ILC conception of these treaties as 'treaties provisionally in force'.[13] Others do not explicitly refer to the ILC but also rely on the conception of these treaties as 'treaties provisionally in force'. Thus, when it comes to substantiating the binding force of *provisionally applied treaties*, they switch to the terminology of 'treaties provisionally in force';[14] 'treaties provisionally in force' are then 'treaties in force' for the purposes of the *pacta sunt servanda* rule.[15] By contrast the terminology of 'provisional application' creates more of a distance between the *pacta sunt servanda* rule and the mechanism under consideration. To say that 'provisionally applied treaties' are legally binding requires explanation; in fact, when ignoring the preparatory work and focusing only on the wording of the two provisions, one could equally maintain the contrary, namely that these treaties, being provisionally applied, do *not* fall within the ambit of the *pacta sunt servanda* rule, given that the rule covers only 'treaties in force'.[16]

However, the question arises whether it is still appropriate to rely on the conception of 'treaties provisionally in force' when it comes to arguing for the legally binding force of treaties which are subject to the mechanism in Article 25. It has been mentioned earlier that the change of name at the 1968–1969 Vienna Conference probably did entail a change of concept, namely to perceive the mechanism not as a subset of entry into force but as a subset of treaty application and performance. The next section will analyse the concepts of 'entry into force' and of a treaty's 'application' in order to clarify their legal implications and possible differences, especially as concerns the question of the binding force of treaties which are either said to be 'in force' or said to be 'applied'.

2.2. *'Entry into Force' and 'Application' in the VCLT 1969*

The starting point of the analysis of the concepts of 'entry into force' and 'application' in the VCLT 1969 is Article 28 on the non-retroactivity of treaties. According to the principle of non-retroactivity, the provisions of a treaty do not apply to any act or fact which took place or any situation

---

[13] Jennings and Watts, *Oppenheim's International Law*, [584]; Lefeber, "Treaties, Provisional Application," [16].

[14] Degan, *Sources of International Law*, 402; Lukashuk, "*Pacta Sunt Servanda*," 516; see also Krenzler, *Vorläufige Anwendung*, 58 (though he wrote prior to the adoption of the VCLT and therefore prior to the adoption of the concept of provisional application).

[15] The terminology of 'provisional entry into force' may make the proposition of the binding force of these treaties *sound* plausible, but it does not *make* it plausible. One could also take the view that 'treaties provisionally in force' are not 'treaties in force' and thus do not fall within the ambit of the *pacta sunt servanda* rule, see the position of Cyprus in the UNGA 6th committee GAOR 22, SR 980 (A/C.6/SR.980) §54.

[16] Geslin, *Application provisoire*, 330.

which ceased to exist before the date of the entry into force of the treaty with respect to that party, unless otherwise agreed. Does it follow from this principle that the duty to apply the treaty to relevant acts, facts and situations arises upon or simultaneously with the treaty's entry into force? A similar question arises with regard to Article 26: is it correct to read the article in a way according to which the duty to perform the treaty in good faith arises *upon* or *due to* the treaty's entry into force? In other words, is the duty to apply the substantive provisions of the treaty implied in, or a consequence of, the treaty's entry into force?

To clarify the relationship between 'entry into force' and the 'performance' or 'application' of treaties, several other provisions of the VCLT will be analysed which relate to the temporal (non)application of a treaty: Articles 70(1)(a) and 72(1)(a), and the caveat to Article 28. Article 28 contains the caveat that treaties can be retroactive if such an intention appears from the treaty or is otherwise established. By the retroactive application of a treaty is understood that once it has entered into force,[17] the treaty will also apply to acts and facts which took place or any situation which ceased to exist prior to its entry into force.[18] In other words, while the treaty applies to these past events, the duties deriving from it arise only after the actual occurrence of the events, at the moment of the treaty's entry into force. Therefore, the caveat which accommodates the retroactive application of treaties shows that the sphere of the temporal application of the treaty can precede its (moment of) entry into force. A similar situation is regulated in the caveat to Article 70(1)(a). There, the temporal application of a treaty can outlast its time in force. Thus, the caveat to Article 70(1)(a) shows that a treaty (or rather some of its provisions) can be applied even after its termination,[19] i.e. that a treaty can be applied without simultaneously being in force. Finally, the converse is also possible: a treaty can be in force without being applied. According to Article 72(1)(a), this is the consequence of the suspension of the operation of a treaty.

---

17 Retroactive application of a treaty tends to commence upon the treaty's entry into force. Due to the freedom of contract, however, it would appear that the negotiating States may choose for the commencement of retroactivity any date or event other than the treaty's entry into force. Thus, examples can be found in State practice, where the retroactive application of a treaty began upon the treaty's provisional application, and not the treaty's entry into force, see Trade Agreement 1973 (Canada-Bulgaria), 977 UNTS 295, Article VIII; Long-Term Trade Agreement, 929 UNTS 85, related letter VI (8 September 1971).

18 Malgosia Fitzmaurice, "Third Parties and the Law of Treaties," *Max Planck Yearbook of United Nations Law* 6 (2002): 74; see also Bindschedler-Robert, "Rétroactivité en droit international public," 185.

19 See e.g., Convention on the Liability of Operators of Nuclear Ships (concluded 25 May 1962, not yet entered into force) *American Journal of International Law* 57 (1963): 268, Article XIX.

In conclusion *being in force* and *being applicable* often coincide. Yet from Articles 70(1)(a) and 72(1)(a) follows that 'entry into force' and the 'temporal application of treaty provisions' are two different phenomena. Accordingly, it is possible that 'entry into force' and 'application' have different legal implications. If so, this may find an expression in the classification of the mechanism as provisional 'application' rather than 'entry into force.' In the next section the concepts of 'entry into force' and 'application' will be analysed further in light of treaty practice and academic writings.[20]

2.3. *'Entry into Force' and 'Application' in Academic Writings and Treaty Practice*

The distinction in treaty practice between entry into force and entry into operation (the latter is used here to signify the beginning of the 'performance' or 'application' of a treaty) is probably best illustrated by the effect of suspensive or dilatory conditions.[21] The effect of these conditions, after a treaty's entry into force, is to condition the treaty's application to relevant acts, facts and situations upon a certain event or date. The 1949 Geneva Conventions, for instance the Geneva Convention Relative to the Protection of Civilian Persons in Time of War,[22] are a good example of the use of a suspensive condition. Although they entered into force on 21 October 1950,[23] many of their substantive provisions, for instance, on the conduct of warfare and the treatment of prisoners of war, only become applicable between the parties in case of an 'international armed conflict', and not upon their entry into force. Thus, the application of these substantive provisions to relevant acts, facts and situations is conditioned, *inter alia,* upon there being an 'international armed conflict'.[24] This clearly shows that a treaty's entry into force does not necessarily involve its performance, i.e. that entry into force does not equal the beginning of the

---

[20] Academic writings on the consequences of 'entry into force' vary substantially mainly because the terminology ('becoming binding', 'becoming operative', 'sphere of temporal application') is used in an inconsistent manner.

[21] Such a condition has been defined as an "[é]vénement futur et de réalisation incertaine, qui suspend ... la naissance d'un droit..." *Dictionnaire de la Terminologie de Droit International Public* (Paris: Sirey, 1960), 144.

[22] Geneva Convention relative to the Protection of Civilian Persons in Time of War (adopted 12 August 1949, entered into force 21 October 1950) 75 UNTS 287 (Geneva Convention IV).

[23] Information provided by the depositary of the four Conventions (Switzerland) http://www.eda.admin.ch/eda/de/home/topics/intla/humlaw/gecons.html

[24] Common Article 2(1) 1949 Geneva Conventions. This is a simplified explanation of one of the possibilities under which the Conventions become operative, as there are

application of the treaty's substantive provisions to relevant acts, facts and situations.[25]

What 'entry into force' does instead is to designate the moment when the treaty becomes binding[26] and acquires full legal force as a legal act.[27] This involves a set of legal implications. First, consent is now irrevocable.[28] When a State changes its mind over a treaty and does not want to become a party to it anymore, prior to the treaty's entry into force consent to be bound can simply be revoked.[29] However, as a consequence of entry into force, either the consent needs to be invalidated, or the treaty terminated (both in accordance with the treaty's own provisions or the law of treaties). Accordingly, upon entry into force the mere revocation of consent generally will not do. Second, along with the treaty's provisions on termination and invalidity, all final clauses of the treaty become applicable upon its entry into force and becoming binding. This includes the rules on amendment and modification, on interpretation etc. Third, the treaty's entry into force implies the (possibly continuing) duty not to defeat the treaty's object and purpose.[30] Thus while entry into force may in practice frequently coincide with the beginning of the application of the treaty to relevant acts, facts and situations, this really is a *coincidence* as opposed to a *consequence* or implication of 'entry into force' (as has been shown above by reference to the 1949 Geneva Conventions and the effect of suspensive conditions). Yet what is an implication or consequence of 'entry into force' is the duty to refrain from acts defeating the treaty's object and purpose.[31]

---

several other conditions or situations in which the Conventions or certain of their provisions become operative, according to common Articles 2 and 3.

[25] Paul Guggenheim and Krystyna Marek, "Völkerrechtliche Verträge," in *Wörterbuch des Völkerrechts*, vol. 3, 2nd ed., Karl Strupp and Hans J. Schlochauer (Berlin: De Gruyter, 1962), 537; Mahiou, "Article 24 VCLT 1969," 1040.

[26] Aust, *Modern Treaty Law*, 162; McNair, *Law of Treaties*, 191; UN Summary of Practice of the Secretary General as Depositary of Multilateral Treaties (hereinafter 'UN SecGen Summary of Practice') [157], http://untreaty.un.org/English/Summary.asp.

[27] Reuter, *Introduction au droit des traités*, [107].

[28] Aust, *Modern Treaty Law*, 120; Joseph Nisot, "L'article 18 de la Convention de Vienne sur le Droit des Traités," *Revue Belge de Droit International* 6 (1970/2): 503; UN SecGen Summary of Practice, [157].

[29] Aust, *Modern Treaty Law*, 120; Nisot, "L'article 18 de la Convention de Vienne sur le droit des traités," 503; UN SecGen Summary of Practice, [157].

[30] ILC, Draft articles on the law of treaties: text as finally adopted by the Commission on 18 and 19 July 1966, UN Doc A/CN.4/190, Final Commentary on Article 23 [pacta sunt servanda], 211, §4.

[31] If the State was already under such a duty prior to the treaty's entry into force (see Article 18), the consequence of entry into force is that the duty continues to apply (the duty under Article 18 terminates upon the treaty's entry into force for the respective State, see the title of Article 18 and 18(b)).

Fourth, the treaty's entry into force means that the matter has become one of international law and no longer (if it did so before) belongs to the sphere of the reserved domain of jurisdiction.[32] Fifth, it also implies that between the parties to the treaty, the matter is governed by treaty law, and to the extent that the treaty is *lex specialis*, ceases to be one of customary international law.

In sum, academic opinion[33] and treaty practice support the above result of the VCLT analysis: that 'entry into force' and 'entry into operation' are two different phenomena, which can but do not have to occur simultaneously. Moreover, 'entry into force' and 'application' have different legal implications. While 'becoming binding' is a consequence of 'entry into force', 'immediate application' of the treaty's substantive provisions is not. Since practice confirms[34] and commentators[35] agree that the mechanism under consideration is about the *application* of a treaty's provisions, the question arises whether it is still appropriate to rely on one of the consequences of 'entry into force' – i.e. the fact that the treaty becomes binding – as an argument for the binding force of these treaties.

2.4. *Does 'Application' Imply That the Treaty is Binding?*

The question therefore is whether treaty application (like the treaty's entry into force) necessarily implies that the treaty is binding. In other words, the question is whether an agreement to apply a treaty necessarily implies States being bound by such an agreement. It would appear that the concept of a treaty's 'application' in terms of binding force would be broader than that and would not necessarily imply that States are legally bound to apply the treaty. Theoretically speaking (and unlike a treaty's entry into force) a treaty's application can be agreed as a soft law undertaking. Thus, an undertaking to apply a treaty can mean either full

---

32 On the reserved domain of jurisdiction in general see *Nationality Decrees Issued in Tunis and Morocco (Advisory Opinion)* PCIJ Series B, No. 4, 24. See also Georg Nolte, "Article 2(7)," in *The Charter of the United Nations: A Commentary*, ed. Bruno Simma, 2nd ed. (Oxford: Oxford University Press, 2002), [27].

33 Briggs, *Law of Nations*, 865; TO Elias, *Law of Treaties*, 39; Guggenheim and Marek, "Völkerrechtliche Verträge," 537; Mahiou, "Article 24 VCLT 1969," 1040; McNair, *Law of Treaties*, 191; *Introduction au droit des traités*, [108]; "Harvard Draft," 787.

34 CoE and BIICL, eds., *Treaty Making*, see the responses by Denmark, 153; Iceland, 192; Ireland, 196; Lithuania, 211; Romania, 241; Sweden, 267; UK, 290; Nash, "Contemporary Practice of the United States," 917.

35 Krenzler, *Vorläufige Anwendung*, 9, 57; Erich Lettow, "Die völkerrechtliche Bindung nicht ratifizierter Verträge" (PhD diss., University of Bonn, 1954), 58; Loibl, "The Energy Charter Treaty," 576; Sondaal, "Dutch Treaty Practice," 225; Michie, "Provisional Application," 31.

performance of the treaty, as though one were legally bound to do so, or performance of the treaty 'to the extent possible or convenient', meaning that one may not be legally but morally or politically bound to do so. Therefore, since the mechanism is now conceived as a subset to 'application', reliance on the assimilation to 'entry into force' and 'becoming binding upon entry into force' may not be advisable when one attempts to explain the legally binding force of provisionally applied treaties.

To the extent that commentators rely not only on the conception of 'provisional entry into force' but also refer to the ILC the following is submitted. The ILC conception of the mechanism and its binding force as 'treaties provisionally in force' is outdated given the fact that the 1968–1969 Vienna Conference moved away from this concept and instead regarded the mechanism as a subset of a treaty's application. Yet the ILC position on the binding force of these treaties, i.e. that these treaties are binding and fall within the ambit of the *pacta sunt servanda* rule, was shared by the majority of States delegates at the 1968–1969 Vienna Conference, as has been shown above. Accordingly, reference to the ILC deliberations as support for the view that provisionally applied treaties are legally binding would be appropriate if it relied on the ILC position and the ILC's authority, but less so if it relied on the ILC's conception of the mechanism.

2.5. *Conclusion*

The argument that provisionally applied treaties are binding because they are like treaties in force (namely 'treaties provisionally in force') is problematic because it could be said to rely on an outdated conception of the mechanism and to disregard the change of name and concept at the 1968–1969 Vienna Conference from 'provisional entry into force' to 'provisional application'.

The next argument for the legally binding force of provisionally applied treaties relies on a general intention of States and international organisations to be bound by these treaties.

3. The Intention of the Participants to be Bound by Provisionally Applied Treaties

The next section will be devoted to the thesis that provisionally applied treaties generally[36] are binding due to the parties' intention to be bound

[36] While many authors argue that provisionally applied treaties are legally binding, without allowing room for exceptions, Montag, *Völkerrechtliche Verträge*, 59, explicitly

during the period of provisional application.[37] More precisely, it is 'agreements on provisional application' (as distinct from the treaty awaiting its entry into force) which are said to be binding due to a corresponding intention of the parties.[38] This distinction is relevant because the main proponent of the thesis (Montag) follows the understanding according to which provisional application is *always* based on a separate collateral agreement, whether it is actually agreed in a separate agreement or in the treaty itself (*negotium* approach).[39] The general intention to be bound is deduced from three different propositions which will now be analysed. The starting point is the proposition that Article 25 regulates these agreements on provisional application, and that the regulation of these agreements by international law indicates that such agreements are binding.[40]

3.1. *The Argument that Agreements on Provisional Application are Legally Binding because they are "Governed by International Law"*

It is argued that the regulation of agreements on provisional application in Article 25 implies that these agreements are 'governed by international

leaves room for exceptions. Since, according to him, the binding force of these agreements depends upon the intention of the parties, he contends that there must be room for exceptions in order to accommodate the possibility that in a given case States would intend not to be legally bound by a provisionally applied treaty. See also van Panhuys, "The Netherlands Constitution and International Law," 94; Mahnoush H. Arsanjani and W. Michael Reisman, "Provisional Application of Treaties in International Law: The Energy Charter Treaty Awards," in *The Law of Treaties Beyond thee Vienna Convention*, ed. Enzo Cannizzaro (Oxford: Oxford University Press, 2011), 101. For authors who put forward the view of the binding force of provisionally applied treaties in a general statement without mentioning possible exceptions see, e.g., Krieger, "Article 25," [29]-[30]; Villiger, *Commentary*, [4]; Mathy, "Article 25 VCLT 1969," 651; Caroline Laly-Chevalier, *La violation du traité* (Brussels: Bruylant, 2005), 40; Jennings and Watts, *Oppenheim's International Law*, [584] fn. 1; see also Butler, *The Law of Treaties in Russia and the Commonwealth of Independent States*, 126.

[37] Montag, *Völkerrechtliche Verträge*, 51; Krenzler, *Vorläufige Anwendung*, 57.

[38] Montag, *Völkerrechtliche Verträge*, 48–50; contrast Krenzler, *Vorläufige Anwendung*, 38–41.

[39] For the use of this terminology in the context of provisional application see Mathy, "Article 25 VCLT 1969," 649–650. The general distinction between '*negotium*' and '*instrumentum*' has been introduced in the following way: "With regard to any legal transaction one can distinguish between the thing itself, which as the object of the transaction is the *negotium*, and the form of the transaction, the *instrumentum*" (present author's translation) Olivier Jouanjan, "Der Beitrag der Wissenschaften zur künftigen Verfassung der EU," *Basler Schriften zur Europäischen Integration* 66 (2003): 15. "According to the well-established dichotomy, the former [*negotium*] relates to the substance, the *causa*, the legal justification, while the latter [*instrumentum*] is but its proof, its evidence" or envelope, see Giovanni Distefano, "The Conceptualization (Construction) of Territorial Title in the Light of the International Court of Justice Case Law," *Leiden Journal of International Law* 19 (2006), 1053, fn. 63.

[40] Montag, *Völkerrechtliche Verträge*, 50.

law'.[41] This, it is said, distinguishes these agreements from non-legally binding agreements since the latter as a rule are not governed by international law.[42] For the premise of this argument, that non-legally binding agreements are not governed by international law, Montag relies on Schachter who in turn put this view forward as being based on state practice[43] and assumed that this proposition "would command general agreement". This last assumption may be questioned because it is contested in academic writings whether or not non-legally binding agreements are governed by international law. As a starting point, many authors agree that "non-legally binding agreements may give rise to some 'legal' consequences",[44] not by themselves but by virtue of the principles of good faith and estoppel.[45] This (legal?) effect of soft law has been described in many different ways,[46] one of which was to say that principles of international law can apply to some of the consequences of non-legally binding agreements.[47] Some writers go further and suggest that, in addition to their consequences, the non-legally binding agreements themselves are governed

41 For this criterion see Article 2(1)(a). The argument is developed in this context by Montag, *Völkerrechtliche Verträge*, 50. It is submitted that if indeed these agreements were regulated in the VCLT, this would require their recognition and treatment as treaties by the Convention, since the VCLT, as its title indicates, regulates 'treaties'.

42 Montag, *Völkerrechtliche Verträge*, 50, based on Schachter, "Nonbinding International Agreements," 300–01.

43 Ibid., 301.

44 Aust, *Modern Treaty Law*, 53 (though he uses this wording to formulate the question whether in fact these agreements can give rise to legal consequences).

45 Aust, *Modern Treaty Law*, 53–55; John F. O'Connor, *Good Faith in International Law* (Dartmouth: Aldershot, 1991) 113; Gruchalla-Wesierski, "Understanding Soft Law," 62–3; Münch, "Non-Binding Agreements," 11; Thürer, "Soft Law," 457. It is not clear whether the applicability of these principles is seen as *legal* consequence of these agreements or not, see Spinner "Über die *völkerrechtlichen* Wirkungen, die auch eine bloß politisch verbindliche Vereinbarung haben kann, scheint noch wenig Klarheit zu bestehen." Bruno Spinner, "Bemerkungen zur Mitteilung der Direktion für Völkerrecht und des Bundesamtes für Justiz betreffend den Abschluss von Staatsverträgen," *Schweizerisches Jahrbuch für Internationales Recht* XLIV (1988): 36, fn. 13. Cautioning against "letting (the) law come in by the back door" when applying these principles in a sweeping way is Bothe, "Legal and Non-Legal Norms," 94–5. He moves on to say: "'Good faith' is a legal concept, and basing respect for non-legal obligations on a legal concept would not seem to be appropriate."

46 Thürer calls it "the immediate legal effects" of soft law in the field of good faith, see Thürer, "Soft Law," [4a] 457; Gruchalla-Wesierski, "Understanding Soft Law," 45; According to Senden "[the concept of legal effect] covers not only legally binding force *sensu stricto*, but also other possible legal effects of soft law. In short: legal effect may come about not only through a legal instrument or act of itself (legally binding force), but also by way of the operation of other legal mechanisms", such as e.g. the principles of good faith or estoppel (indirect legal effects). Linda Senden, *Soft Law in European Community Law* (Oxford: Hart Publishing, 2004), 235.

47 Gruchalla-Wesierski, "Understanding Soft Law," 45.

by international law.[48] Accordingly, the premise of this argument touches upon the highly complex question of the normative framework for such agreements. An attempt at providing an answer would seem to require first a clarification as to the nature of those agreements or provisions (political, moral, legal etc.). Additionally, it may be necessary to clarify whether it is valid to find legally relevant not the agreements but only the consequences flowing therefrom.[49] In other words it may be necessary to clarify how it is that soft law may give rise to certain legal consequences via the principles of good faith and estoppel and whether this does not in fact mean that these legal principles do apply to soft law agreements. And if these legal principles do apply to soft law agreements, does this in turn mean that soft law agreements are governed by international law, or not, or that they are governed by international law but in a different way to legally binding agreements?

The argument itself is that Article 25 regulates 'agreements on provisional application',[50] and Montag surmises from this 'regulation' that agreements on provisional application are governed by international law and therefore legally binding. Indeed, if Article 25 treated or mentioned those agreements as treaties, for instance by setting out a rule of the law of treaties applicable to them (for example, as in Article 60(5) the exception made for "treaties of a humanitarian character"), or by explicitly acknowledging their binding force (as in Article 3(a), for example, with regard to international agreements outside of the scope of the VCLT 1969), then 'agreements on provisional application' could be said to be governed by the law of treaties and therefore governed by international law. Upon careful examination, however, Article 25 does not seem to do that. According to its title, Article 25 regulates 'provisional application', and not 'agreements on provisional application'. Moreover, if the provision would be concerned with regulating those agreements, one would expect them to be mentioned as 'agreements'. However, the wording of Article 25, namely that the provisional application of a treaty (and its termination) can be 'agreed' by the negotiating States, means that the existence of 'agreements on provisional application' can at best be inferred. This is not merely playing with words. The point is that while Article 25 implies the existence of

[48] Eisemann, "Engagements Non-Contraignants," [43]; See also Virally, "La distinction entre textes internationaux ayant une portée juridique dans les relations mutuelles entre leurs auteurs et textes qui en sont dépourvus," 347–8, 345 fn. 6; and Thürer, "Soft Law," 460, 453.

[49] See also Klabbers, *The Concept of Treaty in International Law*, 111–12.

[50] Montag, *Völkerrechtliche Verträge*, 50.

agreements on provisional application, it does not regulate those agreements in their own right and does not treat them as treaties. In other words, in Article 25, States can agree to provisionally apply a treaty, in the same way in which they can agree on a means of expressing consent to be bound (see Article 12(1)b or 13(b), for example), on reservations or on termination. Clearly, these are agreements, but they are not, in the VCLT, seen as agreements in their own right, as treaties, but as 'informal agreements' collateral to and concerning a treaty.[51] Thus, it is submitted that the subject of 'regulation' in Article 25 is the mechanism of provisional application and not 'agreements on provisional application.'

By way of conclusion, in light of the difficulties relating to both the argument and its premise, it is submitted that the view that agreements on provisional application are governed by Article 25, and that they are consequently governed by international law and therefore legally binding, is not entirely convincing.

3.2. *The Argument that the Purpose of Provisional Application Implies a Legally Binding Obligation*

The next proposition relying on the intention to be bound during the period of provisional application points to the purpose of provisional application which can, it is contended, only be achieved by means of legally binding undertakings.[52] The purpose of provisional application is mainly seen in the securing of the benefits associated with the treaty.[53] Montag, for example, argues that these benefits are best secured if the parties are legally bound to observe the treaty;[54] otherwise, legal uncertainty would arise as to whether anyone performed the treaty or would honour the others' performance. These 'benefits of the treaty' are not defined but it would appear that they result from the performance or application of the treaty. Therefore, when saying that these benefits can only be achieved by way of legally binding agreements, Montag touches upon the 'compliance' debate.[55] By 'compliance' is understood "the conformity to the rules,

---

51 Jean Salmon, "Les accords non-formalisés ou '*Solo Consensu*'," *Annuaire Français de Droit International* XLV (1999): 2–4, especially "Accords informels subsidiaires prévus par un traité, distincts du consentement à être lié par le traité".

52 Montag, *Völkerrechtliche Verträge*, 51.

53 It is also seen in the immediate application of the treaty preceding its entry into force, Montag, *Völkerrechtliche Verträge*, 51.

54 Ibid.

55 On the debate see Dinah Shelton, ed., *Commitment and Compliance* (Oxford: Oxford University Press, 2000); Edward C. Luck and Michael W. Doyle, eds., *International Law and*

laws and norms of a particular regime."[56] In this debate, the significance of different factors in enhancing and hindering compliance was discussed, and the influence of legally binding norms on compliance remains contested.[57] Some commentators even raise the question whether a norm's binding force has any relevance for State conduct.[58] Thus, to the extent that Montag's 'purpose of provisional application' is understood as involving the treaty's performance or compliance with it, his view of a legally binding obligation being the *only* means of achieving this purpose may find some criticism in the compliance debate, and if put forward today his view would probably benefit from a discussion of these matters.[59]

Leaving that aside, Montag's assessment of what States wish to achieve with provisional application is convincing. Since in the long-run they opted for a treaty, i.e. a legally binding undertaking, in order to regulate the matter at hand, it is certainly reasonable to assume that this is what they might want during provisional application, too, when they bring the application of the treaty forward in time: legally binding force and legal certainty. Of course, the possibility of enforcing a breach of the legally binding undertaking, which is what ultimately provides legal certainty and distinguishes a legally binding from a non-legally agreement, would not appear to have been relied upon often in practice during provisional application. But this is not specific to provisional application; in general, States are said to regard legal remedies as a last resort and to prefer the exhaustion of other remedies, such as negotiation or the use of political,

---

Organization: Closing the Compliance Gap (Lanham: Rowman & Littlefield, 2004), 5; Abram Chayes and Antonia Handler Chayes, "On Compliance," *International Organization* 47 (1993), 175; see also Harlan Grant Cohen, "Finding International Law: Rethinking the Doctrine of Sources," *Iowa Law Review* 93 (2007–2008): 70.

56 Luck and Doyle, *International Law and Organization*, 5.

57 Henkin's famous statement that "almost all nations observe almost all principles of international law and almost all of their obligations almost all of the time" *How Nations Behave: Law and Foreign Policy*, 2nd ed. (New York: Columbia University Press, 1979), 47 can be juxtaposed to statements according to which "empirical evidence suggests that treaties are poor predictors of state practice", and that, at least in areas such as Human Rights or Environmental Law "[t]he link between treaty accession and compliance is severed completely." Harlan G. Cohen, "Finding International Law: Rethinking the Doctrine of Sources," *Iowa Law Review* 93 (2007–8): 95.

58 "Does international law make a difference as to how countries behave?" see Peter M. Haas, review of *International Law and Organization: Closing the Compliance Gap*, by Edward C. Luck and Thomas Doyle, eds., *American Journal of International Law*, 102 (2008): 226.

59 According to Bothe, the compliance debate began in the 1980s, Michael Bothe, "Compliance," last modified October 2010, in *MPEPIL online*, ed. Rüdiger Wolfrum, [2]. Accordingly, when Montag's book (*Völkerrechtliche Verträge*) was published in 1986, the debate was a recent development.

economic and other pressures.[60] Moreover, in the case of provisional application, there would appear to be additional reasons for this attitude, given its precarious nature[61] and its easy terminability. Thus, the fact that thus far States would not appear to have frequently relied on what legal certainty in practice consists of, does not exclude that ultimately legal certainty is what States might want during the period of provisional application.

Accordingly, while Montag's argument today might require some discussion in light of the compliance debate, his assessment of the overall purpose of provisional application appears plausible. Yet, it leaves open how to proceed when wishing to determine in individual cases whether an agreement on provisional application is legally binding or not.

3.3. *The Argument that Provisionally Applied Treaties are Legally Binding on the Basis of Legitimate Expectations* ('Vertrauensschutz')

Montag further argues that the States' intention to be bound during the period of provisional application also follows from the principle of legitimate expectations[62] (also known as '*protection de la confiance*' or '*Vertrauensschutz*').[63] He suggests that the expression of consent to provisionally apply a treaty, as well as the treaty's subsequent actual provisional application, both create a legitimate expectation amongst the other States concerned that, during the period of provisional application, treaties will be performed as if they were in force.[64] Concerning the expression of consent to provisionally apply a treaty he argues that States need to be able to rely on this declaration if it is supposed to be of any value. With regard to the actual provisional application of the treaty, he asserts that the application of a treaty to acts, facts and situations during the period of provisional application creates the legitimate expectation(s) of other States, that in similar future situations the treaty will equally be applied to acts, facts and

---

60 E.g. Jonathan Charney, "Commentary," in *Commitment and Compliance*, ed. Dinah Shelton (Oxford: Oxford University Press, 2000), 116.

61 Montag, *Völkerrechtliche Verträge*, 51. See also Reuter, *Introduction au droit des traités*, [111] (who designates the undertaking to provisionally apply a treaty as a 'precarious' one).

62 Montag, *Völkerrechtliche Verträge*, 51–52.

63 Robert Kolb uses the term 'legitimate expectations' in "Principles as Sources of International Law," *Netherlands International Law Review* LIII (2006): 20; and "protection de la confiance légitime' in "la bonne foi en droit international public," *Revue Belge de Droit International* (1998/2): 684.

64 Montag, *Völkerrechtliche Verträge*, 52.

situations during the period of provisional application, unless that application remains an exception.

3.3.1. *Does the Relevant Conduct Give Rise to Legitimate Expectations?*

Before analysing these different assertions, the principle of legitimate expectations will be introduced. The principle means that certain expectations, raised by a legal subject's conduct towards its partners or the community at large, have legal effects.[65] It also means that rights and obligations can flow from social interactions in order to protect the legitimate expectations which one legal subject has raised towards other such subjects through its conduct.[66] The principle of legitimate expectations is often seen as an aspect or application of the broader principle of good faith.[67] Additionally, it is said to be an essential element of the law of treaties,[68] and to play an important role in the stages preceding the treaty's entry into force,[69] i.e. also in the provisional application of treaties.

Suppose that in international law conduct which gives rise to legitimate expectations is legally relevant and protected by the law. It follows that if States have concluded an agreement, i.e. given a legal promise, it is not only because of the principle of good faith in its broader application, but also due to the principle of legitimate expectations, that the States' (legitimate) reliance on such an agreement is protected by international

---

65 Jörg Paul Müller, *Vertrauensschutz im Völkerrecht* (Köln: Carl Heymanns Verlag, 1971), 1.

66 Kolb, "La bonne foi en droit international public," 685.

67 See e.g. Kolb, "La bonne foi en droit international public," 684–85; Jean-Didier Sicault, "Engagements unilatéraux,"*Revue General de Droit International Public* 83 (1979): 683–85; Paul Reuter, *Droit International Public*, 6th ed. (Paris : Presses Universitaires de France, 1983), 24; Cheng, *General Principles of Law*, 137. In case law, 'good faith' and 'legitimate expectations' or 'confidence' have been linked to one another in the following cases: *Nuclear Tests (New Zealand v France)* [1974] ICJ Rep 457 (hereinafter '*Nuclear Tests (New Zealand v France)*') 473 [49]; *Military and Paramilitary Activities in and against Nicaragua (Nicaragua v United States of America) (Jurisdiction and Admissibility)* [1984] ICJ Rep 392, 418 [60]; Dissenting Opinion, Judge Torres Bernárdez, *Fisheries Jurisdiction (Spain v Canada)* [1998] ICJ Rep, 432, 675 [251]; Separate Opinion, Judge Lauterpacht, *Case of Certain Norwegian Loans (France v Norway)* [1957] ICJ Rep 9, 53.

68 Montag, *Völkerrechtliche Verträge*, 51–52; see also Müller, *Vertrauensschutz im Völkerrecht*, 104–33. This is suggested to follow, for example, from the rule of fundamental change of circumstances. The fact that a fundamental change of circumstances can be invoked as a ground for terminating the treaty means that the law protects the expectation that circumstances, relevant for and existing at the conclusion of the treaty, would not change.

69 Montag, *Völkerrechtliche Verträge*, 52; Müller, *Vertrauensschutz im Völkerrecht*, 104–33; 154ff.; 164ff.; 191ff.; see also Kolb, "La Bonne Foi en Droit International Public," 688–93.

law. Yet, the kind of protection afforded depends necessarily on what has been agreed. As Schwarzenberger has stated: "Every consensual engagement ... raises expectations that, in due course, the parties will comply *with its terms*."[70] (Emphasis added). Whether these terms merely oblige the conduct of further negotiations[71] or, on the contrary, contain a substantive, precisely-defined obligation capable of third-party assessment, will depend on what the parties want, the circumstances at hand etc. Therefore, being subjected to the principles of good faith and legitimate expectations does not indicate the substance of what has been agreed. In other words, the fact that one can rely on the content of the agreement does not reveal precisely what that content is (other than being a legally protected position, i.e. a position not contrary to *jus cogens* etc.).

In conclusion, it is submitted that Montag overstretches the principle of legitimate expectations in order to deduce an intention to be bound and ultimately the binding force of rights and obligations during the period of provisional application. In individual cases, the principle of legitimate expectations may help clarify the extent or precise object of an implied or ambiguous expression of an intention to be bound.[72] However, it is submitted that it would be problematic to apply the principle in a sweeping manner to all cases of provisional application, in order to overcome the uncertainty in academic writing which surrounds the precise legal meaning of the terms 'provisional application'.

The same would seem to apply to the proposition that the actual application of the provisionally applied treaties amounts to conduct which creates the legitimate expectation that the State so conducting itself will repeat the conduct in future similar situations. Since the States have previously agreed on the provisional application, any subsequent conduct will need to be assessed first and foremost by reference to the agreement. If the agreement is a legally binding one, then the expectation of performance of the agreement is legally protected and ensured due to the existence of enforcement mechanisms. If the agreement is more of a hortatory and aspirational nature, then its performance would not

---

[70] Georg Schwarzenberger, "The Fundamental Principles of International Law," *Recueil des cours de l'Académie de droit international de La Haye* 87 (1955): 295.

[71] The obligation to negotiate (*pactum de negotiando*) is subject to the principle of good faith: Aust, *Modern Treaty Law*, 31; Ulrich Beyerlin, "Pactum de Contrahendo, Pactum de Negotiando," in *Encyclopedia of Public International Law*, vol. 3, ed. Rudolf Bernhardt (Amsterdam: North Holland, 1997), 857. See also O'Connell, *International Law*, 202; Degan, *Sources of International Law*, 504.

[72] Kolb, "La bonne foi en droit international public," 683.

necessarily give rise to legitimate expectations in the future because it is clear that such conduct depends to a much greater extent on the prevailing circumstances at that time. Therefore, it is submitted that it is crucial when determining legitimate expectations to do so against the background of the terms of the relevant agreement.

Finally, Montag appears to omit showing that any expectations raised during provisional application are *legitimate*.[73] This, however, is a crucial point in the analysis of legitimate expectations, as the following quotation makes clear:

> Zu behaupten, ein Staat sei grundsätzlich an die Erwartungen gebunden, die er mit seinem Verhalten bei einem anderen Staat erweckt, wäre ... verfehlt ... Die Frage bleibt stets, wo die Grenze zwischen dem rechtlich schützenwerten Vertrauen und der rechtlich irrelevanten Spekulation auf ein bestimmtes zukünftiges Handeln eines anderen Rechtssubjektes zu ziehen ist. Maßstäbe zur Bestimmung dieser Grenze sind aus einer Gesamtschau der Bereiche des Völkerrechts zu gewinnen, in denen sich Konkretisierungen des Vertrauensprinzip im positiven Recht feststellen lassen.[74]

Accordingly, for the above reasons Montag's recourse to the principle of legitimate expectations is problematic and ultimately not entirely convincing. Leaving the specific conduct behind which has been suggested to give rise to legitimate expectations, a few more thoughts on the principle and its application in this context will now be developed.

3.3.2. *Legitimate Expectations and Good Faith as Source of Obligations*

As previously mentioned, it is from the legitimate expectations that Montag derives the States' intention to be bound during the period of provisional application. In a legal system equipped with a law-maker, it is conceivable that the law attaches specific consequences to a conduct giving rise to expectations, when this is seen as a reasonable balance of interests. In such a case, the conduct in question is perceived as creating a certain 'responsibility' and the expectations in turn are protected by the law and become 'legitimate'. However, it is submitted that on the international legal plane, it is not entirely convincing to infer from certain expectations an intention to be bound. This would amount to arguing that, because States have certain expectations and want these to be protected by law, they also have an intention to be bound – since this intention will bring

---

[73] Montag, *Völkerrechtliche Verträge*, 52.

[74] Müller, *Vertrauensschutz im Völkerrecht*, 255–56. See also Elisabeth Zoller, *La bonne foi en droit international public* (Paris: Pedone, 1977), 349, 350.

about the protection they want. Without question, States pursue certain interests when having recourse to provisional application. But it would be more in line with generally accepted methodology to ascertain by reference to the terms employed and the underlying circumstances,[75] whether these interests did form an intention to be bound, instead of presenting these interests in terms of 'legitimate expectations' and to deduce therefrom an intention to be bound.

This paraphrasing in terms of 'legitimate expectations' may involve a further problem. Admittedly, Montag does not say that the legitimate expectations or the principle of good faith themselves are the formal source of the rights and obligations (assumed to be binding) during the period of provisional application. Instead he identifies conduct which gives rise to legitimate expectations and deduces therefrom an intention to be bound. Yet, the net result of this would appear to be that the principle of good faith, in its application as the principle of legitimate expectations, gives rise to substantive rights and obligations. The question whether the principle of good faith can be the source of obligations is contested. The ICJ takes a narrow position according to which the principle of good faith, while being "one of the basic principles governing the creation and performance of legal obligations"[76] ... "is not in itself a source of obligations where none would otherwise exist."[77] By contrast, some writers consider the principle as a source of minor collateral or accessory obligations, such as obligations to cooperate/consult/inform, pre- or post-conventional obligations to maintain a status quo etc.[78] Be that as it may, there would appear to be little support, including in some of the monographs on legitimate expectations[79] or good faith,[80] for the view that the principles can be the source of fully-fledged substantial obligations. Yet

---

75 *Aegean Sea Continental Shelf* [1978] ICJ Rep 3, 39 [96]; *Maritime Delimitation and Territorial Questions between Qatar and Bahrain (Jurisdiction and Admissibility)* [1994] ICJ Rep 112 (hereinafter '*Qatar v Bahrain Case 1994*') 121 [24].
Aust, *Modern Treaty Law*, 20; Christine Chinkin, "A Mirage in the Sand? Distinguishing Binding and Non-Binding Relations Between States," *Leiden Journal of International Law* 10 (1997): 231; Fitzmaurice and Elias, *Law of Treaties*, 25; cf. Jennings and Watts, *Oppenheim's International Law*, [582]; Widdows, "Agreement in International Law," 137–144.

76 *Nuclear Tests (New Zealand v France)*, 473 [49].

77 *Border and Transborder Armed Actions (Nicaragua v Honduras) (Jurisdiction and Admissibility)* [1988] ICJ Rep 69, 105 [94]; *Land and Maritime Boundary between Cameroon and Nigeria (Preliminary Objections)* [1998] ICJ Rep 275, 297 [39].

78 Kolb, "La bonne foi en droit international public," 681–84.

79 Müller, *Vertrauensschutz im Völkerrecht.*

80 Zoller, *La bonne foi en droit international public*, 350–54. For Kolb's position see note 78 (in chapter 3) above.

this would seem to be the result of Montag's argument, if, irrespective of the specific content of the agreement on provisional application, the principle of legitimate expectations led States to be bound during the period of provisional application.

3.4. *Evaluation and Conclusion*

Montag's approach differs from many in that he does not rely on the ILC commentary and its authority but develops other arguments for the binding force of provisionally applied treaties, or, in his view, for the binding force of agreements on provisional application. The strength of this approach is to regard intention as the decisive criterion for determining the binding force of these agreements, thereby aligning these agreements with other agreements in international law[81] and the general approach taken when determining their binding force and legal nature.[82] The weakness of the approach is the inconsistency it creates by deducing a general intention to be bound from general considerations[83] after stating that intention really only can be established on a case-by-case basis.[84] Looking at a general intention creates the difficulty of establishing indications thereof, and not all indications so presented are equally convincing. An example of a less convincing indication is the recourse to the principle of legitimate expectations which could be seen as sidestepping the uncertainty that surrounds the notion and legal implications of provisional application in academic writings. More convincing is the approach that identifies the overall purpose of provisional application as a way of 'immediately securing the benefits of the treaty'. Indeed, if States choose in the long-term to regulate the matter in question by treaty, i.e. a legally binding agreement, then it is conceivable, or possibly even likely, that they would choose a legally binding agreement also for the period of provisional application,[85] given that they bring forward in time the application of a treaty whose entry into force they are unwilling to await. So understood, this would appear to be a plausible approach to establishing a general

[81] See also Haro F. van Panhuys, "The Netherlands Constitution and International Law," *American Journal of International Law* 58 (1964): 93.

[82] For the general approach on determining the binding force of an agreement in international law, see e.g., Jennings and Watts, *Oppenheim's International Law*, parts 2–4, [582] 1202; Fitzmaurice and Elias, *Law of Treaties*, 5; 26; Aust, *Modern Treaty Law*, 20; 33.

[83] Montag, *Völkerrechtliche Verträge*, 51.

[84] Ibid., 50.

[85] See also Villiger, *Commentary*, Article 25, [4].

intention of States that have recourse to provisional application, and might be useful when answering the question of the binding force and legal nature of provisionally applied treaties in a generalised and approximate manner. Thus, the great value of this approach is that it introduces the criterion of intention into the debate and provides an initial possible response to the question under consideration. Yet it is an initial response because the approach leaves open the question of how to determine the meaning of provisional application and an accompanying intention to be bound (or the absence thereof) in an individual case.

4. The (Collateral) Agreement Approach

Finally, the argument is put forward that provisionally applied treaties are binding because provisional application is seen as based on an agreement. More precisely, the first variant of this argument submits that provisionally applied treaties are binding because provisional application is based on an agreement, and agreements "are the basis for creating legal obligations under international (treaty) law"[86] or because all agreements between States, possibly with the exception of *modus vivendi*, are subject to the principle of *pacta sunt servanda*.[87] The second variant argues that provisionally applied treaties are binding because provisional application is based on a separate, collateral and binding agreement.[88] This is suggested to be the case whether provisional application is actually agreed in a separate agreement, in the treaty itself or brought about by a notification to the depository of the treaty. In other words, the *negotium* approach[89] looks beyond such notifications/final clauses and distinguishes them from an underlying separate agreement. In terms of binding force, this view draws a clear distinction between the main treaty and the separate collateral agreement. The main treaty, on the one hand, is awaiting its entry into force and therefore is not, in terms of binding force or legal effects, seen as being implicated in bringing about its own provisional

86 Krieger, "Article 25," [30]; see also *Kardassopoulos v Georgia* (06/07/2007), [209].

87 Arsanjani and Reisman, "Provisional Application," 101.

88 Pritzkow, *Energiesektor*, 57–58; Meißner, *Vollmacht und Ratifikation*, 90; Kraus, "Système et Fonctions," 359.

89 By this is understood the conception of provisional application as *always* being based on a separate collateral agreement, whether it is actually agreed in a separate agreement or in the treaty itself in one of its final clauses. For the general distinction between *instrumentum* and *negotium* see note 39 (in chapter 3) above.

application.[90] The separate collateral agreement, on the other hand, is seen as entering into force upon signature (agreement in simplified form/ executive agreement), as becoming binding on the parties to it, and as incorporating the provisions of the main treaty subject to provisional application.[91]

The main problem with regard to this argument is that its supporters often assume, but do not show, that those (collateral) agreements are binding in international law.[92] For some of these writers, the binding force seems to follow from having labelled this collateral agreement as either an 'agreement in simplified form',[93] or an 'administrative agreement',[94] although neither name,[95] nor form,[96] are decisive factors when it comes to determining the binding force or nature of an agreement in international

[90] Mathy, "Article 25 VCLT 1969," (2006) [25]; See also Laly-Chevalier, *Violation du Traité*, 37–8.

[91] Pritzkow, *Energiesektor*, 57–58; ibid [25]; Kraus, "Système et Fonctions," 359; Meißner, *Vollmacht und Ratifikation*, 90; See also Laly-Chevalier, *Violation du Traité*, 37–8.

[92] Mathy, "Article 25 VCLT 1969," 652 and 651; Krieger, "Article 25," [29]; Arsanjani and Reisman, "Provisional Application," 101. See also Kraus, "Système et Fonctions," 359; Meißner, *Vollmacht und Ratifikation*, 90.

[93] See e.g., Pritzkow, *Energiesektor*, 57. Agreements in simplified form can be distinguished from formal treaties in the following way: "international engagements which are ratified by the head of State after legislative approval are formal treaties; engagements not so ratified and approved are agreements in simplified form." Wildhaber, "Executive Agreements," in Bernhardt, *Encyclopedia of International Law*, vol. 2, 313. See also Holloway, *Modern Trends in Treaty Law*, 69.

[94] Kraus, "Système et Fonctions," 359; Meißner, *Vollmacht und Ratifikation*, 90. As regards the (American) term 'executive agreements' McNair points out that it is used to denote different phenomena, McNair, *Law of Treaties*, 65. In this vein, the entry on 'executive agreements' in the encyclopedia of international law sets out to define "agreements in simplified form", and uses both terms interchangeably, Luzius Wildhaber, "Executive Agreements," 312ff. Following this approach, for a definition reference is made to the above definition of agreements in simplified form.

[95] Article 2(1)(a) defines a treaty as a "written agreement ... *whatever its designation*" (emphasis added). *South West Africa Cases* (*Ethiopia v South Africa; Liberia v South Africa*) (*Preliminary Objections*) [1962] ICJ Rep 319, 331; Fitzmaurice and Elias, *Law of Treaties*, 9; Klabbers, *The Concept of Treaty in International Law*, 44; Denys P. Myers, "The Names and Scope of Treaties," *American Journal of International Law* 51 (1957): 575–6.

[96] Article 2(1)(a) defines a treaty as a "written agreement ... *whether embodied in a single instrument or in two or related instruments*" (emphasis added). Additionally, Article 3(a) clarifies that despite Article's 2(1) definition of a treaty as a "written agreement", treaties can be concluded orally without this affecting their legal force though excluding the appliability of the VCLT to them. *Aegean Sea Continental Shelf* 39 [96]; *Case Concerning the Temple of Preah Vihear* (*Cambodia v Thailand*) (*Preliminary Objections*) [1961] ICJ Rep 17, 31; Fitzmaurice and Elias, *Law of Treaties*, 11; Klabbers, *The Concept of Treaty in International Law*, 46.

law.[97] Other writers suggest that this (collateral) agreement is binding just as every other international agreement.[98] Thus, the legally binding force of the (secondary) agreement is *presumed*, on the premise that such a presumption exists with regard to international agreements in general. This approach is problematic, because the generally accepted view is that there is no presumption,[99] be it for[100] or against[101] the binding force of international agreements. According to the generally accepted view, the parties' intention to be bound is required for an international agreement to have binding force, and this needs to be established on a case-by-case basis. Thus, while agreements *can* be 'the basis for creating legal obligations under international (treaty) law'[102], they do not have to be or they are not automatically so, since this depends upon the intention of the participants to the agreement.

By way of conclusion, the agreement or *negotium*[103] approach is questionable. The failure to show that the (separate collateral) agreements *are* binding is problematic,[104] if the approach is used in order to argue for the existence of binding rights and obligations during the period of provisional application. Also, all the collateral agreement approach seems to do is to transpose the problem of the binding force of those rights and obligations from the level of the main treaty to the level of the collateral agreement – without solving it. However, the agreement approach is not only used as an argument for the view that provisionally applied treaties are binding. It also serves as an explanation of the legal effects and binding force of treaties awaiting their entry into force, once the binding force of their provisions has been otherwise established. In those instances, the binding force of these treaties is *explained* by reference to a separate collateral agreement, not submitted as necessarily following therefrom.

---

97 *Qatar v Bahrain Case 1994* [23]; Christine Chinkin "A Mirage in the Sand? Distinguishing Binding and Non-Binding Relations Between States," *Leiden Journal of International Law* 10 (1997): 229; Kingsley Igweike, "The Definition and Scope of 'Treaty' in International Law," *Indian Journal of International Law* 28 (1988): 252; Wildhaber, "Executive Agreements," 314.

98 Mathy, "Article 25 VCLT 1969," 652; Arsanjani and Reisman, "Provisional Application," 101.

99 Münch, "Non-Binding Agreements," 1.

100 Mann, "Reflections on a Commercial Law of Nations," *British Yearbook of International Law* 33 (1957): 30–1; Klabbers, *The Concept of Treaty in International Law*, 118.

101 Fawcett, "The Legal Character of International Agreements," 400.

102 Krieger, "Article 25," [30].

103 See note 39 and 89 (in chapter 3) above.

104 See also Giorgio Gaja, "Provisional Application of Treaties," Report of the International Law Comission on the Work of its Sixty-Third Session (2011), Official Records of the General Assembly, Sixty-Six Session (Supplement No. 10), A/66/10, Annex C, [4].

In light of the above criticism, this may be a more suitable role for the (collateral) agreement approach to play.

5. Conclusion

It cannot be concluded from the arguments considered above that provisionally applied treaties are necessarily legally binding. The most convincing approach deduces a general intention of States to be bound from the overall purpose of provisional application. From this it follows that generally, provisionally applied treaties (or the rights and obligations subjected to provisional application) are legally binding, but that there may be some exceptions to this.

Certainly, the view that these treaties are legally binding finds support in the negotiating record of the 1968–69 Vienna Conference on the Law of Treaties[105] as shown in chapter 1, and will be further tested against practice in chapter 4. Before doing so, the next part of this chapter will turn to the difficulty to which this view gives rise: if provisionally applied treaties are thought to be generally legally binding, the question arises how this can be so, given that normally only 'treaties in force' are legally binding, see Article 26. Therefore, the next part of the chapter will analyse different explanations as to how a treaty, during the period of provisional application and thus *prior* to its entry into force, can nevertheless be conceived as legally binding or producing substantial legal effects.

B. Explanations for the Legal Effects of a Treaty Awaiting its Entry into Force

6. Introduction

Given that a provisionally applied treaty is not in force, academic opinion often turns to the legal construct underlying provisional application in order to explain the (here for the sake of reasoning assumed) legally binding force of the rights and obligations set out in the treaty. When provisional application is agreed in a separate collateral agreement, for example, in a protocol to the main treaty as in GATT,[106] there is virtual unanimity

105 Michie, "Treaties in South African Law," 5.

106 Protocol of Provisional Application of the General Agreement on Tariffs and Trade (adopted 30 October 1947, entered into force 1 January 1947) 55 UNTS 308.

among the supporters of the view that provisionally applied treaties are legally binding on two points: first, that this separate agreement is the construct underlying provisional application; second, that this agreement is the source of the legally binding rights and obligations assumed to exist during the period of provisional application. However, when there is no such actual separate collateral agreement, and provisional application is agreed upon in a final clause of the treaty, or is brought about by a unilateral notification of provisional application, then disagreement arises as to the construct underlying provisional application and the explanation for the assumed existence of legally binding rights and obligations during the period of provisional application. These different views and explanations will be analysed in the following section, in order to understand how the rights and obligations of a provisionally applied treaty can be seen as legally binding.

6.1. *A Collateral Agreement as Legal Construct and Formal Source*

As already mentioned,[107] the *negotium* approach assumes that provisional application is always based on an agreement, irrespective of the instrument which may actually bring about the provisional application. This agreement is seen as the formal source of the rights and obligations assumed to exist during the period of provisional application. As the case may be, the separate agreement is seen as entering into force upon signature or as oral agreement, and as being binding upon the parties to it.[108] It has also been suggested that the separate agreement incorporates those provisions of the main treaty which are subjected to provisional application.[109] Through the incorporation into the separate, informal and binding agreement, the binding force of these provisions on the parties to the separate agreement can be explained. Alternatively, when provisional application is agreed in a final clause of the treaty, it has been suggested to sever the clause from the treaty in order to see it for what it is: a special (separate) agreement to resort to provisional application.[110]

---

[107] See note 39 and 89 (in chapter 3) above.

[108] Montag, *Völkerrechtliche Verträge*, 49, 61; Mathy, "Article 25 VCLT 1969," (2006) 1066–67; see also Laly-Chevalier, *Violation du Traité*, 37–8. Several ILC members expressed this view (speaking of 'agreements in simplified form): ILC, Summary record of the 791st meeting, UN Doc A/CN.4/SR. 791, Tsuruoka, §27; Ago, §42.

[109] Vignes, "Une notion ambiguë: la mise en application provisoire des traités," 192; Laly-Chevalier, *Violation du Traité*, 37–8.

[110] Meißner, *Vollmacht und Ratifikation*, 90.

The approach that provisional application is always based on an underlying agreement on provisional application is in line with the wording of Article 25(1), and is convincing. Even when provisional application is brought about by a unilateral declaration or notification, it is still based on the underlying earlier agreement of the relevant States and international organisations to allow recourse to provisional application concerning the treaty in question,[111] including the agreement that such application may be triggered for individual participants by unilateral declarations to such an effect.

Moreover, the approach offers a possible answer to the question how the rights and obligations of a treaty awaiting its entry into force can nevertheless be seen to be legally binding. Of course, the approach also highlights the 'paradox' or problems caused by provisional application for constitutional law: that a treaty, expression of consent to be bound by which is subject to a complex internal law procedure, requiring parliamentary approval and/or the adoption of implementing legislation, can be provisionally applied and legally binding, possibly without that procedure having taken place, for instance merely upon the treaty's signature.[112] If only parts of the treaty are subject to provisional application, or the treaty is only applied provisionally to a limited extent, for instance on the basis of a limitation clause, then the treaty's provisional application might be less problematic under constitutional law.[113]

Be that as it may, the *negotium* approach[114] is certainly capable of explaining the assumed existence of binding rights and obligations during the period of provisional application – by substituting the treaty not in force with another formal source, the separate collateral agreement. The next section will examine whether there are other possible explanations for the (assumed) existence of binding rights and obligations set out in a provisionally applied treaty.

6.2. *Other Legal Constructs and Substitute Sources*

In this section the view is presented which, in contrast to the above *negotium* approach, provides several explanations as to the legal construct

---

[111] Lorand Bartels, "Legal Constraints on the EU's Ability to Withdraw EPA Preferences under Regulation 1528/2007," Briefing Note, European Centre for Development Policy Management 27 (2011): 3.

[112] See also Sondaal, "Dutch Treaty Practice," 228.

[113] See the text following note 324 in chapter 1 above.

[114] See note 39 and 89 (in chapter 3) above.

underlying provisional application as well as to the (assumed) binding force of the rights and obligations set out in the provisionally applied treaty. A difference to the *negotium* approach only arises if provisional application is not agreed in an actual separate collateral agreement. According to this view, the different instruments bringing about provisional application, for example, a unilateral notification of provisional application,[115] serve as underlying legal construct and substitute formal sources for the treaty not in force (*instrumentum* approach).[116] Also when provisional application is brought about by the final clause of a treaty, this final clause is seen as the relevant instrument[117] and in conjunction with Article 24(4) appears in some instances to serve as explanation for the binding force of the provisionally applied rights and obligations.[118]

6.2.1. *The Notification or Declaration of Provisional Application*

Provisional application can be effected by a unilateral notification or declaration, and the question arises whether this unilateral notification or declaration can serve as a substitute formal source for the treaty awaiting its entry into force, so as to explain the binding force of the rights and obligations set out therein during their provisional application.

According to a widely held view unilateral acts in general can, under certain circumstances, be the formal source of obligations of the declaring State in international law.[119] Thus, the first issue that arises is whether the notification or declaration of provisional application qualifies as a unilateral act. Since the legal effects of such notifications/declarations are predetermined by the treaty and the final clause inviting them, it is questionable whether such notifications and declarations are 'autonomous' or 'independent' unilateral acts.[120] They could be seen as 'unilateral'

---

115 Michie, "Provisional Application," 49–50; Sondaal, "Dutch Treaty Practice," 226.

116 Michie, "Provisional Application," 57–58; Krenzler, *Vorläufige Anwendung*, 38–41; Sondaal, "Dutch Treaty Practice," 225–26.

117 Michie, "Provisional Application," 54; Krenzler, *Vorläufige Anwendung*, 38–41 (prior to the adoption of the VCLT 1969 yet based upon the rule which today is expressed in Article 24(4)).

118 Michie, "Provisional Application," 48; Sondaal, "Dutch Treaty Practice," 226.

119 *Nuclear Tests* (*New Zealand v France*), [46]-[49]; ILCs 'Guiding Principles applicable to unilateral declarations of States capable of creating legal obligations' (hereinafter 'ILC Guiding Principles'), http://untreaty.un.org/ilc/texts/instruments/english/draft%20articles/9_9_2006.pdf; Wilfried Fiedler, "Unilateral Acts in International Law," in Bernhardt, *Encyclopedia of Public International Law*, vol. 4, 1018.

120 Geslin, *Application provisoire*, 188–92. In general, i.e. not in the context of notifications or declarations to apply a treaty provisionally, against the classification as unilateral

only in form, but, in substance, rather an application of the *common intention of the parties* as expressed in the treaty.[121] Put more succinctly: unilateral in form but not in substance. Yet, the criterion of 'autonomy' or 'independence' was excluded from the definition of a unilateral act in the ILC's "Guiding Principles applicable to unilateral declarations of States capable of creating legal obligations".[122] Thus, since 'autonomy' does not seem to be a necessary feature of a unilateral act, the absence of this would not amount to a fatal argument against the classification of the declaration or notification as a unilateral act.

But even when classified as unilateral acts, doubts may arise as to the appropriateness of the declaration/notification as a substitute formal source for a treaty not in force. This is so if one perceives the relations under a provisionally applied treaty as 'treaty relations', resulting from a meeting of minds rather than from a unilateral undertaking.[123] Furthermore, unilateral acts as such only create obligations but not any rights for the declaring State.[124] Yet the application of a treaty, provisional or not, could involve *reciprocal* or *synallagmatic* rights and obligations (*do ut des*), and unilateral acts are not apt to account for those[125] and their interdependence as regards different legal aspects such as their creation or consequences of breach etc.

Finally, when a treaty is in force, it is the treaty and not the act of expressing consent to be bound which is regarded as the formal source of the rights and obligations contained in the treaty.[126] Therefore, even if the provisionally applied treaty is not in force, and one may feel the need to find a substitute formal source for the (nevertheless assumed to be

---

act due to lack of 'autonomy' or 'independence': Paul de Visscher, "Cours de droit international public," *Recueil des cours de l'Académie de droit international de La Haye*, 163 (1972): 121; see also Degan, *Sources of International Law*, 279, 280. Contrast: Fiedler, "Unilateral Acts in International Law," 1019; Hugh Thirlway, "Concepts, Principles, Rules and Analogies: International and Municipal Legal Reasoning," *Recueil des cours de l'Académie de droit international de La Haye*, 294 (2002): 334–336.

121 de Visscher, "Cours de droit international public," 121.

122 ILC Guiding Principles; see also Cedeño's 5th Report on Unilateral Acts of States, UN Doc A/CN.4/525, §§52–54.

123 Geslin, *Application provisoire*, 189–90.

124 It follows from the sovereign equality of States that one State cannot oblige another State without the other State's consent (6th principle, UNGA Res 2625 (XXV) (24 October 1970) on Friendly Relations'). See also the title of the ILC's Guiding Principles: "Guiding Principles applicable to unilateral declarations of States capable of creating legal *obligations*" (emphasis added), and Guiding Principles, [9]; Hafner, "Provisional Application," 596.

125 Butler, *Law of Treaties*, 126.

126 Geslin, *Application provisoire*, 191.

binding) rights and obligations contained therein, this does not make the declaration or notification of provisional application a more convincing formal source than the comparably 'unilateral' expression of consent to be bound in case of a treaty in force. While it is correct that both are implicated and necessary for bringing about the treaty or its provisional application, they are the trigger or precondition for certain legal effects (similar to the expression of consent to be bound by the treaty) and thus should not be confused with the legal act itself (the treaty).

By way of conclusion, it has been shown that the unilateral act of the notification or declaration of provisional application seems ill-suited to create anything but obligations for the declaring State; also, it would not be able to explain the meeting of minds upon which the treaty-relations, provisional or not, would seem to rest. It is submitted, therefore, that the unilateral declaration or notification of provisional application can trigger the provisional application of a treaty but is not in itself a basis or substitute formal source of the provisionally applied rights and obligations that would help explain their binding force during provisional application.

6.2.2. *The Final Clause in Which Provisional Application is Agreed and Reference to Article 24(4)*

When provisional application is agreed upon in the treaty itself in one of its final clauses, sometimes reference is made to Article 24(4) and those final clauses which take effect from the moment of the adoption of the text of a treaty as explanation for the legally binding force of the rights and obligations of a provisionally applied treaty. Article 24(4) provides that 'the provisions of a treaty regulating [...] matters arising necessarily before the entry into force of the treaty apply from the time of the adoption of the text'. A final clause on provisional application would certainly fall thereunder, and its application would then bring about the provisional application of the treaty. The sole difference being that Article 24(4) normally leads to the application of *procedural* treaty provisions prior to the treaty's entry into force, for instance on its authentication, expression of consent to be bound etc., whereas in the case of a final clause of provisional application, Article 24(4) would enable the application of *substantive* treaty provisions.[127]

While the point has been made earlier that 'application' does not necessarily imply binding force, it is submitted that in the context of

---

[127] Krenzler, *Vorläufige Anwendung*, 40.

Article 24(4), in the normal course of events the applied provisions are binding on the future parties. Of course the future parties enjoy freedom of contract and can draw up any regime they see fit to regulate the effect of treaty provisions that concern matters arising prior to the treaty's entry into force. But in the normal course of events, the States would want the procedural provisions regulating the process of bringing the treaty into force to bind them, otherwise these provisions might not be able to fulfil their function and the treaty's entry into force might not succeed. This is confirmed by academic writings according to which final clauses on these matters are legally binding,[128] and by the Harvard Draft which already specified that these final clauses had to be complied with by the future parties.[129]

However, while there may be agreement that these final clauses are legally binding, the source of their legal force is not entirely clear. Already in the ILC deliberations, the matter of the formal source of these clauses was and remained unresolved.[130] Waldock once mentioned[131] that he had raised the problem of the effect of these final clauses on several occasions, hoping to obtain an answer from the Commission. He went on to summarise the Commission's position in the following way:

> The Commission seemed to regard them [i.e. final clauses with pre-ratification effects, Article 24(4)] as some kind of esoteric mystery: it agreed that they had some force, but no one seemed to be clear as to its source.[132]

Waldock's summary of the ILC debate, where he found agreement as to the legal force of such final clauses but uncertainty as to the source of such force, is also valid for relevant academic writings, given the myriad of different explanations provided for the assumed binding force of such

[128] Rosenne, "Final Clauses", [19] see also [3]; Cheng, *General Principles of Law*, 109; see also Nisot, "La force obligatoire des traités signés," 879–80.

[129] Harvard Draft, commentary Article 9, 779.

[130] The Final ILC Draft Article 21 did not mention the matter, nor did the Commentary, although the matter had been raised on several occasions in the ILC and had been regulated in draft articles or mentioned in commentaries by every Special Rapporteur: Brierly's 1st Report, UN Doc A/CN.4/23, Article 11(4), 224, and commentary, 243; Lauterpacht's 1st Report, UN Doc A/CN.4/63, commentary Article 5, 109–110; Fitzmaurice's 1st Report, UN Doc A/CN.4/101, Articles 30(2), 42(4) and Commentary thereto, §107; Waldock's 1st Report, UN Doc A/CN.4/144, Article 9(2)d, commentary §7. For different views of ILC members on the source of the legal force of final clauses on matters mentioned in Article 24(4) see especially Meetings: ILC, Summary record of the 644th meeting, UN Doc A/CN.4/SR.644, and Summary record of the 645th meeting, UN Doc A/CN.4/SR.645.

[131] UN Doc A.CN.4/186 and Add. L 107 & L 115; A/CN.4/SR. 849, §81 (discussing Article 56 [Application of a Treaty in Point of Time]).

[132] Ibid.

final clauses. These explanations range from the assumption that the legal effects of the final clauses stem from either the signed but unratified treaty itself,[133] to a retroactive effect of the treaty,[134] from a tacit agreement collateral to the treaty,[135] to customary or general international law,[136] or from assumptions that the legal effects are the result of either the consent expressed at the time of the adoption of the text[137] to the act of signing the treaty.[138]

In light of this it is clear that the reference to the legal force of some final clauses prior to the treaty's entry into force, as expressed in Article 24(4), is a 'shortcut' to an answer to the question where the binding force comes from when provisional application is agreed in the final clause of a treaty: this reference makes clear that these treaties are legally binding without necessarily saying how so. If one is interested in how the legally binding force can be explained, the reference to Article 24(4) resembles the substitution of one unknown variable (the legal force of treaties during the period of provisional application) by another (the legal force of certain final clauses prior to the treaty's entry into force). However, from those provisions in the VCLT under which a treaty either has legal effects on a State for whom it is not in force (e.g., Article 18)[139] or is applied to a State for whom it is not in force (Article 24(4) and Articles 35 and 36), Article 24(4) probably comes closest to provisional application: under both mechanisms (i.e., Article 24(4) and Article 25) certain provisions of a treaty are applied and (at least for the purposes of the present analysis) legally binding prior to the treaty's entry into force. For this reason, some of the explanations for the binding force of treaty provisions provided in the context of Article 24(4) will now be analysed, to the extent that they

---

133 Cheng, *General Principles of Law*, 109; Nisot, "La force obligatoire des traités signés," 879.

134 Sinclair, *Vienna Convention*, 86–7.

135 Mahiou, "Article 24 VCLT 1969," 15.

136 For this position in the ILC, ILC, Summary record of the 644th meeting, UN Doc A/CN.4/SR.644, A/CN.4/SR.644, Verdross, §20; at the Vienna Conference, OR 1968: CoW 26 Iraq §17.

137 TO Elias, *Law of Treaties*, 37; in the ILC, Summary record of the 645th meeting, UN Doc A/CN.4/SR.645, Waldock, §16.

138 McNair, *Law of Treaties*, 203; Paul V. McDade, "The Interim Obligation between Signature and Ratification of a Treaty," *Netherlands International Law Review* 32 (1985): 9–10; Rogoff, "Unratified Treaty," 267.

139 Because the obligation not to defeat a treaty's object and purpose generally does not involve the duty to apply the treaty's provisions to relevant acts, facts and situations, the explanations provided in academic writings for the (limited) effect of the treaty under Article 18 (through those provisions which determine its object and purpose) will not be taken into account for the purposes of the following analysis.

might appear helpful also in the context of provisional application. First, the approach is examined which understands the legal effect of treaty provisions prior to the treaty's entry into force as a partial, anticipated entry into force of the treaty.

6.2.2.1. *Partial, Anticipated Entry into Force of the Treaty*

According to this approach, obligations arising under a treaty not yet in force can be conceptualised as a partial and anticipated entry into force of the treaty.[140] In the context of (today) Article 24(4), G Fitzmaurice first formulated the problem (of treaty provisions being applied although the treaty providing for them is not yet in force) followed by his explanation of those legal effects:

> Logically, a treaty which, *ex hypothesi*, is not yet in force, cannot provide for its own entry into force – since, until that occurs, the clause so providing can itself have no force. The real truth is that, by a tacit assumption invariably made, the clauses of a treaty providing for ratification, accession, entry into force, and certain other possible matters, are deemed to *come into force separately and* at once, *on signature ... even though the substance of the treaty does not.*" (Emphasis added)[141]

Thus, his explanation of the legal effects of some of a treaty's provisions prior to the treaty's entry into force is that those provisions are subject to an anticipated entry into force, separate from the remainder or 'the substance' of the treaty, which will come into force at a later point, for example, upon expression of consent to be bound or another event.

The question arises whether this approach could be used to explain the (assumed) binding force of rights and obligations during the period of provisional application. If so, the binding force of rights and obligations during the period of provisional application would be perceived and explained as a partial, anticipated entry into force of that part of the treaty which is subjected to provisional application. In other words, provisional application would be assimilated with a (partial, anticipated) entry into force. At this point, it may be useful to recall the first argument discussed in this chapter, the argument that provisionally applied treaties are like treaties in force and are therefore binding. The result of the above discussion was that 'application' and 'entry into force' were two different concepts, and that the mechanism under consideration was more closely

---

[140] Cheng, *General Principles of Law*, 109; Fitzmaurice's 1st Report, UN Doc A/CN.4/101, Commentary Article 42, 127–8.

[141] Fitzmaurice's 1st Report, UN Doc A/CN.4/101, Commentary Article 42, 127–8; see also Cheng, *General Principles of Law*, 109 and Briggs, *Law of Nations*, 867.

related to the concept of 'application' than 'entry into force', which is reflected in the terminology finally chosen at the 1968–1969 Vienna Conference ("provisional *application*"). Therefore, in light of the conceptual differences between 'entry into force' and 'application', the understanding of treaty obligations enumerated in Article 24(4) as a partial, anticipated entry into force is not well suited to serve as an explanation of the assumed binding force of provisionally applied treaties.

6.2.2.2. *Retroactive Effect of the Treaty*

According to another view, it is by virtue of a retroactive effect of the treaty that those final clauses regulating the "mechanics of treaty-making"[142] (i.e. those procedural provisions enumerated in Article 24(4)) are applicable from the adoption of the text of the treaty and prior to the treaty's entry into force.[143] The question arises whether this explanation could be also applied to the provisional applicability and (assumed) legal force of some of the substantive provisions of a treaty prior to the treaty's entry into force. To answer this question, it may be useful to recall the above delimitation between provisional application and retroactivity: the commonality of both mechanisms is that the sphere of temporal application of the treaty precedes the treaty's entry into force. The difference between the two is the moment in time when the duty to apply the treaty to such acts, facts and situations arises. In case of a retroactive application, the duty arises *ex post facto*, i.e. after such acts, facts and situations have actually occurred. Thus it is upon the treaty's entry into force, for example, that the duty arises to apply the treaty to *past* acts, facts and situations which occurred prior to the treaty's entry into force. By contrast, provisional application is non-retroactive. Provisional application means that the treaty is applied prior to its entry into force, but it is applied only to acts, facts and situations *of the present and the future*. (Thus in case of provisional application, the treaty does not apply to acts, facts and situations of the past.)

Since provisional application aims at an application of the treaty's provisions to acts, facts and situations of the *present and the future*, this aim cannot be achieved by agreeing on a retroactive application of the treaty's provisions since this latter agreement would only mean that the treaty's provisions covers acts, facts and situations *of the past*.[144] Therefore, the

[142] Term employed by McNair, *Law of Treaties*, 203.

[143] Sinclair, *Vienna Convention*, 86–7.

[144] Bindschedler-Robert, "Rétroactivité en droit international public," 187, fn. 8, distinguishes retroactivity from provisional application in exactly this point, i.e. that

existence of legally binding rights and obligations during provisional application cannot be explained by reference to a retroactive effect of the treaty.[145]

6.2.2.3. *Legal Effect of a Signed but Unratified Treaty*

Although it is generally agreed that treaties, as a rule, do not have obligatory force prior to their entry into force, some writers suggest that Article 24(4) and 25 are an exception to that rule.[146] The following quotation begins with a statement of the rule and then moves on to the exception:

> La doctrine et la pratique internationale sont unanimes pour admettre qu'un Etat n'est lié par les obligations découlant d'un traité qu'à partir du moment où ce dernier est entré en vigueur, sous réserve de l'effet immédiat de certaines clauses et de la mise en application du traité à titre provisoire.[147]

According to these writers, a signed but unratified treaty produces certain legal effects:

> [...] malgré que le traité, de par ses termes exprès, appelle des ratifications, *il produira*, avant le dépôt de ces dernières, *les effets juridiques* que ses stipulations indiquent comme devant intervenir alors.[148]

Unfortunately, there is little information as to how these effects of a signed but unratified treaty can be explained. But the terminology used to describe the phenomenon could signify that the 'signed but unratified treaty' is seen as the formal source of the rights and obligations.[149] Alternatively, some explain these rights and obligations as an 'effect of signature' or the effect that international law attaches to signature.[150]

---

provisional application has *ex nunc* effects (i.e. consists of an immediate applicability as opposed to awaiting e.g. the entry into force and then applying the treaty retroactively to events from the past). It is also for this reason, and rightly so, that Nascimento rejects Sinclair's approach, i.e. to see Article 24(4) as a case of a retroactive application of a treaty, do Nascimento e Silva, "Le Facteur Temps et les Traités," 229.

[145] For the same reason the view has to be rejected according to which Article 24(4) would be a retroactive application of the treaty, see the argument by Silva in the preceding footnote.

[146] See e.g. Rogoff, "Unratified Treaty," 268 and fn. 13.

[147] Philippe Cahier, "L'obligation de ne pas priver un traité de son objet et but avant son entrée en vigueur," in *Mélanges Fernand Dehousse*, vol. 1 (Paris: Fernand Nathan, 1979), 31.

[148] Nisot, "La force obligatoire des traités signés," 879.

[149] See e.g. Rogoff, "Unratified Treaty," 284, 268, 288ff; Cf. McNair who entitles a section 'Effects of a Treaty which has been Signed and Awaits Ratification before its Entry into Force' but adds in a footnote (3) "It is possible that it is more correct to speak of the effects of the signature of the treaty than to speak of the effects of the treaty itself while awaiting ratification", McNair, *Law of Treaties*, 203; see also O'Connell, *International Law*, 223.

[150] McNair, *Law of Treaties*, 199; Kelsen, *Principles of International Law*, 467–478.

On this understanding, to give effect to the rights and obligations set out in a treaty not in force is an effect that international law attaches to signature, in accordance with an agreement between the parties to such an effect.

Admittedly, legally binding substantive rights and obligations may go beyond what is usually associated with the effects of a signed but unratified treaty, given that these tend to be of a procedural nature[151] or limited to the rather indirect effect of the treaty's provisions in the obligation to abstain from conduct that might frustrate the object and purpose of the treaty, Article 18. While this might seem to be a difference of category rather than degree, namely the difference between the substantive and procedural effects of a treaty, the underlying problem is the same: the problem is to explain the existence of *any* legal rights and obligations set out in a treaty awaiting its entry into force, be they procedural or substantive. The fact that one might be more used to the procedural provisions of a treaty being applied prior to its entry into force, rather than its substantive provisions, would not in itself be a convincing reason for rejecting the possibility that the binding force of substantive treaty provisions could result from a signed but unratified treaty.

In conclusion, the legally binding force of provisionally applied rights and obligations might be explained by reference to the recognised legal effects of signed and unratified treaties, when the concept is understood to cover also substantive legal rights and obligations.

6.2.2.4. *Consent at the Time of the Adoption of the Text of the Treaty*

According to another view, the binding force of final clauses specified in Article 24(4) is explained by reference to the consent given of States at the time of the adoption of the text of the treaty. Compared with the legal effects of a signed but unratified treaty, this is probably the better explanation because it is more in line with Article 24(4). According to Article 24(4), it is from the time of the adoption of the text of the treaty, that the final clauses falling under Article 24(4) apply. Of course, if the text of the treaty is adopted by signature, no material difference arises between the two approaches. Yet, if the text of the treaty is adopted by some other means that precedes the treaty's signature (for instance by initialling, consensus or majority vote), then the explanation of these effects by reference to the effects of a signed but unratified treaty technically fails.

---

151 Reservations to the Convention on the Prevention and Punishment of the Crime of Genocide (Advisory Opinion) [1951] ICJ Rep 15.

Therefore, in order to be in conformity with Article 24(4), the view is preferred which sees the legal basis of the effects of a treaty described in Article 24(4) in the consent expressed at the time of the adoption of the text of the treaty.

In the following section, some practical considerations in support of the obligatory force of the provisions of a treaty awaiting its entry into force will be developed.

6.2.2.5. *Practical Reasons for Treating a Treaty not in Force as a Treaty*

The first such practical consideration in support of the legally binding force of rights and obligations of a treaty awaiting its entry into force is the need for a speedy or urgent regulation of a matter by international law. This may be a good reason why States may be inclined to regard such an instrument as a treaty, at least in the international law sphere,[152] even though the usual treaty-formation process is not terminated and the treaty accordingly has not yet entered into force. A reasonably developed legal system can be expected to provide for the need to enact law in situations of urgency or emergency. In internal legal systems, this is sometimes achieved simply by accelerating the usual legislation procedure, i.e. by shortening deliberation periods of parliamentary committees, chambers or parliament as a whole.[153] In international law, the quickest mode of entry into force is by a one-step procedure, if the treaty enters into force immediately upon the adoption/authentication of the text of the treaty, for example, by signature. Frequently, however, a State's internal law may require parliamentary approval of the treaty or implementing legislation.[154] This will be accommodated in the international law sphere by recourse to a two-step procedure for the entry into force of the treaty, allowing for a lapse of time between, for example, the signature of the treaty and (international) ratification, either for all participants or at least

152 See Blix, *Treaty-Making Power*, 297.

153 To provide a German example: during the period of 'terrorism' organised by a group of left-wing radical government-opponents especially in the 1960s and 70s, a piece of legislation was 'created' in approximately 30 hours, simply by accelerating the normal procedures, i.e. renouncing the usual deliberation periods which normally take several weeks if not months, see Eckhart Klein, *Gesetzgebung ohne Parlament?* (Berlin: De Gruyter, 2004), 19.

154 This participation of constitutional organs in the treaty-making procedure is a matter of the constitutional law of each State, touching upon the separation of powers and checks and balances between these organs, see e.g. Rafia Ben Achour, Frikha Imed, and Mounir Snoussi, "Article 14 VCLT 1969," in Corten and Klein, *The Vienna Conventions on the Law of Treaties*, 294.

with regard to the State whose internal law so demands.[155] Therefore, internal law requirements can significantly delay the treaty's entry into force. Yet they are beyond the reach of international law and for this reason, international law cannot accelerate or shorten this part of the treaty-making procedure. Therefore, if constitutional law delays the entry into force of a treaty[156] and turns into a stumbling block when international law would need to be adopted swiftly in a situation of urgency or emergency, this may well create the need to regard or treat an instrument as a treaty although it has not (yet) entered into force.

Additionally, there is an *argumentum a majore ad minus* which may support this approach. The starting point of the argument is the effects of treaties on third States. Possibly because of State sovereignty and the principle *pacta tertiis nec prosunt nec nocent*, the effects of treaties on third States are often divided in two groups: first, the creation of rights and obligations by the treaty for a third State, and second, mere factual – as opposed to legal – repercussions of the treaty on the third State. However, in practice, it would seem that this is not simply a black and white issue, but rather one shrouded in many shades of grey.[157] Accordingly, it is suggested here that the third State can be affected by such a treaty in a legal way, without having agreed to incur rights and obligations set out in the treaty to which it is not a party. Examples of this are so-called 'objective regimes',[158] or objective legal personalities of international organisations which were created by treaty.[159]

One recent example of an international institution whose legal effects on third States have been the subject of much controversy, because they are said to be broader than that of many institutions possessing

---

[155] Bolintineanu, "Expression of Consent," 680.

[156] On the problem of delay in securing final acceptance of international conventions in general see Ruda, *Final Acceptance*, 8–10.

[157] Alan Boyle and Christine Chinkin, *The Making of International Law* (Oxford: Oxford University Press, 2007), 239; see also Reuter, *Introduction au droit des traités*, [151], [160].

[158] On these see e.g. G. Fitzmaurice, Fourth report on the Law of Treaties, UN Doc A/CN.4/120.

[159] E.g. the UN, see *Reparation for Injuries Suffered in the Service of the United Nations (Advisory Opinion)* [1949] ICJ Rep 174 (hereinafter '*Reparations Case*') 185; see also Article 4(1) of the Rome Statute of the International Criminal Court. The various US techniques, such as 'inspiring' the adoption of several UN Security Council resolutions on the jurisdiction of the ICC (e.g. SC Res 1422, 12.07.2002), as well as the practice of concluding bilateral Status of Forces Agreements, in order to avoid the ICC's jurisdiction over US soldiers according to Article 12(2)(a) Rome Statute imply the US' acknowledgement of the objective legal personality of the ICC. See Boyle and Chinkin, *The Making of International Law*, 240–41.

international objective personality,[160] may be the International Criminal Court created by the Rome Statute.[161] At least this is a claim put forward by the US. The US found its capacity to exercise judicial jurisdiction over its own nationals potentially diminished by a court or international organisation of which it was not a member.[162] It is submitted here that the effects of the Rome Statute on the US could be seen as not merely factual reflections but as affecting the US's legal power to exercise judicial jurisdiction over its soldiers with regard to specific crimes.[163] From that would follow that the US is legally affected by a treaty to which it is a third State, i.e. by a legal act which strictly speaking should not produce *legal* effects on third States.

Possibly another example of treaties producing legal effects on third States without their consent can be found in Article 2(6) UN Charter. The article is sometimes interpreted as requiring non-parties to apply some of the principles set out in the UN Charter.[164] The Article reads as follows:

> The Organization shall ensure that states which are not Members of the United Nations act in accordance with these Principles so far as may be necessary for the maintenance of international peace and security.

If the Article is understood as establishing an enforcement duty for the UN against non-member States which act contrary to the UN Charter Principles on the maintenance of international peace and security, then

---

160 By this is meant the fact that certain international organisations, despite their being set up by a treaty (and treaties generally do not have *legal* effects on third States, see Article 34) are seen as having *objective* international personality i.e. a personality which exists with regard to *all* States, not only the States parties to the treaty which set up the institution. As a result of the objective legal personality of the UN the ICJ stated that the UN had the capacity to bring a claim to recover reparation for damages suffered against a (then) non-member State, Israel. (The damages were suffered as a result of the killing of a UN official in the new city of Jerusalem), see *Reparations Case* preceding footnote.

161 Rome Statute of the International Criminal Court (entered into force 1 July 2002) 2187 UNTS 91.

162 See the 2002 US Fact Sheet on the ICC (first item under the heading: "Significant Problems With the ICC Treaty"), http://www.usembassy.at/en/download/pdf/icc_pa.pdf.

163 See Article 5(1)(a)-(c) Rome Statute.

164 This, however, is the minority view, put forward e.g. by Hans Kelsen, *The Law of the United Nations* (London: Stevens & Sons, 1950), 107. Against this view see e.g. Briggs, *Law of Nations*, 871; Philip C. Jessup, "Modernization of the Law of International Contractual Agreements," *American Journal of International Law* 41 (1947): 388. For legal effects as a matter of customary international law: Patrick Daillier, Mathias Forteau and Alian Pellet, *Droit international public*, 8th ed. (Paris: LGDJ, 2009), 381; Abdullah El Erian, "The Legal Organization of International Society," in *Manual of Public International Law*, ed. Max Sørensen (London: McMillan, 1968), 80. For political as opposed to legally binding effects: Christian de Visscher, *Théories et réalités en droit international public,* 4th ed. (Paris: Pedone, 1970), 287.

the non-member States themselves would be under a legal duty to conform to those UN Charter Principles. There can only be enforcement if there is a legal duty to be enforced in the first place.[165]

The *argumentum a majore ad minus* based on these examples could flow in the following way: these examples show that third States in some instances are either affected by a treaty in their *legal* position (yet without agreeing to incur rights or obligations set out in the treaty), or even required to conform to some of the treaty's provisions as a matter of treaty law – while being a stranger to the treaty. If this is the case, then the fact that in some instances States may be bound to comply with a treaty (as a matter of treaty law) prior to the treaty's entry into force seems perfectly acceptable, even more so since in these instances the States are not strangers to the treaty. On the contrary, these States have undertaken the first steps in becoming a party to the treaty or even have expressed an intention to apply some of its provisions provisionally prior to its entry into force.

6.3. *Conclusion*

The supporters of the view that provisionally applied treaties are legally binding have a choice when it comes to explaining their view. Either they revert to the *negotium* (or separate collateral agreement) approach. Its advantage is that it provides a solution for the problem of the legal effects of a treaty not in force by reference to a substitute formal source, namely the separate collateral agreement. Its disadvantage is that it could be said to resort to a legal fiction, by relying on a separate collateral agreement in all instances of provisional application, whether or not there may actually be such a separate agreement.

Alternatively, supporters of the view that provisionally applied treaties are legally binding can revert to the (modified) *instrumentum* approach. (It is a modified *instrumentum* approach because the unilateral declaration or notification of provisional application is not suited to serve as a formal source of the rights and obligations contained in a legally binding provisionally applied treaty.) According to this approach, only if there exists a separate agreement on provisional application this is seen as the formal source of the binding rights and obligations during provisional application. If, however, provisional application is agreed in a final clause of the treaty, then the basis of the legal effects of these rights and

165 See also Kelsen, *Law of the United Nations*, 107.

obligations could be seen in the consent expressed by States at the time of the adoption of the text of the treaty. In comparison to the *negotium* approach, the advantage of this approach is that it makes do without legal fictions. Its disadvantage could be seen to involve the legally binding force of substantive treaty provisions, thereby possibly going beyond the usual understanding of the ambit of the rule expressed in Article 24(4).

It is submitted that the problem of the legally binding force of rights and obligations of a treaty awaiting its entry into force probably is one of convention and definition. In the end it is a matter of convention or agreement among States whether it is from the treaty's entry into force, signature or the adoption of the text of the treaty – or any other subsequent event – that they want the treaty to deploy the agreed legal effects. Or to say it with Jennings and Watts: it is State practice that demonstrates which sources amount to law-making processes.[166] From this perspective, there is nothing to prevent States from regarding a provisionally applied treaty as a law-generating process, as long as they make clear that this is the case, or with regard to which of these treaties this should be the case.

7. Conclusion

This chapter considered the view that provisionally applied treaties are legally binding. Its division into two parts reflects the two main aspects covered by academic writings in this regard, on the one hand arguments for the legally binding force of these treaties (which attempt to demonstrate that provisionally applied treaties are legally binding), on the other hand explanations for the binding force of these treaties (which take the binding force of these treaties as a given and seek to render this binding force comprehensible). The most convincing argument deduces a general intention of States to be bound from the overall purpose of provisional application. From this it would follow that generally, provisionally applied treaties (or the rights and obligations subjected to provisional application) are legally binding, but that there may be some exceptions to this – a result that will shortly be tested against relevant practice.

The second part of the chapter allowed examining the question of the binding force of the rights and obligations of a treaty awaiting its entry

[166] Jennings and Watts, *Oppenheim's International Law*, introduction and part 1, [9]. For this reasoning specifically with regard to custom Chin L. Lim and Olufemi Elias, "Withdrawing from Custom and the Paradox of Consensualism in International Law," *Duke Journal of Comparative and International Law* 21 (2010–2011): 144–45, and n7.

into force. At first sight, the legally binding force of provisionally applied treaties is difficult to square with the rule that treaties prior to their entry into force do not have obligatory force, at least if treaty obligations (and their binding force) are normally seen to 'flow from the treaty' itself.[167] Researching explanations often used in the context of Article 24(4) helped to overcome conceptions of the binding force or legal effects of treaties prior to their entry into force, along the lines that 'the effect could not be derived from the treaty but only from general international law since the treaty was not yet in force'. It led to the understanding mentioned earlier that the problem of the legally binding force of rights and obligations of a treaty awaiting its entry into force probably is one of convention and definition; i.e. that it is a matter of convention or agreement among States whether it is from the treaty's entry into force, signature or the adoption of the text of the treaty – or any other subsequent event – that they want the treaty to deploy the agreed legal effects. This leads on to the general question why treaties are legally binding (i.e. the question of the basis of legal obligation), which then also concerns provisionally applied treaties but is certainly not a problem specific to provisional application. So understood, the legally binding force of provisionally applied treaties does not raise any particular issues and provisionally applied treaties can be seen as a law-generating process demonstrated by State practice.

Having looked at some of the arguments for and against the legally binding force of provisionally applied treaties advanced in academic writings, the analysis now turns to the practice of States and international organisations in this regard. The next chapter will examine whether in practice States and international organisations regard provisionally applied treaties as legally binding, and whether or not there are in their treaty practice any clear manifestations of an intention to be bound by these treaties.

167 Rogoff, "Unratified Treaty," 289; Alfred Verdross and Bruno Simma, *Universelles Völkerrecht*, 3rd ed. (Berlin: Duncker & Humblot, 1984), 68.

CHAPTER FOUR

THE BINDING FORCE OF PROVISIONALLY APPLIED TREATIES IN THE PRACTICE OF STATES AND INTERNATIONAL ORGANISATIONS

1. Introduction

The present chapter will examine the practice of States and international organisations concerning the binding force of treaties during the period of provisional application. In the first part of the chapter, the views expressed by them as derived, for example, from statements, opinions of legal advisers, pleadings, and responses to questionnaires, on the binding force of these treaties will be examined. In the second part of the chapter, their treaty practice will be analysed, by reference to their intention to be bound (or not) during provisional application.

A. The Views Expressed by States and International Organisations

States and international organisations have expressed different views on the binding force of provisionally applied treaties. First, statements in support of the view that these treaties are legally binding will be examined as well as their conceptual underpinning.

2. The View that Provisionally Applied Treaties Are Legally Binding

As seen in the first chapter of this book, the view that provisionally applied treaties are legally binding received substantial support at the 1968–1969 Vienna Conference on the Law of Treaties: At least a dozen States present at the Vienna Conference expressly supported the applicability of the *pacta sunt servanda* principle to provisionally applied treaties and their understanding did not meet any objections. The Conference President of the Plenary Meetings, when summarising and closing the debate on the Article on *pacta sunt servanda* even concluded that "all delegations were agreed" on the interpretation according to which provisionally applied treaties fell within the ambit of the *pacta sunt servanda* principle.[1] The following will briefly look at the conceptual underpinning of this view as expressed at the 1968–1969 Vienna Conference before then moving on to analysing the support for this view in practice since then.

2.1. *The 1968–1969 Vienna Conference*

At the 1968–1969 Vienna Conference, after the change of terminology from 'provisional entry into force' to 'provisional application', an article was proposed[2] in order to clarify the continued applicability of the *pacta sunt servanda* principle to these treaties (despite the change of terminology).[3] The proposed article reads as follows: "Every treaty applied provisionally in whole or in part is binding on the contracting States and must be performed in good faith."[4]

The similarity to the *pacta sunt servanda* article in wording and structure is deliberate. As concerns its placement in the VCLT, the proposed article was intended to follow the article on *pacta sunt servanda* in order to specify the maxim's ambit.[5] So understood, the *pacta sunt servanda* principle not only covers treaties in force but also provisionally applied treaties. According to this proposal the binding force is perceived to be a feature of all provisionally applied treaties and could even be said to form part of the definition of provisional application.

It is possible that this understanding can be traced back to the ILC's understanding of the binding force of these treaties, which has been previously considered but which will be briefly recapitulated for present purposes. The ILC expressed its view on the binding force of these treaties in its commentary on *pacta sunt servanda*.[6] In that commentary there is a passage which relates to the words 'in force' as they still today appear in Article 26: "[e]very treaty *in force* is binding on the parties to it…" (Emphasis added). The ILC, then still speaking of 'treaties provisionally in force', clarified the binding force of these treaties by stipulating "the words 'in force' of course cover treaties in force provisionally … as well as treaties which enter into force definitively…"[7] This is essentially what the above Yugoslav

[1] See note 227 in chapter 1 above.
[2] UN Doc A/Con.39/L.24, entailed in UN Doc A/Conf.39/11/Add.2, 268.
[3] See the Yugoslav delegation's explanation of its amendment, Vienna Conference, OR 1969: Plen. 12: Yugoslavia §§50–51.
[4] UN Doc A/Con.39/L.24.
[5] Ibid.
[6] ILC, Draft articles on the law of treaties: text as finally adopted by the Commission on 18 and 19 July 1966, UN Doc A/CN.4/190, Commentary on final draft article 23, 211.
[7] Ibid., 211 §3.

article proposal says, i.e. both approach the matter of the binding force of provisionally applied treaties as one of the ambit of the *pacta sunt servanda* rule. The Yugoslav delegate, when introducing his amendment on the binding force to the 1968–1969 Vienna Conference, explicitly referred to the ILC's position on the matter.[8]

Many of the statements that adhere to this understanding of the binding force of provisionally applied treaties were made at the 1968–1969 Vienna Conference. Some of them preceded the change of terminology from 'provisional entry into force' to 'provisional application.'[9] Most statements, however, were made as a consequence of the change of terminology, in order to clarify and expressly underline the (continued) applicability of the *pacta sunt servanda* principle to provisionally applied treaties.[10] Finally, a few other statements made at the 1968–1969 Vienna Conference supported this view in passing when making a point which necessarily presupposed the applicability of the *pacta sunt servanda* principle to provisionally applied treaties.[11]

In the following support for this view and conceptual underpinning in practice since the 1968–1969 Vienna Conference will be analysed.

2.2. *Institutional Responses to the 2007–2008 Questionnaire*

In order to obtain a better sense of the practice, I drew up a questionnaire and sent it, between December 2007 and summer 2008, to legal advisers and treaty experts of States and international organisations.[12] The questionnaire was sent to 159 States and 18 international organisations by email. The 26 answers received in response to the questionnaire were mainly given in a private capacity, but, to the extent that the responses were classified as 'institutional', they will be attributed to the relevant State or international organisation.

The questionnaire also contained a question concerning the binding force of provisionally applied treaties, and the affirmative institutional answers received to this question will now be analysed. The question was phrased in the following way: "Does the principle of *pacta sunt servanda*

[8] Vienna Conference, OR 1969: Plen. 12: Yugoslavia §50.

[9] Ibid., OR 1968: CoW 26, Israel §44.

[10] Ibid., OR 1968: CoW 28, Ecuador §50; COW 29, Indonesia §59. OR 1969: Plen. 11: UK §58; Plen.12: Norway §§33–34; Colombia §45; Yugoslavia §50; Romania §58; Ukrainian Soviet Socialist Republic §61; Plen. 29: Poland §§2–3. See also OR 1969: Plen. 12: Israel §62.

[11] Ibid., OR 1969: Plen. 11: Guatemala §53; Iran §62.

[12] For the questionnaire and relevant background information see the 'appendix' and the 'acknowledgements'.

apply to treaties during the period of their provisional application, i.e. are treaties binding during the period of their provisional application?" The question received 18 responses, given by Government legal advisers, with 12 being affirmative, including four institutional responses, one of which was qualified to the effect that there may be limits to the binding force of these treaties (without further information).

The same question received seven clear responses from legal advisers to international organisations, five of which were affirmative (of which one related to commodity agreements and will be discussed in that context), including one institutional response.

It follows that the view that these treaties are legally binding or covered by the *pacta sunt servanda* principle was not only supported by States at the 1968–1969 Vienna Conference but receives also current support from States and an international organisation.

2.3. *Responses to the Council of Europe Questionnaire*

In a Council of Europe questionnaire on States' expression of consent to be bound,[13] one of the questions posed was whether, in the State's respective legal system, the provisional application of a treaty prior to its entry into force is possible, and if so under what conditions.[14] Although the question does not, directly or indirectly, touch upon the problem of the binding force of treaties during the period of provisional application, some of the answers still seemed to express the underlying understanding that provisionally applied treaties in general are legally binding. The following section will analyse how some of the responses created this impression and whether it is appropriate to regard them as a possible expression of this view (i.e. the view that provisionally applied treaties are legally binding). It is to be noted that the responses to the questionnaire reflect official government positions[15] and, therefore, count as state practice.

The answers entail statements which, in various ways, can be seen to demonstrate the assumption that provisionally applied treaties are considered to be legally binding. Also they are phrased in a very broad and general manner, without any qualifications, preconditions or exceptions. These two factors will now be analysed in more detail.

---

[13] The questionnaire, Government responses thereto and an analysis thereof can be found in: CoE and BIICL, eds., *Treaty Making*.

[14] CoE and BIICL, eds., *Treaty Making*, Appendix 1, question 15, 316.

[15] Reinhard Hilger and Guy de Vel, "Introduction," in *Treaty Making*, CoE and BIICL, eds., x.

One way in which that assumption is demonstrated is the recourse to treaty language when the undertaking of provisional application is described. Thus, some States have recourse to treaty language when specifically describing the undertaking of provisional application. An example of this would be to speak of the 'performance' or 'fulfilment' of '*obligations*' or '*treaty obligations*' under, or from the moment of, the treaty's provisional application.[16] Statements of this kind, due to the wording employed, create the impression of legally binding obligations, allowing for the conclusion that provisionally applied treaties are, thus, considered to be legally binding. Alternatively, States have recourse to treaty language when describing the way in which they accept the undertaking of provisional application. An example of this would be to say that the respective State '*binds*' or '*obliges*' itself to a treaty's provisional application.[17] It is submitted that when a State binds itself to a treaty's provisional application, such a treaty will be legally binding on the respective State during its provisional application.

In conclusion, the recourse to treaty language as demonstrated above could be seen to indicate that the respective States regard provisionally applied treaties as legally binding.

This impression is reinforced when the statements phrased in treaty terminology are joined by preconditions concerning provisional application (for example, requiring that the internal legal situation which the treaty requires has to exist or to be provided for provisional application to take place).[18] Provisional application so conditioned can only take place if the necessary internal legal framework either already exists or has been put in place. It is submitted that this rigid attitude towards the implementation of provisionally applied treaties is reminiscent of the implementation attitude towards legally binding agreements and thus adds to the impression already created by the recourse to treaty language that provisionally applied treaties are considered legally binding. This is so because the timely existence of an appropriate internal legal framework is a necessity only with regard to legally binding agreements. Only with regard to legally binding agreements can there exist a legal obligation to bring internal law into conformity with the (legally binding) international

---

[16] See CoE and BIICL, eds., *Treaty Making*, the Netherlands' statement, 223, Denmark, 153, and Lithuania, 211.

[17] See CoE and BIICL, eds., *Treaty Making*, Ireland, 196, and Andorra, 111.

[18] CoE and BIICL, eds., *Treaty Making*, response by Denmark, 153, and Lithuania, 211; see also the Netherlands' response, 223.

agreement. A failure to do so may amount to a breach and give rise to state responsibility.[19] By contrast, as regards soft law agreements, both compliance and implementation[20] are not legally required. Approached from an interpretative point of view, it could be said that a considerable degree of discretion is bestowed upon the participants of a soft law agreement as regards interpretation, including the interpretation and decision as to how and when to perform the soft law agreement.[21] This means that the implementation of soft law, whether by legislative or other means,[22] can occur gradually, only after a long time, or not at all.[23] Of course timely implementation may occur – but in general implementation is not a necessity which need be taken care of *prior* to the coming into effect of the soft law agreement. All in all, the attitude towards the implementation of soft law agreements is therefore typically flexible or relaxed. Regarding the existence of the necessary internal legal framework as a precondition of provisional application therefore is reminiscent rather of the rigid implementation attitude associated with legally binding agreements than of the flexible attitude associated with soft law agreements.

---

19 This formulation is chosen as it seems to depend on the kind of obligation whether 'wrong' implementation in itself constitutes a breach, or whether the implemented legislation needs to be applied to a specific case and this application does not conform to the result agreed upon in the international obligation, see State Responsibility Articles, commentary to article 12 [12], http://untreaty.un.org/ilc/texts/instruments/english/commentaries/9_6_2001.pdf; see also Harvard Draft, commentary to Article 20, 979; Jennings and Watts, *Oppenheim's International Law*, [21].

20 On a preliminary note, soft law agreements produce effects not only in the international but also the national arena, see Chinkin, "Challenge of Soft Law," 863. With soft law agreements implementing legislation is not a legal duty: Gruchalla-Wesierski, "Understanding Soft Law," 66–7; Hillgenberg, "Fresh Look at Soft Law," 501; Charles Lipson, "Why are some International Agreements Informal?," *International Organization* 45 (1991): 535; Christoph Schreuer, "Die innerstaatliche Anwendung von internationalem 'Soft Law' aus rechtsvergleichender Sicht," *Österreichische Zeitschrift für öffentliches Recht und Völkerrecht* 34 (1983): 246.

21 Patricia Birnie, Alan Boyle and Catherine Redgwell, *International Law and the Environment*, 3rd. ed. (Oxford: Oxford University Press, 2009), 35; see also Virally, "La deuxième décennie des Nations Unies pour le développement," 29.

22 Sometimes, the effects of soft law in the national arena are limited to being an interpretative aid in the application of internal law by domestic courts, administrations and legislative authorities, see Thürer, "Soft Law," 458. Soft law, however, can also have broader effects, being, for instance, a point of reference for governmental policies and the adoption of new legislation, see Christine Chinkin, "A Hard Look at Soft Law," *American Society of International Law Proceedings* 82 (1988): 391; Gruchalla-Wesierski, "Understanding Soft Law," 65–7. See especially Schreuer, "Die innerstaatliche Anwendung von internationalem 'Soft Law'," 243ff. (whose article is devoted to the incorporation of soft law into internal law).

23 Roberto Andorno, "The Invaluable Role of Soft Law in the Development of Universal Norms in Bioethics," 2, http://www.unesco.de/1507.html?&L%20=%200.

Thus the impression that provisionally applied treaties are considered legally binding, initially created by the recourse to treaty language by some States when describing the undertaking of provisional application, can be seen to be further corroborated when provisional application is conditioned upon the existence (or provision) of the relevant internal legal framework. In conclusion, responses to the Council of Europe questionnaire which have one or both of these features can be seen as support for the view that provisionally applied treaties are legally binding.

2.4. *Opinions of Legal Advisers*

Two Government statements made in different contexts also seem to express the underlying understanding that provisionally applied treaties are generally legally binding. They both presuppose in a general statement the legally binding force of provisionally applied treaties as if this force was self-evident. The first of these statements is entailed in a Memorandum by the then Canadian Legal Bureau of the Department of External Affairs concerning a treaty between the US and Canada.[24] This treaty appeared to have been applied by both sides, although it had not yet entered into force, nor had its provisional application been formally agreed. The Memorandum concludes on this point that there may be some evidence for a provisional application but adds that this is far from conclusive. It then moves on to consider whether there has been a material breach of the treaty by the US, and clarifies that this possibility can only be entertained on the assumption that the treaty indeed had been provisionally applied. For present purposes, the doubts on the facts as to whether or not the treaty actually had been provisionally applied by the parties are irrelevant. What is relevant, however, is the legal argument involved, namely that the provisionally applied treaty is considered a sufficient basis for there to be a (material) breach of the treaty which would open to Canada the option of invoking Article 60.[25] Since only a legally binding agreement can give rise to the possibility of invoking Article 60 in case of a material breach,[26]

---

[24] See Maurice Copithorne, "Canadian Practice in International Law," *Canadian Yearbook of International Law* XVI (1978): 366–67.

[25] More precisely Canada may have had the option of invoking the customary corollary to Article 60 given that the US at the relevant time was not a party to the VCLT 1969.

[26] This already follows from the wording of Article 60 which both in the title as well as the main body of the article speaks of the material breach of a 'treaty'. The term 'treaty', for the purposes of the Convention, is defined in Article 2(1)(a), as an instrument which *inter alia* is 'governed by international law'. This phrase, according to the ILC, was understood to mean that the relevant parties intended the instrument to be *legally* binding, Commentary

this argument necessarily presupposes the legally binding force of the provisionally applied treaty. Furthermore, it should be noted that the only precondition for there to have been a material breach is the assumption that the treaty has been provisionally applied. There is no further precondition, for example, requiring that in that specific instance provisional application would have needed to be legally binding in order for there to be a (material) breach of the treaty during this period. This could be taken to indicate that the legally binding force of the provisionally applied treaty is simply assumed, which in turn may possibly be a manifestation of the underlying understanding that provisionally applied treaties in general are legally binding.

The other Government statement that seems to be indicative of the underlying understanding that provisionally applied treaties are generally legally binding was made by the then Deputy Legal Adviser of the United States' Department of State, Mr Feldman.[27] In his written reply to the questions of a Senator following testimony before the Senate Committee on Foreign Relations,[28] he explains the two ways in which provisional application can be agreed: either in a separate agreement, which he qualifies as an Executive Agreement, or in the treaty itself, in a provision on provisional application. The legally binding force of such an (separate) Executive Agreement is clear. These agreements "are regarded by both the Government of the United States and other states as treaties for the purposes of international law."[29] With regard to the provision on provisional application the Deputy Legal Adviser clarifies in passing that "such a provision itself constitutes a binding international agreement..." Thus no matter how provisional application is agreed (in a separate (Executive) Agreement or in a final clause of the treaty) he presupposes that this agreement is legally binding. If the agreement to resort to provisional application is legally binding, then States are bound to provisionally apply the treaty in question, which is a different way of saying that they are bound by the provisionally applied treaty (to the extent that they agreed to provisionally apply it). Accordingly, it is submitted that the statement seems to express the underlying understanding that provisionally applied treaties in general are legally binding.

---

to ILC Final Draft Article 2(1)a, UN Doc A/CN.4/190, 189 [6]. It is submitted that Canada must have regarded the provisionally applied treaty as legally binding otherwise it could not have considered a recourse to Article 60 as a response to its breach.

27 Nash, "Contemporary Practice of the United States," 931–33.

28 For this and any of the following information see ibid.

29 Aust, *Modern Treaty Law*, 196. See also McNair, *Law of Treaties*, 64.

It can be concluded with regard to the statements made in the response to the 2007–2008 questionnaire and to the Council of Europe questionnaire as well as the statements by the Government legal advisers, that from their content, wording and general tone, including the absence of any preconditions or exceptions to the binding force of provisionally applied treaties, they may evidence the underlying understanding that provisionally applied treaties are generally legally binding.

2.5. *Support in other 'Sources'*

After having presented the evidence found in the practice of States and, to a lesser extent, of international organisations for the understanding that provisionally applied treaties are generally or by definition legally binding, further evidence of such an understanding will be examined, based on pronouncements by the ILC or individual ILC members, arbitral tribunals, as well as statements by legal advisers or treaty experts which were made in a private capacity.

2.5.1. *The Understanding of the ILC and Some of its Members*

Reference has already been made to the ILC commentary on *pacta sunt servanda* in which the ILC expresses the view that treaties subject to the mechanism under consideration are by definition legally binding. To be clear, the ILC used the terminology of 'provisional entry into force' rather than 'provisional application', but there is no doubt that by this the ILC meant the mechanism currently under consideration. By defining 'treaties provisionally in force' as treaties which were deemed to be 'in force' for purposes of the rule of *pacta sunt servanda*, the commentary basically stipulates that 'every treaty provisionally in force is binding on the parties to it and must be performed in good faith'.[30] Some individual ILC members also voiced this view prior to the adoption of the commentary to the final draft articles.[31] Thus, both individual ILC members as well as the ILC commentary support the understanding that provisionally applied treaties (as they are called today) are by definition legally binding.

---

30 ILC, Draft articles on the law of treaties: text as finally adopted by the Commission on 18 and 19 July 1966, UN Doc A/CN.4/190, commentary to final draft Article 23, 211.

31 ILC, Summary record of the 791st meeting, UN Doc A/CN.4/SR.791, Tsuruoka, §27; Bartoš, §24; see also ILC, Summary record of the 790th meeting, UN Doc A/CN.4/SR.790, Waldock, §90.

2.5.2. *The* Yukos *and* Kardassopoulos *Tribunals*

In a long anticipated arbitral award, the *Yukos* Tribunal held that it had jurisdiction over the merits of the claims brought by Hulley Enterprises Limited, Yukos Universal Limited and Veteran Petroleum Limited against the Russian Federation on the basis of the provisionally applied 1994 Energy Charter Treaty.[32] In the context of assessing the effect that should be given to the limitation clause in Article 45(1) ECT, the *Yukos* Tribunal based parts of its reasoning on the "principle that provisional application of a treaty creates binding obligations".[33] Although technically, the Tribunal's jurisdiction is limited to the claims submitted for its decision, the Tribunal did not limit its view to the notion of provisional application in the 1994 ECT but referred to 'provisional application' in general, and thus clearly supports the view that provisionally applied treaties are legally binding.

Similarly, the *Kardassopoulos* Tribunal found that it had jurisdiction to decide the case brought by Kardassopoulos against Georgia on the basis of the provisionally applied 1994 Energy Charter Treaty.[34] With regard to the provisional application of a treaty as a whole the Tribunal held that this "imports the application of all its [the treaty's] provisions *as if they were already in force*...."[35] The emphasised legal fiction at the end of the quotation implies two typical features of treaty provisions in force, namely that they are binding on the parties to the treaty and that they must be performed by them in good faith. Thus, the Tribunal understood the notion of such provisional application as involving legally binding obligations just as if the treaty and its provisions were already in force. Moreover, the Tribunal's interpretation of what provisional application means, when it concerns a treaty as a whole, is not limited to the notion of provisional application as employed in the 1994 Energy Charter Treaty. Rather, the interpretation is said to reflect the "generally accepted understanding"[36] of what the provisional application of a treaty as a whole means. Accordingly, the Tribunal expressly endorsed the view that the binding force of these treaties is implicit in the very notion of provisional

---

[32] *Yukos Universal Ltd v Russian Federation* (30 November 2009). In this Award, the Tribunal discussed the separate claims of the three Claimants in separate arbitrations as a single set of proceedings, except where circumstances distinct to particular Claimants necessitated separate treatment, see [2] of the Award.

[33] *Yukos Universal Ltd v Russian Federation* (30 November 2009), [314] 116.

[34] 2080 UNTS 95.

[35] *Kardassopoulos v Georgia* (6 July 2007), [219].

[36] Ibid.

application, at least when the provisional application concerns the treaty as a whole.

2.5.3. *Personal Responses to the 2007–2008 Questionnaire*

In the 2007–2008 questionnaire, the question on the binding force of treaties during the period of provisional application was phrased in the following way: "Does the principle of *pacta sunt servanda* apply to treaties during the period of their provisional application, i.e. are treaties binding during the period of their provisional application?" The question received 18 responses by Government legal advisers, with 12 being affirmative, including eight responses given in private capacity.

Relevant for present purposes are the eight responses according to which treaties are legally binding during the period of provisional application. Of these eight responses, three were joined by a 'disclaimer' to the effect that the response was either purely personal, based on limited direct experience or of an assumptive nature. Furthermore, one response affirmed the applicability of the *pacta sunt servanda* principle by stating that "the consequences of non-compliances ... are different from a treaty in force", without going into anymore detail.

The same question received seven responses from legal advisers to international organisations, five of which were affirmative (although one related to commodity agreements and will be discussed in that context), including three given in a private capacity. Relevant for present purposes are the three responses according to which treaties are legally binding during the period of provisional application. Of these, two were joined by a 'disclaimer' that the respondent had limited direct experience in the matter.

When taking the responses to the 2007–2008 questionnaire together (i.e. adding the institutional responses to the ones given in private capacity), there are two points which can be made with regard to the above results. First, the majority of responses by both legal advisers to States and international organisations affirms that provisionally applied treaties are legally binding.[37] Second, most of these respondents agree that the matter of these treaties' legally binding force can be affirmed in a general way. This conclusion is deduced from the fact that the responses, with two

[37] While the qualifications and disclaimers should not be taken lightly, the responses so qualified are still affirmative. Therefore, this 'generalisation' (i.e. counting them towards the total number of affirmative responses) seems justified.

exceptions, are phrased in a general manner without any preconditions or qualifications concerning the legally binding force of provisionally applied treaties.

2.6. *Evaluation: Provisionally Applied Treaties as* 'Pacta' *and the Role of Intention*

After having presented the material found which supports the view that provisionally applied treaties are legally binding, it is time to examine this view and its implications in more detail. This view is at times expressed by saying that provisionally applied treaties fall within the ambit of the *pacta sunt servanda* principle or are covered thereby.[38] In those instances, provisionally applied treaties are posited to be '*pacta*', i.e. posited to be legally binding. This is most apparent in the Article proposed at the 1968–1969 Vienna Conference, according to which "[e]very treaty applied provisionally in whole or in part is binding on the contracting States and must be performed in good faith."[39] Thus, binding force forms part of the definition of a provisionally applied treaty; in the same way, in which treaties are by definition legally binding, so too are provisionally applied treaties.

In the final analysis whether an agreement in international law falls within the so defined category depends upon the intention of the States and/or international organisations concerned. Only if intended to be legally binding will the agreement be a 'treaty' or a 'provisionally applied treaty'. Terminology, by contrast, is not decisive. Only because something is called a 'treaty', does not make it a treaty – and the same would be true for a provisionally applied treaty, as defined by this view.

In conclusion, when provisionally applied treaties are posited to be '*pacta*', this view defines 'provisional application' by reference to binding force. Only if intended to be legally binding, will a treaty be subject to the mechanism under consideration properly so called. On this understanding, it is submitted that it might be useful to have recourse to a different terminology when not intended to be legally binding, so as to avoid confusion and respect the definition of 'provisional application' as presupposed by this view.

---

[38] On statements to such effects made at the 1968–1969 Vienna Conference see note 226 and the text following note 218, all in chapter 1 above; for the ILC position, see e.g. Final Commentary on Article 22, ILC, Draft articles on the law of treaties: text as finally adopted by the Commission on 18 and 19 July 1966, UN Doc A/CN.4/190, 210, §1 and Final Commentary on Article 23, 211, §3.

[39] UN Doc A/Con.39/L.24.

2.7. *Conclusion*

In conclusion, the view according to which provisionally applied treaties are legally binding has received ample and continuous support in practice, ranging from the 1968–1969 Vienna Conference (or even the ILC) to the 2007–2008 questionnaire, and the recent pronouncements by the *Kardassopoulos* and *Yukos* Tribunals. Furthermore, there is a good deal of support for the understanding, that the binding force forms part of the definition of provisionally applied treaties or that provisionally applied treaties are defined as legally binding. On this understanding binding force, and therefore an intention to be bound, is a necessary requirement for there to be provisional application properly so called. Accordingly, on this understanding, intention would appear to play a key role in determining whether or not a treaty is subject to provisional application as defined by strands of this view.

After this brief evaluation and conclusion, the next view expressed by States and international organisations on the binding force of these treaties will be assessed.

3. The View that Provisionally Applied Treaties are not Legally Binding

Only a small number of statements would appear to support the view that provisionally applied treaties are 'not legally binding'[40]. While the statements agree that provisionally applied treaties are not covered by the *pacta sunt servanda* rule, they have different views on the legal effects these treaties may produce (if any). According to one view, the obligations which may arise under a provisionally applied treaty come under the heading of the obligation not to defeat a treaty's object and purpose prior to its entry into force, as laid down in Article 18. According to the other view, provisionally applied treaties are morally or politically binding, but not legally. In other words, they are considered to be soft law. Finally, some statements limit themselves to excluding the applicability of the *pacta sunt servanda* rule to provisionally applied treaties, without

40 The expression 'not legally binding' is used in a broader way than the expression non(-legally) binding. The former simply excludes that the treaty is binding; this leaves open the option that the treaty may have indirect effects through Article 18 or be non-legally binding, i.e. only have soft law effects. As previously mentioned, the notion 'non-legally binding' is limited to describing the effects of soft law agreements. Thus the expression non-legally binding would not include the effects of a treaty via Article 18.

further specifying what legal effects these treaties are considered to have instead.[41]

3.1. *Provisional Application is Similar to Article 18*

It may be recalled that India rejected the view that provisionally applied treaties fall within the ambit of the *pacta sunt servanda* rule during the discussion at the 1968–1969 Vienna Conference. Instead it maintained that the obligations which may arise under a provisionally applied treaty fall under the heading of the obligation not to defeat a treaty's object and purpose prior to its entry into force. Since the matter of the applicability of the *pacta sunt servanda* principle to provisionally applied treaties was not brought to a vote, it is not clear how much support there actually was for each of these views. Yet the course of the debate shows that India's view failed to attract any support in the statements made on the matter by at least a dozen delegations. Nor does there seem to have been subsequent support in other state practice, based on the present research. A possible reason for this may be the *argumentum ad absurdum* which this understanding prompts, namely the question why there is a need for provisional application at all, if it produces the same legal consequences as the obligation not to defeat a treaty's object and purpose pending its entry into force.

Be that as it may, based on the present research the view, according to which the obligations which may arise under a provisionally applied treaty fall under the heading of the obligation today codified in Article 18, seems to find only little support in practice.

3.2. *Provisionally Applied Treaties are Considered to be Soft Law*

By contrast to the above opinion, the view according to which provisionally applied treaties are morally or politically binding, but not legally binding, has recently been endorsed in State practice. In the *Yukos* arbitration, which was brought by three shareholders of the Yukos Oil Corporation OJSC against the Russian Federation on the basis of the provisionally applied 1994 Energy Charter Treaty, the Russian Federation argued that "the provisional application of treaties does not give rise to legally enforceable rights and obligations", thus supporting the view that the rights and obligations of a provisionally applied treaty are non-legally binding.[42]

[41] Cyprus GAOR 22, SR 980, UN Doc A/C.6/SR.980, §54.

[42] See the position of the Russian Federation as summarised in the Claimants' Skeleton Argument, parts of which are reprinted in *Yukos Universal Ltd v Russian Federation*

Furthermore, in the *Kardassopoulos* arbitration brought against Georgia on the basis of, *inter alia,* the provisionally applied 1994 Energy Charter Treaty, Georgia rejected the view that the provisionally applied ECT could be legally binding by arguing that this would render its ratification and entry into force meaningless. Georgia then moved on to submit that provisional application is a soft law undertaking which is aspirational in nature and not binding:

> It is ... submitted that the provisional application of a treaty must be aspirational in nature, rather than capable of binding the state with the consequence of potential sanctions before the treaty has actually entered into force.[43]

This statement describes typical soft law features, such as (the undertaking being "aspirational in nature" as opposed to obligatory and) the fact that a breach of the undertaking does not give rise to state responsibility and sanctions. Moreover, this statement on the soft law character is not limited to the ECT's provisional application but concerns "the provisional application of a treaty" in general. Thus, Georgia's position would seem to relate to provisionally applied treaties in general.

The position according to which provisionally applied treaties are morally or politically binding – but not legally – has also found some support in the responses to the relevant question in the 2007–2008 questionnaire. Two responses given by Government legal advisers, in their private capacity, support this view, and it is noteworthy that certainly one of these Governments would generally be considered as 'experienced and conscientious' in the conduct of its foreign relations. Therefore, this additional neutral support[44] should quell, somewhat, any doubts that may arise with regard to the Russian Federation's or Georgia's position on the matter, given that it provided these States with another objection against the jurisdiction of the respective Tribunals.

In analysing the support for the view according to which provisionally applied treaties are morally or politically binding – but not legally – binding, the above provisos apply, to the extent that here the absence of

---

(30 November 2009), [72] 31 ([13] of the Skeleton Argument, see also [14]). According to the Economist, the Russian Federation *inter alia* argued that it never ratified the 1994 ECT, Economist 12 May 2007, 72.

43 *Kardassopoulos v Georgia* (6 July 2007), [76].

44 'Neutral' here means that none of the States for which the respondents generally act as legal advisers are implicated, at the time of writing, in, for instance, arbitration proceedings under the ECT.

binding force is seen as part of the definition of provisional application. Accordingly, such a definition is not to be interpreted in a literal manner. A literal interpretation of the view would mean that the mere usage of the terms 'provisional application' would automatically exclude the legally binding force of the agreement subjected to such provisional application. It has been submitted that such an interpretation has to be rejected since it is irreconcilable with the role intention plays in international law concerning the binding force (or otherwise) of international agreements. As has been pointed out earlier, such a definition does not render the criterion of intention obsolete. On the contrary, the definition ultimately relies on intention when determining whether or not a treaty is subject to provisional application properly so called. Since provisionally applied treaties so understood are by definition non-legally binding, only those agreements are subjected to 'provisional application' properly so called, which are intended to have soft law effects during their provisional application. Finally, on the basis of the 2007–2008 questionnaire, it is conceivable that this position presumes in general the absence of an intention to be bound during provisional application out of respect for the rule of law and the internal legal procedures which normally need to be completed before consent is expressed, the treaty becomes effective and is applied. The absence of legal force of a provisionally applied treaty would, so understood, be a consequence of a missing intention to be bound, in recognition of the fact that the internal legal procedures which normally need to take place before the treaty becomes effective and is applied have not yet been completed.

3.3. *Conclusion*

By way of conclusion, the view according to which provisionally applied treaties are not legally binding would seem to receive considerably less support in practice than the opposing view. Of its two strands, the support for the view that the effects of provisional application come under the heading of Article 18 would appear to be negligible. By contrast, the view that provisionally applied treaties are non-legally binding and have soft law character has received more as well as recent support, both in investment arbitrations as well as outside this context, by Government Adviser in personal capacity of 'neutral' States, i.e. States that are not implicated in current proceedings brought against them on the basis of a provisionally applied treaty. To the extent that the absence of binding force and an intention to be bound is understood to form part of the definition of provisional application, on this understanding, too, intention would appear to play a key role in determining whether or not provisional application is given.

4. The View that Provisionally Applied Treaties can be Legally Binding or Non-Legally Binding

According to this third view provisionally applied are not a class of treaties with regard to which the matter of the binding force could be either affirmed or rejected in a general way. Rather, the binding force of these treaties varies.

4.1. *International Practice*

This view draws its support mainly from recent practice. One such instance is the response by Spain to a questionnaire which the Secretariat of the EC Council of Ministers[45] circulated in the 1990s to the then fifteen Member States on "[...] les procédures internes des Etats Membres pour la conclusion d'accords internationaux approuvés selon une procédure simplifiée ou d'accords juridiquement non obligatoires".[46] Under the section which deals with the provisional application of treaties, Spain explains the internal procedure for the provisional application of treaties, and thereby draws a distinction between provisionally applied treaties which are binding, and provisionally applied treaties which are non-legally binding. More precisely it is with regard to publication that Spain specifies that only binding provisionally applied treaties need be published in the Spanish "Boletín Oficial"; for provisionally applied treaties which are non-legally binding the publication is unnecessary.[47] This would seem to be an unambiguous statement to the effect that according to the Spanish understanding, provisionally applied treaties may come in both forms: they can be either binding or non-legally binding, and both types of provisionally applied treaties are recognised and accommodated in the Spanish internal treaty-making procedure.

Further support for this view can be found in American practice and, more precisely, from two separate incidents of American practice.

---

[45] See Aust, *Modern Treaty Law*, 38 (the summary of government responses which is available from the Council of Ministers upon request does not seem to entail any information of this kind).

[46] PESC/SEC 899 (09 August 1996).

[47] Ibid., 10.

First, there is a report from 2002 by which the then American Secretary of State submitted amendments to a treaty[48] to the then American President for transmittal to the Senate for its advice and consent to ratification.[49] The letter describes the amendments to the treaty and an accompanying memorandum of understanding (hereinafter 'MOU') which provides for the provisional application of several of the amendments pending their entry into force. The letter explicitly and unequivocally states that the MOU is non-legally binding.[50] As has been explained earlier, if the agreement on provisional application is non-legally binding, then the agreement subject to such provisional application will not be legally binding, since States are not bound to provisionally apply the agreement. Thus, classifying the MOU as non-legally binding is tantamount to saying that the amendments subject to this provisional application will not be legally binding (during this period pending their entry into force).

The information that provisionally applied treaties can equally be (legally) binding is taken from a statement by the then Deputy Legal Adviser of the (American) Department of State[51] to which reference has been made earlier. It may be recalled that the then Deputy Legal Adviser in his written reply to the questions of a Senator following testimony before the Senate Committee on Foreign Relations,[52] explained the two ways in which provisional application can be agreed. He states that each of the relevant agreements is either explicitly or implicitly legally binding. When provisional application is agreed in a separate agreement, he labels the separate agreement as an (American) Executive Agreement. Since these are by definition 'treaties' as far as the international law sphere is concerned,[53] this label implies their binding force. When provisional application is agreed upon in the treaty itself, in one of its final clauses, he explicitly classifies this to be a 'binding international agreement'. In short, whether provisional application is agreed by way of a separate agreement or in a final clause in the treaty itself, he seems to regard these agreements as binding.

---

48 Treaty on Fisheries between the Governments of Certain Pacific Island States and the Government of the United States of America (entered into force 2 April 1987) 2176 UNTS 93.

49 "Treaty Affairs," *Digest of United States Practice in International Law* 2002, B3, 186.

50 Ibid., 189.

51 The then Deputy Legal Adviser was Mark B Feldman; for his statement see Nash, "Contemporary Practice of the United States," 931–33.

52 For this and any of the following information see ibid.

53 Aust, *Modern Treaty Law*, 196; see also McNair, *Law of Treaties*, 64.

4.2. *Support in other 'Sources'*

Furthermore, this view finds support in two of the responses to the relevant question in the 2007–2008 questionnaire, which were given by legal advisers to international organisations, in their private capacity. According to both the binding force of provisionally applied treaties is subject to certain conditions. For one of them the binding force is subject to the condition of reciprocity. So understood a provisionally applied treaty is binding if the other party/parties equally consider it to be binding. For the other adviser the binding force of the provisionally applied treaty depends upon the binding force of the agreement on provisional application. If the agreement on provisional application is binding, then the provisionally applied treaty is binding, too. In short, when the respective condition is met, then the binding force of a provisionally applied treaty is affirmed. Yet in the reverse situation, i.e. if the condition is not met, it would seem that the provisionally applied treaty would not be regarded as binding. So understood provisionally applied treaties can be either binding or non-legally binding, and accordingly these responses are interpreted as adhering to the view that the binding force of these treaties can vary and is not entailed in the notion of 'provisional application'.[54]

Finally, it is possible that Reuter, as an ILC member, adhered to this view. Reuter in the ILC once submitted that the binding force of provisionally applied treaties could vary. According to him, the binding force of (all) provisionally applied treaties could vary from the most stringent to the most lenient undertakings. Unfortunately, it does not become clear whether he considers the lenient undertaking to be 'lenient but legally binding' or 'lenient and non-legally binding'. Only if it is the latter could he be said to fully endorse the view according to which provisionally applied treaties can be binding or non-legally binding. Yet since the relevant passage is not clear in that aspect, it remains ambiguous whether he endorsed the view that the binding force of provisionally applied treaties varies to its full extent, i.e. by including non-legally binding agreements in the range of 'lenient' undertakings of provisional application.

4.3. *Evaluation and Conclusion*

By way of evaluation and conclusion on this third view the following is submitted. In contrast to the above views, the determination of the

---

54 For a similar approach in academic writings see van Panhuys, "The Netherlands Constitution and International Law," 94.

binding force of an agreement is, according to this understanding, *not* decisive for its classification as a provisionally applied treaty. Therefore, there is no need to first determine the agreement's binding force by recourse to the criterion of intention in order to then classify it accordingly as a provisionally applied treaty (or not). Since the notion of provisional application so understood is not linked to the binding force of the agreement, the binding force of provisionally applied treaties can vary, or put differently: provisionally applied treaties can be binding or non-legally binding.

While the support for this view in practice is recent it is quantitatively rather low. Nevertheless, the Spanish statement, as well as the responses given by the legal advisers to international organisations in their private capacity, seems to be explicit and unequivocal endorsements of this view. Moreover, the distinction between binding and non-legally binding provisionally applied treaties would appear to be so common in Spanish practice as to being rooted and accommodated in internal treaty procedures. Finally, since it has been mentioned earlier that some statements were of an assumptive nature and not based on ample direct experience of the matter, it is worthwhile underlining that Spain is one of the States that resorts to provisional application most frequently.[55] With regard to the responses given by two legal advisers to international organisations, in their private capacity, it should be mentioned that one of them is a famous expert in the law of treaties,[56] and the other works for an organisation which is generally recognised as an important global player. While the answers of course are given in a private capacity, it is assumed that they are informed by the practice of the institution and thus benefit from the broad involvement and experience which that particular institution has in treaty-making. In conclusion this view may not rely on great quantitative support. Yet qualitatively speaking the support seems explicit and unequivocal, is fairly recent, and based on direct experience in provisional application.

---

[55] This is based on treaties which are registered in the UN Treaty Series. Also, in its response to the Council of Europe questionnaire, Spain makes the point that "in practice provisional application is often allowed." (263) It is the sole State saying so in the Council's questionnaire project, and the statement can be contrasted with responses by seven other States to the effect that they have recourse to provisional application only in exceptional circumstances, see CoE and BIICL, eds., *Treaty Making,* Andorra, 111; Belgium, 127; France, 167; Greece, 183; Italy, 203; Luxembourg, 214; and Turkey, 281.

[56] In general no names will be given in relation to the 2007–2008 questionnaire since responses thereto were provided on condition of anonymity.

5. The Provisional Entry into Force and Application of Commodity Agreements

In the context of commodity agreements, the terms 'provisional entry into force' and 'provisional application' are used to denote different phenomena.[57] Provisional entry into force tends to relate to the treaty, more precisely its status, and can be contrasted with the treaty's definitive entry into force. Provisional application, on the other hand, seems to be reserved to a State's individual and unilateral undertaking to provisionally apply a commodity agreement, which will be entailed in a notification to the depositary, and can be contrasted to expressions of consent to be bound in instruments of ratification, acceptance, approval or accession.[58] Thus, while usually the terms 'provisional entry into force' and 'provisional application' are used synonymously,[59] this is different in the context of commodity agreements, where the former relates to the treaty's effects prior to its definitive entry into force, and the latter to the individual undertaking of a State to give effect to the treaty pending its definitive entry into force. This specific use of terminology, which invites a separate analysis of provisional entry into force and provisional application, is the reason why statements on commodity agreements are analysed separately

---

57 Institutional response of a commodity organisation to question I(1)(b) of the 2007–2008 questionnaire. The following authors explicitly make this point: Bhupinder S. Chimni, *International Commodity Agreements* (London: Croom Helm, 1987), 83; see also Pierre-Michel Eisemann, *L'Organisation Internationale du Commerce des produits de base* (Brussels: Bruylant, 1982), 285. The following authors make the point implicitly (by applying the distinction in the terminology they use): Kabir-ur-Rahman Khan, *The Law and Organisation of International Commodity Agreements* (Boston: Martinus Nijhoff Publishers, 1982), 345; Christian Tomuschat, "Commodities," in Bernhardt, *Encyclopedia of Public International Law*, vol. 1, 690.

58 Some commodity agreements expressly say that consent to be bound can be provisional, by way of a notification of provisional application, or definitive, by way of 'classic' means of expressing consent to be bound namely an instrument of ratification, acceptance, approval or accession, see, e.g., Coffee Agreement 1994 (concluded 30 March 1994, entered into force 1 October 1999) 827 UNTS 3, Article 2(5); Coffee Agreement 2001 (concluded 28 September 2000, entered into force provisionally on 1 October 2001 and definitively on 17 May 2005) 2161 UNTS 308, Article 2(5); Coffee Agreement 2007 (concluded 28 September 2007, entered into force 2 February 2011) Article 2(5); Cocoa Agreement 1980 (concluded 19 November 1980, entered into force 1 August 1981) 1245 UNTS 221, Article 2(i); Cocoa Agreement 1986 (concluded 25 July 1986, entered into force 20 January 1987) 1446 UNTS 103, Article 2(4); Cocoa Agreement 1993, 1766 UNTS 3, Article 2(4); Cocoa Agreement 2001 (concluded 2 March 2001, entered into force 2 November 2005) 2229 UNTS 2, Article 2(4); Rubber Agreement 1987 (entered into force provisionally on 29 December 1988, and definitively on 3 April 1989) 1521 UNTS 3, Article 2(2) and (3).

59 Geslin, *Application provisoire*, 127, 139–40.

from the other statements examined above.[60] Yet, prior to beginning the analysis of statements on the legal implications of both provisional entry into force and provisional application in the context of commodity agreements, the notion of commodity agreements will be introduced and an explanation provided as to why provisions on provisional entry into force and provisional application are a standard feature of these agreements.[61]

5.1. *Introduction*

Commodity agreements are commercial treaties, and the term is used here to denote sectoral trade agreements on a multilateral basis relating to raw material and food stuffs such as tin, rubber, tropical timber, jute and jute products, sugar, coffee, cocoa, grains and olive oil, to name but a few.[62] Historically, the emphasis of commodity agreements has been on price stabilisation[63] due to the volatility that commodity prices were subjected to.[64] Price stabilisation and market regulation were to be achieved through mechanisms such as buffer stocks[65] and export quotas.[66] Yet over time the

[60] The analysis of the above agreements rested on the assumption that the terms 'provisional application' and 'provisional entry into force' (or whatever terminology was used to describe the giving effect to a treaty's provisions prior to its entry into force) are used interchangeably, as normally seems to be the case in practice (outside the special case of commodity agreements), see preceding footnote.

[61] Tomuschat, "Commodities," 690.

[62] Gerold Herrmann, "Commercial Treaties," in Bernhardt, *Encyclopedia of Public International Law*, vol. 1, 680.

[63] UNCTAD, Intergovernmental Producer-Consumer Cooperation in Commodities in Mid1990s – A Handbook on International Commodity Agreements, Arrangements and Study Groups (New York, 1998) (hereinafter 'UNCTAD Handbook'), 1; See also Erik Chrispeels, "Simplifying International Commodity Agreements," in *International Commodity Organisations in Transition*, ed. Erik Chrispeels (London: Cameron May, 2002), 357; Edward Quill, "The Failure of International Commodity Agreements," *Denver Journal of International Law and Policy* 22 (1993–1994): 505; Herrmann, "Commercial Treaties," 680.

[64] Offer and demand in commodities were not easily balanced because of, *inter alia*, the amount of time needed in these products to react to market developments as well as a lack of exchange of information between and among producing and consuming countries, see Montag, *Völkerrechtliche Verträge*, 56.

[65] "Buffer stocks aim at ensuring that the price remains within a given price range by selling when the market price exceeds the maximum intervention price and by buying when the price falls below the minimum price." Gerhard Loibl, "International Economic Law," in *International Law*, 3rd ed., ed. Malcom D. Evans (Oxford: Oxford University Press, 2010), 740; Herman Walker, "The International Law of Commodity Agreements," *Law and Contemporary Problems* 28 (1963): 394; Tomuschat, "Commodities," 688.

[66] Export quotas are a further device for market regulation and may, for example, be combined with buffer stocks to support their operation. "Generally, export control measures have as their starting point national basic quotas or basic export tonnages determined on the basis of the volume of the average exports in a number of preceding years. Before the beginning of each quota year, the competent council [of the relevant

emphasis has shifted away from these economic commodity agreements towards administrative agreements which mainly confine themselves to consultative functions, acting as a centre for the collection, exchange and publication of information, promoting studies and encouraging consumption.[67] Finally, there are also "developmental" commodity agreements which focus on cooperation in production, consumption and development of rare commodities, such as tropical timber and jute.[68] All types of commodity agreements, whether economic, administrative or developmental, regularly provide for provisional entry into force and provisional application, and the underlying situation which creates the need for the recourse to these mechanisms would appear to be the following.

5.1.1. *The Need for Provisional Entry into Force and Provisional Application*

First, commodity agreements are concluded for a limited period of time.[69] Thus, whether their period of application will be extended or not, at one point or another they will terminate upon a certain date or event. Second, commodity agreements have stringent entry into force requirements such as participation in the treaty by those States which together are responsible for 70% percent of the trade in the respective commodity in order to ensure the effectiveness[70] of these agreements. More precisely, definitive entry into force is conditioned upon an expression of consent to be bound by States representing a minimum percentage (usually above 50%) of the world trade in the relevant commodity.[71] Many agreements furthermore require the expression of consent to be bound by a minimum number of exporting and importing States.[72] Because of these stringent entry into force requirements and the fact that commodity agreements frequently require parliamentary approval or the fulfilment of other lengthy constitutional procedures prior to an expression of consent to be bound on the

commodity organization] adopts a comprehensive estimate as to prospective world demand and distributes the global quantity thus calculated among members in proportion to their basic quotas, thereby fixing the annual quota or quotas in effect." Tomuschat, "Commodities," 688.

67 UNCTAD Handbook, 1, see also Loibl, "International Economic Law," 740.

68 Quill, "The Failure of International Commodity Agreements," 505. See also UNCTAD Handbook, 1.

69 This is so in response to changing world economic conditions, see Tomuschat, "Commodities," 690.

70 On the effectiveness of international commodity agreements see, e.g., ibid and Chimni, *International Commodity Agreements*, 83.

71 Chimni, *International Commodity Agreements*, 83; Tomuschat, "Commodities," 690.

72 Chimni, *International Commodity Agreements*, 83.

international plane, the entry into force of the successor agreement can be delayed until long after the termination of the predecessor agreement. Thus, a legal gap could arise between the predecessor and successor commodity agreement. Third, commodity agreements establish international organizations,[73] legal regimes and research or development projects whose proper functioning is averse to long interruptions or gaps between predecessor and successor agreement. More precisely, with regard to these international organizations, commodity agreements serve as a constitutive instrument,[74] and delay or uncertainty of the entry into force of the successor commodity agreement would certainly be problematic for the continued proper functioning of the organization.[75] Thus, already in order to enable the continued existence of the commodity institutions the relevant agreements provide for the possibility of their provisional entry into force, upon a certain event or by agreement of the relevant States.[76] Furthermore, with regard to economic commodity agreements it is evident that their aim of market regulation and prize stabilization can only be pursued effectively if done so in a continuous manner. Equally, the continuous interest in the functions performed on the basis of administrative and developmental commodity agreements, including the pivotal information exchange as well as ongoing research and developmental projects, means that interruptions in the underlying treaty regime are ideally avoided. Accordingly, stop-gap measures are introduced,[77] such as the provisional entry into force of the successor agreement if the stringent requirements for its definitive entry into force are not fulfilled upon the termination of the predecessor agreement.

5.1.2. *The Operation of Provisional Entry into Force and Provisional Application*

The way in which provisional entry into force and provisional application help to bridge gaps between predecessor and successor commodity

---

[73] Palitha K.B. Kohona, "Some Legal Problems Relating to the Implementation of International Commodity Agreements," *Indian Journal of International Law* 21 (1981): 550–51; see also Henry G. Schermers and Niels M. Blokker, *International Institutional Law*, 4th ed. (Boston: Martinus Nijhoff Publishers, 2004), 35 fn. 136 (on the International Coffee Organization).

[74] Kohona, "Implementation of International Commodity Agreements," 551.

[75] Geslin, *Application provisoire*, 50, 52.

[76] Ibid.; Eisemann, *L'Organisation Internationale du Commerce des produits de base*, 285.

[77] An example of another stop-gap measure is the extension of duration of the 'old' agreement where appropriate.

agreements will now be explored. Frequently, for the treaty's provisional entry into force, the aforementioned stringent requirements for definitive entry into force, in terms of participating exporting and importing States and/or the requirement that they represent a certain percentage of the world trade in the respective commodity, stay the same.[78] The sole difference is that those States that deposit declarations of provisional application will be considered to have satisfied the requirements for *provisional* entry into force, while only those States that deposit instruments expressing their consent to be bound by the treaty, i.e. instruments of ratification, acceptance, approval or accession, will be taken into account as satisfying the requirements for the *definitive* entry into force of the commodity agreements. Alternatively, in some cases for the treaty's provisional entry into force, the stringent entry into force requirements in terms of numbers and trade percentage are lowered,[79] in addition to the fact that declarations of provisional application will count towards achieving these requirements alongside instruments expressing consent to be bound. Both mechanisms describe the default provisional entry into force rule of commodity agreements (i.e. provisional entry into force is brought about by the fulfilment of certain criteria concerning the participation of importing and exporting countries). Alternatively, in case the numerical and percentage requirements for the treaty's provisional entry into force cannot be met by the time the predecessor agreement expires, States which either expressed their consent or deposited a declaration of provisional application can agree to bring the treaty into force between themselves, be it provisionally or definitively.[80]

The above shows that in the complex entry into force stipulations of commodity agreements 'provisional application' and 'provisional entry into force', while designating different phenomena, are linked. They are linked in that a State's unilateral declaration of provisional application counts towards achieving the stringent numerical requirements for the treaty's provisional entry into force. They are also linked in that a State making such a declaration is entitled, together with States having expressed their consent to be bound by the treaty, to agree to put the treaty in force among themselves, be it provisionally or definitively, in case

[78] Chimni, *International Commodity Agreements*, 83.

[79] Ibid. See, e.g., the UNCTAD International Tropical Timber Agreement (concluded 27 January 2006, entered into force 7 December 2011) UN Doc TD/TIMBER.3/12, Article 39(1), (2).

[80] UN SecGen Summary of Practice, [239].

the stringent numerical requirements for the treaty's provisional entry into force are not met.

Against the background of these preliminary remarks on the function of provisional entry into force and provisional application in commodity agreements, the statements as to their legal force can now be analysed.

5.2. *The Binding Force of Commodity Agreements Provisionally in Force*

No statement has been found which is explicitly limited to the binding force or legal effects of commodity agreements provisionally in force. Nevertheless, there are two statements contained in UN publications which seem to have been made with the specific understanding of provisional entry into force in the context of commodity agreements in mind.[81]

---

[81] One of these statements, following the introductory paragraph on provisional entry into force which is not explicitly limited to provisional entry into force in commodity agreements, acknowledges that "provisional entry into force is a mechanism *usually* employed in commodity agreements", Final Clauses of Multilateral Treaties Handbook 66, section K.2. (Emphasis added). Further testament to the assumption that the statement was drafted with the specific use of 'provisional entry into force' in the context of commodity agreements in mind is the fact that the greater part of the statement, following the general introduction, is confined to commodity agreements. Moreover, the only example given in the entire paragraph is a provisional entry into force clause of a commodity agreement. With regard to both statements the assumption that they were drafted with the specific use of 'provisional entry into force' in the context of commodity agreements in mind mainly rests on the following two reasons. First, both statements distinguish between 'provisional entry into force' and 'provisional application'. As has been mentioned earlier, this distinction is typical and broadly recognised in the context of commodity agreements. However, not one instance of an agreement has been found outside of the context of commodity agreements which would apply this distinction in the sense that 'provisional entry into force' would relate to the treaty and its status, whereas provisional application would be used to designate a State's unilateral declaration to give effect to the treaty prior to its (definitive) entry into force. Similarly, academic writings outside the field of commodity agreements do not generally maintain that the terms 'provisional entry into force' and 'provisional application' would need to be distinguished (nor do they simply apply the distinction without explaining it). Thus, the distinction between 'provisional entry into force' and 'provisional application' does not seem to exist outside the context of commodity agreements. Second, the fact that the very first sentence in the statements on 'provisional application' associates the mechanism with a unilateral declaration is also typical for commodity agreements. While of course this is one way in which provisional application in general can be effected, it would not necessarily be the first way coming to mind when explaining provisional application outside the context of commodity agreements. A glance at Article 25 would seem to confirm that the explanation of provisional application by immediate reference to a unilateral declaration is less inspired by the general understanding of the notion (Article 25 does not once refer to a unilateral declaration) than by the notion's specific use in commodity agreements – possibly for the reason that this specific use may predate the adoption and entry into force of the VCLT 1969 (and simply may not have been adjusted). On this reasoning see also Michie "Provisional Application," 78, the text preceding footnote 392.

Thus, they implicitly seem to relate specifically to commodity agreements. One such statement is published in the "Final Clauses of Multilateral Treaties" Handbook.[82] It provides that upon provisional entry into force, a treaty "creates *obligations* for the parties that agreed to bring it into force in such manner" (emphasis added).[83] This recourse to treaty terminology might well be an indication that commodity agreements which are provisionally in force are regarded as legally binding. The other statement is taken from the glossary attached to the UN Treaty Collection Treaty Reference Guide[84] and can be seen to confirm this first impression. According to it, a treaty provisionally in force is "binding" upon the parties to it.[85] Moreover, "the nature of the legal obligations resulting from provisional entry into force would appear to be the same as the legal obligations in a treaty that has entered into force" since "it is the criteria for formal entry into force that have not been met but the legal standard of the obligations remains."[86] According to this statement a commodity agreement would appear to be legally binding whether it is provisionally or definitively in force. The reason adduced for this is that provisional entry into force means nothing but the failure to meet the stringent definitive entry into force criteria. Thus, the legal standard of the obligations contained in the commodity agreement remains the same, namely that they are (legally) binding also when the treaty is provisionally in force.

In conclusion, these are the only two statements which may be seen to implicitly express an opinion on the binding force or legal effects of commodity agreements provisionally in force. So understood they can be seen as supporting the view that commodity agreements provisionally in force are legally binding.

5.3. *The Legal Effects of the Provisional Application of Commodity Agreements*

After having analysed the views found on the legal effects of a commodity agreement which is provisionally in force, the question arises whether States which provisionally apply such an agreement are legally bound

82 UNOLA Final Clauses Handbook, 2003, http://treaties.un.org/doc/source/publications/FC/English.pdf.

83 UNOLA Final Clauses Handbook, 66, section K.2.

84 Available at http://treaties.un.org/Pages/Overview.aspx?path=overview/glossary/page1_en.xml.

85 Section 17.2. on 'provisional entry into force'.

86 Ibid.

by it. This question seems to be contested in practice. According to one view States, upon a declaration or notification of provisional application concerning a commodity agreement, *largely* have the same rights and obligations under that agreement as States which have expressed their consent to be bound by it. Thus, based on this understanding, States which provisionally apply a commodity agreement are bound by it. They are obliged to perform it in good faith – to the extent that such performance is consistent with existing 'laws and regulations', at least if the commodity agreement in question contains a limitation clause concerning its provisional application by States. By contrast, the opposing view understands the provisional application of a commodity agreement to amount broadly speaking to a soft law undertaking, involving moral or political implications rather than legally binding obligations.

5.3.1. *The View that Provisional Application of Commodity Agreements Involves Legally Binding Rights and Obligations*

Several statements have been found in the practice of States and international organisations which support the former view. In an institutional response given on behalf of the sole commodity institution which participated in the 2007–2008 questionnaire, the view was expressed that States which provisionally apply a commodity agreement are legally bound to do so, and that the *pacta sunt servanda* principle applies during that period. In addition to that it was explained that the consequences of breach are the same whether a State has declared to provisionally apply the commodity agreement or expressed its consent to be bound by it. The view that a declaration of provisional application binds the State legally, as opposed to morally or politically, has also been expressed by the then Assistant Legal Adviser for Treaty Affairs to the US Department of State, as the following statement illustrates:

> It is very difficult, if not impossible, to perceive any valid basis for considering the effect of the deposit of a declaration of provisional application as being limited to "moral implications". There does not appear to be any basis for such an interpretation either in the provisions of the Convention itself or in generally recognized treaty law and practice.[87]

[87] The statement is taken from a memorandum written by Charles Bevans, "Law of Treaties and Other International Agreements," *Digest of United States Practice in International Law* 2 (1974): § 2, 235. Bevans originally expressed the view when, as Assistant Legal Adviser for Treaty Affairs, performing the US's duties as a depositary of the 1971 Food Convention. As the view of a depositary, the statement does not amount to US practice in

Thus, in the above quotation the then Assistant Legal Adviser declares as unfounded and completely rejects the view according to which the effects of a declaration of provisional application could be moral rather than legal. In the part following the above quotation he moves on to show the contrary, namely that States provisionally applying the Convention in question largely have the same rights and obligations as States which have expressed their consent to be bound by it. Admittedly, this part of his statement, in which he affirms the *legal* effects of declarations of provisional application, relates specifically to the Convention in question.[88] Thus, his memorandum does not contain an explicit statement which would affirm the legal consequences of declarations of provisional application with regard to commodity agreements in general. However, in light of the above complete and unequivocal rejection of the opposing view it is rather likely that underlying the statement affirming the legal consequences of declarations of provisional application with regard to the Convention in question, is the view that declarations of provisional application concerning commodity agreements *in general* involve legally binding rights and obligations, and oblige a State to perform the treaty.

Finally, further support for this view, albeit limited to the binding force of a specific treaty, can be found in a Report of the Secretary General on 'Examples of Precedents of Provisional Application…' requested in the context of the negotiations of UNCLOS.[89] In that report the Secretary General expresses the opinion that a State's provisional application of the 1968 Sugar agreement[90] involves "the *full range* of *rights*, *duties* and responsibilities […] thereby coming into operation before the Agreement entered into force definitively." (Emphasis added)[91] Thus, in this quotation

---

treaty-matters. However, the memorandum has been selected by the Department of State for inclusion in a "Digest of US Practice in International Law". The inclusion of the memorandum in such a publication implies that the State Department regards the memorandum as reflecting the US view and practice regarding declarations of provisional application and their legal effects. Thus, it is on this latter basis that the memorandum is regarded as US practice. See C. E. Maw, "Introduction," *Digest of United States Practice in International Law* 1 (1973): iii.

88 Food Aid Convention 1971 (concluded 29 March 1971, entered into force 18 June 1971) 22 UST 971. Bevans, "Law of Treaties and Other International Agreements," 236.

89 'Examples of Precedents of Provisional Application, Pending their Entry into Force, of Multilateral Treaties, Especially Treaties which have Established International Organizations and/or Regimes' requested by the Committee on the Peaceful Uses of the Sea-bed and the Ocean Floor Beyond the Limits of National Jurisdiction, UN Doc A/AC.138/88 of 12 June 1973 (hereinafter 'Precedents of Provisional Application').

90 International Sugar Agreement 1968 (concluded 3 December 1968, entered into force provisionally on 1 January 1969, and definitively on 17 June 1969) 654 UNTS 3.

91 Precedents of Provisional Application, 579.

the Secretary General explicitly says that 'rights' and 'duties' are involved in a State's provisional application (he even says they are involved in their 'full range') so that there can be little doubt that the he regards a State's provisional application of the 1968 Sugar agreement as involving legally binding rights and obligations, prior to the treaty's definitive entry into force for the respective State.

These are the three statements found of States and international organisation which would seem to support the view that commodity agreements are legally binding when provisionally applied by a State. In the following section further evidence of this understanding will be examined. This further evidence is derived from actors whose statements do not amount to 'practice' of States and international organisation. Yet these statements were made by 'sources' who are likely to be informed by practice and for this reason are relevant to the analysis at hand, for example, the views expressed by a former UN legal adviser (on commodity agreements) and the summary of practice of the UN Secretary General as depositary of multilateral treaties, given that these multilateral treaties include commodity agreements and the declarations of provisional application relating thereto.

The summary of practice of the UN Secretary General leaves no doubt that the UN Office of Legal Affairs, when discharging the Secretary General's depositary tasks,[92] regards declarations or notifications of provisional application as (legally) binding instruments.[93] On several occasions and in different contexts, the summary of practice mentions notifications or declarations of provisional application as examples of legally "binding instruments" which, for instance, "will create new obligations, or increase or limit existing ones."[94] While the summary of practice does not limit these statements to notifications or declarations of provisional application in the context of commodity agreements, the statement certainly includes these,[95] so that it also expresses a view on the binding force of a commodity agreement which a State is applying provisionally based on a notification or declaration to such an effect.

Finally, the view that States which provisionally apply a commodity agreement largely enjoy the same rights and obligations as States which

---

92 Aust, *Modern Treaty Law*, 328 and Richard Caddell, "Depositary," last modified June 2006, in *MPEPIL online*, ed. Rüdiger Wolfrum, [13].

93 UN SecGen Summary of Practice [105], [149], see also [120].

94 Ibid.

95 See, e.g., the reference in ibid [149c] to [238]–[240].

expressed their consent to be bound by the agreement is confirmed in a statement of a former UN official.[96] (His views can be regarded as those of an expert in the field since he acted as legal adviser at commodity conferences convened to negotiate international commodity agreements and assisted international commodity organisations with the interpretation of their agreements and rules.[97]) In a piece which provides suggestions on how to simplify international commodity agreements, the former adviser submits that the distinction between a State's provisional and definitive application of commodity agreements should be abandoned, given that States "have the same obligations, financial or otherwise, in an ICO [international commodity organisation] regardless of whether they apply the agreement on a provisional or a definitive basis."[98]

In conclusion only few statements have been found expressing the view according to which States provisionally applying commodity agreements largely enjoy the same rights and obligations as States which have expressed their consent to be bound by it. However, all of the statements found are unqualified and unconditioned, and the overall support for the view in these statements is unequivocal. Also, although two of the three statements date back to the 1970s, there is also one recent statement which forcefully expounds this view. Hence, together with the further recent support found in the views expressed by experts in the field, it would seem that the support voiced for this view in statements is continuous and unequivocal.

5.3.2. *The View that a Declaration of Provisional Application is Non-Legally Binding*

The opposing view regards declarations of provisional application in the context of commodity agreements as non-legally binding. Following such a declaration, States may be politically or morally bound to apply the treaty pending its entry into force for them, but they are not legally bound to do so.

This view seems to have been advanced, albeit cautiously, in a legal opinion of the Secretariat of the United Nations.[99] The Executive Director of the International Cocoa Organisation had sought the Secretariat's advice *inter alia* on the question whether a notification of "intention to

---

96 Chrispeels, "Simplifying International Commodity Agreements," 357.
97 Ibid., 349.
98 Ibid., 357.
99 1976 UN Juridical Yearbook 221, no. 24.

apply the agreement provisionally" can be considered the legal equivalent to a "notification of provisional application".[100] It is in this context that the Secretariat expounded its view on the nature and effects of declarations of provisional application in the context of commodity agreements – after admitting that it was "not fully informed about what 'provisional application' and 'provisional entry into force' mean[t] in the actual practice of commodity organizations."[101] On the basis of its knowledge of some instances in which States provisionally applying a commodity agreement failed to strictly comply with the agreement's terms (but these States were still counted towards the provisional entry into force requirements), the Secretariat put forward the view that provisional application may mean "only that pending ratification States *will do their best*, within their existing legislation, to apply the agreement."[102] (Emphasis added). Thus, the Secretariat does not explicitly say that a declaration of provisional application involves morally or politically, rather than legally, binding obligations. However, its recourse to the hortatory phrase, that "States will do their best" would seem to suggest that the Secretariat regards these as soft undertakings rather than legally binding ones, even if it is very cautious in advancing this view.[103]

Further support for the view that a State's provisional application of a commodity agreement does not involve legally binding obligations can be found in the United Nations' "Final Clauses of Multilateral Treaties" Handbook. The handbook sets out that it is possible for a State to provisionally apply a treaty also after the treaty's (provisional or definitive) entry into force. It is in this context that the handbook expresses the view that such provisional application comprises the possibility "to give effect to the treaty *without incurring the legal commitments under it.*"[104] (Emphasis added). When a treaty does not give rise to legal commitments or obligations for a State which has declared that it will provisionally apply the treaty this would seem to imply that the State upon such declaration is not legally bound by the treaty. While the statement by its wording leaves open whether provisional application could have another meaning than the one just summarised, this is the only meaning or explanation provided

[100] Ibid. (see the heading and the last question which was submitted for advice).

[101] Ibid., 222, no. 24.

[102] Ibid.

[103] The relevant paragraph contains at least three 'disclaimers' expressing the Secretariat's uncertainty surrounding the meaning of 'provisional application' in the practice of commodity agreements.

[104] UNOLA Final Clauses Handbook, 44, section G.2.

by the handbook of instances where a State applies a treaty provisionally after the treaty's (provisional or definitive) entry into force.

Finally, the most explicit support for the view that declarations of provisional application in the context of commodity agreements do involve morally or politically, but not legally binding obligations can be found in statements which relate to declarations of provisional application of specific commodity agreements. First, the then legal advisers of the EEC Commission apparently perceived a declaration of provisional application concerning the 1971 Food Aid Convention as being limited to moral implications.[105] More precisely the advisers are quoted to have wanted "the '*moral*' implications of the declaration of provisional application to be translated into some binding, inescapable formal obligation", by requiring the respective country to deposit an instrument of ratification instead of the declaration of provisional application. This clearly shows that the then legal advisers of the EEC perceived a declaration of provisional application concerning the 1971 Food Aid Convention as involving moral implications rather than legally binding obligations. The second statement advancing this view has been expressed by a Working Party during the drafting of the 1962 Wheat Agreement.[106] The Working Party in charge of 'Legal and Drafting' submitted the view that the notification of provisional application by a government under the respective draft provision of the Convention "would not give rise to legal rights and obligations..."[107] Instead a "Government will only have legal rights and obligations after the deposit of its instrument of acceptance of accession."[108] This statement, again, makes clear that the relevant Working Party perceived notifications of provisional application concerning the 1962 Wheat Agreement as not giving rise to legal rights and obligations under the Convention. Admittedly these last two statements were made in the context of declarations or notifications of provisional application concerning specific commodity agreements. Nevertheless it is not inconceivable that the statements express a general view on the matter given the overall similarity in drafting and content that the clauses on entry into force and notifications or declarations of provisional application in commodity agreements share.

---

105 The view of the legal advisers of the then EEC is mentioned in the introduction to a memorandum by Bevans, "Law of Treaties and Other International Agreements," § 2, 235.

106 444 UNTS 3, for the statement see "Developing International Economic Law," *Whiteman Digest of International Law* 14, § 10, 665.

107 Ibid.

108 Ibid.

In conclusion statements which support the view according to which declarations of provisional application involve morally or politically – but not legally – binding obligations are similarly rare as the above statements supporting the opposing view. Three out of the four statements found which advance the non-legally binding view were made in the 1970s. Thus, little recent support was found for this view in statements by States and international organisations. Moreover, it is rather tentatively that the UN Secretariat puts forward this view, admitting beforehand that it is "not fully informed about what 'provisional application' ... mean[s] in the actual practice of commodity organizations."[109] All in all, the support found for this view mainly dates back to the 1970s and is not always wholehearted or unequivocal.

5.3.3. *Evaluation and Conclusion*

There are several points which can be made with regard to the above summary of statements on the nature and effects of declarations of provisional application concerning commodity agreements. First, with regard to statements by States and international organisations, there is in terms of quantity no clear majority or minority view. Yet the statements supporting the non-legally binding effects overall seem less recent, and they are not always expressed in a wholehearted manner. By contrast, the statements advancing the view of the legally binding effects of declarations of provisional application are all unequivocal in their support. Also, while some date back to the 1970s, one statement is rather recent. When the views expressed by experts in the field are taken into account, there is even more recent support for this view. Overall, then, the support for the view which ascribes legal nature and legal effects to declarations of provisional application, prevails. One possible explanation of this result would be that the matter of the binding force of declarations of provisional application was contested in the 1970s, but that since then the view that they involve legally binding rights and obligations has won ground.

Second, as an aside, it is noteworthy that the UN in its different statements adheres to both opposing views. The fact that these different views are put forward during the same decade would seem to show that different views on the nature and effects of declarations of provisional application

[109] UN Juridical Yearbook 222 (1976), no. 24.

exist within the UN, so that this would not appear to be a case of a change of position over time.

Finally, a theoretical point can be made when analysing the views on the nature and effects of declarations of provisional application, and for the sake of argument it will be assumed that declarations of provisional application give rise to moral rather than legal obligations. This, it is submitted, can create problems of logical consistency with the above view on the binding force of commodity agreements provisionally in force. It may be recalled that the sole view found on the binding force and effects of commodity agreements provisionally in force was that these agreements are legally binding and largely involve the same rights and obligations as treaties which are definitively in force. The consistency problem arises because declarations of provisional application can help bring about the provisional entry into force of a commodity agreement. If indeed these declarations are understood to give rise to moral rather than legal implications, then the absurd situation could arise whereby a commodity agreement upon its provisional entry into force is legally binding although this provisional entry into force rests solely on non-legally binding declarations of provisional application.[110] Thus, the commodity agreement would be legally binding although not a single participant would be legally bound by the agreement, due to the moral, rather than legal, effects ascribed to declarations of provisional application. This situation is highly hypothetical, but the problem of logical consistency is real. It already arises if only half of the States (or a few more) make declarations of provisional application. Is it then possible to regard the treaty which, with the help of these declarations, enters into force provisionally as a legally binding treaty? The simple solution to this dilemma may be that the above view on the legally binding force of commodity agreements provisionally in force is incorrect. But if it is correct, then it may be interesting to see whether in practice there is a solution to this problem of logical consistency, or whether indeed declarations of provisional application concerning commodity agreements generally give rise to *legal* consequences so that the problem does not arise. It will be for a further analysis of commodity agreements under a different angle in the second part of this chapter to examine whether indeed the problem of logical consistency arises in the practice of commodity agreements.

---

110 See also the anonymous article "Three International Commodity Agreements," *British Yearbook of International Law* 35 (1959): 243–44.

6. Conclusion

This conclusion will begin with the last subject of analysis, namely commodity agreements that have been analysed separately from other agreements due to their different use of terminology. With regard to the provisional entry into force of commodity agreements statements have been found which would appear to suggest that these agreements are largely regarded as legally binding. While it seems to have been contested in the 1970s whether declarations of provisional application concerning commodity agreements have only moral implications or involve legally binding obligations, the evidence would suggest that, since then, these declarations have come to be perceived as involving legally binding rights and obligations for the relevant States under the commodity agreement in question. Thus, to the greater part the views expressed by States and international organisations on provisional entry into force and provisional application in the field of commodity agreements indicate that both nowadays are seen to involve legally binding obligations.

By contrast, the views expressed by States and international organisations on the legal nature and binding force of provisional application in general, diverge. The above analysis has shown that there are at least three different views on the matter. According to one view, provisionally applied treaties are legally binding; another considers them 'not legally binding';[111] and a third view holds that they can be binding or non-legally binding. Following the discussion of academic writings in chapters 2 and 3, the first two views derived from statements from States and international organisations are not surprising, to the point that the majority view derived from statements is the majority view in academic writings, and the same is true for the first minority view. However, the above third view derived from statements, that these treaties can be both, either binding or non-legally binding would not appear to be put forward or discussed in academic writings on the matter. This would appear to be a new result derived from the above analysis.

To the extent that the first two views are understood to include binding force, or the absence thereof, in the definition of provisional application, they would appear to rely on the criterion of intention, upon which generally the binding force (or absence thereof) in an international law agreement depends. Therefore, the next part of the chapter will take a closer

[111] On the use of this term, see note 40 (in chapter 4) above.

look at the intention of States and international organisations to be bound (or not) during the period of provisional application by examining their treaty practice in this regard.

B. The Binding Force of Provisionally Applied Treaties: Treaty Practice and the Intention of the 'Parties'

7. Introduction

This part of the chapter considers the binding force of provisionally applied treaties by reference to the intention of the parties. Practice, case-law and academic opinion agree that intention is the main criterion for establishing the binding force of agreements in international law in general. In addition, the criterion also seems to be relied upon to some extent in practice in the specific context of provisional application as has been shown earlier. It may seem odd at first to try answering the question of the binding force of provisionally applied treaties *in general* by reference to the criterion of intention, given that such intention normally relates to an individual agreement, i.e. to *just one* instance of provisional application. Clearly, applied in this way the criterion of intention does not provide any information as to a 'general intention' or view of States and international organisations concerning the binding force of provisionally applied treaties. It is for this reason that the intention of States and international organisations will be analysed with regard to a multitude of agreements on provisional application, in order to gain an overview of the binding force of provisionally applied treaties and to understand patterns and regularities, including the frequency or rarity of an intention to be bound during that period.

8. The Wording and Content of Agreements on Provisional Application

In the following section the parties' intention to be bound (or otherwise) will be established by reference to the wording and content of agreements on provisional application. By these is meant the agreement specifically concerning provisional application, whether expressed in a final clause of the treaty or in an agreement which is separate to the main treaty such as an exchange of notes.[112] As regards the wording of these agreements a distinction can be made between those agreements which are phrased in treaty language and those which are phrased in non-treaty language; the former will now be analysed.

8.1. *Agreements Using Treaty Language, Form or Nomenclature*

More precisely the following part will examine agreements which are phrased in treaty language and whose form and nomenclature, at least sometimes, may entail further indications as to the parties' intention to be bound. It is these rather formal indications of an intention to be bound which all of these agreements have in common. Some display additional indications of an intention to be bound. Their content may either be potentially indicative of an intention to be bound, or, in rare cases, the content (and wording thereof) clearly expresses the parties' intention to be bound during provisional application. These categories will now be examined in more detail, starting with those agreements whose content is not necessarily indicative of an intention to be bound.

8.1.1. *Agreements Whose Content is not Necessarily Indicative of an Intention to be Bound*

The typical content of brief provisional application clauses would not appear to be indicative of an intention to be bound. Frequently, recourse

---

[112] It is submitted that the agreements on provisional application may express an intention to be bound (or otherwise) whether they are contained in a separate agreement or in a final clause of the treaty. In the latter case it is not disputed that a hard instrument can contain soft clauses. Thus while it is clear that the treaty as such is intended to be binding upon its entry into force (hard instrument), the clause providing for provisional application may still contain non-treaty language and thereby express the intention not to be legally bound during provisional application (soft clause). Examples of provisionally applied treaties which contain soft clauses (and thus clearly could have contained – but did not – a soft clause on provisional application) were mainly found in Aviation agreements, see, e.g.: UK–Iceland Air Transport Agreement 1950, 95 UNTS 277, soft clause: Article 10(1) [dispute settlement], final clause on provisional application in treaty language: Article 14(2); Belgium–Greece Air Transport Agreement 1949, 137 UNTS 215, soft law clause: Article 9 [consultations], final clause on provisional application in treaty language: Article 14; UK–Colombia Air Services Agreement 1947, 160 UNTS 297, soft clause: Article 10(1) [dispute settlement], clause on provisional application in treaty language: Article 13(b); UK–Spain Air Services Agreement 1950, 398 UNTS 101, soft clauses: Articles 12(a) [dispute settlement], 13 [use of best endeavours to reach agreement upon certain minimal facilities to be offered at airports...]; UK–Panama Aviation Agreement 1951, 560 UNTS 143, soft clause: Article X(1) [dispute settlement], clause on provisional application in treaty language: Article XIII(2); Canada–Netherlands Air Transport Agreement 1974, 987 UNTS 113, soft clause: Article XVII(1) [dispute settlement], clause on provisional application in treaty language: Article XXI.

is had to a 'short formula of agreeing on provisional application', a typical example of which would be the following:

"This agreement shall be applied provisionally from 1st January 2006."[113] Or

"This agreement shall enter into force provisionally on the date of signature, and definitively as soon as it has been ratified by both Contracting Parties."[114]

Thus the short formula agreement in its simplest form consists of two elements: the undertaking of provisional application and its commencement. Often there is also a reference to the treaty's entry into force,[115] be it within the provisional application clause or within its direct vicinity. This would appear to be the typical minimal content of agreements on provisional application, and this minimal content as such would not seem to be useful for establishing the intention of the parties to the agreement.

In other instances the agreement on provisional application is more detailed and contains additional elements of regulation or information concerning provisional application, for example, on the termination of provisional application[116] or the reason why recourse was had to this mechanism in the present instance.[117] Another addendum is a limitation clause, i.e. a clause according to which the treaty shall be provisionally applied 'only to the extent that it is compatible with internal law'. The effect of limitation clauses and of the power of unilateral termination on agreements on provisional application, and the question whether these features allow any conclusions on the authors' intention to be bound by them has been examined in chapter two under theoretical aspects. Since the analysis of practice in the present chapter has not produced any new insights, the result of the above analysis remains valid, namely that these features generally do not (individually or combined) provide any indication as to the existence or absence of an intention to be bound.

---

[113] Netherlands–UK Pipeline Agreement 2005, 2398 UNTS 251, Article 20(2). For a similar example in a multilateral treaty see, e.g., "Mir" Inter-State Television Agreement 1993, 1971 UNTS 11, Article 15(1).

[114] UK–Argentina Air Services Agreement 1946, 164 UNTS 53, Article 12(1); see also Belgo-Luxembourg Economic Union–Morocco Investment Agreement 1965, 620 UNTS 171, Article 8(1).

[115] Alternatively, the reference is sometimes to the method of expressing consent to be bound by the respective treaty or both (entry into force and expression of consent).

[116] UK–Iceland Air Transport Agreement 1950, 95 UNTS 277, Article 14.

[117] See, e.g., agreements which provide for provisional application and are concluded under the auspices of the Council of Europe, such as e.g. Convention on the Elaboration of a European Pharmacopoeia, CETS No. 50, Article 17.

Following this short introduction to the typical content of agreements on provisional application and its general insignificance for determining an intention to be bound, an analysis of the wording of these agreements will now be undertaken, starting with agreements which are separate from the main treaty.

8.1.1.1. *Provisional Application in a Separate Agreement*

When provisional application is brought about by a separate agreement, this agreement can take different forms. Most frequently, it is either a protocol or an exchange of notes, but there are also instances in which the agreement on provisional application is contained in a final act to the conference adopting the treaty in question. (On a technical note it may be added that the following analysis of protocols and exchanges of notes is limited to those instances in which the sole purpose and content of these separate agreements consists in providing for provisional application; this means that all manifestations of an intention to be bound would seem to relate to the treaty's provisional application.[118])

Some protocols of provisional application are drafted in treaty language throughout the entire body of the agreement, i.e. the preamble (the Parties have *agreed* as follows), the main part regulating the substance of the agreement (*shall; undertake; agree* etc.) and the final formal part of a treaty, the *testimonium*[119] ('*done at*'; and when the text was drawn up in different languages it is remarked that these are '*equally authentic*'). According to the guidance notes on treaty and non-treaty language of some governments,[120] these are all unambiguous examples of treaty language, and it is explicitly advised to use them only when concluding a legally binding agreement. Besides the language, the form of some of these protocols may also be an indication of an intention to be bound by them, for instance, when the agreement displays a formal *testimonium* usually used at the end of treaties, since (in this form) it does not generally appear in non-legally binding agreements.[121] Finally the nomenclature, which is employed either in the title of the agreement or in its main body in order to refer to the agreement, may also be indicative of an intention

[118] The deliberations, which are developed under section 2.1.1.3., apply *mutatis mutandis* to the other instances (when provisional application is agreed in a separate agreement but the separate agreement also regulates other matters).

[119] See Aust, *Modern Treaty Law*, 441.

[120] See, e.g., FCO, *Treaties and MOUs*, and US State Department, "Non-Binding Documents".

[121] Ibid., 444 (on MOUs).

to be bound.[122] Some of these undertakings indeed refer to themselves as 'agreements'[123] which again is treaty language and a term governments explicitly advise using solely when drafting a legally binding agreement.

All the above indications of intention, i.e. wording, form and nomenclature, point in the direction that these agreements on provisional application were intended to be legally binding. Given that the sole purpose of these agreements is to bring about the provisional application of another treaty (and indeed this is what their entire content is about), it seems unlikely that these manifestations could relate to anything but the undertaking of provisional application. Thus, it is submitted that in instances such as these, there are good grounds for assuming that the parties to these agreements intended to be legally bound to provisionally apply the treaty in question.

Provisional application of a treaty may also be agreed in an exchange of notes following the conclusion of the treaty. When the wording in both notes consists of treaty language, this would seem to be the main indication of an intention to be bound. In addition, the nomenclature used in an exchange of notes may be indicative. The clause determining the nature of the agreement resulting from this exchange,[124] in particular, lends itself to an expression of intention through recourse to either treaty or non-treaty language. Thus, when it is said that "both notes shall be regarded as constituting an *agreement*"[125] between the two Governments the nomenclature would seem to entail another clear indication of an intention to be bound.[126] Admittedly, the form of an exchange of notes does not change even if the resulting agreement is not intended to be legally binding.[127] Nevertheless, it is submitted that the consistent recourse to treaty language in an exchange of notes as well as in the nomenclature used would

---

122 UN Treaty Reference Guide, Part I, Introduction., http://treaties.un.org/Pages/Overview.aspx?path=overview/definition/page1_en.xml.

123 See, e.g., the *Agreement* Providing for the Provisional Application of the Draft International Customs Convention on Touring ... 1949, 45 UNTS 149 (emphasis added).

124 See, e.g., Richard K. Gardiner, *Treaty Interpretation* (Oxford: Oxford University Press, 2008), 78 (according to whom an Exchange of Notes is "usually identifiable as a treaty *by a specific statement in the notes that together they are to constitute an agreement*" (emphasis added).

125 See the Netherlands–Japan Exchange of Notes 2008 concerning the Provisional Application of the Agreement on Social Security 2008, http://www.minbuza.nl/en/Key_Topics/Treaties/Search_the_Treaty_Database?isn=010627.

126 See also Aust, *Modern Treaty Law*, 27.

127 Ibid., 445.

seem to be a strong indication of the parties' intention to be legally bound to provisionally apply the treaty in question.[128]

As has already been mentioned, sometimes agreements on provisional application are entailed in the Final Act of the conference which adopted the treaty in question. While a Final Act is mainly a summary of the proceedings of the conference,[129] there is nothing to prevent the conference participants from including any agreements supplementing the treaty in the Final Act if they see fit to do so.[130] These agreements may be legally binding or non-legally binding, and the manifestations of intention are the same as with any other agreement. One of the most famous examples of a Final Act entailing an (non-legally binding) agreement is the 1975 Helsinki Final Act of the Conference on Security and Co-operation in Europe.[131] Relevant for present purposes is the Final Act of the Helsinki Summit Conference (10 July 1992) which entails the States' agreement on the provisional application of the Treaty on Conventional Armed Forces in Europe (hereinafter "CFE").[132] While the text itself is referred to as being a "document",[133] it is "agreed" among the "States Parties" and not by the 'Conference'. This creates the possibility that the States Parties may have had recourse to their treaty-making capacity when entering into the agreement, a possibility which would not have existed had the document's author been the 'Helsinki Summit Conference' since it is unlikely that the Conference is endowed with international legal personality. The consistent recourse to treaty language (other than the reference to the text being

[128] With regard to the Agreement in the form of an Exchange of Letters concerning the provisional application of the trade and trade-related provisions of the Euro-Mediterranean Agreement establishing an Association between the European Communities and their Member States, of the one part, and the Arab Republic of Egypt, of the other part ([2003] OJ L 345/115) Michie quotes an EC Council Decision which seems to entail an explicit expression of the EC's intention to be bound during provisional application ([2003] OJ L 345/113); Michie, "Provisional Application," 66.

[129] UN Treaty Handbook, 60, http://treaties.un.org/doc/source/publications/THB/English.pdf. See also Aust, *Modern Treaty Law*, 92.

[130] This would seem to follow from the freedom of contract (and form) which is firmly established in public international law.

[131] The 1975 Helsinki Final Act is available at http://www.osce.org/documents/mcs/1975/08/4044_en.pdf.

[132] When the Treaty was adopted in November 1990, a protocol of provisional application (forming an integral part of the CFE treaty) was also agreed, see ILM 30 (1991): 67. This, however, only provided for the partial provisional application of the treaty. By contrast, the above 1992 agreement entailed in the Final Act relates to "all of the provisions of the Treaty", see [1] of the agreed text available at the US Department of State website, http://www.state.gov/s/l/65828.htm.

[133] Agreed text [5].

a "document") is an indication that the States Parties might well have intended to rely on their treaty-making capacity and to enter into a legally binding agreement. The word 'shall' is used six times throughout the five paragraphs of the text, four times relating to the CFE treaty's provisional application. Moreover, the basis for such provisional application is referred to as "the *agreement* reached by all States Parties" – as opposed to an 'understanding' or 'arrangement'. In light of all these signs, it is suggested that the States Parties may well have intended to be legally bound by the provisional application of the entire CFE treaty.

In conclusion to the analysis of separate agreements on provisional application in general, it is submitted that the consistent recourse to treaty language, nomenclature and form amounts to a strong indication of the States' intention to be bound during provisional application. This is even more convincing when the separate agreement is solely concerned with provisional application, since then all of these manifestations of intention necessarily relate to provisional application.

8.1.1.2. *Provisional Application Brought about by a Declaration or Notification*

It has been mentioned in the third chapter that sometimes provisional application is effected by a unilateral declaration or notification. For the clause on provisional application in the respective treaty this means that it does not express an agreement among all States to actually have recourse to provisional application but rather an agreement on the possibility to have recourse to provisional application if individual States so wish. Or to put it differently, here recourse to provisional application is 'subsidiary' in that it does not begin automatically at a certain time but needs to be triggered by a declaration or notification to such an effect. This involves the choice for every State whether or not to have recourse to provisional application. This choice notwithstanding (i.e. once the provisional application is triggered) the basic question remains whether the treaty is intended to be binding during its period of provisional application. In order to find an answer to that question the wording of the clauses inviting declarations or notifications of provisional application has been analysed. Sometimes, in addition to that, the text of the declarations or notifications was taken into account, if any were made and are accessible to the public.

Some clauses inviting declarations or notifications of provisional application are clearly drafted in treaty language. Examples of these are all clauses which use "shall" in relation to provisional application, such as the clause according to which a State may declare that "the provisions of this

Protocol *shall* apply to it on a provisional basis"[134] or that "it [the State] *shall* apply the treaty provisionally".[135] It is submitted that this treaty language would seem to indicate that the parties intended to be legally bound to provisionally apply the treaty once such a declaration of provisional application was made. Less clear, however, are the cases were the auxiliary verb in relation to provisional application is "will", whereas "shall" is used consistently in the remainder of the agreement.[136] Although "will" belongs to the 'code words' intended to manifest an intention, there are divergent views among governments as to which intention it actually does manifest. The UK and Canada use it to express an intention not to be legally bound.[137] By contrast, the US considers that its use does not necessarily signify an intention not to be bound.[138] It even advises against its use in non-legally binding agreements so as to avoid confusion.[139] Thus, based on the US guidelines, "will" could be used to manifest an intention to be legally bound whereas the UK and Canada would employ it to manifest the exact opposite. (The recourse to the word "will" is particularly problematic when the regulation of provisional application is contained in a brief final clause and the word "will" is the sole factor manifesting an intention.) The declarations or notifications often simply repeat the text of the clause inviting them so they are not particularly helpful in clarifying the meaning of "will" in the respective treaty clause.[140] In some instances

---

[134] Protocol No. 14 to the Convention for the Protection of Human Rights and Fundamental Freedoms, amending the Control System of the Convention, CETS 194,Article 7; see also Agreement for the Implementation of the Provisions of the United Nations Convention on the Law of the Sea of 10 December 1982 relating to the Conservation and Management of Straddling Fish Stocks and Highly Migratory Fish Stocks (adopted 4 August 1995, entered into force 11 December 2001) 2167 UNTS 3, Article 41; Agreement on the International Dolphin Conservation Programme 1998, [2005] OJ L 348/28, Article XXIX, the provisional application of which, upon such a declaration, may have been intended to be legally binding in light of the predominant (though not consistent) use of treaty terminology.

[135] Central European Free Trade Agreement 1992, see ILM 34 (1995): 8, Article 40(4).

[136] See, e.g., the Convention on Early Notification of a Nuclear Accident, 1439 UNTS 275, Article 13, and the Convention on Assistance in the Case of a Nuclear Accident or Radiological Emergency, 1457 UNTS 133, Article 15. See also Privileges and Immunities Agreement of the International Tribunal for the Law of the Sea 1997 (adopted 23 May 1997) 2167 UNTS 271, Article 31.

[137] FCO, *Treaties and MOUs*, 16. For Canadian Practice see Hugh M. Kindred et al., *International Law Chiefly as Interpreted and Applied in Canada*, 5th ed. (Toronto: Emond Montgomery, 1993), 88.

[138] US State Department, "Non-Binding Documents".

[139] Ibid.

[140] See, e.g., the declarations made pursuant to Article 13 of the Convention on Early Notification of a Nuclear Accident available at http://www.iaea.org/Publications/Documents/Conventions/cenna_reserv.pdf and the declarations made pursuant to

further information was found[141] or obtained upon request which suggests that in those instances "will" was used in order to manifest an intention to be legally bound. However, without any further information of this kind the word "will" alone would not seem a reliable indication of intention for the above reasons.

By way of conclusion it is submitted that the recourse to (uncontested) treaty language in the clause inviting declarations or notifications of provisional application would seem to indicate that the States intended the respective treaty to be legally binding during its period of provisional application.

8.1.1.3. *Provisional Application Agreed in the Treaty Itself*

States more frequently agree on provisional application within the treaty itself than by way of a separate agreement. Often such an agreement 'within the treaty itself' is contained in a final clause. Technically it may also be drawn up in a document of its own which is then designated to form 'an integral part' of the treaty.[142] In both instances intention to be bound is mainly manifested in the recourse to treaty language. Most frequently, the auxiliary verb 'shall' is employed (the treaty 'shall' be applied provisionally), or alternatively recourse is had to 'agree' or 'undertake' (the States 'agree' or 'undertakc' to provisionally apply the treaty). If provisional application is agreed according to the above-mentioned typical short formula 'this agreement shall be applied provisionally from [date/event]', it may well be that the sole manifestation of intention within that agreement lies in the "*shall* be applied provisionally". Put more generally, if the agreement on provisional application is drafted according to this short formula, the possibilities to manifest an intention to be bound are rather

Article 15 of the Convention on Assistance in the Case of a Nuclear Accident or Radiological Emergency respectively, available at http://www.iaea.org/Publications/Documents/Conventions/cacnare_reserv.pdf.

141 With regard to Article 35(4) of the Council of Europe Protocol Amending the European Convention on Transfrontier Television, CETS 171, the explanatory memorandum provides such further information, at [15]. Aust explains that while explanatory memoranda do not amount to authoritative interpretations, they are "approved by the government experts involved in drafting the respective instruments" and he suggests that "they provide an invaluable guide" to the respective instrument's interpretation, see Aust, *Modern Treaty Law,* 237–8. Thus, based on the committee's expertise this explanatory report contains a strong indication that the parties to the protocol regarded it as legally binding during its provisional application.

142 See, e.g., the Protocol on the Provisional Application of Certain Provisions of the Treaty on Conventional Armed Force in Europe, ILM 30 (1991): 67, which according to Article I(3) of the CFE treaty forms an integral part of the treaty.

limited – especially when compared to the various possibilities which exist when provisional application is agreed in a separate agreement whose sole purpose and content is to bring about the treaty's provisional application (recourse to treaty language, form and nomenclature). Nevertheless, it is submitted that if States did not intend to be bound during provisional application, they simply could express this intention also in the above short formula by recourse to typical soft law phrases, such as 'the parties *intend* to apply the treaty provisionally', 'the parties *shall endeavour* to apply the treaty provisionally' or '*shall seek* to apply the treaty provisionally'. After all, 'soft clauses in hard treaties' are a familiar feature in treaty practice.[143] Therefore, even if the manifestation of an intention to be bound consists in just one word, such recourse to treaty language would seem to be deliberate and accordingly would seem to indicate the parties' intention to be bound during provisional application.[144]

8.1.1.4. *Conclusion*

The above analysis of the wording, form and nomenclature of agreements on provisional application would seem to indicate that those are ways in which an intention to be bound during provisional application can be expressed. While this may seem to be a truism it is not as far as agreements on provisional application are concerned. In previous academic analyses, to the extent that the criterion of intention has been found relevant,[145] it has not been established by reference to the wording (form and

[143] See e.g. *Oil Platforms (Islamic Republic of Iran v United States of America) (Preliminary Objections)* [1996] ICJ Rep 803[52], in which the ICJ seems to have considered Article I of the Iran–US Treaty 1955 as a 'soft clause'. The Court then found it had jurisdiction to entertain the dispute on the very basis of that treaty [53], and thus clearly saw the treaty as such a legally binding instrument, albeit as one possibly containing a soft clause in Article I. For academic writings on soft clauses in hard treaties see especially Sztucki, "International Soft Law," 551–52, 560–61; see also Alan Boyle, "Some Reflections on the Relationship of Treaties and Soft Law," *International & Comparative Law Quarterly* 48 (1999): 902; Christine Chinkin, "Normative Development in the International Legal System," in *Commitment and Compliance*, ed. Dinah Shelton (Oxford: Oxford University Press, 2000), 25–6.

[144] With regard to the 1990 Protocol on the Provisional Application of Certain Provisions of the Treaty on Conventional Armed Forces in Europe a possible confirmation of this view has been found in an Article-by-Article Commentary published on the website of the US Office of the Under Secretary of Defence for Acquisition, Technology, and Logistics. If the views expressed in the Commentary were attributable to the US government, then this would amount to an indication of an intention to be bound by the Protocol at least by the US. The Commentary is at http://www.dod.mil/acq/acic/treaties/cfe/artbyart/analysis_provisional.htm.

[145] See Montag, *Völkerrechtliche Verträge*, 50–2; van Panhuys, "The Netherlands Constitution and International Law," 94.

nomenclature) of agreements on provisional application. In this sense the above analysis is a novelty. Its interim result would seem to be twofold. First, in the case of the type of agreement analysed above (the agreement is phrased in treaty language and its content is not necessarily indicative of an intention to be bound) States and international organisations would seem to intend to be bound to provisionally apply the respective treaty. Second, this type of agreement would seem to be the one to which States and international organisations have most frequent recourse to when agreeing on provisional application. Thus it would seem that in the majority of cases (i.e. whenever recourse is had to the above described type of agreement) States and international organisations intend to be legally bound to provisionally apply a treaty.

8.1.2. *Agreements Whose Content may be Indicative of an Intention to be Bound*

After having analysed agreements whose content is not indicative of an intention to be bound, those agreements whose content may potentially be indicative of such an intention will now be examined. A common feature of such agreements is that they regulate provisional application in more detail than the frequently encountered short formula of 'this agreement shall be provisionally applied...' Hence, this more detailed regulation, its content and additional wording may contain further indications of intention. The following analysis will identify some common features or contents of these agreements which have been found to be potentially indicative of intention.[146] First to be considered will be those instances in which the additional indication of intention lies in the reference to 'rights and/or obligations' relating to provisional application.

8.1.2.1. *'Rights and Obligations' During Provisional Application*

Some agreements employ terms such as 'rights' and/or 'obligations' when referring to the period of provisional application. These terms are 'treaty language', and can be an indication that the parties considered provisional application as involving legally binding rights and obligations – as if the treaty was in force. Examples of the use of these terms when specifically referring to the period of provisional application can be found in treaties

146 Commodity agreements are not included in the following analysis, since their use of the terms 'provisional application' and 'provisional entry into force' deviates from the general understanding of these terms. For this reason they will be analysed in a section concerned specifically with what they are, namely a 'special case' of the regime of provisional application and provisional entry into force.

setting up (or amending) Satellite Organisations,[147] in the Protocol of Provisional Application of the European Monetary Agreement[148] as well as the 1994 Energy Charter Treaty[149] (hereinafter 'ECT').[150] In the Energy Charter Treaty, the undertaking of the signatory Governments to provisionally apply the treaty, Article 45(1), is in other subsections of the same article referred to as an 'obligation' to do so. It is submitted that this recourse to treaty language, seeing that it occurs repeatedly, would seem to be deliberate. As such it could be seen as an expression of the parties' understanding that they are bound to provisionally apply the ECT, or put differently, that they are bound by the ECT during provisional application (to the extent that they agreed to this).[151] Accordingly, this would be an additional indication of an intention to be bound, alongside the recourse to treaty language in the clause expressing the agreement to have recourse to provisional application in Article 45(1) ECT.[152]

The other examples explicitly refer to 'rights and obligations' of States which so far have only provisionally applied the respective treaty and provide a legal regime applicable to such 'rights and obligations' in case of

---

[147] Agreement relating to the International Telecommunications Satellite Organization 'INTELSAT' (concluded 20 August 1971, entered into force 12 February 1973) 1220 UNTS 22, Article XX(c); Convention Establishing the European Telecommunications Satellite Organization EUTELSAT (concluded 15 July 1982, entered into force 1 September 1985) 1519 UNTS 175, Article XXII(d); Agreement relating to the International Telecommunications Satellite Organization (as amended, entry into force 30 November 2004), 2004 ATS 30, Article XVIII.

[148] Adopted 5 August 1955. Text is available at <http://www.minbuza.nl/en/key-topics/treaties/search-the-treaty-database>.

[149] Energy Charter Treaty, 2080 UNTS 95.

[150] Compare the EU–US Passenger Name Record Agreement 2007, [2007] OJ L 204/18, [9] where it is not entirely clear whether or not 'obligations' arise under the agreement from the commencement of provisional application, i.e. the date of signature. On this agreement and its predecessors in general from an EU perspective see Valsamis Mitsilegas, *EU Criminal Law* (Oxford: Hart Publishing, 2009), 298–308.

[151] The extent to which the ECT is provisionally applied varies. According to the first option, the ECT as a whole is provisionally applied (Article 45(1)), yet due to the limitation clause the actual extent to which this is done may vary from signatory to signatory (since a signatory agrees to apply the ECT provisionally "to the extent that such provisional application is not inconsistent with its constitution, laws or regulations". According to the second option, as provided for in Article 45(2), only part VII of the ECT is provisionally applied concerning its "Structure and Institutions". This enables signatories to participate in the institutional framework which is set up by the ECT, but means that they (or their investors) cannot derive any other benefits from the ECT (such as benefits which could be derived from the ECT's investment promotion and protection regime or its dispute settlement procedures), see Article 45(2)(b).

[152] See also the *Yukos* Tribunal, according to which Article 45(1) establishes a binding obligation, *Yukos Universal Ltd v Russian Federation* (30 November 2009), 227, [262] 98.

termination of the provisional application.[153] Such a regulation would appear to show that the parties considered it at least a possibility that 'rights' and 'obligations' would be generated during provisional application. Accordingly it would seem to follow that they perceived the provisionally applied treaty as a legally binding agreement.

After having dealt with clauses which directly or indirectly refer to 'rights and/or obligations' of States relating to provisional application, the next section will analyse clauses which specify the conduct expected during that period in a more concrete manner.

8.1.2.2. *Specification of Conduct Expected During Provisional Application*

The following agreements have in common that they do entail further specifications as to the conduct expected during the period of provisional application. In theory any kind of conduct is conceivable, but in practice this often concerns the payment of financial 'contributions'. The payment of these contributions may, for instance, arise under provisionally applied treaties which set up an international organisation.[154] Alternatively such payments may arise in the context of bilateral reciprocal agreements such as the commercial fishing protocols which the EC frequently concludes with third States, usually belonging to the African, Caribbean and Pacific Group States (ACP States).[155] In those agreements the financial contribution is given in return for fishing opportunities granted by a third State to the EC. Since these protocols are of a limited duration, new agreements pending their entry into force are frequently provisionally applied so as to enable the 'continuity of the fishing activities of the Community vessels'.[156] This is based on the understanding that financial payments "must"

153 See, for instance, the Protocol of Provisional Application of the European Monetary Agreement (concluded and entered into force 5 August 1955) Article 7(2).

154 Protocol of Provisional Application of the European Monetary Agreement, Article 6; Implementation Agreement 1994, 1836 UNTS 3, Annex, Section 1, No. 12(c). See also Convention on the Establishment of the International Institute for the Management of Technology 1971 (concluded 6 October 1971, entered into force 28 October 1974) 995 UNTS 164, Article 15(2), (3).

155 See, e.g., the 2nd paragraph of the Agreement on the Provisional Application of the Protocol Establishing the Fishing Opportunities and the Compensation Provided for in the Agreement between the European Economic Community and the Government of the Republic of Guinea-Bissau on Fishing off the Coast of Guinea Bissau for the period of 16 June 2001 to 15 June 2006, [2002] OJ L 19/34; the 2nd paragraph of a similar EC–Angola agreement [2002] OJ L 351/91; the 2nd paragraph of a similar EEC–Senegal agreement [2002] OJ L 349/45 as well as the agreements listed in the following footnote.

156 See, e.g., paragraph 4 of the 'preamble' of the Council Decision of 12 February 2008, [2008] OJ L 48/37: "In order to guarantee the continuation of fishing activities by the Community vessels, it is essential that the new ... Agreement should be applied as quickly

be made in return, also during the period of provisional application.[157] By way of conclusion, it is submitted that a duty to pay financial contributions during the period of provisional application such as in the above examples, i.e. when phrased in compelling treaty language, can be seen as an indication of the States' intention to be bound during provisional application (at least to the payment of these contributions).[158]

In contrast to the above cases, the conduct expected during provisional application may equally consist in an omission, for example, the non-collection of certain taxes as provided for, by way of implication, in a 1971 exchange of notes between Colombia and Brazil.[159] The agreement provides (for provisional application and) that it will enter into force on "the date on which the two Governments notify each other of the fulfilment in each country of the requirements related to its ratification." It then specifies the consequences of a notification that the requirements relating to ratification have not been fulfilled, by providing that upon such a

as possible. Both parties have therefore initialled an Agreement providing for ... provisional application..." See also paragraph 3 of the Council Decision of 15 November 2007, [2007] OJ L 331/3: "It is necessary to guarantee the pursuit of fishing activities from the date of expiry of the previous Protocol until the date of entry into force of the [new] Protocol..." These or similar provisions are often found in the 'preamble' of Council Decisions on the conclusion and provisional application of the relevant protocols or agreements.

[157] See, e.g., the 2nd paragraph of the Agreement on the Provisional Application of the Protocol Setting out, for the Period from 18 January 2005 to 17 January 2011, the Fishing Opportunities and the Financial Contribution Provided for by the Agreement between the European Economic Community and the Republic of Seychelles on Fishing off Seychelles, [2005] OJ L 348/3; the penultimate paragraph of a similar EEC–Madagascar agreement [2007] OJ L 331/5; the penultimate paragraph of a similar EEC– Côte d'Ivoire agreement [2008] OJ L 48/39; the penultimate paragraph of the Agreement on the Provisional Application of the Fisheries Partnership Agreement between the European Community and the Republic of Guinea Bissau for the period 16 June 2007 to 15 June 2011 [2007] OJ L 342/3; see the penultimate paragraph of a similar EC–Mozambique Agreement [2007] OJ L 331/33.

[158] Regulations concerning financial contributions during provisional application are varied and range from the above full payment duty couched in treaty language over 'payment possible within budgetary regulations' (International Institute of Refrigeration Agreement 1954), 826 UNTS 191, Article XXXIV(3).) or voluntary contributions (see Decision 2 (2003) ATCM XXVI (Madrid), available at <http://www.ats.aq/devAS/info_measures_listitem.aspx?lang=e&id=298> on the 'Provisional Application of Measure 1 (2003)', paragraph 6) - to no payment at all. The question may arise whether no payment at all or voluntary contributions during provisional application implies that the undertaking is less serious and thus possibly not intended to be legally binding. While a duty to make financial contributions during the period of provisional application, when couched in imperative or treaty language, may be a manifestation of an intention to be bound, it is not a necessary prerequisite for there to be such an intention. This also follows from Article 25 which provides for the possibility of applying only parts of a treaty provisionally.

[159] See Michie, "Provisional Application," 65 and fn 337 (despite considerable efforts, the exchange of notes mentioned there could not be found).

notification "both parties *shall be free* to require the ... enterprises of the other party to pay the taxes which were not collected while the agreement was in force provisionally" (emphasis added). The fact that only upon such notification both parties '*shall be free*' to require the payment of taxes would seem to imply that without such notification (i.e. during provisional application) the parties are not free to do so. In other words, the consequences of the notification would seem to imply that, until such notification, the two States are *obliged* not to require the payment of these taxes during provisional application. Therefore, this would seem to be another case where the description of the conduct expected during provisional application can be seen as indicating an intention to be bound during this period.[160]

After having analysed clauses which specify the conduct expected during provisional application, a different aspect of the content of the regulation of provisional application will now be examined, namely clauses on compulsory judicial dispute settlement.

8.1.2.3. *Legal Dispute Settlement and Provisional Application*

The following section will examine the provisional application of *legal* dispute settlement clauses in treaties[161] and the provisional application of arbitration agreements. The question to be analysed is whether the linking of provisional application with legal dispute mechanisms, i.e. mechanisms resulting in a decision which is *binding* upon the parties to the dispute, is an indication of the State's intention to be bound by those provisionally applied agreements.

The underlying reasoning with regard to the provisional application of arbitration agreements is the following. Arbitration agreements contain the parties' consent to arbitration.[162] In other words such an agreement contains the parties' consent to a legal dispute settlement mechanism resulting in a decision which is *binding* on the parties.[163] To the extent that the States parties are willing to provisionally apply such an agreement throughout the entire arbitral proceedings, including the rendering of the binding award, such provisional application would seem to imply the

160 See Michie, "Provisional Application," 65.

161 A *legal* dispute settlement mechanism is one which is compulsory and leads to a binding decision on the dispute which is based on the application of legal rules and principles, see Charles H. Brower, "Arbitration," last modified February 2007, in *MPEPIL online*, ed. Rüdiger Wolfrum, [3]; see also Brownlie, *Principles of International Law*, 701.

162 Malcom Shaw, *International Law*, 6th ed. (Cambridge: Cambridge University Press, 2008), 1051.

163 Brower, "Arbitration," [3]–[4].

parties' *consent to be bound* by the tribunal's decision. This in turn would seem to be a strong indication for the parties' intention to be bound also by the provisionally applied arbitration agreement expressing such consent.[164] (In other words it would appear unlikely that States would agree to a legally binding dispute settlement mechanism by way of a soft law agreement). Therefore, due to the subject-matter of these agreements (and to the extent that the parties are willing to base the entire arbitral proceedings on the provisionally applied agreement) provisionally applied arbitration agreements, such as the one between Belgium and the Netherlands regarding the Iron Rhine Railway dispute,[165] may well be intended to be legally binding on their parties.

Furthermore, the provisional application of treaties will be analysed which include clauses on *legal* dispute settlement. By these are meant clauses which provide for the jurisdiction of the ICJ or an arbitral tribunal over disputes arising out of the interpretation or application of the respective (provisionally applied) treaty. The agreement on provisional application sometimes links the treaty's legal dispute settlement mechanism to the period of provisional application. To the extent that this link results in the applicability of the legal dispute settlement mechanism to disputes which arise out of the treaty's provisional application, it is submitted that this may be seen as an indication of the States' intention to be bound by the treaty during provisional application.[166] The reason for this is twofold. First, as has been mentioned above, consent to a dispute settlement procedure which results in a *binding* decision would seem to imply consent to be bound by the decision and therefore would seem to involve a legally binding agreement expressing this consent. Accordingly, the content of the provisionally applied dispute clause (namely the expression of consent *inter alia* to be bound by the court's or tribunal's decision) may be a strong indication that the States intend to be bound by the provisionally applied dispute settlement clause. Second, the provision for *legal* dispute settlement mechanisms concerning disputes arising out of the treaty's

---

164 Thirlway, "The Law and Procedure of the International Court of Justice 1960–1989 Part Three," 8, fn. 28 (on special agreements referring a case to the ICJ).

165 *Iron Rhine Arbitration* (*Belgium v Netherlands*) available at <http://www.pca-cpa.org/showpage.asp?pag_id=1155>.

166 Outside the specific context of provisional application, a legal dispute settlement clause is seen as an indication of an intention to be bound by Aust, *Modern Treaty Law*, 34; Fawcett, "Legal Character of International Agreements," 388; Mann, "Reflections on a Commercial Law of Nations," 31; Thirlway, "The Law and Procedure of the International Court of Justice 1960–1989 Part Three," 7–8.

provisional application would seem to express the State's view that the dispute and the underlying agreement are suitable to adjudication or arbitration. It is generally agreed that only legally binding agreements can be at the heart of judicial or arbitral proceedings.[167] Therefore, these clauses would appear to show that States regard the respective provisionally applied treaty as containing legally enforceable rights and obligations. Furthermore, these clauses would seem to indicate that States regard the provisionally applied treaty as one by whose application (in addition to the application of other relevant treaty and customary law), the court or tribunal will arrive at a decision with regard to the dispute. Accordingly, the availability of the treaty's legal dispute settlement mechanism for disputes arising out of the treaty's provisional application would seem to be a strong indication that the States considered the provisionally applied treaty to be legally binding.

An example of an agreement in which the legal dispute settlement mechanism is available during the period of provisional application is the Protocol of Provisional Application of the 1964 Fisheries Convention.[168] According to this Protocol "[t]he provisional application of the provisions of the Fisheries Convention by a Contracting Party will entail the establishment of the list of arbiters".[169] The protocol then moves on to explicitly provide that the arbitration procedure set out in the Fisheries Convention[170] (also) applies to disputes which are raised by the provisional application of the Convention. Based on the above, this provision which extends the arbitration procedure to disputes arising out of the Convention's provisional application would seem to be an indication that States intended the Convention to be legally binding during the period of provisional application.

Another example of such a clause, albeit worded in a more indirect manner, can be found in the 1994 Energy Charter Treaty. The relevant

---

167 One could rephrase this by saying that only legally binding agreements can be the 'basis' of a judicial decision, basis meaning '*Anspruchsgrundlage*', i.e. meaning that the provisionally applied treaty can be the source of rights and obligations, and moreover that it is law on the basis of which or by application of which the dispute in question will be decided – as opposed to disputes which are decided *ex aequo et bono*, see Article 38(2) ICJ statute. See Bothe, "Legal and Non-Legal Norms," 87; Chinkin, "Challenge of Soft Law," 866; Eisemann, "Engagements Non-Contraignants," [44]; Separate Opinion, Judge Lauterpacht, *Case of Certain Norwegian Loans* (*France v Norway*) [1957] ICJ Rep 9, 48–51.

168 Fisheries Convention 1964 (concluded 9 March 1964, entered into force 15 March 1966) 581 UNTS 57.

169 Protocol of provisional application of the Fisheries Convention (concluded 9 March 1964, entered into force 18 March 1964) 581 UNTS 76, Article 2(1).

170 Fisheries Convention 1964, 581 UNTS 57, Article 13.

clause provides that upon termination of the provisional application the obligation to apply the Charter's provisions on dispute settlement with regard to investments made during such provisional application shall "*remain* in effect" for a certain period.[171] Although the precise content of this obligation is contested,[172] a straightforward interpretation of the wording of the clause would suggest that the Charter's dispute settlement provisions already are "in effect" during the period of provisional application; only against this background it is reasonable to provide that they "*remain*" in effect also upon the termination of provisional application (for a limited duration).[173] Among the variety of procedures and *fora* available under the dispute settlement provisions of the ECT are *legal* dispute settlement mechanisms as defined above, i.e. compulsory proceedings leading to a legally binding decision on the dispute based on the application of legal rules and principles.[174] In light of the above, this would seem to be an indication that the parties intended to be legally bound also during provisional application, at the very least by that part of the 1994 Energy Charter Treaty with regard to which recourse to the dispute settlement provisions is stipulated, i.e. Part III on 'Investment Protection and Promotion'.[175]

---

[171] Article 45(3)(b) ECT.

[172] Georgia argued in the jurisdictional phase of the *Kardassopoulos* case that the Tribunal did not have jurisdiction *ratione temporis* to hear the case in relation to acts which had occurred during the ECT's provisional application (and thus prior to its entry into force), *Kardassopoulos v Georgia* (6 July 2007), [71]; Andrew Hutcheon and James Spencer, "Provisional Application of the Energy Charter Treaty," *European and Middle Eastern Arbitration Review* 25 (2008) (who raise the question whether the provisionally applied ECT would amount to consent to arbitration); Wälde submits that the provisionally applied ECT involves consent to arbitration, Thomas Wälde, "International Investment under the 1994 Energy Charter Treaty," in *The Energy Charter Treaty*, ed. Thomas Wälde (London: Kluwer Law International, 1996), 314. In the following arbitral awards, the respective Tribunals based their jurisdiction on the provisionally applied ECT: *Petrobart Limited v the Kyrgyz Republic*, SCC Case No 126/2003 (29 March 2005) (first instance) 15–17, affirmed T 5208–05 (19 January 2007)(Court of Appeal); *Plama Consortium Limited v Republic of Bulgaria*, ICSID Case No. ARB/03/24, Decision on Jurisdiction (8 February 2005); *Kardassopoulos v Georgia* (6 July 2007), *Yukos Universal Ltd v Russian Federation* (30 November 2009).

[173] Niebruegge, "Provisional Application of the Energy Charter Treaty," 367; Hafner, "Provisional Application," 602.

[174] See Article 26(4), (6), (8).

[175] By contrast, the reverse conclusion is not helpful for gaining indications of the absence of an intention to be bound. In other words it is submitted that the absence of a clause on a legal dispute settlement mechanism does not amount to an indication of an intention not to be legally bound by the agreement. This is so because the possibility to submit disputes to a *legal* dispute settlement mechanism is (at best) a sufficient condition for there to be a legally binding agreement, but not a necessary one. If this were otherwise, a great number of agreements could not be considered legally binding due to States'

It may be added that in some instances the clause linking the *legal* dispute settlement mechanism to the period of provisional application can be worded in a slightly ambiguous manner. As a consequence, its precise meaning and content may be open to different interpretations, including the question whether certain preparatory acts stipulated to take place during the period of provisional application were aimed at getting the procedure up and running for the treaty's entry into force or (whether they were aimed) at enabling recourse to the procedure also during provisional application.[176] Yet leaving these difficulties pertaining to individual cases aside, it is submitted more generally that clauses according to which *legal* dispute settlement mechanisms, i.e. arbitration or judicial settlement, are clearly available also during the period of provisional application may be an expression of the States' intention to be legally bound during provisional application, since they imply that the disputes arising out of the provisionally applied treaties are suited to such procedures.[177]

8.1.2.4. *Conclusion*

The above analysis of agreements on provisional application which regulate provisional application in a more detailed manner has shown that these details sometimes provide further indications as to an intention to be bound during provisional application. This further indication may result from the fact that the parties associate 'rights and/or obligations' with provisional application, that the conduct expected during provisional application would seem to reveal a sense of obligation (such as the duty to make financial contributions if it is phrased in treaty language), or from the availability of *legal* dispute settlement mechanisms during provisional application.

After having examined cases in which the agreement's content may be potentially indicative as to an intention to be bound during provisional application, the next section will outline provisional application clauses which express the intention to be bound in a clear and sometimes even explicit manner.

---

general reluctance to subject themselves to *legal* dispute settlement mechanisms. Accordingly, the absence of such clauses does not affect the possibly legally binding nature of the agreement in question. See also Klabbers, *The Concept of Treaty in International Law*, 78.

[176] See, e.g., the "Economic Partnership Agreement between the CARIFORUM States, of the one part, and the European Community and its Member States, of the other part" 2008, [2008] OJ L 289/I/3, Articles 216(1), 221(1).

[177] See also Aust, *Modern Treaty Law*, 34 (not in the specific context of provisional application).

8.1.3. *Agreements Whose Content is Explicit as to an Intention to be Bound*

As just indicated, there are instances in which the agreement on provisional application would seem to clearly express an intention to be bound during provisional application. In very rare cases this intention could virtually not be made any clearer in that the agreement states that during provisional application the parties "shall be *bound*" (emphasis added) by the treaty's provisions,[178] or that during provisional application the treaty "shall be deemed to be in *full force and effect*..." (emphasis added).[179] More frequently the intention to be bound is expressed in a 'legal fiction' along the lines that the treaty will be provisionally applied 'as if it had entered into force'.[180] It is submitted that such a fiction[181] expresses an intention to be bound since the foremost quality of a treaty in force is that it is binding upon the parties to it, as can be seen in the beginning of Article 26: "Every treaty in force is *binding* upon the parties to it..." (emphasis added). Another example of this drafting technique is when the position of a State provisionally applying the treaty is assimilated to that of States for which the treaty has entered into force. Particularly clear are those cases in which it is set out that States provisionally applying the treaty and being provisional members to the institution and organs set up by the treaty shall have the 'same rights and obligations' as other (non provisional) members, "including the obligation to contribute to the administrative budget of the institution."[182]

The above examples are instances in which the intention to be bound during the period of provisional application has been expressed not merely by recourse to treaty language but also by making comparatively explicit statements to such an effect. It would appear to be very difficult to

---

[178] Protocol of provisional application of the Fisheries Convention, 581 UNTS 76, Article 2(2).

[179] Greece–Ethiopia Agreement on Reciprocal Tax Exemptions on Income earned by Greek and Ethiopian Maritime Shipping Enterprises 1962 (concluded 7 November 1962) 550 UNTS 179, note I. See also an agreement between the same parties on Reciprocal Tax Exemptions on Income Earned by Greek and Ethiopian Air Transport Companies (concluded 7 November 1962) 550 UNTS 189, note I.

[180] Protocol of Provisional Application of the European Monetary Agreement, Article 1(a), 6. See also the Netherlands–OECD Agreement on the Provisional Participation of the Netherlands in the Activities of the Organisation, (1961) 22 Tractatenblad, no. 126, 3, Article 1.

[181] By this is meant the assimilation of a provisionally applied treaty to a treaty in force.

[182] Agreement Relating to the Implementation of Part XI of the United Nations Convention on the Law of the Sea of 10 December 1982, 1836 UNTS 3, Annex, sec. 1, no. 12(c).

convincingly contend that these treaties do not carry binding force during provisional application. Yet it should be added that these agreements constitute the minority among provisional application agreements drafted in treaty language.

8.1.4. *Conclusion*

The above analysis of agreements on provisional application phrased in treaty language has shown that these agreements can be categorised according to their different manifestations of intention and the explicitness of each. The simplest or basic manifestation of an intention to be bound consists in the recourse to treaty language, form and nomenclature (to the extent possible)[183] in the agreement on provisional application ('this treaty *shall* be applied provisionally; provisional application *shall* terminate' etc). The second category are those agreements whose content, in addition to the above recourse to the treaty language, entails further indications of an intention to be bound. In the third category belong those agreements on provisional application which evidence the most explicit expression of an intention to be bound, either in the form of statements which state that the provisionally applied treaty shall be binding upon its parties or by recourse to a 'legal fiction' according to which the provisionally applied treaty shall be applied 'as if it were in force.'

Broadly speaking, the increasing explicitness of the indications of intention from the first to the third category is inversely proportionate to the frequency of the instances found per category. In other words, the most explicit cases would appear to be less frequent in practice. Most frequent, by contrast, seem to be the short formula agreements on provisional application ('this treaty shall be applied provisionally from [date/event]')[184] where the manifestation of an intention may consist of just one word.

After having analysed agreements on provisional application which are phrased in treaty language, agreements on provisional application which are phrased in *non*-treaty language will now be examined.

---

183 If the agreement on provisional application is contained in a separate agreement the sole purpose of which is to bring about the provisional application of the main treaty, then further indications of an intention may be entailed in the form of this separate agreement and the nomenclature used. If, by contrast, the agreement is contained in a final clause of the treaty, then the manifestation of an intention to be bound is essentially limited to the recourse to treaty language within that clause.

184 See this chapter 8.1.1.

8.2. *Agreements using Non-Treaty Language or Form*

The next section will examine agreements on provisional application in non-treaty language, beginning with instances where provisional application is agreed in a separate agreement.

8.2.1. *Provisional Application in a Separate Agreement*

When provisional application is agreed in a separate agreement, these agreements can take different forms. Instances have been found in which the agreement was contained in an exchange of letters,[185] a memorandum of understanding[186] or in a Final Act of the conference at which the relevant treaty was adopted.[187] In the exchange of letters it was suggested that the parties "should" (not "shall") apply the treaty in question provisionally, and that the initial letter together with the affirmative answer would constitute an "understanding" (not "agreement") which would "come into effect" (not into "force") on a given date.[188] Similarly, the parties of the memorandum of understanding stated they "intend" (not "undertake" or "agree") to apply the respective treaty provisionally, and the MOU was "dated" (not "done").

Admittedly, these differences may seem rather subtle. However, when analysed in light of the guidance notes issued by some governments on the use of treaty and non-treaty language, it becomes clear that these 'agreements' were drafted according to the book and are almost model cases of agreements drawn up in non-treaty language following, as they

---

[185] UN–US Agreement on Provisional Application of the Cooperation Service Agreement for the Contribution of Personnel to the International Criminal Tribunal for the Former Yugoslavia, 1823 UNTS 335. (Admittedly, the fact that the agreement has been registered by the UN secretariat *ex officio* would seem to suggest that the UN regards the agreement as legally binding. Nevertheless, it is submitted that in the analysis of the exchange of letters indications of an intention not to be bound as expressed in the wording and nomenclature outweigh the fact of registration, on the basis that registration speaks to the intention of the UN (*ex officio* registration) whereas the wording and nomenclature used would seem to manifest the intention of both sides.)

[186] Memorandum of Understanding Provisionally Applying the Treaty on Fisheries between certain Pacific Island States and the United States of America 2002. The only place in which the text of the MOU could be found is the following website: http://iea.uoregon.edu/pages/view_treaty.php?t=2002-MemorandumOfUnderstanding-1987-FisheriesPacificIslandsUS.EN.txt&par=view_treaty_html.

[187] Final Act of the Eleventh Antarctic Treaty Special Consultative Meeting, ILM 30 (1991): 1460 (for the agreement on provisional application see the Final Act's penultimate paragraph, 1461).

[188] 1823 UNTS 336–337.

do, the instructions with great diligence and care.[189] With regard to the MOU it should be added that it is drafted in a very simple form, omitting, as is generally done, the formal formula often used in the final paragraph of treaties (*testimonium*).[190] Finally, the nomenclature used for the agreements is also typical for non-legally binding agreements. Of course the nomenclature is not *decisive* when analysing the intention to be bound by the participants,[191] but it may still be *indicative* of the intention and may be taken into account when the different manifestations of intention are assessed.[192] Here, the nomenclature used by the participants when referring to their 'agreements', "memorandum of understanding" in the one case and, as has already been pointed out, "understanding" in the other, would seem to be another deliberate recourse to non-treaty language. All of these indications point to the conclusion that the agreements on provisional application would appear not to have been intended to be legally binding.[193] It is submitted that from this it follows that the participants did not intend to be legally bound to provisionally apply the agreement in question.[194]

As has already been mentioned, sometimes agreements on provisional application are contained in the Final Act of the conference which adopted the treaty in question. Relevant for present purposes is the 11th

---

189 The one exception to this is that the participants of the MOU are referred to as "Parties", not 'participants' or 'governments', in deviation from the UK and US guidance notes, see FCO, *Treaties and MOUs*, 16, and US State Department, "Non-Binding Documents".

190 Aust, *Modern Treaty Law*, 444.

191 See the definition of a treaty in Article 2(1)(a). See also the jurisprudence of the ICJ and PCIJ: *South West Africa Cases (Ethiopia v South Africa; Liberia v South Africa)(Preliminary Objections)* [1962] ICJ Rep 319, 331; *Customs Regime between Germany and Austria (Advisory Opinion)* PCIJ Series A/B No 41, 47.

192 FCO, *Treaties and MOUs*, 15; UN Treaty Reference Guide, Part I, Introduction (on the title of an agreement). The guide is available at: http://treaties.un.org/Pages/Overview.aspx?path=overview/definition/page1_en.xml.

193 With regard to the memorandum of understanding a statement of the US (being a party to the MOU) confirms the result of this analysis, see "Treaty Affairs," in *Digest of United States Practice in International Law*, 2002, B3, 187. For academic support of the result of this analysis see a note on the International Environmental Agreements Database project website (the website's data is provided by Professor Mitchell, University of Oregon), http://iea.uoregon.edu/page.php?query=treaty_info&mitch_id=3558.

194 Contrast, Michie, "Provisional Application," 69, according to whom States will still be legally bound to provisionally apply a treaty even if the engagement to do so is contained in a non-legally binding agreement. He bases this contention on the principle of good faith. It is submitted here that the binding force of an agreement is first and foremost dependent on the intention of States. If the intention of the States not to be legally bound to provisionally apply a treaty is clearly expressed, as in the above example, then *pacta sunt servanda* should not be let in through the backdoor via the principle of good faith, compare Bothe, "Legal and Non-Legal Norms," 94–5.

Antarctic Treaty Special Consultative Meeting at which the States parties adopted the 1991 Protocol on Environmental Protection to the Antarctic Treaty.[195] In the penultimate paragraph of the Final Act the (Special Consultative) Meeting agreed on the Protocol's provisional application pending its entry into force.[196] Although the agreement is not entirely free from treaty language (the meeting "*agreed*"...), the non-treaty language and drafting elements predominate (the meeting agreed that it was "*desirable*" to ensure the protocol's effective implementation at an early date...; that it was "desirable" to apply Annexes I-IV ... "to the extent practicable"). As a result of the language used and the recourse to the self-judging rider ("to the extent practicable"), the undertaking is extremely vague and would not seem to entail any (immediate) obligation to act and help bring about the desired result. Based on all of the above, it is submitted that the Meeting did not intend to create a legally binding obligation to provisionally apply the Protocol on Environmental Protection to the Antarctic Treaty.[197]

Another possibly non-legally binding agreement which has been concluded at the margin of an international conference[198] can be found in the 1979 'Resolution on Long-Range Transboundary Air Pollution'.[199] Although the wording of the paragraph dealing with provisional application is not entirely free from treaty language, the undertakings relating to provisional application are rather weak. First, the 'Signatories to the Convention' do not so much decide to provisionally apply the Convention but merely that they 'shall initiate' the 'provisional implementation' of the Convention 'as soon as possible'. Moreover, the undertaking pending the Convention's entry into force is not to 'carry out the obligations arising from the Convention' but only to do so 'to the maximum extent possible'. It is submitted that the predominant element in the shaping of provisional application in the 1979 Resolution is the recourse to soft law techniques and

---

[195] See the preamble of the protocol; for the protocol see the website of the Antarctic Treaty Secretariat: <http://www.ats.aq/documents/recatt/Att006_e.pdf>.

[196] Final Act of the Eleventh Antarctic Treaty Special Consultative Meeting, see ILM 30 (1991): 1461.

[197] Laura Pineschi, "The Madrid Protocol on the Protection of the Antarctic Environment and its Effectiveness," in *International Law for Antarctica*, eds. Francesco Francioni and Tullio Scovazzi, 2nd. ed. (The Hague: Kluwer Law International, 1996), 265–66.

[198] High-Level Meeting within the Framework of the ECE on the Protection of the Environment (13 November 1979) resulting in the signing of the Convention on Long-Range Transboundary Air Pollution, 1302 UNTS 217.

[199] Reprinted in Evgeny Chossudovsky, *"East-West" Diplomacy for Environment in the United Nations* (New York: United Nations Institute for Training and Research, 1989), 235.

wording as a result of which the undertaking of provisional application is rather vague and weak. This would seem to indicate that the signatories to the Convention did not intend to be legally bound to provisionally apply the Convention in question.

Coming to the end of this analysis, it should be mentioned that locating these agreements on provisional application, which are drafted in non-treaty language and contained in a document separate from the treaty, is often a difficult task. If the above analysis is correct, then the non-treaty language, form and nomenclature are manifestations of an intention not to be legally bound by the agreement. This would mean that these 'arrangements' are not covered by the duty of registration with the UN Secretariat under Article 102 UN Charter. Thus, these arrangements are not generally published in the UN Treaty Series, nor normally published on the national plane. It follows that it is rather difficult to make an approximate statement about the frequency or rarity of these separate agreements on provisional application in non-treaty language. While it is correct to state that less than a handful of these arrangements have been found, which can be contrasted with the number of separate legally binding agreements on provisional application, it is not clear to which extent this reflects the realities of international practice.

8.2.2. *Provisional Application Agreed in the Treaty Itself*

There are also instances of agreements on provisional application in non-treaty language which are contained in the treaty itself, in a final clause.[200] These 'soft-clauses' on provisional application in otherwise hard instruments seem to be even less frequent and also less recent than the similar 'soft agreements' which are drawn up in a separate document. As has been explained earlier, the possibilities of finding an express intention is more limited the shorter the agreement on provisional application is. Thus, if the agreement is contained in a final clause and, in addition to that, recourse was had to the 'short formula of agreeing on provisional application', then the manifestation of intention may well be limited to just one word. Nevertheless, the surprise of breaking the almost 'regular' recourse to treaty language in provisional application clauses makes these cases stand out. After innumerable instances of 'shall apply the treaty

200 Sweden–Brazil Air Transport Agreement 1947 (concluded 14 November 1947) 94 UNTS 139, Article XII; Brazil–Chile Air Transport Agreement 1947 (concluded 4 July 1947) 971 UNTS 321, Article XIII.

provisionally', phrases such as "shall endeavour" or "shall seek" to apply the treaty provisionally, would appear to be of a different nature. The wording of these clauses was also compared to that of other articles of the treaty, which confirmed that indeed the clause on provisional application was worded in a different manner, namely in soft language, than the remainder of the treaty (which was worded in treaty language). Based on this, it is submitted that the States concerned had recourse to such a soft clause in a hard treaty in order to express their intention not to be legally bound to provisionally apply the treaty in question.

8.2.3. *Conclusion*

A close analysis of agreements on provisional application shows that some are phrased in non-treaty language. Those contained in the final clause of a treaty stand out because they are so unusual, and because the remainder of the treaty is phrased in treaty language and is, overall, a 'hard instrument'. These soft clauses thus seem to express the intention not to be legally bound to provisionally apply the treaty. When the agreement on provisional application in non-treaty language is contained in a separate instrument which is solely concerned with provisional application, this instrument sometimes displays further indications of an intention not to be legally bound. Such indications can be contained in the nomenclature used to designate the 'agreement' (for example, 'understanding' or 'memorandum of understanding') or consist in the omission of the testimonium which is typical for non-legally binding agreements. The evidence suggests that these agreements in non-treaty language are by far less frequent than those in treaty language, with the caveat that this is an impression rather than an exact statement due to difficulties in finding non-binding separate agreements as a result of their rather limited publication.

8.3. *Provisional Entry into Force and Provisional Application Clauses in Commodity Agreements*

The following section will analyse provisional entry into force and provisional application clauses in commodity agreements. It was mentioned earlier that commodity agreements have a distinct use of these two terms: provisional entry into force is used when the agreement and its status is referred to; provisional application is used when the undertaking of individual States is referred to. It is because of this distinct use of terminology, and because different legal consequences have been attached to the two mechanisms, that commodity agreements, and their relevant clauses, are analysed separately from the other agreements above. First, the meaning of provisional entry into force will be analysed in light of its regulation and role within commodity agreements.

8.3.1. *The Legal Effects and Binding Force of Commodity Agreements Provisionally in Force*

It is a common feature of sugar,[201] coffee[202] and cocoa[203] agreements to provide in their article containing definitions of terms used in the agreement, a definition of the term 'entry into force'. In that provision 'entry into force' is defined broadly as the day on which the treaty enters into force, be it provisionally or definitively, unless otherwise specified. Thus unless otherwise specified,[204] no distinction is drawn between the treaty's provisional and definitive entry into force; the same provisions apply and the same legal consequences attach to both. The entry into force of commodity agreements is relevant, *inter alia,* in the economic provisions of commodity agreements, dealing with the buffer stock,[205] export quotas[206] and import restrictions.[207] The agreement's entry into force may also be relevant for determining when certain payments will be due.[208] In light of the first and foremost quality of an agreement in force, namely that it is binding and has to be performed by the parties to it in good faith as Article 26 states, the following is submitted. If a commodity agreement contains such a general assimilation of provisional entry into force to definitive entry into force – i.e. if in terms of provisions applicable to them and the legal consequences that attach to them *generally* no difference is

201 1968 Agreement, 654 UNTS 3, Article 2(26); 1977 Agreement, 1064 UNTS 219, Article 2(22); 1984 Agreement, 1388 UNTS 3, Article 2(10); 1987 Agreement, 1499 UNTS 31, Article 2(10); 1992 Agreement, 1703 UNTS 203, Article 2(8).

202 1962 Agreement, 469 UNTS 169, Article 2(12); 1968 Agreement, 647 UNTS 3, Article 2(12); 1976 Agreement, 1024 UNTS 3, Article 3(11); 1983 Agreement, 1333 UNTS 119, Article 3(11); 1994 Agreement, 1827 UNTS 3, Article 2(11); 2001 Agreement, 2161 UNTS 308, Article 2(11).

203 1972 Agreement, 882 UNTS 67, Article 2(s); 1975 Agreement, 1023 UNTS 253, Article 2(s); 1980 Agreement, 1245 UNTS 221, Article 2(p); 1986 Agreement, 1446 UNTS 103, Article 2(7); 1993 Agreement, 1766 UNTS 3, Article 2(7); 2001 Agreement, 2229 UNTS 2, Article 2(7).

204 Provisions in which it is "otherwise specified" are usually the agreements' stipulations on provisional and definitive entry into force and their respective requirements as set out in the final clauses, see, e.g., Article 45 of the 2001 coffee agreements, 2161 UNTS 308.

205 See, e.g., Article 27(3)a, 27(4)a, 31(2)b of the 1980 Cocoa Agreement.

206 See, e.g., Article 31 and 33 of the 1976 Coffee Agreement.

207 See, e.g., Article 45(4) of the 1976 Coffee Agreement.

208 See, e.g., Article 25(3) of the 1976 Coffee Agreement, or Article 23(3) of the 1980 Cocoa Agreement; see also Article 55 of the 1976 Coffee Agreement.

drawn between the two – then a treaty provisionally in force would seem to be intended to be similarly binding as a treaty definitively in force.

The conclusion that a commodity agreement containing such a clause suggests an intention to be bound also when it is provisionally in force, would seem to find support in data available on the performance of the 1972 Cocoa Agreement. While the agreement was provisionally in force, the Council decided to suspend the voting rights of Algeria, Honduras and Venezuela due to their non-payment of the annual member contribution.[209] The payment of the annual member contribution in that agreement is clearly phrased as a legally binding obligation,[210] and the suspension of voting rights as a consequence of non-payment would seem to be a sanction for the breach of the obligation. So understood, this sanction would seem to evidence that the 1972 cocoa agreement was legally binding and involved binding rights and obligations for its members while being provisionally in force.

This conclusion may find further confirmation in the fact that the International Cocoa Organization concluded a headquarters agreement with the UK in March 1975,[211] again during the period in which the 1972 cocoa agreement was provisionally in force. This would seem to show that both the UK and the International Cocoa Organization perceived the organisation as possessing treaty-making capacity during the period in which the treaty was provisionally in force. While of course institutions exist which are, or were, based on non-legally binding agreements,[212] these institutions normally are not endowed with the capacity to conclude legally binding international agreements.[213] Thus because the International Cocoa Organization was capable of concluding, in its own capacity, a legally binding agreement, this would seem to indicate that the

---

209 See EX(REP) 7 of 11 November 1974 as referred to in Pierre Michel Eisemann, "L'Accord International sur le Cacao," *Annuaire Français de Droit International* 21 (1975): 762 fn. 112.

210 1972 Cocoa Agreement, 882 UNTS 67, Article 22(2).

211 UK–International Cocoa Organization Headquarter Agreement 1975 (concluded 26 March 1975) 990 UNTS 141.

212 The 'Organization for Security and Cooperation in Europe' has its origins in the 'Conference on Security and Cooperation in Europe', at the end of which the participating States decided to have regular follow-up meetings without establishing the Conference as an international organization, Schermers and Blokker, *International Institutional Law*, [30] and fn. 79.

213 See also Ignaz Seidl-Hohenveldern, "Internationale Organisationen aufgrund von Soft Law," in *Recht zwischen Umbruch und Bewahrung: Völkerrecht, Europarecht, Staatsrecht: Festschrift für Rudolf Bernhardt*, eds. Ulrich Beyerlin et al. (Berlin: Springer, 1995), 230.

organisation's constituent instrument, while being in force provisionally, was itself a legally binding agreement, establishing an organisation with international legal personality and the capacity to conclude treaties.[214]

In conclusion, the above would seem to point in the direction that commodity agreements which contain a clause assimilating the agreement's provisional entry into force to its definitive entry into force may largely be intended to be legally binding during the period in which the agreement is provisionally in force.

8.3.2. *The Legal Implications of Provisional Application of Commodity Agreements*

The next section will analyse provisional application clauses of commodity agreements in order to establish what it means, in terms of legally binding force, when a State declares that it will provisionally apply a commodity agreement. It is a common feature of cocoa,[215] sugar[216] and olive oil[217] agreements that a State which has made a declaration of provisional application thereupon 'shall be regarded as a provisional member'. This raises the question whether 'being regarded as a provisional member' is intended to mean that such a State by and large has the same rights and obligations as a member, and therefore has the same legal status as a State which has expressed its consent to be bound by the commodity agreement. Such an overall parity in legal status would, for instance, concern the benefit of voting rights in the Council of the organisation or the obligation to contribute annually to the budget of the organisation.

Some agreements explicitly specify that a State making a declaration of provisional application shall be regarded as a provisional member "with all the rights and obligations of a member".[218] Provisions of this kind

---

214 See also Schermers and Blokker, *International Institutional Law*, [36] (who regard as proof of Interpol's intergovernmental status the fact that it has concluded a headquarters agreement with France).

215 See, e.g., 1972 Agreement Article 66(3); 1975 Agreement, Article 68(1), (2); 1980 Agreement Article 65(1), (2); 1986 Agreement Article 69(1), (2); 1993 Agreement Article 55(1), (2).

216 See, e.g., 1968 Agreement Article 62(2); 1977 Agreement Article 74(1), (2); 1984 Agreement Article 37(1), (2); 1987 Agreement Article 38(1), (2); 1992 Agreement Article 39(1), (2).

217 See, e.g., 1963 Agreement, 495 UNTS 3, Article 36(8); 1979 Agreement, 1219 UNTS 135, Article 45(1), (2); 1986 Agreement, 1445 UNTS 13, Article 54(1), (2); 1993 Protocol, 1763 UNTS 319, Article 7(1), (2); 2005 Agreement, [2005] OJ L302/47, Article 41(2).

218 See, e.g., in the following Olive Oil Agreements: 1963 Agreement Article 36(8); 1979 Agreement Article 45(1), (2); 1993 Protocol Article 7(1), (2).

clarify that a State which provisionally applies the commodity agreement in question enjoys 'rights' and 'obligations' under the treaty, which would seem to indicate that such States are bound by the commodity agreement in question during that period. Some differences, however, remain between States which provisionally apply a commodity agreement containing such a clause and States which have expressed their consent to be bound by the agreement. One of the remaining differences would be the working of the limitation clause if the provision on provisional application entails one. This would mean that the State is bound to apply the commodity agreement only to the extent that such application is in accordance with "its laws and regulations".[219] Thus, to the extent that such application runs counter to existing laws and regulations, the State would not be obliged to apply the commodity agreement. A further difference to States which have expressed their consent to be bound by the agreement is that the provisional membership (and provisional application) is stipulated to terminate at a set date if the formal instrument of consent to be bound has not by then been deposited with the UN Secretary General.[220] Yet besides these differences, States which have made a declaration of provisional application and thus have become provisional members of the organisation generally have the same rights and obligations as States which have expressed their consent to be bound and are (definitive) 'members' of the organisation, as a result of the clause to such an effect. Therefore, clauses to such an effect would seem to be a strong indication that States which provisionally apply the commodity agreements in question are legally bound by them.

In other instances the question whether being a 'provisional member', as a result of a declaration of provisional application, creates parity between it and an actual 'member' of a commodity organisation, would appear to be implicitly answered. In those instances, the provision at the beginning of the commodity agreement, which contains definitions of terms used, may be helpful in establishing what 'provisional membership'

---

[219] See, e.g., the Third Extension of the 1983 Coffee Agreement, Coffee Council Resolution 355 (concluded and entered into force 1 October 1992) [4], and the Fourth Extension of the 1983 Coffee Agreement, Coffee Council Resolution 363 (concluded and entered into force 1 October 1993) [3].

[220] See, e.g., Extension of the 1983 Coffee Agreement, 1546 UNTS 389, Coffee Council Resolution 347 (03 July 1989), [6]; Second Extension 1983 Coffee Agreement, 1651 UNTS 572, Coffee Council Resolution 352 (concluded 28 September 1990, entered into force and 1 October 1991), [5]; Third Extension 1983 Coffee Agreement, 1691 UNTS 449, Coffee Council Resolution 355, [4], Fourth Extension 1983 Coffee Agreement, Coffee Council Resolution 363, [3]; see also the 1963 Olive Oil Agreement, Article 36(8).

and 'provisional application' entail. There, a 'member' is defined as a 'contracting party',[221] and a 'contracting party' is defined as a State which has either expressed its consent to be bound by the agreement or which has made a declaration of provisional application.[222] As a result of the application of these definitions, it would seem that a 'member', due to being a contracting party, could be both, a State which has expressed its consent to be bound or a State which has made a declaration of provisional application. As a consequence thereof it would seem that States which provisionally apply commodity agreements of this kind are generally regarded as 'members'. Thus whenever the rights or obligations of members are specified in conventions of this kind, this would seem to also cover States which provisionally apply the agreement in question. Accordingly, a State which provisionally applies such an agreement would, as a member, have the right to cast the votes it holds in the Council, and would be under the obligation to contribute towards the organisations' budget or to follow the obligations set out concerning the production of or trade in the relevant commodity. While commodity agreements of this kind do not contain a provision which explicitly states that provisional members have the same rights and obligations as members, this would seem to be the result of an application of the definitions given at the beginning of these agreements. The remaining differences to States which have already consented to be bound would be as outlined above, including the working of a limitation clause or the possibility that the provisional application will terminate at a set date if by then the instrument expressing consent to be bound by the commodity agreement has not been deposited with the UN Secretary General.

By way of conclusion, it is submitted that when commodity agreements provide, explicitly or implicitly, that States which provisionally apply the agreement generally have the same rights and obligations as States which have expressed their consent to be bound by the agreement, this may be an indication that such provisional application is intended to legally bind the relevant States.

Some commodity agreements contain another regulation of provisional application which would seem to indicate that provisional application is intended to be legally binding. It has been mentioned above that

---

221 See, e.g., the following cocoa agreements: 1980 Agreement Article 2(j); 1986 Agreement Article 2(13); 1993 Agreement Article 2(12); 2001 Agreement Article 2(12).

222 See, e.g., the following cocoa agreements: 1980 Agreement Article 2(i); 1986 Agreement Article 2(4); 1993 Agreement Article 2(4); 2001 Agreement Article 2(4).

some agreements define 'Contracting Parties' as either States which have expressed their consent to be bound or States which have made a declaration of provisional application. Sometimes this provision alternatively speaks of States 'which have consented to be bound by the agreement provisionally or definitively'.[223] In other words, these provisions seem to express the underlying understanding according to which a declaration of provisional application is a provisional expression of consent to be bound. It is submitted that recourse to the phrase 'consent to be bound' when referring to a declaration of provisional application would be another indication that such provisional application is intended to be legally binding. Otherwise, there would appear to be little room to speak of a provisional 'consent to be *bound*'.

8.3.3. *Conclusion*

In conclusion, the treaty wording used with regard to both, provisional entry into force and provisional application would seem to be an initial indication that States intend to be bound by a commodity agreement provisionally in force and upon a declaration of provisional application, i.e. when they apply a commodity agreement provisionally. The frequent use of drafting techniques and definitions which generally assimilate a commodity agreement's provisional entry into force to its definitive entry into force, and a provisional member (upon a declaration of provisional application) to a member (upon expression of consent to be bound (definitively)) would appear to be an indication of such an intention to be bound with regard to those agreements which contain such assimilating provisions. Thus, based on this analysis, it would seem that the above-mentioned concern of logical inconsistency does not seem to arise in practice. By the concern of 'logical inconsistency' is meant the problem which might arise if declarations of provisional application would not have legally binding effects but rather moral or political ones. If commodity agreements are considered to be legally binding upon their provisional entry into force, then this binding force would be difficult to explain if the provisional entry into force was brought about solely by declarations of provisional application – and these were not intended to be legally binding but limited to moral or political implications. However, the above

[223] See, e.g., the following cocoa agreements: 1980 Agreement Article 2(i); 1986 Agreement Article 2(4); 1993 Agreement Article 2(4); 2001 Agreement Article 2(4); see also the 1987 Rubber Agreement Article 2(2); see also the following coffee agreements: 1994 Agreement Article 2(5); 2001 Agreement Article 2(5); 2007 Agreement Article 2(5).

analysis would seem to indicate that States have an intention to be (legally) bound when making a declaration of provisional application with regard to commodity agreements containing such assimilation clauses so that at least in those instances the problem of logical inconsistency would not seem to arise.

8.4. *Conclusion*

The result of the analysis of agreements of provisional application by reference to intention is that in these agreements, intention would appear to be manifested in the same way as in other international law agreements, thus by the wording and nomenclature used, the content of the agreement etc. Furthermore, there would appear to be a high degree of consistency in this practice: the great majority of agreements analysed seem to be intended to be legally binding, although there is a minority of instances in which there would appear to be a deliberate use of manifestations of an intention not to be legally bound. It is difficult to say whether this is an emanation of the result obtained in the first part of the chapter, that there exist different views on the binding force of these treaties, or whether this is simply that practice 'by nature' would not necessarily be entirely consistent, because States and international organisations could normally deviate from a generally accepted notion (supposed it did exist) if need be.

Finally, the result is also interesting in terms of underlying expectations one might have had, at least in the case of the present researcher, and possibly also by those who criticise that the meaning and effects of 'provisional application' are not clear: originally it was thought that the key to the understanding of the binding force of provisionally applied treaties would lie in the notion of provisional application, and that sufficient research would bring to the light the meaning of the notion in this regard. Yet, the above research suggests, that it is possible that the key to understanding the binding force of provisionally applied treaties may lie outside the notion of provisional application, in the usual ways of manifesting an intention to be bound (or the absence thereof). This could be so, whether the binding force of a specific provisionally applied treaty is in issue or even the meaning of provisional application in general.

Finally, with regard to the provisional entry into force and provisional application of commodity agreements it may be added that no instance has been found in the present research in which the relevant clauses were worded in soft-law terminology or in which a manifestation not to be bound by the commodity agreement provisionally in force or during a commodity agreement's provisional application had been otherwise manifested within the agreement. Thus, it is conceivable that commodity agreements not only have a distinct use of the terms 'provisional entry into force' and 'provisional application' but also that in this specific field of international law, there may be a uniform and consistent use of the terms which is reserved for those instances in which there is an intention to be bound by the treaty prior to its definitive entry into force and during its provisional application.

9. Evaluation and Conclusion

The purpose of this chapter was to examine what practice suggests regarding the binding force of provisionally applied treaties. When researching practice as attempted here, several difficulties arise, ranging from the fact that practice goes hand in hand with pragmatism and is not made with a view to fit within the different possible theoretical categories, or that it is at times contradictory, to the inevitable limitations that a single researcher will encounter (such as access to material, scarcity of time and possibly means etc.). Nevertheless, academic research should not be divorced from practice but take it into account to the extent possible, and for this reason the above research on practice was undertaken, despite its difficulties and limitations.

The result of the analysis of the views of States and international organisations on the binding force of provisionally applied treaties was that there exist different opinions: according to one view, provisionally applied treaties are generally binding, possibly even so defined; according to the opposing view they are non-legally binding, possibly also so defined; and according to the third, provisionally applied treaties can be binding or non- legally binding. Based on the above research, the first view (generally legally binding) enjoys by far the most support in practice. The result of the analysis of agreements on provisional application by reference to intention is that most of the agreements examined were intended to be legally binding, with a small minority of cases which seemed to be intended not to be legally binding.

On the basis of publicly available practice material as well as information obtained from the 2007–2008 questionnaire, it is clear that uncertainty surrounds the notion of provisional application. The above research also confirms that different opinions exist on the binding force of provisionally applied treaties (as the *Kardassopoulos* and *Yukos* arbitrations already indicated). Nevertheless, no traces were found of a debate on the matter, at least in cases where the potential recourse to provisional application is discussed (this may be different if a dispute arises *ex post* with regard to a provisionally applied treaty such as the ECT). To the extent that material was made available[224] or has been found on discussions among States concerning whether or not to have recourse to provisional application with regard to a particular treaty,[225] or to a certain group of treaties,[226] the question of the binding force of treaties during that period did not arise. Given that these discussions frequently contain a legal analysis of the mechanism of provisional application, one might expect that the matter of the binding force of these treaties would be raised. Yet, while questions were raised with regard to the mechanism,[227] and tensions are

---

224 I followed up the possibility mentioned in an article by David Sagar ("Provisional Application in an International Organization," *Journal of Space Law*, 27 (1999): 99 fn. 1) to request the Inmarsat documents cited in the article from the Inmarsat Legal Office. I am indebted to Ms Jenny Ray (Inmarsat) who kindly provided access to many of the requested documents.

225 See, e.g., the discussion of a provisional application of Protocol no. 14 to the Convention for the Protection of Human Rights and Fundamental Freedoms by the CAHDI as contained in the document CM(2009)56 addendum of 31 March 2009. For earlier discussions of the use of provisional application with regard to protocols amending the ECHR which again contain a legal discussion of the mechanism, but do not address the question of the binding force, see, e.g., CDDH-GDR(2003)031 available at <http://www.coe.int/t/e/human_rights/cddh/3._committees/07.%20other%20committees%20and%20working%20groups/archives/06.%20guaranteeing%20human%20rights%20(cddh-gdr)/01.%20working%20documents/2003/2003_031_en.asp#TopOfPage> and CDDH-GDR(2003)020 <http://www.coe.int/t/e/human_rights/cddh/3._committees/07.%20other%20committees%20and%20working%20groups/archives/06.%20guaranteeing%20human%20rights%20(cddh-gdr)/01.%20working%20documents/2003/2003_020_en.asp#TopOfPage>.

226 The Legal Commission of the International Civil Aviation Organization (ICAO) considered whether or not to have recourse to provisional application with regard to existing and future amendments to the Chicago Convention, see A32-WP/10 LE/1 of 30/6/98, Agenda Item 35 [4.2], available at www.icao.int/icao/en/assembl/a32/wp/010.pdf.

227 The following statements illustrate the scepticism which is often expressed with regard to provisional application. In order to properly understand the statements it is necessary to mention that in Inmarsat the term 'rapid implementation' was used instead of 'provisional application' "to ease the consideration of the subject for Parties who had difficulty with agreeing to provisional application." Sagar, "Provisional Application in an International Organization," [47]. See, e.g., a Statement by the Representative of the Inmarsat Party of Japan stressing that "it [Japan] has strong concerns on the introduction of rapid implementation." Assembly/12/Report Annex 32. See also the Statement by the Representative of the Party of Costa Rica "In relation to rapid implementation, Costa Rica would have problems..." Assembly/12/Report Annex 14. Finally, a legal adviser to an international organisation mentioned in the context of responding to the 2007–2008 questionnaire that several States Parties to the relevant organisation had expressed "strong doubts on the legality of this practice [provisional application] when it concerns the constitutive instrument" of an international organisation.

mentioned in terms of the effect of provisional application on a State's internal law,[228] the matter of the binding force is not addressed.

The impression that there would not seem to be a big debate in practice on the binding force of provisionally applied treaties appears to be reinforced by the answers of legal advisers, given in their private capacity, to a question in the 2007–2008 questionnaire. The question relates to the above quoted question on the binding force of treaties during provisional application. Thus first it was asked "Does the principle of *pacta sunt servanda* apply to treaties during the period of their provisional application...?", and this was followed by the question "In your experience, is this position contested among States and/or international organizations?". The question received a total of twelve responses from Government legal advisers. Only one of these was affirmative (given in a private capacity), saying that it was contested in practice whether the principle of *pacta sunt servanda* applied to provisionally applied treaties.[229] A similar pattern emerges when looking at the responses on the same question by legal advisers to international organisations. The question received in total six responses by legal advisers to international organisations, given largely in their private capacity, and none of these was affirmative. Accordingly, awareness of the difference of opinion among the respondents is rather low. But this is only a snapshot in time, taken after the *Kardassopoulos* but prior to the *Yukos* award, and it is possible that the answers would have been different if given after the *Yukos* award.

The explanation of this phenomenon, if indeed it is one, may be that even if the notion of provisional application is surrounded by uncertainty, including the matter of the binding force of these treaties, States and international organisations may get by this in practice due to the possibility of expressing an intention to be bound (or not) in the usual ways, for instance by the wording, nomenclature and content of the undertaking. Therefore, even if in the abstract the meaning of the notion might not be clear, in concrete cases this would not necessarily need to pose a problem given that negotiators would discuss concrete treaty provisions with the usual indications of an intention to be bound (or not), and either agree or disagree on them. However, this is only to explain the possible absence of discussions surrounding the binding force of these treaties for instance

---

[228] See, e.g., CM(2009)56 add. [38].

[229] Seven were negative (three institutional responses and four given in a private capacity), two were to the effect that the respondent did not have any direct relevant experience, and two were unclear.

when considering recourse to the mechanism. Thus, this is not to say that the matter of the binding force of these treaties does not require clarification. It clearly does require clarification, given that treaties not only affect States and international organisations, but also the rights and obligations of individuals and companies, investments by investors etc.

Finally, based on the above research on the provisional entry into force and provisional application of commodity agreements, it appears that both terms imply an intention to be legally bound by the commodity agreement if the relevant clause is worded in treaty language and contains clauses generally assimilating the agreement's provisional entry into force to its definitive entry into force, and/or a provisional member to a (definitive) member. More generally, in the above research on commodity agreements no instance has been found in which there has been recourse to soft law language in the clauses on provisional entry into force and provisional application, nor has any other manifestations of an intention not to be legally bound been found within these agreements. Accordingly, it is conceivable that in the field of commodity agreements the terms 'provisional application' and 'provisional entry into force' are used only when there is an intention to be legally bound during those periods.

CONCLUDING REMARKS

Provisional application is an established mechanism of the law of treaties, despite the fact that many States would appear to have recourse to provisional application only in exceptional circumstances.[1] The possibility to bring forward in time the application of a treaty's provisions, while the treaty itself is not (yet) in force, has many diverse uses.[2] These range from remedying administrative issues, such as problems with planning and the possibly late commencement of treaty negotiations,[3] to responding to international crises, emergencies and other situations of urgency. In this latter case provisional application serves a purpose similar to that of emergency statutes in internal law,[4] and fulfils an important function in the international legal system. The purpose of the present book has been to examine the binding force of treaties during the period of their provisional application in theory and practice, given that this is debated in academic writings and contested in practice. The question is highly relevant because it concerns the stability and certainty of treaties subject to this mechanism, and because it determines the rules applicable to the regime of provisional application.

The purpose of the first chapter was to provide an introduction to provisional application. The natural starting point of any analysis in the law of treaties is the relevant provision in the VCLT 1969. Article 25 does not explain the meaning or effect of provisional application. Thus, the drafting history of Article 25 and the concomitant conceptualisation of provisional application was examined in an attempt at gaining a better understanding of the provision and its underlying mechanism. Furthermore, provisional application was analysed from an internal law perspective, because internal law can affect a treaty regime on the international plane,[5] including the content and features of agreements on provisional application.[6]

---

1 CoE and BIICL, eds., *Treaty Making*, see responses by Andorra, 111; Belgium, 127; France, 167; Greece, 183; Italy, 203; Luxembourg, 214; and Turkey, 281; contrast Spain, 263.

2 For a very good overview see Krieger, "Article 25," [1]-[8].

3 Remiro Brotóns, "The Spanish Constitution and International Law," *Spanish Yearbook of International Law* IX (2003): 43. See also Thomas Sägesser, "Die vorläufige Anwendung völkerrechtlicher Verträge," *Recht* 21 (2003): 91.

4 It does so in the sense that normal (lengthy) procedures can be reduced to a bare minimum, e.g., to produce a piece of legislation in a few days' time.

5 See Article 46. Bolintineanu, "Expression of Consent," 679.

6 Aust, *Modern Treaty Law*, 182.

Finally, the drafting history and the issues raised throughout the conceptualisation – be it the name of the mechanism, the constraints imposed by constitutional law, such as the need for a power of unilateral termination etc. – have been used in arguments that address the question of the legal character of these treaties. Thus, the first chapter was an introduction to provisional application and to several of its features; it also prepared the ground for the second and third chapters in which some of these features were analysed more closely when examining the arguments for and against the legally binding force of these treaties.

There is one point that deserves special mention with regard to the drafting history of Article 25. Until recently it was contested in academic writings whether the change of name at the 1968–1969 Vienna Conference from 'provisional entry into force' to 'provisional application' meant that these treaties were not anymore regarded as 'treaties in force' for the purposes of the *pacta sunt servanda* rule, according to which 'treaties in force' are binding. Now the debate can be closed because the position of the 1968–1969 Vienna conference on the binding force would appear to be clear.[7] In a string of (until recently apparently ignored) interpretative declarations to such effect, at least a dozen State delegates supported the view according to which 'provisionally applied' treaties fall under the ambit of the *pacta sunt servanda* rule – and their statements on the matter remained unopposed.[8] Most importantly, the President of the Plenary Meetings said that "in the light of the interpretative statements [...] made, it was obvious that the expression 'treaty in force' also covered treaties applied provisionally...".[9] Thus, any other position on the Vienna preparatory work would appear difficult to sustain. While some academic writings refer to the preparatory work of the 1968–1969 Vienna Conference,[10] this point would not appear to have been made thus far. Also, the overall significance of the Vienna Conference position for the debate, both in terms of the theoretical conception of the view that provisionally applied treaties are binding and for the view's support in practice, does not seem to have been sufficiently acknowledged.

The subsequent two chapters examined the theoretical debate and the arguments for and against the legally binding force of these treaties.

---

[7] See the comprehensive research by Mathy, "Article 25 VCLT 1969," 652, fn. 105. On this more generally, see the text to notes 232–241 in chapter 1 above.

[8] On this see note 226 in chapter 1 above.

[9] Vienna Conference, OR 1969: Plen. 12: §63.

[10] See note 236 in chapter 1 above.

More precisely, chapter two examined some of the arguments against the legally binding force of provisionally applied treaties. Their underlying assumption is that provisionally applied treaties are more similar to soft law agreements than treaties, due to certain features. One such feature is the power of a party to unilaterally terminate an agreement on provisional application (Article 25(2)). The other is the possibility of invoking internal law that conflicts with the provisionally applied treaty (a reverse of the general rule expressed in Article 27). The primary question discussed is whether this discretion prevents the provisionally applied treaty from having legally binding force, or whether a "discernible realm of obligation"[11] remains despite this discretion. Chapter two discussed these features in detail, by assessing their effect on the binding force of an undertaking within and outside the context of provisional application. Eventually, the criterion of 'third party interpretation' was used, i.e. whether the agreement is by reference to its substance capable of adjudication (then legally binding) or "inherently unsuited to adjudication"[12] (then non-legally binding). It was shown that these features do not render the undertaking unsuited to adjudication, so that they would not appear to exclude the legally binding force of these agreements.[13] However, if a limitation clause is intended to allow the invocation of legislation that has been adopted after the conclusion of the agreement (on provisional application) or after the commencement of provisional application, then this would enable the 'obligor' unilaterally to modify or exclude the provisional application of the treaty. This would make the undertaking similar to a 'potestative condition' where the obligor itself can determine whether and to which extent it is bound. Accordingly, the point may be reached where the undertaking may not be intended to be legally binding (or be incompatible with the nature of a legal obligation, since one is not bound to anyone other than oneself). It is not clear whether this interpretation of limitation clauses has been used in practice. But even if so, this would be an argument only against the binding force of these specific instances, and not against the binding force of provisionally applied treaties *in general*. All in all, the discretion allowed by provisional application does not necessarily exclude the legally binding nature of provisionally applied treaties, nor express an intention not to be bound.

---

11 Widdows, "What is an Agreement in International Law," 124.

12 Chinkin, "Challenge of Soft Law," 862.

13 See the text to notes 194–198 in chapter two above.

Chapter three continued the theoretical analysis by exploring in its first part some of the arguments put forward for the legally binding force of these treaties. Among these is the proposition that provisionally applied treaties are binding in much the same way as treaties in force. This is based on and developed from academic writings which either refer to the ILC conception of the mechanism in support of the view that these treaties are legally binding (for instance the ILC commentary to *pacta sunt servanda* according to which the words 'in force' in that Article also covered 'treaties provisionally in force'),[14] or rely on the terminology of 'provisional entry into force' when it comes to substantiating their view.[15] Thus, in part this proposition relies on a conceptual assimilation of provisionally applied treaties to treaties in force. The analysis looked at the concepts of 'entry into force' and 'application' in the VCLT and academic writings, and its result was that the ILC *conception* of the mechanism and its binding force as 'treaties provisionally in force' is outdated given the fact that the 1968-1969 Vienna Conference moved away from this concept and instead regarded the mechanism as a subset of a treaty's application.[16] Yet the ILC *position* on the binding force of these treaties, i.e. that these treaties are binding and fall within the ambit of the *pacta sunt servanda* rule, was shared by the majority of States delegates at the 1968–1969 Vienna Conference, as has been shown above.[17] Accordingly, reference to the ILC deliberations as support for the view that provisionally applied treaties are legally binding would be appropriate if it relied on the ILC *position* and the ILC's *authority*, but less so if it relied on the ILC's *conception* of the mechanism. Yet overall, additional reliance on the position of the 1968–1969 Vienna Conference (which confirmed that 'treaties in force' also covered treaties provisionally applied) would enhance the validity of this argument, given that ultimately it was the decision of the attending States delegates whether or not to accept the propositions submitted by the ILC to the law of treaties conference.

Furthermore, the argument was discussed according to which States generally intend to be bound by treaties during their provisional application.[18] While not every way in which such a 'general intention' was established has been found entirely convincing, the overall assumption has its

---

14 Final Commentary on Article 23, see ILC, Draft articles on the law of treaties: text as finally adopted by the Commission on 18 and 19 July 1966, UN Doc A/CN.4/190, 211, §3.

15 See note 14 in chapter 3 above.

16 See the text between notes 35 and 36 (sections 2.4. and 2.5.) in chapter 3 above.

17 See the text to notes 8 and 9 in chapter 4 above.

18 See section 3 of chapter 3 above, i.e., the text to notes 36–85 (of chapter 3).

merits, if it is understood in the following way: since in the long-run States opted for a treaty, i.e. a legally binding undertaking, in order to regulate the matter at hand, it is reasonable to assume that this is, generally, what they might want during provisional application, too, when they bring the application of the treaty forward in time: legally binding force and legal certainty. From this it would follow that provisionally applied treaties generally are intended to be legally binding, but that there would also be room for exceptions. Yet, this approach did not further specify how in individual cases such an intention to be bound (or the absence thereof) could be established.

In the second part of chapter three, explanations for the legally binding force or effects of treaties prior to their entry into force were examined, both specific to the context of Article 25 but also inspired from Article 18, 24(4) etc. At first sight, the legally binding force of provisionally applied treaties is difficult to square with the rule that treaties prior to their entry into force do not have obligatory force, at least if treaty obligations (and their binding force) are seen to 'flow from the treaty' itself once the treaty is in force.[19] (For instance in the context of Article 18, conceptions are found according to which these effects of the treaty cannot be derived from the treaty but only, for example, from general international law since the treaty is not yet in force. In reverse conclusion, this could be taken to mean that once the treaty is in force, its obligations and their binding force can be/are derived therefrom.) Consideration of these issues led to the understanding that the problem of the legally binding force of the rights and obligations of a treaty awaiting its entry into force probably is one of convention; i.e. that it is a matter of convention or agreement among States whether it is from the treaty's entry into force, signature or the adoption of the text of the treaty – or any other subsequent event – that they want the treaty to deploy the agreed legal effects.[20] This leads on to the general question why treaties are legally binding (i.e. the question of the basis of legal obligation), which then also concerns provisionally applied treaties. Yet since this is not a problem specific to provisional application, it does not need special attention in this context. So understood (and against the impression of first sight), the legally binding force of provisionally applied treaties does not raise any particular issues, and provisionally applied treaties can in the words of Jennings and Watts be

[19] Rogoff, "Unratified Treaty," 289; Alfred Verdross and Bruno Simma, *Universelles Völkerrecht*, 3rd ed. (Berlin: Duncker & Humblot, 1984), 68.

[20] See the text to notes 166 and 167 in chapter 3 above.

seen as a 'law-generating process' demonstrated by State practice.[21] This would appear to be unproblematic as long as States and international organisations make clear that this is the case, or with regard to which of these treaties this should be the case.

The analysis of the theoretical debate on the binding force of these treaties in chapters two and three was complemented by an analysis of practice in chapter four. A broad notion of practice was adopted so as to be able to look at what States, and to a lesser extent international organisations, 'say' and 'do'. Thus, first, statements by States and international organisations were examined to learn about their view(s) on the matter. The result of this was that there seemed to exist three different views: the majority view according to which provisionally applied treaties are legally binding, the first minority view according to which they are non-legally binding, and the second minority view according to which they can be both, either legally binding or non-legally binding. The first two corresponded to views put forward in academic writings. Yet, the third view would appear not to have been put forward or discussed in academic writings thus far and is different in that legally binding force (or the absence thereof) is not a defining feature of provisional application so understood.[22]

Thereafter, the binding force of provisionally applied treaties was examined by reference to the intention of the parties. More precisely, the intention of States and international organisations was analysed with regard to a multitude of agreements on provisional application, in order to gain an overview of the binding force of provisionally applied treaties and to understand patterns and regularities, including the frequency or rarity of an intention to be bound during that period. The result of this analysis was that intention would appear to be manifested in the same way as in other international law agreements, thus by the wording and nomenclature used, the content of the agreement etc. Furthermore, there would appear to be a high degree of consistency in this practice: the great majority of agreements analysed seem to be intended to be legally binding, although there is a minority of instances in which there would appear to be a deliberate use of manifestations of an intention not to be legally bound. The overall meaning of this result seems to be that the key to

---

[21] See note 166 in chapter 3 above.

[22] Those academic writings which mention the possibility of (exceptionally) non-legally binding provisionally applied treaties (see, e.g., the references in note 36 in chapter 3 above.) could be seen to come close to this view, but can be distinguished from it to the extent that provisionally applied treaties are generally seen to be legally binding.

understanding the binding force of provisionally applied treaties might not be the notion of provisional application itself,[23] but the usual manifestations of an intention to be bound (or otherwise), in the respective agreement on provisional application (i.e. language; nomenclature; form). Thus, an analysis thereof might help both to answer the question of the binding force of a specific treaty subject to provisional application as well as possibly the binding force of these treaties in general (when looking at a multitude of them).

With regard to the academic debate on the binding force of provisionally applied treaties, the following points can be made. First, it is noteworthy that many positions on the binding force of these treaties are phrased in broad and general terms. 'Provisionally applied treaties' *in general* are said to be legally binding or not. Either way it is rare that exceptions or qualifications to those positions are spelt out.[24] Thus, in these writings the impression is created that provisional application is a mechanism which always has the same effects with regard to binding force, and accordingly that provisionally applied treaties are a class of treaties which all share the same binding force (be it legally binding or not). Similarly, some of the arguments developed for each position concern so-called '*general* features' of provisionally applied treaties, for instance the possibility to invoke internal law, or are based on the object and purpose of provisional application *in general*.[25] From these arguments, positions on the binding force of 'provisionally applied treaties in general' are derived. Accordingly, it would appear that a large amount of academic debate in the case of provisional application deviates from the general approach that the binding force of agreements in international law has to be determined on a *case by case* basis, by reference to manifestations of an intention to be bound (or otherwise). Instead, the academic debate is, in large part,

---

[23] The expectation that the notion of provisional application might be the key to understanding the binding force and legal nature of provisionally applied treaties could underlie the interest in the notion of provisional application, and the criticism that this notion is not defined in the VCLT 1969 or ambiguous. For this criticism see, e.g., Hafner, "Provisional Application," 595; Rogoff and Gauditz, "Provisional Application," 51; Vignes, "Une notion ambiguë: la mise en application provisoire des traités," 181.

[24] For these exceptions see, e.g., Montag, *Völkerrechtliche Verträge*, 59. See also Arsanjani and Reisman, "Provisional Application," 101; van Panhuys, "The Netherlands Constitution and International Law," 94.

[25] A drawback of this approach would appear to be that sometimes features or commonalities are taken to be 'general' although they may only concern a specific sub-type of provisionally applied treaties (such as commodity agreements). Thus, generalisations are formulated and conclusions drawn with regard to provisionally applied treaties in general which for this reason may be inappropriate or too broad.

seemingly based on the underlying assumption that provisionally applied treaties are in a class of their own, all sharing the same binding force.

Within the confines of this research it would not appear that academic writings have questioned why this should be so, or where this broadly accepted underlying assumption comes from. It is possible that the perception of provisionally applied treaties as a class of treaties which all have the same binding force is a result of the ILC's position, as expressed in its commentary to the final draft Article. It may be recalled that the ILC stated that 'these treaties' produce legal effects and fall within the ambit of the *pacta sunt servanda* rule.[26] Of course it is difficult to prove that this is the origin of the perception. However, what is clear is that States[27] and commentators alike refer to the ILC position and commentary as support for their own position as to the binding force of provisionally applied treaties. An alternative or additional origin of this assumption could be the regulation of provisional application in the VCLT, which may raise the expectation that the mechanism (at least by default) produces the same effects whenever resort to it is had.

Be that as it may, based on the foregoing, the following conclusions can be drawn. The view that provisionally applied treaties are not legally binding is a minority view in academic writings and in practice. Similarly, the view according to which provisionally applied treaties can be either legally binding or not only enjoys little support in practice. By contrast, to say that provisionally applied treaties are legally binding would appear to enjoy most support both in academic writings and in practice.

Such a statement can be given two different meanings. First, it could be a description of the (assumed or shown) fact that most provisionally applied treaties are legally binding, thus be a *descriptive* statement. This seems to be corroborated in practice, given that most of the provisionally applied treaties examined for the present book appeared to be intended to be legally binding. Such a position could theoretically be based, for instance, on the approach that States and international organisations generally intend to be legally bound during the provisional application of a treaty.[28]

---

26 Final Commentary on Article 22, see ILC, Draft articles on the law of treaties: text as finally adopted by the Commission on 18 and 19 July 1966, UN Doc A/CN.4/190, 210, §1 and Final Commentary on Article 23, 211, §3.

27 See the delegates' statements at the Vienna Conference 1968–69: OR 1968: CoW 29 Chile §32; Norway §58; Indonesia §59; OR 1969: Plen. 11: UK §58; India §70; Plen. 12: Yugoslavia §50; Romania §57; also one respondent in the 2007–2008 questionnaire referred to the ILC commentary.

28 Montag, *Völkerrechtliche Verträge*, 51; Krenzler, *Vorläufige Anwendung*, 57.

Alternatively, to say that provisionally applied treaties are legally binding could be intended to state the rule or definition according to which provisionally applied treaties are legally binding, and thus be a *prescriptive* statement.[29] This could be based on the position of the 1968–1969 Vienna Conference (that despite the change of name, these treaties still were regarded as 'treaties in force' for the purposes of the *pacta sunt servanda* rule) in conjunction with the ILC position and some more recent support in practice such as the pronouncements of the *Yukos* Tribunal[30] or the institutional responses to the 2007–2008 questionnaire.

Both positions appear tenable in terms of theoretical conception and support in practice. However, in both instances it should be made clear – and this might have been missing in previous academic analyses – that ultimately, the binding force of these treaties depends upon the intention of the parties. In other words, to say that these treaties are legally binding still requires that in every individual instance of provisional application, the intention of the (future) parties to be bound (or not) has to be ascertained.[31] In this sense the binding force and legal nature of provisionally applied treaties is similar to that of any other agreement in international law.

[29] An example of this is the position expressed at the 1968–1969 Vienna Conference when stating that the phrase "treaties in force" in Article 26 also covers provisionally applied treaties (thereby positing provisionally applied treaties as *pacta*).

[30] *Yukos Universal Ltd v Russian Federation* (30 November 2009), [314] 116.

[31] If meant as a descriptive statement, in order to know whether the specific agreement follows the majority of agreements on provisional application or is an exception; if meant as a prescriptive statement, in order to know whether this is a case (or not) of provisional application properly so called.

APPENDIX

BACKGROUND INFORMATION ON THE 2007–2008 QUESTIONNAIRE

Between December 2007 and summer 2008, 159 States and 18 international organizations were contacted by email with the questionnaire attached. As a result, twenty completed questionnaires were received, as well as some brief 'freestyle' written statements summarizing the participant's experience with the provisional application of treaties. In addition, six interviews were conducted (on the basis of the questionnaire).

Telephone numbers and email addresses were generally obtained from the website of the Ministry in charge of treaties (or international organization). Alternatively, attempts were made to obtain these from the Embassy of the relevant country in the United Kingdom. Finally, in some instances, contact was facilitated by my former supervisors.

2007–2008 Questionnaire

Questionnaire on the Provisional Application of Treaties

This questionnaire is subdivided into four parts: I: General; II: *Pacta sunt servanda*; III: Implementation; IV: Miscellaneous. You are most welcome to raise any issues you feel would be of interest to the project. Please note that not all questions may be equally relevant to your institution's practice. With regard to questions which tend to relate to States (concerning e.g. the separation of powers between the executive and the legislature), Legal Advisers to international organizations are very welcome to answer them from their perspective if they wish to do so. The questionnaire is intended to elicit personal responses, i.e. responses drawing from your own personal experience. However, institutional rather than personal responses are also welcome. Furthermore, if you feel that there might be someone else working in a different institution that you would recommend as being well-placed to respond to this questionnaire or any questions therein, I would be most grateful if you could forward it to them and/or inform me accordingly in part IV at the end of the questionnaire. Finally, part IV allows you to specify the level of confidentiality you feel appropriate with regard to the information provided.

To answer a question, move the mouse to the grey answer field underneath the question and left-click on it once (for further information on this, left-click on the first answer field and press F1). Due to time constraints relating to my PhD, it would be very much appreciated if you could **return the completed questionnaire by the 03.03.08.** Please do not hesitate to contact me should any questions arise. For further information on my research, please visit [information has been removed].

I. *General*

1. *Terminology & the Clause Providing for Provisional Application*

In this questionnaire, the term 'provisional application' refers to instances where a treaty is applied prior to its entry into force, whether the participant[1] has expressed its consent to be bound by the treaty or not, and whether the participant has implemented the treaty into internal law[2] by legislation and/or acts of the executive or not.

a) Does this accord with your understanding of the term? *Please explain.*

b) Is there a difference between 'provisional application' and 'provisional entry into force'? *If yes, please explain.*

c) Does it make a (legal) difference whether the clause providing for provisional application is contained in the treaty itself or in a separate instrument, e.g. a protocol, resolution, final act etc? *If yes, please explain.*

2. *Bilateral and Multilateral Treaties:*

a) Is there a difference in practice of States and international organizations between bilateral and multilateral treaties with regard to provisional application? *If yes, please explain.*

b) Is it a purely unilateral decision to provisionally apply a multilateral treaty, or is there a need to obtain consent from the other participant(s) for which the treaty either is already in force or is provisionally applied? If not, how else is this done?

3. *Situations Underlying Provisional Application:*

In what situations does your State or international organization have recourse to provisional application in both the international and internal spheres of law?

---

[1] The term 'participant' refers to a State or international organization participating in the provisional application of a treaty.

[2] The term 'internal law' is used with regard to international organizations as well as States. With regard to States, it is used generically, and comprises all laws and regulations in force within a State, regardless of the authority adopting or creating the law, or the level at which the law operates (central, federal etc.).

International sphere of law:

Internal sphere of law (do factors such as parliamentary approval of/consent to the treaty, implementing legislation etc. play a role? If so, how?) *Please specify the legal system to which you are referring.*

4. *Position with Regard to Provisional Application:*

Is your State or international organization in favour of provisional application or not? Why?

5. *Provisional Application and Internal Law*

a) Does your State's or international organization's internal law regulate the provisional application of treaties? *If so, please provide further information on/ reference to the relevant provision(s) of your State's or international organization's internal law.*

b) Does a description of your State's or international organization's practice in the field of provisional application exist, for instance in a guide on treaty-making, or with regard to States in a digest of State practice (or similar) published by, for example, your Ministry of Foreign Affairs? *If so, please provide further information on/reference to it.*

c) Does provisional application in your State create 'separation of powers' issues, in the sense that – through provisional application – the government has more powers in respect of provisionally applied treaties than it has relating to treaties (fully) in force? (This might be at the expense of other constitutional organs, such as parliament, because provisional application could mean a treaty is (provisionally) applied regardless of the absence of parliamentary approval or implementing legislation. These parliamentary actions might be deferred to a later point in time, e.g. when the treaty enters into force. Besides this 'deferral' of parliamentary powers relating to treaties, it is also possible that provisional application could end before any of these parliamentary actions take place (and the treaty does not enter into force at all)).

d) Are you aware of any cases in your State's courts or courts affiliated to your international organization involving provisionally applied treaties? *If so, please provide further information on/reference to them.*

e) Are you aware of any debates concerning provisional application in parliament, special committees thereof, or in an organ of an international organisation? *If such information is not confidential, kindly provide information on/references to such debates.*

II. *Pacta Sunt Servanda*

1. *The Binding Force of Treaties During the Period of Provisional Application:*

a) Does the principle of *pacta sunt servanda* apply to treaties during the period of their provisional application, i.e. are treaties binding during the period of their provisional application? *Please explain.*

b) In your experience, is this position contested among States and/or international organizations? *If yes, please explain.*

c) If they are binding, are the consequences of breach (of a provisionally applied treaty) the same as those of a treaty that is (fully) in force? *If not, please explain.*

2. *Compliance with Treaties During the Period of their Provisional Application:*

a) Do States and/or international organizations tend to comply with treaties during the period of their provisional application? *Please explain.*

b) Is this compliance different from compliance with treaties that are (fully) in force? *If so, please explain.*

3. *Breaches of a Treaty During the Period of its Provisional Application:*

a) Are you aware of any instances of breach of a treaty during the period of its provisional application? *If yes, please provide examples.*

b) If so, is this frequent or infrequent?

III. *Implementation of Provisionally Applied Treaties into Internal Law*

1. *Limitation Clauses and their Effect:*

Frequently, a provision on provisional application is accompanied by a clause establishing a hierarchy between the provisionally applied treaty and internal law. Examples of such clauses, sometimes called 'limitation clauses', are the following:

> "All such States and entities shall apply this Agreement provisionally *in accordance with their national or internal laws and regulations*, with effect from…" [Article 7(2) Agreement Relating to the Implementation of Part XI of the United Nations Convention on the Law of the Sea (UNCLOS), emphasis added]
>
> "… undertake to apply provisionally on and after January 1, 1948 Part II of that Agreement *to the fullest extent not inconsistent with existing legislation.*" [Protocol of Provisional Application of the General Agreement on Tariffs and Trade (GATT), Article 1b, emphasis added]

a) If there is no further specification, as in the second example from the GATT protocol (which simply refers to "existing legislation"), do such clauses refer only to 'internal law' existing at the time when that clause comes into effect/at the time of the commencement of provisional application, or do they also refer to internal law enacted any time thereafter? (In other words, if a State subsequently adopts internal law that restricts the application of the provisionally applied treaty, will such a subsequent law validly limit the extent of the provisional application for that State on the international plane?) *Please explain.*

b) Do limitation clauses exempt States from any implementation, or is in your State a distinction drawn between implementing legislation passed by parliament on the one hand and implementing acts adopted by the executive (the government and/or the administration) on the other? Or would a specific effect such as the latter depend upon the specific wording of the clause? *Please explain.*

c) How do States and international organizations in a multilateral treaty which contains a limitation clause know about the extent of other participants' undertakings (and possibly obligations) under the treaty during its provisional application? Do these clauses create an element of uncertainty? *Please explain.*

d) In a multilateral treaty which contains a limitation clause, is there a mechanism safeguarding the reciprocity of the undertakings (comparable to e.g. Article 21(1)b Vienna Convention on the Law of Treaties 1969), or do no such concerns arise? *Please explain.*

2. *Absence of Limitation Clauses:*

a) In the absence of limitation clauses, are treaties implemented into your State's or international organization's internal law during the period of their provisional application? If so, how?

b) Is there a difference between implementing legislation passed by parliament and implementing acts adopted by the executive (government or administration)? *Please explain.*

3. *Unilateral Declarations or 'Reservations'*

Have you come across unilateral declarations made upon the signature of a provisionally applied treaty or upon the notification of the participation in the provisional application of a treaty along the following lines:

> ".. the Government of Japan implements the said Agreement during the period of provisional application *within the limitations of its internal legislation and budgets.*" [Japanese declaration made upon notification of the provisional application of the 1993 International Cocoa Agreement, emphasis added]
>
> (*If not, please move on to part IV, Miscellaneous*)

a) Are such declarations made frequently or infrequently?

b) In your experience, in what situations do States or international organizations have recourse to them? Does it matter whether the clause providing for provisional application contains a limitation clause? *Please explain.*

c) Is it open to any State/international organization with regard to any treaty subject to provisional application to formulate such a declaration, or are such declarations the outcome of specific circumstances and negotiations, limited to certain treaties or kinds of treaties? *Please explain.*

d) Are other States and/or international organizations participating in the provisional application of the treaty able to react to such declarations? If so, how?

IV. *Miscellaneous:*

1. *Confidentiality and Anonymity:*

The information provided will remain anonymous. If you so wish, your (specific) institutional affiliation will not be mentioned. Please indicate below, if this is the case.

All further requests you may have regarding confidentiality will be respected.

2. *Categorisation of the Information Provided:*

For the purpose of analysing the information provided, could you kindly specify whether your responses are personal or institutional:

3. *Suggestion of Another Expert on the Provisional Application of Treaties:*

If you are able to suggest any other expert that you believe will be able to provide answers to this questionnaire, particularly in relation to other jurisdictions or international organizations, please provide their title, full name and contact details.

4. *Comments or Suggestions:*

Are there any comments or suggestions relating to the questionnaire you would like to make?

5. *Research Results:*

Do you wish to be informed of the research results in due course?

Thank you very much for your participation. Your expertise, experience, time and consideration are truly appreciated.

BIBLIOGRAPHY

Books and Monographs

Anzilotti, Dionisio. *Cours de droit international.* Vol. 1. Translated by Gilbert Gidel, Paris: Sirey, 1929.

Aust, Anthony. *Modern Treaty Law and Practice.* 2nd ed. Cambridge: Cambridge University Press, 2007.

Bernhardt, Rudolf, ed. *Encyclopedia of Public International Law.* Vol. 4. Amsterdam: Elsevier, 2000.

Bernhardt, Rudolf, ed. *Encyclopedia of Public International Law.* Vol. 3. Amsterdam: Elsevier, 1997.

Bernhardt, Rudolf, ed. *Encyclopedia of International Law.* Vol. 2. Amsterdam: Elsevier, 1995.

Bernhardt, Rudolf, ed. *Encyclopedia of Public International Law.* Vol. 1. Amsterdam: North-Holland, 1992.

Birnie, Patricia, Alan Boyle and Catherine Redgwell. *International Law and the Environment.* 3rd ed. Oxford: Oxford University Press, 2009.

Bittner, Ludwig. *Die Lehre von den völkerrechtlichen Vertragsurkunden.* Stuttgart: Deutsche Verlagsanstalt, 1924.

Blix, Hans. *Treaty-Making Power.* London: Stevens & Sons Limited, 1960.

Bluntschli, Johann Caspar. *Droit international codifié.* Translated by MC Lardy. 3rd ed. Paris: Librairie Guillaumin, 1881.

Boyle, Alan and Christine Chinkin. *The Making of International Law.* Oxford: Oxford University Press, 2007.

Briggs, Herbert W. *The Law of Nations.* 2nd ed. London: Stevens & Sons, 1953.

Brownlie, Ian. *Principles of International Law.* 7th ed. Oxford: Oxford University Press, 2008.

Butler, William E. *The Law of Treaties in Russia and the Commonwealth of Independent States: Text and Commentary.* Cambridge: Cambridge University Press, 2002.

Cheng, Bin. *General Principles of Law.* London: Stevens & Sons, 1953.

Chimni, Bhupinder S. *International Commodity Agreements.* London: Croom Helm, 1987.

Chinkin, Christine. *Third Parties in International Law.* Oxford: Clarendon Press, 1993.

Chossudovsky, Evgeny. *"East-West" Diplomacy for Environment in the United Nations.* New York: United Nations Institute for Training and Research, 1989.

Corten, Olivier and Pierre Klein, eds. *Les Conventions de Vienne sur le Droit des Traités: commentaire article par article.* 3 vols. Brussels: Bruylant, 2006.

Corten, Olivier and Pierre Klein, eds. *The Vienna Conventions on the Law of Treaties: A Commentary.* 2 vols. Oxford: Oxford University Press, 2011

Council of Europe and British Institute of International and Comparative Law, eds. *Treaty Making: Expression of Consent by States to be Bound by a Treaty.* London: Kluwer Law International, 2001.

Cummins Sally J. and David P. Stewart, eds. *Digest of United States Practice in International Law 2002.* Washington, DC: International Law Institute 2003.

D'Amato, Anthony. *The Concept of Custom in International Law.* Ithaca, NY: Cornell University Press, 1971.

Daillier, Patrick, Alain Pellet, and Mathias Forteau,. *Droit international public.* 8th ed. Paris: Librairie Générale de Droit et de Jurisprudence, 2009.

David, Arie E. *The Strategy of Treaty Termination.* New Haven: Yale University Press, 1975.

de Visscher, Charles. *Théories et réalités en droit international public.* 4th ed. Paris: Pedone, 1970.

Degan, Vladimir D. *Sources of International Law*. The Hague: Martinus Nijhoff Publishers, 1997.
Dehousse, Fernand. *La ratification des traités*. Paris: Recueil Sirey, 1935.
Dictionnaire de la terminologie de droit international public. Paris: Sirey, 1960.
Dörr, Oliver and Kirsten Schmalenbach, eds. *Vienna Convention on the Law of Treaties: A Commentary*. Heidelberg: Springer, 2012.
Eisemann, Pierre Michel. *L'Organisation Internationale du Commerce des produits de base*. Brussels: Bruylant, 1982.
Elias, Olufemi A. and Chin Leng Lim. *The Paradox of Consensualism in International Law*. The Hague: Kluwer Law International, 1998.
Elias, Taslim Olawale. *Modern Law of Treaties*. Dobbs Ferry: Oceana Publications, 1974.
Field, David Dudley. *Outlines of an International Code*. 2nd ed. New York: Baker, Voorhis & Company, 1876.
Fiore, Pasquale. *International Law Codified: and its Legal Sanction*. New York: Baker, Voorhis & Company, 1918.
Fitzmaurice, Malgosia and Olufemi A. Elias. *Contemporary Issues in the Law of Treaties*. Utrecht: Eleven International Publishing, 2005.
Frangulis, Antoine F. *Théorie et pratique des traités internationaux*. Paris: Académie Diplomatique Internationale, 1934.
Gardiner, Richard K. *International Law*. London: Pearson Longman, 2003.
——. *Treaty Interpretation*. Oxford: Oxford University Press, 2008.
Gautier, Philippe. *Essai sur la Définition des Traités entre Etats*. Brussels: Bruylant, 1993.
Geslin, Albane. *La mise en application provisoire des traités*. Paris: Pedone, 2005.
Haraszti, György. *Some Fundamental Problems of the Law of Treaties*. Budapest: Akadémiai Kiadó, 1973.
Harris, David J. *Cases and Materials on International Law*. 6th ed. London: Sweet & Maxwell, 2004.
Henkin, Louis. *How Nations Behave: Law and Foreign Policy*. 2nd ed. New York: Columbia University Press, 1979.
Hertslet, Edward. *Map of Europe by Treaty*. Vol. 3. London: Butterworths, 1875.
Holloway, Kaye. *Modern Trends in Treaty Law*. London: Oceana Publications, 1967.
Ipsen, Knut: *Völkerrecht*. 5th ed. Munich: C.H. Beck, 2004.
Jennings, Robert Yewdall and Arthur Watts, eds. *Oppenheim's International Law*, Vol. 1. 9th ed. Harlow: Longman, 1992,
Jessup, Philip C. *A Modern Law of Nations*. New York: The Macmillan Company, 1949.
Kelsen, Hans. *Principles of International Law*. 2nd ed. New York: Holt Rinehart and Winston Inc., 1967.
——. *The Law of the United Nations*. London: Stevens & Sons, 1950.
Khan, Kabir-ur-Rahman. *The Law and Organisation of International Commodity Agreements*. Boston: Martinus Nijhoff Publishers, 1982.
Kindred, Hugh M. et al. *International Law Chiefly as Interpreted and Applied in Canada*. 5th ed. Toronto: Edmond Montgomery Publications, 1993.
Klabbers, Jan. *The Concept of Treaty in International Law*. The Hague: Kluwer Law International, 1996.
Klein, Eckart. *Gesetzgebung ohne Parlament?*. Berlin: De Gruyter, 2004.
Krause-Ablaß, Wolf-Dietrich. *Intertemporales Völkerrecht*, Hamburg: Alfred Metzner Verlag, 1970.
Krenzler, Horst-Günther. *Die vorläufige Anwendung völkerrechtlicher Verträge*. Freiburg im Breisgau: Rota-Druck, 1963.
Laly-Chevalier, Caroline. *La Violation du Traité*. Brussels: Bruylant, 2005.
Lauterpacht, Hersch, ed. *Oppenheim's International Law*. 8th ed. London: Longmans, Green & Co, 1955.
Leigh, Monroe, Merritt R. Blakeslee, and L. Benjamin Ederington, eds. *National Treaty Law and Practice. Studies in Transnational Legal Policy*, no. 30. Washington, DC: American Society of International Law, 1999.

Lettow, Erich. "Die völkerrechtliche Bindung nicht ratifizierter Verträge." PhD diss., University of Bonn, 1954.

Luck, Edward C. and Michael W. Doyle, eds. *International Law and Organization: Closing the Compliance Gap*. Lanham: Rowman & Littlefield, 2004.

McNair, Arnold Duncan. *The Law of Treaties*. Oxford: Clarendon Press, 1961.

Meißner, Hans-Otto. *Vollmacht und Ratifikation bei völkerrechtlichen Verträgen nach Deutschem Recht*. Göttingen: Vandenhoeck & Ruprecht, 1934.

Michie, Andrew Gordon. "The Provisional Application of Treaties with Special Reference to Arms Control, Disarmament and Non-Proliferation Instruments." LL.M. thesis, University of South Africa, 2004.

Mitsilegas, Valsamis. *EU Criminal Law*. Oxford: Hart Publishing, 2009.

Montag, Frank. *Völkerrechtliche Verträge mit vorläufigen Wirkungen*. Berlin: Duncker & Humblot, 1986.

Moore, John Basset. *A Digest of International Law*. Vol. 2. Washington, DC: Government Printing Office, 1906.

Müller, Jörg Paul. *Vertrauensschutz im Völkerrecht*. Köln: Carl Heymanns Verlag, 1971.

O'Connell, Daniel P. *International Law*. Vol. 1. London: Stevens & Sons Limited, 1965.

——. *International Law*. Vol. 1, 2nd ed. London: Stevens & Sons, 1970.

O'Connor, John F. *Good Faith in International Law*. Dartmouth: Aldershot, 1991.

Phillimore, WGF. *Three Centuries of Treaties of Peace*. London: John Murray, 1917.

Picone, Paolo. *L'applicazione in via provvisoria degli accordi internazionali*. Naples: Casa Editrice Dott. Eugenio Jovene, 1973.

Poirat, Florence. "Le traité comme acte juridique." PhD diss., Université Panthéon Assas, 1997.

Pritzkow, Sebastian. *Das völkerrechtliche Verhältnis zwischen der EU und Russland im Energiesektor*. Heidelberg: Springer, 2011.

Reuter, Paul. *La Convention de Vienne du 29 Mai 1969 sur le Droit des Traités*. Paris: Librairie Armand Colin, 1970.

——. *Droit International Public*. 6th ed. (Paris: Presses Universitaires de France, 1983)

——. *Introduction au Droit des Traités*. 2nd ed. Paris: Presses Universitaires de France, 1985.

Roe, Thomas and Matthew Happold. *Settlement of Investment Disputes under the Energy Charter Treaty*. Cambridge: Cambridge University Press, 2011.

Rovine Arthur W., ed. *Digest of US Practice in International Law 1974*. Washington, DC: Department of State Publication, 1975.

Ruda, José María. *The Final Acceptance of International Conventions*. Muscatine, IA: The Stanley Foundation, 1976.

Russell, Ruth B. *A History of the United Nations Charter*. Washington, DC: Brookings Institution, 1958.

Sand, Peter H. *Lessons Learned in Global Environmental Governance*. Washington, DC: World Resources Institute, 1990.

Scelle, Georges. *Précis de Droit des Gens*. Vol. 2. Paris: Sirey, 1934.

Schermers, Henry G. and Niels Blokker. *International Institutional Law*. 4th ed. Boston: Martinus Nijhoff Publishers, 2004.

Schmidt, Bruno. *Über die völkerrechtliche clausula rebus sic stantibus sowie einige verwandte Rechtsnormen*. Leipzig: Dunker & Humblot, 1907.

Schwarzenberger, Georg. *International Law*. Vol. 1. 3rd ed. London: Stevens & Sons, 1957.

——. *International Law*. Vol. 3. London: Stevens & Sons, 1976.

Senden, Linda. *Soft Law in European Community Law*. Oxford: Hart Publishing, 2004.

Shaw, Malcom N. *International Law*. 6th ed. Cambridge: Cambridge University Press, 2008.

Shelton Dinah, ed. *Commitment and Compliance*. Oxford: Oxford University Press, 2000.

Sinclair, Ian McTaggart. *The Vienna Convention on the Law of Treaties*. 2nd ed. Manchester: Manchester University Press, 1984.

Smets, Paul F. *La conclusion des accords en forme simplifiée*. Brussels: Bruylant, 1969.

United Nations. *UN Final Clauses of Multilateral Treaties-Handbook*. New York: United Nations, 2003.
Vamvoukos, Athanassios. *Termination of Treaties in International Law: the Doctrines of Rebus Sic Stantibus and Desuetude*. Oxford: Clarendon Press, 1985.
Verdross, Alfred and Bruno Simma. *Universelles Völkerrecht: Theorie und Praxis*. 3rd ed. Berlin: Duncker & Humblot, 1984.
Verwey, Delano R. *The European Community, the European Union and the International Law of Treaties*. The Hague: T.M.C. Asser Press, 2004.
Villiger, Mark Eugen. *Customary International Law and Treaties*. Dordrecht: Martinus Nijhoff Publishers, 1985.
——. *Commentary on the 1969 Vienna Convention on the Law of Treaties*. Leiden: Martinus Nijhoff Publishers, 2009.
Whiteman, Marjorie M. *Digest of International Law*. Vol. 14. Washington, DC: Department of State Publication, 1970.
Wolfke, Karol. *Custom in Present International Law*. 2nd ed. Boston: Martinus Nijhoff Publishers, 1993.
Wolfrum, Rüdiger, eds. *Max Planck Encyclopedia of International Law* online edition. Oxford: Oxford University Press, 2008-. http://www.mpepil.com.
World Trade Organization, ed. *GATT Secretariat Guide to GATT Law and Practice*, 6th ed. Geneva: WTO Secretariat, 1994.
Zoller, Elisabeth. *La bonne foi en droit international public*. Paris: Pedone, 1977.

Articles and Chapters

"Three International Commodity Agreements." *British Yearbook of International Law* 35 (1959): 240–244.
Abbott, Kenneth W. and Duncan Snidal. "Hard and Soft Law in International Governance." *International Organization* 54 (2000): 421–456.
Abbott, Kenneth W., Robert O. Keohane, Andrew Moravcsik, Anne-Marie Slaughter, and Duncan Snidal. "The Concept of Legalization." *International Organization* (2000): 401–419.
Achour, Rafia Ben, Frikha Imed, and Mounir Snoussi. "Article 14 VCLT 1969." In Corten and Klein, *The Vienna Conventions on the Law of Treaties : A Commentary*, 288-304.
Akehurst, Michael B. "Custom as a Source of International Law." *British Yearbook of International Law* 47 (1974–75): 1–53.
Anderson, D. H. "Resolution and Agreement Relating to the Implementation of Part XI of the UN Convention on the Law of the Sea." *Zeitschrift für ausländisches öffentliches Recht und Rechtsvergleichung* 55 (1995): 275–289.
Andorno, Roberto. "The Invaluable Role of Soft Law in the Development of Universal Norms in Bioethics." Last modified July 2007. http://www.unesco.de/1507.html?&L%20 =%200
Arsanjani, Mahnoush H. and W. Michael Reisman, "Provisional Application of Treaties in International Law: The Energy Charter Treaty Awards," in *The Law of Treaties Beyond the Vienna Convention*, 86–104. Edited by Enzo Cannizzaro. Oxford: Oxford University Press, 2011.
Asada, Masahiko. "CTBT: Legal Questions Arising from Its Non-Entry-Into-Force." *Journal of Conflict and Security Law* 7 (2002): 85–122.
Aust, Anthony. "The Theory and Practice of Informal International Instruments." *International and Comparative Law Quarterly* 35 (1986): 787–812.
——. "Limping Treaties: Lessons from Multilateral Treaty-Making." *Netherlands International Law Review* 50 (2003): 243–266.
Baxter, Richard R. "International Law 'in her Infinite Variety'." *International and Comparative Law Quarterly* 29 (1980): 549–566.

Bartels, Lorand. "Legal Constraints on the EU's Ability to Withdraw EPA Preferences under Regulation 1528/2007." Briefing Note, European Centre for Development Policy Management 27 (2011): 1–5.

——. "Withdrawing Provisional Application of Treaties: Has the EU Made a Mistake." *Cambridge Journal of International and Comparative Law* 1 (2012): 112–118.

Bederman, David J. "The 1871 London Declaration, *Rebus Sic Stantibus* and a Primitivist View of the Law of Nations." *American Journal of International Law* 82 (1988): 1–40.

Belz, Matthew. "Comment: Provisional Application of the Energy Charter Treaty: Kardassopoulos v. Georgia and improving provisional application in multilateral treaties." *Emory International Law Review* 22 (2008): 727–760.

Bernhardt, Rudolf. "Treaties." In Bernhardt, *Encyclopedia of Public International Law*, vol. 4, 926–933.

Beyerlin, Ulrich. "Pactum de Contrahendo, Pactum de Negotiando." In Bernhardt, *Encyclopedia of Public International Law*, vol. 3, 854–858.

Bindschedler, Rudolf. "Treaties, Reservations." In Bernhardt, *Encyclopedia of Public International Law*, vol. 4, 965–968.

Bindschedler-Robert, Denise. "De la rétroactivité en droit international public." In *Recueil d'Etudes de Droit International en Hommage à Paul Guggenheim*, 184–200. Geneva: Faculte de Droit de l'Universite de Geneve, 1968.

Bishop, William W., "Reservations to Treaties." *Recueil des Cours de l'Académie de la Haye* 103 (1961): 245–341.

Boisson de Chazournes, Laurence, Anne-Marie La Rosa, and Makane Moise Mbengue. "Article 18 VCLT 1969." In Corten and Klein, *The Vienna Conventions on the Law of Treaties : A Commentary*, 369–403.

Bolintineanu, Alexandru. "Expression of Consent to be Bound by a Treaty in the Light of the 1969 Vienna Convention." *American Journal of International Law* 68 (1974): 672–686.

Bothe, Michael. "Legal and Non-Legal Norms." *Netherlands Yearbook of International Law* XI (1980): 65–95.

——. "Compliance." In Wolfrum, *Max Planck Encyclopedia of International Law* online edition. Last modified October 2010. http://www.mpepil.com.

Boyle, Alan E. "Some Reflections on the Relationship of Treaties and Soft Law." *International and Comparative Law Quarterly* 48 (1999): 901–913.

Brower, Charles H. "Arbitration." In Wolfrum, *Max Planck Encyclopedia of International Law* online edition. Last modified February 2007. http://www.mpepil.com.

Browne, Marjorie Ann. "The Law of the Sea Convention and US Policy." Congressional Research Service, 2005. http://www.fas.org/sgp/crs/row/IB95010.pdf

Buffard, Isabelle and Zemanek, Karl. "The Object and Purpose of a Treaty: an Enigma." *Austrian Review of International and European Law* 3 (1998): 311–343.

Caddell, Richard. "Depositary." In Wolfrum, *Max Planck Encyclopedia of International Law* online edition. Last modified June 2006. http://www.mpepil.com.

Cahier, Philippe. "L'obligation de ne pas priver un traité de son objet et but avant son entrée en vigueur." In *Mélanges Fernand Dehousse*, vol. 1, 31–38. Paris: Fernand Nathan, 1979.

Capotorti, Francesco. "L'extinction et la suspension des traités." *Recueil des Cours de l'Académie de la Haye* 134 (1971): 427–587.

Charme, Joni S. "The Interim Obligation of Article 18 of the Vienna Convention of the Law of Treaties: Making Sense of an Enigma." *George Washington Journal of International Law and Economics* 25 (1991–1992): 71–114.

Charney, Jonathan L. "Commentary. Compliance with International Soft Law." In *Commitment and Compliance*. Edited by Dinah Shelton, 115–120. Oxford: Oxford University Press, 2000.

Charpentier, Jean. "Pratique française de droit international." *Annuaire Français de Droit International* XXI (1975): 1014–1077.

Chayes, Abram and Antonia Handler Chayes. "On Compliance." *International Organization* 47 (1993): 175–205.

Chinkin, Christine. "A Hard Look at Soft Law." *American Society of International Law Proceedings* 82 (1988): 371–395.

——. "The Challenge of Soft Law." *International and Comparative Law Quarterly* 38 (1989): 850–866.

——. "A Mirage in the Sand? Distinguishing Binding and Non-Binding Relations Between States." *Leiden Journal of International Law* 10 (1997): 223–247.

——. "Normative Development in the International Legal System." In *Commitment and Compliance*. Edited by Dinah Shelton, 21–42. Oxford: Oxford University Press, 2000.

Chrispeels, Erik. "Simplifying International Commodity Agreements." In *International Commodity Organisations in Transition*. Edited by Erik Chrispeels, 349–358. London: Cameron May, 2002.

Christakis, Theodore. "Article 56 VCLT 1969." In Corten and Klein, *The Vienna Conventions on the Law of Treaties : A Commentary*, 1251–1276.

Cohen, Harlan G. "Finding International Law: Rethinking the Doctrine of Sources." *Iowa Law Review* 93 (2007–8): 67–129.

Condorelli, Luigi. Review of *L'applicazione in via provvisoria degli accordi internazionali*, by Paolo Picone. *Italian Yearbook of International Law* 1 (1975): 382–386.

Copithorne, Maurice. "Canadian Practice in International Law." *Canadian Yearbook of International Law* XVI (1978): 359–377.

Cot, Jean-Pierre. "La bonne foi et la conclusion des traités." *Revue Belge de Droit International* (1968): 140–159.

——. "Margin of Appreciation." In Wolfrum, *Max Planck Encyclopedia of International Law* online edition. Last modified June 2007. http://www.mpepil.com.

Crawford, James. "The Legal Effect of Automatic Reservations to the Jurisdiction of the International Court." *British Yearbook of International Law* 50 (1979): 63–86.

de Visscher, Paul. "Cours de droit international public." *Recueil des Cours de l'Académie de la Haye* 136 (1972): 1–202.

Denza, Eileen. "The Relationship between International and National Law." In *International Law*. 3rd ed. Edited by Malcom D. Evans, 411–438. Oxford: Oxford University Press Oxford, 2010.

Distefano, Giovanni. "The Conceptualization (Construction) of Territorial Title in the Light of the International Court of Justice Case Law." *Leiden Journal of International Law* 19 (2006): 1041–1075.

Do Nascimento e Silva, Geraldo Eulalio. "Le facteur temps et les traités." *Recueil des Cours de l'Académie de la Haye* 154 (1977): 215–297.

Dolzer, Rudolf. "Connally Reservation." In Bernhardt, *Encyclopedia of Public International Law*, vol. 41, 755–756.

Dörr, Oliver. "Codifying and Developing Meta-Rules: The ILC and the Law of Treaties." *German Yearbook of International Law* 49 (2006): 129–164.

Eisemann, Pierre Michel. "Engagements Non-Contraignants." In *Répertoire de Droit International*. Edited by Dominique Carreau, 1–7. Paris: Dalloz, 2001.

——. "Les gentlemen's agreement comme source du droit international." *Journal du Droit International* 106 (1979): 326–348.

——. "L'accord international sur le cacao." *Annuaire Français de Droit International* 21 (1975): 738–766.

El Erian, Abdullah. "The Legal Organization of International Society." In *Manual of Public International Law*. Edited by Max Sørensen, 55–115. London: McMillan, 1968.

Fawcett, James Edmund Sandford. "The Legal Character of International Agreements." *British Yearbook of International Law* 30 (1953): 381–400.

Fiedler, Wilfried. "Unilateral Acts in International Law." In Bernhardt, *Encyclopedia of Public International Law*, vol. 4, 1018–1023.

Fitzmaurice, Gerald. "The Foundations of the Authority of International Law and the Problem of Enforcement." *Modern Law Review* 19 (1956): 1–13.

——. "Hersch Lauterpacht – The Scholar as Judge. Part III." *British Yearbook of International Law* 39 (1963): 133–188.

Fitzmaurice, Malgosia. "Third Parties and the Law of Treaties." *Max Planck Yearbook of United Nations Law* 6 (2002): 37–121.

——. "Dynamic (Evolutive) Interpretation of Treaties." *Hague Yearbook of International Law* 21 (2008): 101; Hague Yearbook of International Law 22 (2009): 3–31.

Gruchalla-Wesierski, Tadeusz. "A Framework for Understanding Soft Law." *McGill Law Journal* 30 (1984–85): 37–88.

Guggenheim, Paul and Krystyna Marek. "Völkerrechtliche Verträge." In *Wörterbuch des Völkerrechts*. Vol. 3. 2nd ed. Edited by Karl Strupp and Hans-Jürgen Schlochauer, 528–544. Berlin: De Gruyter.

Haas Peter M. Review of *International Law and Organization: Closing the Compliance Gap*, by Edward C. Luck and Michael W. Doyle. *American Journal of International Law* 102 (2008): 226–233.

Hafner, Gerhard. "The 'Provisional Application' of the Energy Charter Treaty." In *International Investment Law for the 21st Century: Essays in Honour of Christoph Schreuer*. Edited by Christina Binder, Ursula Kriebaum, and August Reinisch, 593–607. Oxford: Oxford University Press, 2009.

Haraszti, György. "Treaties and the Fundamental Change of Circumstances." *Recueil des Cours de l'Académie de la Haye* 146 (1975): 1–94.

Helfer, Laurence R. "Exiting Treaties." *Vanderbilt Law Review* 91 (2005): 1597–1648.

Herrmann, Gerold. "Commercial Treaties." In Bernhardt, *Encyclopedia of Public International Law*, vol. 1, 677–683.

Hilger Reinhard and de Vel Guy "Introduction." In *Treaty Making: Expression of Consent by States to be Bound by a Treaty*. Edited by Council of Europe and British Institute of International and Comparative Law, ix-xi. London: Kluwer Law International, 2001.

Hillgenberg, Hartmut. "A Fresh Look at Soft Law." *European Journal of International Law* 10 (1999): 499–515.

Igweike, Kingsley. "The Definition and Scope of 'Treaty' in International Law." *Indian Journal of International Law* 28 (1988): 249–263.

Izquierdo Sans, Cristina. "Parliamentary Procedure in the Conclusion of International Treaties in Spain." *Spanish Yearbook of International Law* V (1997): 1–42.

Jacobs, Francis G. "Introduction." In *The Effect of Treaties in Domestic Law*. Edited by Francis G. Jacobs and Shelley Roberts, xxiii-xxxi. London: Sweet & Maxwell, 1987.

Jessup, Philip C. "Modernization of the Law of International Contractual Agreements." *American Journal of International Law* 41 (1947): 378–405.

Jouanjan, Oliver. "Der Beitrag der Wissenschaften zur künftigen Verfassung der EU." *Basler Schriften zur Europäischen Integration* 66 (2003): 12–23.

Kälin, Walter. "Implementing Treaties in Domestic Law: from 'Pacta Sunt Servanda' to 'Anything Goes'?" In *Multilateral Treaty-Making*. Edited by Vera Gowlland-Debbas, 111–128. The Hague: Martinus Nijhoff Publishers, 2000.

Kearney, Richard D. and Robert E Dalton. "The Treaty on Treaties." *American Journal of International Law* 64 (1970): 495–561.

Klabbers, Jan. "Treaties, Conclusion and Entry into Force." In Wolfrum, *Max Planck Encyclopedia of International Law* online edition. Last modified September 2006. http://www.mpepil.com.

——. "New Dutch Law on the Approval of Treaties." *International and Comparative Law Quarterly* 44 (1995): 629–643.

Klaus, Ulrich. "The Yukos Case under the Energy Charter Treaty and the Provisional Application of International Treaties." *Policy Papers on Transnational Economic Law* 11 (2005): 1–8.

Kohona, Palitha Tikiri Bandara. "Some Legal Problems Relating to the Implementation of International Commodity Agreements." *Indian Journal of International Law* 21 (1981): 546–562.

Kolb, Robert. "La bonne foi en droit international public." *Revue Belge de Droit International* (1998/2): 661–732.

——. "Principles as Sources of International Law." *Netherlands International Law Review* 53 (2006): 1–36.
Kraus, Herbert. "Système et fonctions des traités internationaux." *Recueil des Cours de l'Académie de la Haye* 50 (1934): 311–396.
Krieger, Heike. "Article 25: Provisional Application." In Dörr and Schmalenbach, *Vienna Convention on the Law of Treaties: A Commentary*, 407–421.
Lefeber, René. "Treaties, Provisional Application." In Wolfrum, *Max Planck Encyclopedia of International Law* online edition. Last modified October 2006. http://www.mpepil.com.
Legault, LH. "Canadian Practice in International Law during 1979 as Reflected mainly in Public Correspondence of the Department of External Affairs." *Canadian Yearbook of International Law* 18 (1980): 301–336.
Lim, Chin Leng and Olufemi Elias. "Withdrawing from Custom and the Paradox of Consensualism in International Law." *Duke Journal of Comparative and International Law* 21 (2010–2011): 143–156.
Lipson, Charles. "Why are some International Agreements Informal?" *International Organization* 45 (1991): 495–538.
Loibl, Gerhard. "The Energy Charter Treaty: Implementation and Compliance Issues." In *The Energy Charter Treaty*, edited by Thomas Wälde, 565–582. London: Kluwer Law International, 1996.
——. "International Economic Law." In *International Law*. 3rd ed. Edited by Malcom D. Evans, 722–751. Oxford: Oxford University Press Oxford, 2010.
Lukashuk, Igor I. "The Principle of *Pacta Sunt Servanda* and the Nature of Obligation under International Law." *American Journal of International Law* 83 (1989): 513–518.
Mahiou, Ahmed. "Article 24 VCLT 1969." In Corten and Klein, *Les Conventions de Vienne sur le Droit des Traités: commentaire article par article,* 1023–1044.
Mancini, Marina. "Comment" in "Italian Practice Relating to International Law" *Italian Yearbook of International Law* XIII (2003): 317–318.
Mann, Frederick Alexander. "Reflections on a Commercial Law of Nations." *British Yearbook of International Law* 33 (1957): 20–51.
Mathy, Denise. "Article 25 VCLT 1969." In *The Vienna Conventions on the Law of Treaties: A Commentary*. Edited by Olivier Corten and Pierre Klein, 639–654. Oxford: Oxford University Press, 2011.
Maw, CE. "Introduction." *Digest of US Practice in International Law* 1973, Washington, DC: US Government Printing Office, iii.
McDade, Paul V. "The Interim Obligation between Signature and Ratification of a Treaty." *Netherlands International Law Review* 32 (1985): 5–47.
Michie, Andrew Gordon. "The Provisional Application of Treaties in South African Law and Practice." *South African Yearbook of International Law* 30 (2005): 1–32.
——. "The Role of Provisionally Applied Treaties in International Organisations." *Comparative and International Law Journal of Southern Africa* 39 (2006): 39–56.
Mohler, Paul B., Steve Shapiro and Edna Sussman. "Report of the Alternative Dispute Resolution Committee." *Energy Law Journal* 29 (2008): 231–238.
Münch, Fritz. "Comments on the 1968 Draft Convention on the Law of Treaties." *Zeitschrift für ausländisches öffentliches Recht und Rechtsvergleichung* 29 (1969): 1–11.
Myers, Denys P. "The Names and Scope of Treaties." *American Journal of International Law* 51 (1957): 574–605.
Nahlik, Stanislaw Edward. "L'entrée en vigueur des traités internationaux." *Yearbook of the Association of Attenders and Alumni of the Hague Academy of International Law* 31 (1961): 81–95.
——. "The Grounds of Invalidity and Termination of Treaties." *American Journal of International Law* 65 (1971): 736–756.
Nash, Marian. "Contemporary Practice of the United States Relating to International Law." *American Journal of International Law* 74 (1980): 418–432.

Niebruegge, Alex M. "Provisional Application of the Energy Charter Treaty: The Yukos Arbitration and the Future Place of Provisional Application in International Law." *Chicago Journal of International Law* 8 (2007): 355–376.

Nisot, Joseph. "La force obligatoire des traités signés, non encore ratifiés." *Journal du Droit International* 57 (1930): 878–883.

——. "L'article 18 de la Convention de Vienne sur le Droit des Traités." *Revue Belge de Droit International* (1970/2): 498–503.

Nolte, Georg. "Article 2(7)." In *The Charter of the United Nations: A Commentary*. 2nd ed. Edited by Bruno Simma, 148–171. Oxford: Oxford University Press, 2002.

Öhlinger, Theo. "Vertragsabschlußverfahren." In *Lexikon des Rechts: Völkerrecht*. 2nd ed. Edited by Ignaz Seidl-Hohenveldern, 373–384. Neuwied: Luchterhand, 1992.

Oppenheim, Lassa F. "The Science of International Law: Its Task and Method." *American Journal of International Law* 2 (1908): 313–356.

Partsch, Karl J. "International Law and Municipal Law." In Bernhardt, *Encyclopedia of Public International Law*, vol. 2, 1183–1202.

Pellet, Alain. "Article 38." In *The Statute of the International Court of Justice: A Commentary*. Edited by Andreas Zimmermann, Karin Oellers-Frahm, and Christian Tomuschat, 677–792. Oxford: Oxford University Press, 2006.

Pescatore, Pierre. "Conclusion." In *The Effect of Treaties in Domestic Law*. Edited by Francis G. Jacobs and Shelley Roberts, 273–283. London: Sweet & Maxwell London, 1987.

Pineschi, Laura. "The Madrid Protocol on the Protection of the Antarctic Environment and its Effectiveness." In *International Law for Antarctica*. 2nd ed. Edited by Francesco Francioni and Tullio Scovazzi, 261–291. The Hague: Kluwer Law International, 1996.

Plender, Richard. "The Role of Consent in the Termination of Treaties." *British Yearbook of International Law* 57 (1986): 133–167.

Quill, Edward. "The Failure of International Commodity Agreements." *Denver Journal of International Law and Policy* 22 (1993–1994): 503–539.

Reisman, W. Michael. "Procedures for Controlling Unilateral Treaty Termination." *American Journal of International Law* 63 (1969): 544–547.

Remiro Brotóns, Antonio. "The Spanish Constitution and International Law." *Spanish Yearbook of International Law* IX (2003): 27–59.

Rensmann, Thilo. "Article 46 VCLT 1969: Provisions of Internal Law Regarding Competence to Conclude Treaties." In Dörr and Schmalenbach, *Vienna Convention on the Law of Treaties. A commentary*, 775–804.

Ress, Georg. "Verfassung und völkerrechtliches Vertragsrecht." In *Staat und Völkerrechtsordnung: Festschrift für Karl Doehring*. Edited by Kay Hailbronner, Georg Ress, and Torsten Stein, 803–853. Berlin/New York: Springer, 1989.

Rogoff Martin A. "The International Legal Obligations of Signatories to an Unratified Treaty." *Maine Law Review* 32 (1980): 263–300.

Rogoff, Martin A. and Barbara E. Gauditz. "The Provisional Application of International Agreements." *Maine Law Review* (1987) 39: 29–81.

Rosenne, Shabtai. "Final Clauses." In Wolfrum, *Max Planck Encyclopedia of International Law* online edition. Last modified January 2008. http://www.mpepil.com.

Roucounas, Emmanuel. "Uncertainties regarding the Entry into Force of some Multilateral Treaties." In *International Law: Theory and Practice*. Edited by Karel Wellens, 179–193 The Hague: Martinus Nijhoff Publishers, 1998.

Sagar, David. "Provisional Application in an International Organization." *Journal of Space Law* 27 (1999): 99–116.

Sägesser, Thomas. "Die vorläufige Anwendung völkerrechtlicher Verträge durch den Schweizerischen Bundesrat." *Recht* 21 (2003): 85–92.

Salmon, Jean. "Les accords non-formalisés ou '*Solo Consensu*'." *Annuaire Français de Droit International* XLV (1999): 1–28.

Schachter, Oscar. "The Twilight Existence of Nonbinding International Agreements." *American Journal of International Law* 71 (1977): 296–304.

Schreuer, Christoph. "Die innerstaatliche Anwendung von internationalem 'Soft Law' aus rechtsvergleichender Sicht." *Österreichische Zeitschrift für öffentliches Recht und Völkerrecht* 34 (1983): 243–260.

Schwarzenberger, Georg. "The Fundamental Principles of International Law," *Recueil des Cours de l'Académie de la Haye* 87 (1955): 195–383.

Seidl-Hohenveldern, Ignaz. "Internationale Organisationen aufgrund von Soft Law." In *Recht zwischen Umbruch und Bewahrung: Völkerrecht, Europarecht, Staatsrecht: Festschrift für Rudolf Bernhardt.* Edited by Ulrich Beyerlin, Michael Bothe, Rainer Hofmann, Ernst-Ulrich Petersmann, 229–241. Berlin: Springer, 1995.

Seyersted, Finn. "Objective International Personality of Intergovernmental Organizations." *Nordisk Tidsskrift for International Ret* 34 (1964): 1–112.

Shelton, Dinah. "Introduction. Law, Non-Law and the Problem of 'Soft Law'." In *Commitment and Compliance*. Edited by Dinah Shelton, 1–20. Oxford: Oxford University Press, 2000.

——. "International Law and 'Relative Normativity'." In *International Law*. 3rd ed. Edited by Malcom D. Evans, 95–121. Oxford: Oxford University Press Oxford, 2010.

Sicault, Jean-Didier. "Du caractère obligatoire des engagements unilatéraux en droit international public." *Revue Générale de Droit International Public* 83 (1979): 633–688.

Sohn, Louis B. "International Law Implications of the 1994 Agreement" *American Journal of International Law* 88 (1994): 696–705.

Sondaal, Hans H. "Dutch Treaty Practice." *Netherlands Yearbook of International Law* 19 (1988): 179–241.

Spinner, Bruno "Bemerkungen zur Mitteilung der Direktion für Völkerrecht und des Bundesamtes für Justiz betreffend den Abschluss von Staatsverträgen." *Schweizerisches Jahrbuch für Internationales Recht* XLIV (1988): 25–39.

Sztucki, Jerzy. "Reflections on International Soft Law." *Festskrift till L Hjerner*. Edited by Jan Ramberg, Ove Bring, and Said Mahmoudi. 549–575. Stockholm: Norstedts Förlag, 1990.

Thirlway, Hugh. "The Law and Procedure of the International Court of Justice 1960–1989 (Part 1)." *British Yearbook of International Law* 60 (1989): 1–257.

——. "The Law and Procedure of the International Court of Justice 1960–1989 (Part 3)." *British Yearbook of International Law* 62 (1991): 1–75.

——. "Concepts, Principles, Rules and Analogies: International and Municipal Legal Reasoning." *Recueil des Cours de l'Académie de la Haye* 294 (2002): 265–406.

——. "The Sources of International Law." In *International Law*. 3rd ed. Edited by Malcom D. Evans, 95–121. Oxford: Oxford University Press Oxford, 2010.

Thürer, Daniel. "Soft Law." In Bernhardt, *Encyclopedia of Public International Law*, vol. 4, 452–460.

Tomuschat, Christian. "Commodities' Bernhardt, *Encyclopedia of Public International Law*, vol. 1, 686–691.

——. "Obligations Arising for States without or against Their Will." *Recueil des Cours de l'Académie de la Haye* 241 (1993): 209–374.

——. "Article 36." In *The Statute of the International Court of Justice: A Commentary*. Edited by Andreas Zimmermann, Karin Oellers-Frahm, and Christian Tomuschat, 589–657. Oxford: Oxford University Press, 2006.

Trauttmansdorff, Ferdinand. "Der Abschluß völkerrechtlicher Verträge: einige Streiflichter aus der Österreichischen Praxis." In *Völker- und Europarecht, 24. Österreichischer Völkerrechtstag*. Edited by Wolfram Karl and Ulrike Brandl, 127–145. Wien: Verlag Österreich, 2000.

Treviranus, Hans D. "Neue Verfahren zur Vereinfachung und Beschleunigung des Zustandekommens von multilateralen Verträgen." *Friedens-Warte* 59 (1976): 51–62.

Van Panhuys, Haro F. "The Netherlands Constitution and International Law." *American Journal of International Law* 58 (1964): 88–108.

Vignes, Daniel. "Une notion ambiguë: la mise en application provisoire des traités." *Annuaire Français de Droit International* XVIII (1972): 181–199.
Virally, Michel. "La deuxième décennie des Nations Unies pour le développement." *Annuaire Français de Droit International* 16 (1970): 9–33.
——. "La distinction entre textes internationaux ayant une portée juridique dans les relations mutuelles entre leurs auteurs et textes qui en sont dépourvus." *Annuaire de l'Institut de Droit International*, vol. 1, 60 (1983): 328–357.
Walker, Herman. "The International Law of Commodity Agreements." *Law and Contemporary Problems* 28 (1963): 392–415.
Weil, Prosper. "Observations (sur le Rapport Provisoire de M. Virally)." *Annuaire de l'Institut de Droit International*, vol. 1, 60 (1983): 366–373.
——. "Towards Relative Normativity in International Law." *American Journal of International Law* 77 (1983): 413–442.
Wengler, Wilhelm. "Die Abgrenzung zwischen völkerrechtlichen und nichtvölkerrechtlichen Normen im internationalen Verkehr." In *Legal Essays: a Tribute to Frede Castberg*. Edited by Johannes Andenæs, 332–353. Copenhagen: Scandinavian University Books, 1963.
Whitton, John B. "La Règle *Pacta Sunt Servanda*." *Recueil des Cours de l'Académie de la Haye*, vol. 3, 49 (1934): 151–273.
Widdows, Kelvin. "What is an Agreement in International Law." *British Yearbook of International Law* 50 (1979): 117–149.
——. "The Unilateral Denunciation of Treaties Containing No Denunciation Clause." *British Yearbook of International Law* 53 (1982): 83–114.
Wildhaber, Luzius. "Executive Agreements." In Bernhardt *Encyclopedia of International Law*, vol. 2, 312–318.
Zemanek, Karl. "What is Practice and who Makes it." In *Recht zwischen Umbruch und Bewahrung: Völkerrecht, Europarecht, Staatsrecht: Festschrift für Rudolf Bernhardt*. Edited by Ulrich Beyerlin, Michael Bothe, Rainer Hofmann, and Ernst-Ulrich Petersmann, 289–308. Berlin: Springer, 1995.

BIBLIOGRAPHY OF LITERATURE ON THE PROVISIONAL APPLICATION OF TREATIES

Books About the Provisional Application of Treaties

Geslin, Albane. *La mise en application provisoire des traités*. Paris: Pedone, 2005.

Krenzler, Horst-Günther. *Die vorläufige Anwendung völkerrechtlicher Verträge*. Freiburg im Breisgau. Rota-Druck, 1963.

Montag, Frank. *Völkerrechtliche Verträge mit vorläufigen Wirkungen*. Berlin: Duncker & Humblot, 1986.

Picone, Paolo. *L'applicazione in via provvisoria degli accordi internazionali*. Naples: Casa Editrice Dott. Eugenio Jovene, 1973.

Articles and Chapters on or Referring to the Provisional Application of Treaties

"Three International Commodity Agreements." *British Yearbook of International Law* 35 (1959): 240–244.

Anderson, D. H. "Resolution and Agreement Relating to the Implementation of Part XI of the UN Convention on the Law of the Sea." *Zeitschrift für ausländisches öffentliches Recht und Rechtsvergleichung* 55 (1995): 275–289.

Andrés Sáenz de Santa María, Maria Paz. "La aplicación provisional de los tratados internacionales en el Derecho Español." *Revista Española de Derecho Internacional* XXXIV (1982): 31–78.

Arsanjani, Mahnoush H. and W. Michael Reisman, "Provisional Application of Treaties in International Law: The Energy Charter Treaty Awards," in *The Law of Treaties Beyond the Vienna Convention*, 86–104. Edited by Enzo Cannizzaro. Oxford: Oxford University Press, 2011.

Asada, Masahiko. "CTBT: Legal Questions Arising from Its Non-Entry-Into-Force." *Journal of Conflict and Security Law* 7 (2002): 85–122.

Bartels, Lorand. "Legal Constraints on the EU's Ability to Withdraw EPA Preferences under Regulation 1528/2007." Briefing Note, European Centre for Development Policy Management 27 (2011): 1–5.

——. "Withdrawing Provisional Application of Treaties: Has the EU Made a Mistake." *Cambridge Journal of International and Comparative Law* 1 (2012): 112–118.

Belz, Matthew. "Comment: Provisional Application of the Energy Charter Treaty: Kardassopoulos v. Georgia and improving provisional application in multilateral treaties." *Emory International Law Review* 22 (2008): 727–760.

Bindschedler-Robert, Denise. "De la rétroactivité en droit international public." In *Recueil d'Etudes de Droit International en Hommage à Paul Guggenheim*, 184–200. Geneva: Faculte de Droit de l'Universite de Geneve, 1968.

Browne, Marjorie Ann. "The Law of the Sea Convention and US Policy." Congressional Research Service, 2005. http://www.fas.org/sgp/crs/row/IB95010.pdf

Chrispeels, Erik. "Simplifying International Commodity Agreements." In *International Commodity Organisations in Transition*. Edited by Erik Chrispeels, 349–358. London: Cameron May, 2002.

Condorelli, Luigi. Review of *L'applicazione in via provvisoria degli accordi internazionali*, by Paolo Picone. *Italian Yearbook of International Law* 1 (1975): 382–386.

Do Nascimento e Silva, Geraldo Eulalio. "Le facteur temps et les traités." *Recueil des Cours de l'Académie de la Haye* 154 (1977): 215–297.

García Fernández, Francisco Javier. "La aplicación provisional de los tratados." In *La celebración de tratados internacionales por España: Problemas actuales*, 95–101. Madrid: Ministerio de asuntos exteriores, 1990.

Hafner, Gerhard. "The 'Provisional Application' of the Energy Charter Treaty." In *International Investment Law for the 21st Century: Essays in Honour of Christoph Schreuer*. Edited by Christina Binder, Ursula Kriebaum, and August Reinisch, 593–607. Oxford: Oxford University Press, 2009.

Hillgenberg, Hartmut. "A Fresh Look at Soft Law." *European Journal of International Law* 10 (1999): 499–515.

Izquierdo Sans, Cristina. "Parliamentary Procedure in the Conclusion of International Treaties in Spain." *Spanish Yearbook of International Law* V (1997): 1–42.

Kearney, Richard D. and Robert E Dalton. "The Treaty on Treaties." *American Journal of International Law* 64 (1970): 495–561.

Klaus, Ulrich. "The Yukos Case under the Energy Charter Treaty and the Provisional Application of International Treaties." *Policy Papers on Transnational Economic Law* 11 (2005): 1–8.

Kraus, Herbert. "Système et fonctions des traités internationaux." *Recueil des Cours de l'Académie de la Haye* 50 (1934): 311–396.

Krieger, Heike. "Article 25: Provisional Application." In Dörr and Schmalenbach, *Vienna Convention on the Law of Treaties: A Commentary*, 407–421.

Lefeber, René. "Treaties, Provisional Application." In Wolfrum, *Max Planck Encyclopedia of International Law* online edition. Last modified October 2006. http://www.mpepil.com.

——. "The Provisional Application of Treaties." In *Essays on the Law of Treaties: A Collection of Essays in Honour of Bert Vierdag*. Edited by Jan Klabbers and René Lefeber, 81–96. The Hague: Martinus Nijhoff, 1998.

Loibl, Gerhard. "The Energy Charter Treaty: Implementation and Compliance Issues." In *The Energy Charter Treaty*, edited by Thomas Wälde, 565–582. London: Kluwer Law International, 1996.

Mancini, Marina. "Comment" in "Italian Practice Relating to International Law" *Italian Yearbook of International Law* XIII (2003): 317–318.

Mathy, Denise. "Article 25 VCLT 1969." In *The Vienna Conventions on the Law of Treaties: A Commentary*. Edited by Olivier Corten and Pierre Klein, 639–654. Oxford: Oxford University Press, 2011.

Michie, Andrew Gordon. "The Provisional Application of Treaties in South African Law and Practice." *South African Yearbook of International Law* 30 (2005): 1–32.

——. "The Role of Provisionally Applied Treaties in International Organisations." *Comparative and International Law Journal of Southern Africa* 39 (2006): 39–56.

Milić, Milenko. "Privremeno primenjivanje međunarodnih ugovora." *Jugoslovenska revija za međunarodno pravo* XXI (1974): 186–200.

Mohler, Paul B., Steve Shapiro and Edna Sussman. "Report of the Alternative Dispute Resolution Committee." *Energy Law Journal* 29 (2008): 231–238.

Nash, Marian. "Contemporary Practice of the United States Relating to International Law." *American Journal of International Law* 74 (1980): 418–432.

Neri, Sergio. "Sull' 'applicazione provvisoria' dei trattati internazionali non ancora ratificati." *Rivista di Studi Politici Internazionali* 24 (1962): 588–591.

Niebruegge, Alex M. "Provisional Application of the Energy Charter Treaty: The Yukos Arbitration and the Future Place of Provisional Application in International Law." *Chicago Journal of International Law* 8 (2007): 355–376.

Orihuela Calatayud, Esperanza. "Diferencias entre aplicación retroactiva y aplicación de disposiciones convencionales antes de su entrada en vigor." In *Los tratados internacionales y su aplicación en el tiempo*, 35–52. Madrid: Dykinson, 2004.

Pineschi, Laura. "The Madrid Protocol on the Protection of the Antarctic Environment and its Effectiveness." In *International Law for Antarctica*. 2nd ed. Edited by Francesco Francioni and Tullio Scovazzi, 261–291. The Hague: Kluwer Law International, 1996.

Quill, Edward. "The Failure of International Commodity Agreements." *Denver Journal of International Law and Policy* 22 (1993–1994): 503–539.

Reisman, W. Michael and Mahnoush H. Arsanjani M. "What is the Current Value of Signing a Treaty?" In *Human Rights, Democracy and the Rule of Law: Liber Amicorum Luzius Wildhaber*. Edited by Stephan Breitenmoser, Bernhard Ehrenzeller, Marco Sassoli, Walter Stoffel, and Beatrice Wagner Pfeifer, 1491–1513. Zurich: Dike, 2007.

Remiro Brotóns, Antonio. "The Spanish Constitution and International Law." *Spanish Yearbook of International Law* IX (2003): 27–59.

Ress, Georg. "Verfassung und völkerrechtliches Vertragsrecht." In *Staat und Völkerrechtsord nung: Festschrift für Karl Doehring*. Edited by Kay Hailbronner, Georg Ress, and Torsten Stein, 803–853. Berlin/New York: Springer, 1989.

Rogoff, Martin A. and Barbara E. Gauditz. "The Provisional Application of International Agreements." *Maine Law Review* (1987) 39: 29–81.

Roucounas, Emmanuel. "Uncertainties regarding the Entry into Force of some Multilateral Treaties." In *International Law: Theory and Practice*. Edited by Karel Wellens, 179–193 The Hague: Martinus Nijhoff Publishers, 1998.

Sagar, David. "Provisional Application in an International Organization." *Journal of Space Law* 27 (1999): 99–116.

Sägesser, Thomas. "Die vorläufige Anwendung völkerrechtlicher Verträge durch den Schweizerischen Bundesrat." *Recht* 21 (2003): 85–92.

Sohn, Louis B. "International Law Implications of the 1994 Agreement" *American Journal of International Law* 88 (1994): 696–705.

Sondaal, Hans H. "Dutch Treaty Practice." *Netherlands Yearbook of International Law* 19 (1988): 179–241.

Tomuschat, Christian. "Commodities' Bernhardt, *Encyclopedia of Public International Law*, vol. 1, 686–691.

Trauttmansdorff, Ferdinand. "Der Abschluß völkerrechtlicher Verträge: einige Streiflichter aus der Österreichischen Praxis." In *Völker- und Europarecht, 24. Österreichischer Völkerrechtstag*. Edited by Wolfram Karl and Ulrike Brandl, 127–145. Wien: Verlag Österreich, 2000.

Treviranus, Hans D. "Neue Verfahren zur Vereinfachung und Beschleunigung des Zustandekommens von multilateralen Verträgen."*Friedens-Warte* 59 (1976): 51–62.

Van Panhuys, Haro F. "The Netherlands Constitution and International Law." *American Journal of International Law* 58 (1964): 88–108.

Vignes, Daniel. "Une notion ambiguë: la mise en application provisoire des traités." *Annuaire Français de Droit International* XVIII (1972): 181–199.

Walker, Herman. "The International Law of Commodity Agreements." *Law and Contemporary Problems* 28 (1963): 392–415.

Books Referring to the Provisional Application of Treaties

Aust, Anthony. *Modern Treaty Law and Practice*. 2nd ed. Cambridge: Cambridge University Press, 2007.

Bittner, Ludwig. *Die Lehre von den völkerrechtlichen Vertragsurkunden*. Stuttgart: Deutsche Verlagsanstalt, 1924.

Blix, Hans. *Treaty-Making Power*. London: Stevens & Sons Limited, 1960.

Butler, William E. *The Law of Treaties in Russia and the Commonwealth of Independent States: Text and Commentary*. Cambridge: Cambridge University Press, 2002.

Chimni, Bhupinder S. *International Commodity Agreements*. London: Croom Helm, 1987.

Corten, Olivier and Pierre Klein, eds. *Les Conventions de Vienne sur le droit des traités: commentaire article par article*. 3 vols. Brussels: Bruylant, 2006.

Corten, Olivier and Pierre Klein, eds. *The Vienna Conventions on the Law of Treaties: A Commentary*. 2 vols. Oxford: Oxford University Press, 2011

Council of Europe and British Institute of International and Comparative Law, eds. *Treaty Making: Expression of Consent by States to be Bound by a Treaty*. London: Kluwer Law International, 2001.

Daillier, Patrick, Alain Pellet, and Mathias Forteau,. *Droit international public*. 8th ed. Paris: Librairie Générale de Droit et de Jurisprudence, 2009.
Degan, Vladimir D. *Sources of International Law*. The Hague: Martinus Nijhoff Publishers, 1997.
Dehousse, Fernand. *La ratification des traités*. Paris: Recueil Sirey, 1935.
Dörr, Oliver and Kirsten Schmalenbach, eds. *Vienna Convention on the Law of Treaties: A Commentary.* Heidelberg: Springer, 2012.
Eisemann, Pierre Michel. *L'Organisation Internationale du Commerce des produits de base*. Brussels: Bruylant, 1982.
Elias, Taslim Olawale. *Modern Law of Treaties*. Dobbs Ferry: Oceana Publications, 1974.
Ipsen, Knut: *Völkerrecht*. 5th ed. Munich: C.H. Beck, 2004.
Jennings, Robert Yewdall and Arthur Watts, eds. *Oppenheim's International Law*, Vol. 1. 9th ed. Harlow: Longman, 1992,
Khan, Kabir-ur-Rahman. *The Law and Organisation of International Commodity Agreements*. Boston: Martinus Nijhoff Publishers, 1982.
Klabbers, Jan: *The Concept of Treaty in International Law*. The Hague: Kluwer Law International, 1996.
Laly-Chevalier, Caroline. *La Violation du Traité*. Brussels: Bruylant, 2005.
Leigh, Monroe, Merritt R. Blakeslee, and L. Benjamin Ederington, eds. *National Treaty Law and Practice. Studies in Transnational Legal Policy*, no. 30 and no. 33. Washington, DC: American Society of International Law, 1999.
Lettow, Erich. "Die völkerrechtliche Bindung nicht ratifizierter Verträge." PhD diss., University of Bonn, 1954.
Meißner, Hans-Otto. *Vollmacht und Ratifikation bei völkerrechtlichen Verträgen nach Deutschem Recht.* Göttingen: Vandenhoeck & Ruprecht, 1934.
Michie, Andrew Gordon. "The Provisional Application of Treaties with Special Reference to Arms Control, Disarmament and Non-Proliferation Instruments." LL.M. thesis, University of South Africa, 2004. http://uir.unisa.ac.za/bitstream/handle/10500/1920/02dissertation.pdf?sequence=1.
Pritzkow, Sebastian. *Das völkerrechtliche Verhältnis zwischen der EU und Russland im Energiesektor*. Heidelberg: Springer, 2011.
Reuter, Paul. *Introduction au droit des traités*. 2nd ed. Paris: Presses Universitaires de France, 1985.
——. Introduction to the Law of Treaties. 2nd ed. London: Kegan Paul International, 1995.
Roe, Thomas and Matthew Happold. *Settlement of Investment Disputes under the Energy Charter Treaty*. Cambridge: Cambridge University Press, 2011.
Schermers, Henry G. and Niels Blokker. *International Institutional Law.* 4th ed. Boston: Martinus Nijhoff Publishers, 2004.
Schwarzenberger, Georg. *International Law*. Vol. 1. 3rd ed. London: Stevens & Sons, 1957.
——. *International Law*. Vol. 3. London: Stevens & Sons, 1976.
Sinclair, Ian McTaggart. *The Vienna Convention on the Law of Treaties*. 2nd ed. Manchester: Manchester University Press, 1984.
United Nations. *UN Final Clauses of Multilateral Treaties-Handbook*. New York: United Nations, 2003.
Verdross, Alfred and Bruno Simma. *Universelles Völkerrecht: Theorie und Praxis*. 3rd ed. Berlin: Duncker & Humblot, 1984.
Verwey, Delano R. *The European Community, the European Union and the International Law of Treaties*. The Hague: T.M.C. Asser Press, 2004.
Villiger, Mark Eugen. *Commentary on the 1969 Vienna Convention on the Law of Treaties*. Leiden: Martinus Nijhoff Publishers, 2009.
Wolfrum, Rüdiger, eds. *Max Planck Encyclopedia of International Law* online edition. Oxford: Oxford University Press, 2008-. http://www.mpepil.com.
World Trade Organization, ed. *GATT Secretariat Guide to GATT Law and Practice*, 6th ed. Geneva: WTO Secretariat, 1994.

INDEX

www.ingramcontent.com/pod-product-compliance
Lightning Source LLC
LaVergne TN
LVHW020651300926
849161LV00004B/898